Edmund Gillingwater, A. E Murton

## Gillingwater's History of Lowestoft

A Reprint - with a Chapter of More Recent Events by A.E. Murton

Edmund Gillingwater, A. E Murton

**Gillingwater's History of Lowestoft**
*A Reprint - with a Chapter of More Recent Events by A.E. Murton*

ISBN/EAN: 9783337139162

Printed in Europe, USA, Canada, Australia, Japan

Cover: Foto ©ninafisch / pixelio.de

More available books at **www.hansebooks.com**

# GILLINGWATER'S
# HISTORY OF LOWESTOFT.

A reprint: with a chapter
of more recent events by
A. E. MURTON.

LOWESTOFT

mdcccxcvii.

# HISTORY OF LOWESTOFT.

### SECTION I.

### OF THE ISLAND OF LOTHINGLAND.

THIS island (lately become a peninsula) is situated in the most eastern part of Great Britain and in the northern corner of the County of Suffolk. It is bounded by the German Ocean on the east, by the river Yare on the north, by the Waveney on the west, and by the beautiful and spacious water, the lake Lothing on the south; thus encircled by water on every side it is generally called the Island of Lothingland, and would strictly be so, did not a very narrow neck of land (near Lowestoft) intervene, and make it a peninsula. Its length, from north to south, is about ten miles; its breadth from east to west, about six miles; and contains sixteen parishes, viz: Lowestoft, Corton, Gunton, Olten, Ashby, Lound, Fritton, Flixton, Hopton, Somerley, Blundeston, Gorleston, Belton, Burgh, Bradwell, and Herringfleet, of which Lowestoft is the principal, and is the only market town in the island. During the Saxon Heptarchy, this island was part of the kingdom of the East Angles, In respect to the civil government of the county, it is reckoned but a half hundred, the other half being the district of Mutford. They are generally called the half-hundreds of Mutford and Lothingland, but were incorporated as one hundred by an Act of Parliament in 1764, for the better relief of the poor, and for building an house of industry for their use.

In the ecclesiastical division of the county, this hundred was one of the rural deaneries under the archdeacon of Suffolk. Bishop Kennet, in his parochial antiquities, informs us that this office in the church was very ancient, for in one of the laws ascribed to Edward the Confessor, it is provided, that of eight pounds penalty for breach of the king's peace, the king shall have an hundred shillings, the earl of the county fifty, and the dean of the bishop in whose deanery the peace was broken, the other ten; which words can be applied only to the office of rural deans, according to the respective districts which they had in parts of every diocese. At first their office was merely to inspect the manners and behaviour of the inferior clergy and people, but by degrees they became possessed of a power to judge and determine in smaller matters, and the rest they were to report to their ecclesiastical superiors Some time before the Reformation, by the great power of the archdeacons and their officials, the jurisdiction of rural deans declined almost to nothing; and at that period no steps being taken for the restoration of this part of the government of the Church, their name and office unhappily ceased together, notwithstanding attempts have since been made to revive this ancient and useful institution, which in some places have been successful.

Rural Deans of the deanery of Lothingland, Anno 1325, Jeffrey de Boudon, priest, upon the resignation of William de Weston : 1326, John de Wynneferthyng; 1328, John de Thrillo ; 1339, Edmund de Bokenham ; 1376, Roger de Belton.

15 Henry VI. Anno 1535, when the clergy granted a tenth to the king, the deanery of Lothingland paid as follows:—

|  | £ | s. | d. |
|---|---|---|---|
| Vicarage of Lowestoft | 0 | 8 | 8 |
| Rectory of Blundeston | 1 | 6 | 8 |
| Rectory of Somerliton | 1 | 4 | 0 |
| Rectory of Lound | 0 | 16 | 0 |
| Rectory of Belton | 1 | 14 | 8 |
| Rectory of Burgh | 0 | 13 | 4 |
| Rectory of Bradwell | 2 | 16 | 0 |
| Vicarage of Gorleston | 0 | 13 | 4 |
| Vicarage of Yarmouth Parva | 0 | 8 | 8 |
| Rectory of Oldton | 1 | 9 | 4 |
| Rectory of Gunton | 0 | 8 | 8 |
| | £11 | 19 | 4 |

Benefices of 12 merks or under, which did not pay this tenth, and on which the Rectors or Vicars kept personal residence, were Flixton, Fritton, and Ashby.

Why Herringfleet, Corton, and Hopton came to be omitted, does not appear.

This, though apparently a small sum, was in fact, a very considerable one, for thirty pounds now is scarcely an equivalent in value to five pounds at the time of Henry VI.

It has been conjectured by some, that the island took its name from the lake Lothing, but, I apprehend, without any foundation; it seeming more probable that both the island and lake derived their names from Lothbrock, a noble Dane, whose descendants, in order to perpetuate his memory, gave to this part of the kingdom of the East Angles—frequently the seat of war in their descents on the British coast—the name of Luddingland, Lovingland, Luthingland, or as it is now called Lothingland.

This Lothbroth was of royal race, and had two sons, named Ingwar and Hubba. It happened once, as he was alone in a boat hawking for birds near the island on the coast of Denmark, that he was driven by a sudden tempest across the German Ocean and was carried into the mouth of the Yare up as far as Reedham. The inhabitants of the country having discovered the stranger they brought him to Edmund, king of the East Angles, whose palace was at Caister, about ten miles from thence. The king was astonished at the man's figure and fortune, and received him with a countenance and behaviour so engaging that Lothbroch relinquished every desire of returning to his own country again, and was so delighted also with the diversions of the courtiers, particularly that of hunting that he oftentimes accompanied Berno the king's huntsman, in that amusement, in order to become more expert in it; and in a short time made such great proficiency therein, and so far excited the envy of his master that having seduced him into a wood under the pretence of hunting, he privately murdered him. While Lothbroch was missing, a vigilant greyhound which he had kept, guarded his body; but being at last stimulated with hunger he sometimes visited the royal palace, which being observed by the servants, it excited their curiosity to follow him on his return, and they presently discovered the murdered body of Lothbroch. Berno being suspected, was apprehended and found guilty of the crime, and was sentenced, by the order of the king's court, to be put alone into Lothbroch's boat, and without a compass or any other instrument was committed to the mercy of the wind and waves which fortunately carried him to Denmark. The boat being there known he was suspected of having been accessary to the death of Lothbroch; and being examined upon the rack concerning it, he affirmed that the murder was committed by Edmund, king of the East Angles.

The Danes having resolved to revenge the death of Lothbroch upon King Edmund and his subjects, levied an army of 20,000 men made Ingwar, and Hubba (the sons of Lothbroch) commanders in chief of the expedition; and having made every necessary preparation for the voyage, and taken Berno with them as a leader, who knew the country, they immediately embarked and set sail for East England in the year 865, in the tenth year of King Edmund's reign; but meeting with contrary winds they were driven ashore at Berwick upon Tweed, in Scotland, where having committed the most violent outrages, and in some measure gratified their revenge for the murder of Lothbroch, they soon after returned home. But in the following year the relentless Danes re-visited our coasts, when after burning and destroying all they could meet with, and also having greatly harassed and had frequent skirmishes with King Edmund's army, they returned to their own country. The year after, the Danes again renewed their descents on the British coast, and so far succeeded in their enterprises against King Edmund, that they reduced him to the utmost distress; for surrounding him in a certain place in the Island, where he was so inclosed with marshes and rivers, that it was almost impossible for him to escape, he was left to this dreadful alternative, either to surrender to his enemies or fight his way through them. Having resolved upon the latter, he sought out a place most convenient for his design, and having at last discovered a ford (which was called Berneford, from Berno,) and now called Barnby, he passed it, and falling furiously upon his enemies, he routed them with a great slaughter, and compelled them to return immediately to Denmark. (In a field near Barnby, called Bloodmere-field, have been found many ancient beads, spears, etc.) In the succeeding year, the Danes returned again to England, and having committed the most horrid ravages in divers part of it, they came to Ely, where Hubba being left to guard their spoil, Ingwar, with his army entered East England, when, after committing many barbarous cruelties at Thetford, he sent a message to King Edmund, who was then at Eglesdune (now Hoxne, in Suffolk), proposing to him that if he would renounce christianty, pay adoration to his idols, and become his vassal and servant, he would then divide not only his treasure but also his kingdom with him. No sooner did the king receive this message than he marched with his whole army against the Danes and engaging them at a place not far from Thetford, the contending armies fought with great obstinacy from morning till evening, and great numbers were slain on both sides, when the Danes retreated from the field of battle. But the pious king was so exceedingly affected at the fate of so many martyrs who had shed their blood in this battle in defence of the christain faith as well as for the unhappy end for such a numerous body of Pagans that he returned with the shattered remains of his army to Eglesdune with a resolution excited by religious considerations never to engage any more in battle with the Pagans, but if it was necessary to appease their rancour by yielding himself up as a sacrifice for his people and for his christian faith. The army belonging to Ingwar was much diminished from the loss he sustained in this battle; but receiving information of Edmund's retreat he instantly proceeded to Thetford, where, being joined by Hubba with 10,000 men, the brothers united their forces and pursued the unhappy king to Eglesdune, where, taking him prisoner he was martyred in the year 871, in the 29th year of his reign; and with him expired the kingdom of the East Angles.

After the death of Edmund, the Danes settled themselves in Lothingland, to which tract of land they are supposed to have given that name, in remembrance of their ancestor Lothbroch.

The following tradition respecting the death of King Edmund, is current in the parish of Hoxne to this day; namely, that the King, after he had relinquished every intention of opposing the Danes any farther, in consequence of the horrid carnage which the numerous contests between them had occasioned, fled to this village for safety, but finding himself closely pursued by his enemies, was obliged for security, to conceal himself under a bridge in that parish, now called Gold Bridge, so named from the gilt spurs which the king happened to have on whilst there concealed. A newly-married couple that were returning home in the evening, saw, by moonlight, the king's spurs glitter in the water, and immediately discovered him to the Danes, who instantly put him to death. The king, in the warmth of resentment, pronounced a curse upon every couple that should afterwards pass over this bridge to be married. A superstitious regard is paid to this sentence even to this day; as not one will pass over the bridge in their way to the parish church on that occasion. It is now about a thousand years since the event happened, and is a remarkable instance of the length of time which traditions in parishes are sometimes continued.

The Danes, when they got the king into their possession, endeavoured to prevail with him to renounce the christian faith; which he refusing to do, they first scourged him with whips, and afterwards bound him to a stake and shot him to death with arrows. He was first buried in an obscure wooden chapel at Eglesdune (now Hoxne), but being afterwards esteemed a martyr, and canonized by the Church, his bones were removed to Bury St. Edmund's, where a magnificent abbey was erected to his memory.

It appears from that ancient survey of the landed property of this kingdom, the Book of Domesday, that the fee of this hundred was originally in the crown, for that record informs us that Earl Guert (sixth son of Earl Goodwin, brother of Queen Edith, wife of Edward the Confessor. This earl, with Harold his brother, who disputed the crown with William the Conqueror, was slain at the decisive battle of Hastings) held Gorleston, (and probably the whole island), in the reign of Edward the Confessor ; and describing the extent and property of this manor in the time of Edward, and comparing them with the survey made in the reign of William the Conqueror, it says it contained five carucates of land; that there were then twenty villains, now only twelve; five bornars, then five servants, now only four ; then two carucates in demesne, now but one; then cattle for five carucates of land, now only three; then two workhouses, now none; ten acres of meadow land, three salt pans, wood for five hogs, always three hundred sheep, and twenty-four fishermen at Yarmouth.

Both history and tradition informs us that some centuries since, there were numerous and violent disputes between the lords of this island and the men of Great Yarmouth, respecting the privileges of that burgh; and whereas it was alleged that those privileges had been greatly infringed by the said lords of the island.

King John in the ninth year of his reign, granted the burgesses of Yarmouth a charter, whereby it was created a free burgh, the burgesses were thereby invested with many valuable commercial privileges, and empowered to hold it in fee farm (fee farm is a perpetual fixt rent, in ancient times, both in England and France. A ferm signified rent, and land put to farm, was said to be affirmed or arrented) paying to the king and fisheries an annual rent of £55 for ever; for payment whereof they had nothing but the customs arising out of the port, not being allowed to receive any custom of goods bought or sold in the market in Lothingland at any time of the year.

Soon after the granting of this charter, the burgh of Great Yarmouth became most flourishing, and made a more respectable figure in trade and commerce than before; and whilst Yarmouth and Lothingland were both holden in the king's hands, no disputes about customs arose betwixt them, nor do any records now extant mention any suits about them, payable at this or that place, but as the charter had invested the men of Yarmouth with the sole property of their land, as well as their merchandise, they sought to monopolize the trade to themselves, and to hinder the king's tenants of Lothingland from enjoying any part with them. (At this period the only distinction of property was the king's demesne, and the baronies of the nobility, and the rest of the people were vassals either to one or the other, small private estates were entirely unknown, and the yoemen of England did not exist of a century after.)

The granting these privileges to the burgh of Yarmouth, was effectually emancipating the inhabitants ; no sooner, therefore, had this charter passed, than the men of Lothingland, and particularly the inhabitants of Little Yarmouth and Gorleston (much more considerable places than now) began to be alarmed at the acquisitions of their neighbours, and dreaded their future power. In consequence of this grant several infringements were made, and many disputes arose; however, they did not arise to any considerable degree, till about the twelfth year of Henry III., when Roger Fitz-Osbert (the principal branch of the family of the Fitz-Osberts, resided at Somerley Hall in this island) who was then the king's bailiff or warden of Lothingland, endeavoured to draw the trade of herrings and other goods to his own side of the river Yare, and took certain customs in the port of Yarmouth, contrary to the liberties which the burgesses claimed by their charter.

Complaints against these proceedings of the bailiff of Lothingland were exhibited by the burgesses of Yarmouth, and king Henry, willing to terminate the dispute, as being a party concerned, and being also desirous of being informed what customs really belonged to Yarmouth, and what to his manor of Lothingland, sent Martin de Patteshall, an itinerant justice, to determine it, who took an inquisition at Yarmouth upon the oaths of forty-eight persons belonging to the counties of Norfolk and Suffolk, upon which a verdict was found, that all wares ought to be unladen and sold at Great Yarmouth, and that all the haven belonged to the burgesses of Yarmouth; but that small merchandise and provisions of all kinds might be unladen on the Yarmouth or Lothingland side of the river, at the option of the owners or importers thereof. This affair being thus decided, the respective parties continued for some time on more amicable terms, but it was of short duration, for upon king Henry's exchanging the manor of Lothingland, and the rent of the fee-farm of Yarmouth, in 1228, with John de Baliol, for certain lands in Cheshire, it opened a new source of contention; for although the men of Yarmouth had seemingly the advantage in the late decision yet, as a license was given to unlade ships with provisions on either side, and as fish — which was the chief merchandise then carried on — was evidently included in that permission, they soon found, that in reality, they had gained no other advantage than an expensive suit and an ambiguous decree. John de Baliol seems to have been as well apprized of this as of their inability to dispute it with him, for in 1244 he brought a writ against the burgesses for depriving him of his customary tolls in Little Yarmouth, which alarmed them so much, that, two years after, we find them soliciting the king for a new exclusive charter, that all merchandises and wares, as well fish as other commodities, should be sold at Yarmouth only by the hands of the importers thereof.

Whatever were King Henry's motives for thus confining the trade, and injuring the property which John de Baliol undoubtedly had in it, I know not, but he granted the burgesses their request, and gave them a new charter agreeable to their desires; notwithstanding, which, I find the bailiff of Lothingland took the usual customs the very next year, and also continued to do so whilst the manor remained in the hands of the Baliols, and consequently fresh disputes about the customs were continually arising.

In 1259 John de Baliol died, and was succeeded by his son, John de Baloil, afterwards king of Scotland, and it appears that the usual disputes were in agitation during the time he held this manor; but upon his acquiring the kingdom of Scotland, the burgesses of Yarmouth were obliged to submit to so powerful an opponent, for we find he levied the following customs; for every foreign ship, eighteen pence; and of every English ship trading to or from the port of Yarmouth, fourpence; of every cart or horse-load of merchandize passing through his manor a half-penny; and for every last of herrings imported for a foreign merchant, fourpence; of every stall, fourpence; and of every window where bread was placed to sell, fourpence. The last is a remarkable article for a tax; and I can account for it no other way than by supposing the men of Yarmouth used to make bread and send it to be sold at Little Yarmouth and Gorleston for the supply of their herring fleet, in case of necessity.

The manor of Lothingland and fee-farm of Yarmouth being in the hands of the Baliols, by virtue of the above-mentioned exchange, were now in the actual possession of John de Baloil, king of Scots; but upon this king's renouncing his homage to King Edward 1st, all his English estates became forfeited, and by his resignation afterwards of his person, his dignity his kingdom, and all his private states, the said manor of Lothingland, and the fee-farm of Yarmouth, once more reverted to the crown. This was accounted by the burgesses of Yarmouth as a most happy deliverance, they thereby getting rid of a troublesome and powerful neighbour, who not only vigorously supported the rights of his manor, but interfered also with their trade, and was willing to become a partner in their gains; for the Baliols, both father and son, had for many years, by their bailiffs, greatly infringed on the liberties of Yarmouth, by taking customs in that port, contrary to its charters, to the great injury of the burgesses which they were under the necessity of submitting to as being unable to contend with such powerful adversaries. But after the above forfeiture the burgesses of Yarmouth adjudging it to be a seasonable opportunity for having their grievances redressed, made application to King Edward 1st in the 34th year of his reign, to have the charter granted by his predecessor Henry 3rd more clearly explained, and to be expressed in such manner as should leave no room for farther disputes.

The king in order to compromise the difference between the respective parties, requested the assistance of his council; and notwithstanding the opposition from Little Yarmouth and Gorleston, yet it appearing upon enquiry that as the manor of Lothingland and fee-farm of Yarmouth were now in the hands of the said King Edward, and that certain privileges had been granted to the burgesses of Great Yarmouth by the charter of Henry 3rd, therefore his said Majesty, in the year above-mentioned, complied with the request of the burgesses, and both explained and ratified the said charter of King Henry. (The strength of the contest during the whole of this dispute may be summed up in these words: "By this controversy between the burgh of Great Yarmouth and the men of Little Yarmouth and Gorleston, in Lothingland it appears that prescription, seeing they were no burghs, prevailed not to assert and make good a liberty of unlading goods and exposing them to sale in the towns." By the same it is also evident that liberties belonging to free burghs are only to be had and obtained by the king's charter; and that where they were used without it, they were esteemed and judged usurpations, especially if practised and continued to the prejudice and damage of a free burgh. It was observed before, that the fee of this hundred was originally in the crown, and it appears to have continued so, without any interruption, till the time of king Henry 3rd, who, in the twenty-second year of his reign, anno 1238, granted it to John de Baliol and Devergill, his wife, one of the sisters (Ives says nieces) and heiress of John Scot, Earl of Chester and Huntingdon, in exchange for their part of the county of Chester. The reasons which induced king Henry to make this exchange were strictly political; the ancient Earls of Chester being Earls Palatine, bore great sway in any combination of the barons, and this the king, as well as his father, had often experienced. Randulf, the sixth Earl of Chester, uncle and immediate predecessor of John, was not only a man of great power, but of considerable abilities and much integrity; he warmly espoused the cause of king John against the barons, and proved himself a faithful champion to his son, even to the preservation of his person, and the raising him to his father's throne; his attachment to loyalty seemed to proceed from conviction; and, notwithstanding his being so great an advocate for John and Henry, yet, with all the dignity and hardiness of one of the iron barons of that period, he openly rebuked the former in parliament for his criminality respecting the wives and daughters of the nobility, and joined with the Earl of Cornwall to force the latter to seal the new charter of the forest liberties instead of that which he had cancelled at Oxford. Earl John, the last of this family, his successor, adopted his uncle's system, and took part with king Henry upon the great difference between him and Richard, Earl Marshall, in 1233, and, upon the solemnity of Henry's marriage with Eleanor, daughter of Raymund, Earl of Provence, we find him bearing the sword, called Curtana before the king, in token, says Matthew Paris, that, being an Earl Palatine, he had power to restrain the king, if he should be exorbitant. It is no wonder, therefore, that, upon his death, Henry should be desirous of annexing the county of Chester to his crown, especially as he left no issue, and only female relations; and as this earldom was, in some respects, entitled to royal privileges, and a local monarchy, he assumed it into his own hands, "lest so fair a dominion should be divided among women; and in the 31st year of his reign this Earldom annexed to the crown for ever, and remained so till the 21st of Richard 2nd, when by Act of Parliament, it was united to the principality of Wales.")

The manor of Lothingland continued in the crown but a short time; for king Edward 1st in his 34th year, anno 1306, gave it, with all Baliol's English estates, to John de Britainy, Earl of Richmond, his sister's son. (Beatrice, the second daughter of king Henry and his Queen Eleanor, married John, the first Duke of Britainy, son of John, the late Earl of the same family, by whom he had issue, Arthur, duke of Britainy, and John Earl of Richmond, the said nephew. This great and accomplished nobleman was no less famous for his conduct and courage, than for his illustrious descent from one of the ancient Norman families, strengthened in its interests and possessions by several very near alliances to the crown; he also united to those qualifications, great generosity and real goodness.)

The burgesses of Yarmouth, however well pleased they might at first appear with the loss of their old neighbours, quickly found that they had acquired nothing by the exchange, for John de Britainy was no less determined upon a vigorous defence of the rights of his manor than his predecessors; and as he was a much more powerful opponent, so, in the end, he was a much more troublesome one. Previous, however, to the settlement of the manor of Lothingland upon this nobleman, the burgesses of Yarmouth had obtained from king Edward a charter confirming that of his father, and commanding that all fish and other merchandize brought up the river should be sold at Yarmouth only, and that no person whatever should purchase any goods as they were carrying up the stream. Thus, in spite of the absurdity and injustice of making all commercial transactions centre in themselves, under the pretence of their being a free burgh by charter, the men of Yarmouth effectually hindered those of Little Yarmouth and Gorleston from sharing in the trade, which their situation rendered them as equally capable of carrying on to advantage as their neighbours. Such was the state of affairs between the contending parties, when the grant of the manor of Lothingland was given to the Earl of Richmond. Though it appears he took no cognizance of their disputes till the 2nd of Henry 3rd, anno 1328, yet he could not remain so long ignorant of them; though it is probable the distance of his residence (Richmond Castle, in Yorkshire) from this place and the small account a nobleman of his large possessions must naturally make, of so trifling an addition to them, might render him unwilling to engage in an expensive suit, which at best, could procure him very insignificant advantages. However, after repeated application from the inhabitants of Gorleston and Little Yarmouth, and the rest of the tenants of Lothingland (It is evident from Swinden, that the affair was agitated in the 8th and 9th of Edward 2nd, although Ives asserts, that the Earl of Richmond took no notice of it till the 2nd of Edward 3rd. Possibly the earl, from residing at so great a distance, might not personally appear in the prosecution till the time of Edward 3rd; when the suit grew more serious and importunate), about the 8th and 19th of Edward 2nd, the Earl, about the year above mentioned, exhibited a petition to king Edward 3rd.; in which he alleged, that half the haven of Yarmouth belonged to him in right of his manor; and that he ought to have as his ancestors, who held this manor before him, undoubtedly had, the arriving, discharging, and laden of ships, goods and merchandizes, and a free buying and selling for his tenants of Little Yarmouth and Gorleston, as had been the case till king Henry 3rd by his charter to the burgesses, granted that these things should belong solely to Great Yarmouth, and the aforesaid free buying and selling should be done there only; and as the burgesses of Yarmouth claimed all their restrictive power from this charter, the earl wisely considered, that without removing the cause, the effect must still subsist; therefore, in the same petition he attacked the charter itself, and represented to the king, that it had not been rightly granted king Henry not being timely apprized of the destructive tendency such a grant must necessarily have upon the fishing trade, how contrary its dictates were to the common rights of mankind, and, particularly, how injurious to the crown itself, as the original proprietor of the manor of Lothingland. So severe an attack upon the Yarmouth palladium, roused the burgesses from their wonted security, and they were summoned to appear personally before the king and his Council, to make their defence against the Earl and to produce their charters, records, and reasons to the contrary. The burgesses accordingly appeared, and urged in their behalf, that the claims demanded by the Earl were erroneous and ill-grounded: and exhibited several grants given them by preceding kings, as the charter of king John, that of Henry 3rd, the confirmation of the same by Edward 1st, and the decisions in favour of the burgh, in the 8th and 19th of Edward 2nd, in the Exchequer and other courts, all tending to confirm the rights they claimed, and to invalidate the earl's assertions; in which they had ever been victorious.

The burgesses of Yarmouth founded the merits of their cause on the charter which had incorporated them. The men of Lothingland, on ancient customs before those charters existed; alledging that the Manor was part of the ancient demesne of the crown, and that the customs and privileges claimed by the Earl of Richmond and his tenants, are the same as were demanded in the times of Canute and Harold, and the succeeding kings of England, being owners of the said Manor, and by many other pleadings, they asserted their lawful right to those privileges, both by prescription and long-continued possession; but, after hearing the controversy, the cause was determined in favour of Yarmouth, and the burgesses triumphed once more over their rival neighbours.

The ill success of this application did not deter the Earl from making another, which had the same great end in view, the wresting from the burgesses their great Charter of Incorporation; but, after many pleadings and decisions, before the king and council, the parliament and the judges, the Earl had no better success than before; for in the end it only served to strengthen the designs of the men of Yarmouth, by the entire overthrow of the adverse party; the affair being at length finally determined in favour of the burgesses, 5th Edward 3rd, anno 1332.

The men of Lothingland, who had, probably, formed the highest expectations of success, from the great power and credit of their patron, the Earl of Richmond now saw themselves left entirely to the mercy of the elated burgesses, who, on all occasions, exerted their power over them with a malevolence considerably inflamed by the late dissensions; they had also the mortification to see that power fixed upon the strongest and most unalterable basis, by an extensive charter, confirming all their former rights, and adding many valuable liberties to those they already enjoyed.

Thus ended this litigious and destructive controversy, in which the inhabitants of Lothingland had been engaged for more than one hundred years. The motives which actuated each party were strictly the same; the one strove for the continuance of those liberties which Henry's charter had deprived them of; the other, to retain the rights they had acquired, so beneficial to themselves, at the expense of their neighbours. It is not to be doubted, that this was considered by the men of Yarmouth as an object of the highest importance. A grant which gave a restrictive trading power to one place, in prejudice to another, must, of course, draw within its gates all those who wished to advance their interest, or enlarge their property.

The well-being of any commercial town must depend upon the conveniency of its situation for traffic, but, in this case, their opponents were equally fortunate as themselves; the same stream flowing equally between them, and the same conveyance which brought emolument to the one, would have carried opulence to the other. To the final determination of this controversy in their favour, the town of Yarmouth is chiefly indebted for the prosperity it now enjoys; whilst its rivals, Gorleston and Little Yarmouth, are sunk into obscure villages, and particularly the latter, of which hardly anything more than the name remains. In the following year, the earl of Richmond, who had gone over into France, to settle some matters relative to the estate which he there held as earl of Britainy, died in that kingdom, without issue, and was succeeded to his manors and estates by John de Dreux, son of Arthur, earl of Britainy; and he dying in 1342, they were granted by Edward III. to John, duke of Britainy, and earl of Montford in France; who was advanced to this dignity on account of his adherence to the interest of king Edward in that kingdom, for which cause the king of France had seized upon his possessions. (The Commissioners appointed by the king to meet at Great Yarmouth, in order to make enquiry concerning this dispute, and to terminate the differences, were the Bishop of Winchester, Lord Chancellor of England, Lord John

## HISTORY OF LOWESTOFT.

Stoneherd, and John de Cambridge, his justices; Robert de Ufford, Oliver de Ingham, and Ralph Nevel, steward of the king's household. In the roll of this year is the following entry:—Paid to the lord chancellor and others, the king's justices, the time they were at Great Yarmouth, by order of John Pere Brown, £1 2s. 6d., and at the same time paid for bread sent to them 13s. 4d.

After the **above decision, which** established the burgesses of Great Yarmouth, **in the** peaceable possession of all their ancient privileges, the **animosities and** disturbances, which had agitated the contending parties for a **century past,** appear to have subsided; and they maintained a more friendly **intercourse** with each other, without any material interruption, until the reign **of Queen Elizabeth;** but, in the 12th year of the reign of that princess, new **dissensions** arose, which were combated with a considerable degree of violence **and** animosity, between the burgesses of Great Yarmouth, and Sir Henry Jerningham and his tenants, the men of Little Yarmouth and Gorleston, concerning divers liberties claimed by Great Yarmouth, respecting the free fair holden at the said town; and also concerning **a** parcel of waste ground, lying on the south side of the haven's mouth, near the town of Gorleston; which, some time ago, when **the** course of the haven extended to the south of Corton, was situate between **the neck of** the haven and the main sea; and because the said haven **had at this** time a shorter **neck** or passage to the sea, obtained by the **town of Great Yarmouth,** at an immense expense, and was brought further **to the north, conse**quently the above-mentioned waste ground must lie to the **south of the haven's** mouth, as then situated; and as Sir Henry Jerningham **was owner, not only of** the town of Gorleston, but also of the greater part of **Lothingland in which** Gorleston is situated, the claim of the burgesses of **Yarmouth must** materially affect the property of Sir Henry. In order **therefore,** to restore peace and tranquility to the several parties, **the matter in dispute** was referred to the arbitration of Sir Christopher Heydon, and Sir **William** Butts, knights, by virtue of a commission from the Star-Chamber, who finally determined the difference in such a fair and equitable manner, as met with the approbation of both parties.

But, notwithstanding this affair was so amicably adjusted, fresh disputes arose, shortly after, between the town **of** Great Yarmouth and some neighbouring towns, respecting a fair that was held at Gorleston; and as Queen Elizabeth, at that time, happened to be at Norwich, her majesty deputed several **lords** of her retinue to proceed to Yarmouth, and survey the premises; **which orders** being accordingly executed, they made a report thereof to the Queen; and the following letter from the Privy Council, was sent to the Sheriff and Justices of the county of Suffolk, respecting the same.

A copy of the letter sent from the Lords of the Queen's Majesty's Privy Council, to the Sheriff, and also the Justices of Suffolk, in August, 1578, after that the Lord Treasurer, the Lord of Leicester, and others of the Council, had viewed and seen the town; (all these noblemen were elegantly entertained at **the priory, at** the town's expense) the Queen being at Norwich, on her tour at **the time.**

(In **August** 1578, the Queen was expected at Yarmouth, by way of Suffolk, and great preparations were made for her reception and entertainment; particularly, **a silver cup of £16 value, made** in the form of a ship, was intended as a present to **Her** Majesty; but she proceeded no further than Norwich, and from thence the Lords of her retinue came to Yarmouth. In the same year, an annuity of 20s. **a** year, was granted, by the city of Norwich, to John Benne, of Lowestoft, who was lamed with firing off the cannon at Norwich, when the Queen visited that city.)

"After our hearty commendations—Whereas the town of Great Yarmouth **is situated** upon the frontiers of the sea, in the county of Norfolk, near the **county of** Suffolk; and great care has been taken by the ancestors of our **Sovereign** Lady, the Queen's Majesty, for the maintenance and preservation of the **said town,** and divers liberties and privileges have been granted, by the progenitors of **her** majesty, to that intent and purpose; amongst which there is one privilege, granted unto the burgesses of the town of Great Yarmouth, that **no** fair or market should be kept or holden at any place or places within seven leuks (Leuks, leuga, or luca. There are various conjectures concerning the meaning of this word; some making it three, others

B

two, and many only one mile; but with respect to the liberties belonging to the herring fair, the leuk was determined as only one mile; as may be seen in section 4th., when an actual admeasurement of the said distance was ordered to be made,) of the said town, either of fish in general, or herrings in particular, or any other kind of merchandizes, but only at the town of Great Yarmouth which said grants and liberties are thought very necessary to be continued and protected, for that the Yarmouth men do expend great costs and charges upon the haven belonging to the said town. We understanding, nevertheless, that divers and sundry persons heretofore have sought, and do daily seek, to keep and hold a fair, for buying, selling, and delivering herrings, and other fish, and divers other merchandizes, at the town of Gorleston, in the county of Suffolk, which is within the mouth of the said haven of Yarmouth. We have therefore, thought good to charge and require, you that you give due information unto the inhabitants of the said town of Gorleston, and to all other persons repairing thither, that they suffer no such fair or market, or any buying, selling or delivering of herrings, or any other fish or merchandise, at the said town, or at any other place within the said haven of Great Yarmouth, but only at the said town, or in the road of the said town, at any time or times, from the beginning of the herring fair or fishing, now, next ensuing, until the end of the said herring fair or fishing, as they tender Her Majesty's pleasure, and will answer the contrary at their perils. And if you shall receive information of any person or persons, either seller or buyer, that shall be obstinate, or act contrary to this Her Majesty's command, you shall bind the said persons to appear before us, to answer their contempt in that behalf. And, finally, we desire you to use all the good means you can, to see the design of this our letter put in due execution. And so we bid you heartily farewell.

Your loving friends, &c."

From Thetford, the 27th August, 1578.

In consequence of this letter the men of Gorleston, Lowestoft, and other towns upon the coast, in the county of Suffolk, presented a petition to Her Majesty's Privy Council, praying to have this letter recalled. Whereupon the burgesses of Yarmouth sent up immediately to the Privy Council, William Harebrowne and Thomas Damett, with their charters and decrees, to answer the complaints presented by the above-mentioned towns; and succeeded so far in their application as to obtain the following decree, which was issued forth by the Lords of the Privy Council, and which finally determined the dispute. (It appears indisputably evident, from divers charters granted to the town of Great Yarmouth, that the rights and privileges belonging to their herring fair extended to the distance of seven leuks or miles. The principal point in dispute between that town and the town of Lowestoft, was, from what place the said distance was to be measured, whether the quay or the mouth of the haven: when it was proved, and legally determined, about the year 1664, that the said admeasurement should commence at the former place. And, therefore, the town of Lowestoft, and the other towns, pretending to have a right to buy and sell herrings, etc., within the limits of the said seven miles from Great Yarmouth was illegal, and a manifest infringement on the liberties of the town).

"A Decree, made by the Lords and others of the Queen's Majesty's Privy Council, upon a matter in controversy between the town of Great Yarmouth, in the county of Norfolk, and the towns of Little Yarmouth and Gorleston, and other towns, in Suffolk, after divers hearings of both parties; and put in writing and subscribed the four and twentieth day of February, in the one and twentieth year of the reign of our Sovereign Lady, the Queen's Majesty, Elizabeth, and in the year of our Lord one thousand, five hundred and eighty

"Whereas, upon complaint exhibited before us by Henry Gunvyle, of Gorleston, and John Hoo, of Gunton, gent.; William Frenche, of Lowestoft, and John Fox, of Aldborough, merchants; as well in their own names, as also in the names of the inhabitants of the said towns, and of other coast towns of Suffolk, against the bailiffs, burgesses, and commonalty of the town of Great Yarmouth, in the county of Norfolk; the substance of which complaint and controversy consisteth in this: Whether, by the liberties belonging to the said town of Great Yarmouth, all kinds of merchandize, and also herrings and all other fish, being brought into the haven of Great Yarmouth, should, be unladen and discharged at the said town of Great Yarmouth, or elsewhere (saving only to Gorleston and Little Yarmouth, their own proper merchandize, and fish, brought in their own bottoms, and none other; but excepting such ships belonging to these towns as are laden with wool, leather, wool-skins, and other merchandize, whereof great custom ought to be paid, and to be discharged in the port where the Queen's Majesty's trone [a beam to weigh with] and seal called the Coquet do remain). Which liberty is challenged by the said town of Great Yarmouth: and, for support thereof, there have been shewed forth sundry charters, judgments, and decrees, all affirming the said liberties to belong to Great Yarmouth; and not by any allegations for the other parties, justly disproved.

"And, forasmuch, as upon the deliberate hearing of the allegations of both parties, concerning the said controversy, there hath not been shewn before us any sufficient matter to make void the said liberties, challenged by the said town of Great Yarmouth, by virtue of their charters: We do therefore order and decree that the said town of Great Yarmouth, and the bailiffs, burgesses, and commonalty thereof, shall stand possessed of, and quietly hold and enjoy, the said liberties, by them claimed according to their said charters; and that no delivering, buying, or selling of herrings, or any other fish, or any merchandizes, coming into the said haven be made, kept, or holden, but only at the said town of Great Yarmouth, or where the bailiffs, burgesses, and commonalty of the said town will appoint the same to be done, and not elsewhere: excepting only to the said towns of Little Yarmouth and Gorleston, and the inhabitants thereof, liberty to land and receive, at the said towns, all such herrings, and other fish, and merchandizes, as shall be their own, and taken and brought into that haven in their own boats and vessels, without any colouring, fraud, or covyn (saving those ships belonging to the said towns of Little Yarmouth and Gorleston, as are laden with wool, leather, wool-skins, and other things, whereof great customs ought to be paid, which shall be discharged in the port of Great Yarmouth, and at the same place where the Queen's Majesty's trone and seal, called the Coquet) do remain, and not elsewhere.

"And, for the better publication and observation of this our order and decree, we do not only will and require the said complainants to publish the tenor thereof, in the said coast towns, but, also, have ordered, that the justices of assizes of the said county, shall be by us required to give in charge to the Justices of the Peace there, to have good regard, that the same may be performed, and put in the execution, without any manner of disturbance; and, that if any person or persons shall wilfully disobey this order, that then the next justice of the peace of the said county, shall take sufficient bond of the said party to appear before us, and to answer his contempt in that behalf. And this our order and decree shall stand and remain in full force, until such time as the said complainants, or any other persons, in behalf of the said towns, shall justly shew, and prove before us, such good matter as may move us to revoke this our present or derand decree.

"Given at Westminster, the day and year above written,

"(Signed.)

LORD BURLEIGH, LORD LINCOLN, LORD SUSSEX, LORD WARWICK, LORD LEICESTER, LORD HUNSDON, SIR FRANCIS KNOLLY'S, SIR JAMES CROFTE, SIR CHRISTOPHER HATTON, SIR FRANCIS WALSINGHAM, SIR WALTER MILDMAY; T. WILSON, Secretary.

Afterwards in the year 1616 we find the bailiffs of Great Yarmouth petitioning for leave to extend their jurisdiction, or power, on the west side of the haven; but it does not appear, that they ever acquired any authority there till the 20th of Charles II., when Southtown was incorporated with Great Yarmouth; for about that time Sir Robert Paston, being desirous of adjusting the differences which had for so many years subsisted between the town of Great Yarmouth and Little Yarmouth (or Southtown) and Gorleston, brought a bill into the House of Commons in the year 1664, for incorporating the former with Southtown, which was accordingly effected.

And, again, in the 36th of Charles II. a new charter was granted to Great Yarmouth, wherein the said incorporation was confirmed, and other grants and privileges subjoined; and was afterwards confirmed again by another charter, granted in the reign of Queen Anne, and remains incorporated to this day.

It appears from what has been premised, that this island, as part of the ancient demesne of the crown, was held in the time of Edward the Confessor, by Earl Guert; in the time of William the Conqueror, by Earl Warren (about this time a Warren, earl of Surrey, was warden or bailiff of Lothingland, who, it is conjectured, was William de Warren, the second earl of Surrey); and in the time of Henry III., by Roger Fitz Osbert (it also appears that Lowestoft, and also the island, in the reign of King Henry IV. and Henry V. was part of the estate of Michael de la Pole, earl of Suffolk, and passed to his successors) afterwards it descended to the Baliols; but, upon John de Baliol's renouncing his homage to Edward I. and thereby forfeiting all his English estates, it again reverted to the crown, and king Edward I. in the 34th year of his reign gave the island to his nephew John de Britainy, earl of Richmond. In the reign of Queen Elizabeth the greatest part of the island belonged to Sir Henry Jerningham (of Somerly town, in this island, and in whom the family became extinct. Isabel, the sister of Sir Roger Fitz-Osbert, of Somerley, was wife of Sir Walter Jernegan, of Horham, by virtue of which marriage [her brother, Sir Roger, dying without issue] he became possessor of the Somerley estate. This family, in the reign of King John, was settled first at Horham, in Suffolk, afterwards another branch was settled at Stonham Jerningham, in the same county, about the year 1234. The Horham branch, by marriage with the Fitz-Osberts, removed to Somerly which then became the principal seat of the family.) In the reign of Charles II. the part contiguous to Gorleston was in the hands of Sir Robert Paston, knight.

History informs us, that the island of Lothingland has experienced a variety of viscissitudes from the irruptions of the sea; and that the coast which is washed by the German Ocean, was, in former ages, very different in its appearance from which it is at present. A large arm of the sea, at the time when the Romans were in Britain, extended itself, on the north side of the island, several miles westward of the ground whereon Yarmouth is now situated; and the mouth of the Yare, or, rather, arm of the sea, at that time, was very large, and discharged itself into the ocean by two channels, (being separated by the sand-bank on which Yarmouth was afterwards built) the one near Caister, and the other near Gorleston. It is highly probable that before the Christain era, this extraordinary effect of the secret operations of the ocean, had not commenced; and that previous to that period, the Yare discharged itself into the sea by one channel only.

The reason why this sand-bank was not formed before that time, is one of those secrets of Providence which, to us, continues unexplored.

The north-east winds appear to have been the apparent cause of forming the sand-bank at the mouth of that river; and is an inconvenience to which it is subject, even at this present time.

The original name of the bank was, the Cerdick Sand; from Cerdick, a warlike Saxon, who, about the year 495, landed here; and who, after having routed the opposing Britons, and greatly harassed the Iceni with a very grievous war, sailed to the western parts of Britain, where he founded the kingdom of the West Saxons.

The mouth of the former of these channels being entirely choaked up by the north-east winds, the whole stream fell, afterwards, into the latter; and this last-mentioned channel having its entrance so frequently blocked up by the sand-banks formed by these winds, that its course was greatly altered, and extended a considerable distance to the south of Gorleston, before it was able to discharge itself into the sea. These obstructions still continuing, the mouth of the haven kept proceeding still further to the south, till, at last, it reached even to the south of Corton, before it was able to force its passage into the ocean.

The mouth of the haven, from these obstructions, being carried thus far to the south, and having such numerous sands and shallows formed therein, especially between the 10th and 20th of Edward III, that its navigation became extremely dangerous, and but few ships of burthen could enter there with safety; and, consequently, was so detrimental to Yarmouth, that it greatly affected the trade, which for many years had subsisted there, as well as the commerce of the adjacent country.

Whereupon, the bailiffs, burgesses, and commonalty of Great Yarmouth, presented a petition to king Edward III, in the 20th year of his reign, for liberty to cut a new mouth to the haven, nearer to Yarmouth than it was at that time; which petition being granted, a new communication with the ocean was accordingly opened, and confined with piers, opposite to the parish of Corton. This great undertaking was accomplished at an immense expense, and was confined to this place for the space of twenty-six years; (46th of Edward III), when it began again to be so much choked up with sand, that no vessels of any considerable burden could enter, but were obliged to unload their cargoes in an adjoining place, called Kirkley Road, which was near the mouth of the said haven. The king, being informed of the great difficulties which the town of Great Yarmouth laboured under, from the dangerous state of its haven, and how utterly unable they were thereby rendered of paying the fee-farm rent due to his majesty, from the great quantity of merchandise that was obliged to be unladen in the adjoining place called Kirkley Road, and which, by that means, escaped paying the usual customs to Yarmouth, his majesty, in consideration of these misfortunes, was pleased to grant a charter for uniting the said Road of Kirkley unto the port and haven of Yarmouth; (the Yarmouth men were opposed by the adjoining towns six years before they obtained this charter,) upon condition, that the said burgesses of Great Yarmouth would pay to the king and his successors, an additional rent of 100s. yearly: and also granted unto the said burgesses full power to demand and receive the same duties in the said Kirkley road, as in the port and haven of Yarmouth, for ever. (The granting of this charter, for uniting Kirkley road with Yarmouth haven, was one of the principal sources of the great contention which arose between Yarmouth and Lowestoft, about the year 1660, respecting the herring fishery; and gave rise to a law-suit which subsisted several years: the Yarmouth men insisting, that the place called Kirkley Road was not contiguous to the haven, but a part of the main sea, opposite to the town of Kirkley; which town lies to the south of Lowestoft, thereby including the Roads of Lowestoft within the boundary of their liberties. Whereas, it is very evident, from the charter itself, that Kirkley Road was an adjoining place to the haven, and that the mouth of the haven, at that time, discharged itself into the sea, opposite the town of Corton; and, therefore, must be situated a little to the south of that town. This assertion receives still further confirmation from an ancient view of the town of Lowestoft, late in the possession of Thomas Martin, F.S.A , and an old map of this part of the coast, inserted in Ives's Garianonum, where Kirkley Road is placed between Lowestoft and Corton.)

(It is probable that the passage cut throught the cliffs at Lowestoft, a little to the north of the town, called the Cart's Score, and also the foot-path between that Score and the northern light-house, were designed, originally, for the convenience of a communication between Lowestoft and the adjacent country, and the haven's mouth when situated near Corton: and there are several other passages, similiar to the above, between Lowestoft and Yarmouth, which were also formed for preserving a communication between the country and the haven's mouth, according to the several situations which the haven afterwards had.)

It is very evident, to an attentive observer, that the whole of the flat country, which lies between Caister and Burgh, extending about four miles, and forms a considerable part of the water called Braydon, was once covered by the German Ocean; and that the mouth of the Yare, at that time, was an estuary, or arm of the sea, and extended, with considerable magnitude, for many miles up the country. Tradition, the faithful preserver of many a fact which history has overlooked or forgotten, confidently and invariably asserts it; and the present appearance of the ancient bed of the river, from Yarmouth to Harleston, in Norfolk, tends to confirm it. Probably the points of land whereon Beccles, Bungay, and Homersheld are situated, and which protruded themselves into the ancient river, might serve as convenient situations for placing beacons and other signals, announcing the approach of an enemy, at the time when the Romans, Saxons, and Danes invaded and gained possession of the island; and might, from thence give birth to the origin of those towns. The case may be the same in respect to other places situated on points of land on the borders both of the Yare and the Waveney. What is here suggested may receive farther confirmation from an inspection of the above ancient map of Garienis Oestium, or mouth of the Yare, as given in the Ives's Garianonum, (the old map from whence this was taken, remained in a chest called the Hutch, belonging to the Corporation of Yarmouth; and was copied from one still more ancient, which appeared to be in a perishing condition about the time of Elizabeth,) which represents this part of the country as it appeared in the year one thousand; **and which**, also, affords considerable assistance in forming a just conception of **the ancient** boundaries **of these** rivers, at the time when the Romans and **other foreign** invaders were in possession of this island.

The mouth of the Waveney on the south of the island, **was also**, at this time very large, and discharged itself into the ocean between Lowestoft and Kirkley. (Camden speaks of Kirkley as a haven town, and in his **time** very likely it was so; for the Waveney had then not only a communication with the **sea** near Lowestoft, but had also such a depth of water at its entrance as was sufficient to admit vessels of a small draught into it. At a little distance from the mouth of this river, on the south side, is a small inlet running towards Kirkley, and now called Kirkley Ham, and probably is the place **which in** those days was called Kirkley Haven.) The conflux of waters **arising from** the communication which these two rivers **had with the sea**, the one at Yarmouth and the other at Lowestoft, **was so** great, **when they** formed a junction as to render the Waveney navigable some **miles beyond** Harleston in Norfolk. (Blomfield in his history of Norfolk, says **it was** navigable as far as Brockdish, and its opposite village Syleham. That the former place, from the great breadth and depth of the river there, was originally called Broad-ditch; and the latter now called Syleham, is derived from Sail-home, intimating probably that there the navigation terminated. [Swinden says, that in the time of Kett's Rebellion in 1549, a small pinnace was to go up to Weybread with twenty-four men] and, as a corroborating circumstance, anchors have been found, in turning up the ground in the last-mentioned village, which is generally acknowledged as sufficient evidence that some centuries ago large boats and barges had a free and easy access to those places. But when the Yare was reduced to a stream, and all communications between the Waveney and the sea was cut off at Lowestoft, the rivers decreased, and the navigation consequently was more contracted).

After that the sea had considerably receded from the river between Lowestoft and Kirkley, yet it still preserved a small communication with it; **and** therefore, whenever a violent storm arose from the north-west, at the time **when** the waters were intressed by the spring tides, it would flow into the river with great violence, and threaten the adjacent country with an inundation. To guard against these irruptions of the ocean, and prevent the damages that would otherwise ensue, a break-water was erected between Lowestoft and Kirkley, as a security for the low grounds and marshes which laid contiguous to the river.

For it appears, that on the 6th February, 1652, a verdict was **given** by the jury, on a commission of sewers, **of** the number of acres of low grounds in the several towns in Norfolk and Suffolk, which were **subject to** inundations from the sea-breach between Lowestoft and Kirkley; **wherein it** was found that in the parishes of Ellingham and Kirby only, there **were** 482 acres and one rood of low ground subject to those inundations, the annual value whereof was £87 18s. 10d., and which paid **to the** charge of the said breach £7 4s. 9d.; and it was also found, by the said commission of sewers, that in the manor of Earsham there were 418 acres of low grounds liable to inundation from the said sea-breach, valued at £330 and paid £13 10s. 6d. towards repairing the same. (From hence it appears that the defence or fortification, ordered to be **erected** at the sea-breach near Lowestoft, was, in reality, only the reparation **of a** former one. When it was first erected is now unknown. In a violent **storm** and high tide in 1786, the sea was very near breaking into the river, and so much soil was washed away that the old foundations of the above defence were discovered.)

And at a commission of sewers, held at the Swan Tavern, at Lowestoft, the 21st February, 1660, before Sir Thomas Meadows, Knight; Henry Bacon, John Duke, John Garnies, William Cooke, William Cooke, the younger; John Playters, Francis Brewster, William Gooch, John Baispoole, Esquires; Robert London, Thomas London, Philip Hayward, Christopher Reeve, Glover Denny, Gisleham Wollhouse, Henry Jenkenson and Anthony Jenkenson, gentlemen, commissioners; the two following questions were proposed, viz:

"1st. Whether the work at the sea-breach between Lowestoft and Kirkley should stand in its present state until an engineer shall come or not?

"2nd. Whether the fortifications (or fence of the sea-breach) shall be made at Mutford Bridge, or at the sea?"

When it was resolved by the Court and ordered, "That the work and fortifications shall be proceeded upon forthwith without delay; and that the said work and fortification shall be made and done at the sea-shore, where the bank or wall formerly was made, or thereabouts."

It was further ordered by the Court, "That the sum of six hundred pounds should forthwith be raised, for a defence and fortification to be made against the sea-breach at Lowestoft."

And whereas it appeared to the Court, "That the causeway at Mutford Bridge was decayed and broken down, in consequence of the sea-breach at Lowestoft, and made unpassable for foot-passengers, and very dangerous to others; it was therefore ordered, That the same should be repaired immediately out of the first money to be raised, but not to exceed the sum of ten pounds." It was also ordered, "That Henry Bacon, Esquire, should treat with Sir Cornelius Vermewden, or any other engineer at London, to come down to Lowestoft, and view the work and fortification to be made there against the sea-breach, and to take his opinion concerning the same. That Gisleham Wollhouse, of Olton, gent., be treasurer, and Thomas Verdon, of the same place, gent., be surveyor."

Warrants were also issued to the sheriffs of both counties, to warn a jury, to take a view of all such breaches and other decays, within the limits of the said commission, and to make presentments of the same; and, accordingly, amongst many other matters, they presented the sea-breach near Lowestoft, and that it was necessary that a defence against the sea should be made there, otherwise it would be injurious to the owners of the lands betwixt the said sea-breach and Ditchingham Dam. Also, they found the grounds liable to be taxed to the sea-breach, as far as the former jurors found them, viz: to Yarmouth on the Suffolk side, and to Braydon on the Norfolk side. They also found the grounds hereinafter mentioned, as liable to be taxed to the said sea-breach, although omitted in the former levy, viz:

|  | Acres. |
|---|---|
| Lands within the Town of Lowestoft. | 60 |
| Low grounds in Carlton Colville, lying between East Heath and the common drain leading from Kirkley Bridge and against Lowestoft | 20 |
| Several doles in Kirkley, and other low grounds lying against the common, betwixt Lowestoft bounds and inclosed meadows towards Kirkley Bridge | 30 |
| Several inclosed pieces, betwixt divers common doles and Kirkley Bridge, whereof one piece is glebe, belonging unto William Bacon, clerk | 2 |
| Two other pieces, in the tenure of Henry Church | 2 |
| One other piece of glebe, lying next Kirkley Bridge, belonging to the said William Bacon, clerk | 1 |

It was further ordered by the Court, "That against the next sessions of sewers, to be holden at the Swan Tavern, Lowestoft, the 21st June next, a levy be prepared, to be sent to the several towns chargeable to the sea-breach at Lowestoft, at double the proportion which was formerly charged, viz. from the said sea-breach to Beccles Bridge and Gillingham Dam, in the whole level, chargeable at two shillings in the pound; and from the said Bridge and Dam to Ditchingham Dam, sixteen pence in the pound; and those towns which were not charged upon the former levy, to be added to this.

"Also, that the clerk of this commission do issue out warrants to the several petty constables within the towns charged towards the sea-breach at Lowestoft, to collect and pay their several sums to Mr. Gisleham Wollhouse, treasurer, at the White Lion, at Beccles, the 4th day of July next.

The proportion of the several towns charged to the sea-breach at Lowestoft, being the second levy at two shillings in the pound to Beccles Bridge, and sixteen pence in the pound from thence to Bungay Bridge and Ditchingham Dam. (The first levy, at two shillings, and sixteen pence in the pound was made under the former commission in 1652.)

|  | £ | s. | d. |
|---|---|---|---|
| Gorleston | 26 | 17 | 0 |
| South Town | 16 | 4 | 10 |
| Bradwell | 17 | 11 | 8 |
| Burgh Castle | 16 | 10 | 8 |
| Belton | 16 | 8 | 0 |
| Fritton | 16 | 19 | 9 |
| Herringfleet | 9 | 6 | 10 |
| Somerley Town | 8 | 18 | 10 |
| Blundeston | 2 | 1 | 4 |
| Flixton | 7 | 19 | 6 |
| Oulton | 16 | 8 | 9 |
| Carlton Colville | 6 | 15 | 9 |
| Lowestoft | 2 | 0 | 0 |
| Barnaby | 10 | 18 | 2 |
| North Cove | 12 | 17 | 0 |
| Worlingham | 6 | 19 | 4 |
| Beccles | 46 | 8 | 4 |
| Barsham | 6 | 13 | 9 |
| Shipmeadow | 3 | 6 | 8 |
| Mettingham | 14 | 10 | 9 |
| Kirkley | 0 | 9 | 9 |
| Broom | 5 | 18 | 2 |
| Ellingham | 8 | 15 | 11 |
| Gelston | 5 | 17 | 8 |
| Aldeby | 39 | 15 | 2 |
| Burgh | 58 | 18 | 2 |
| Whitacre All Saints | 17 | 19 | 10 |
| Haddiscoe | 52 | 19 | 10 |
| Thorp next Haddiscoe | 28 | 0 | 8 |
| Ranningham | 7 | 9 | 4 |
| Thurlton | 14 | 14 | 7 |
| Loddon | 10 | 11 | 6 |
| Toft Monks | 21 | 8 | 9 |
| Langlie | 13 | 1 | 0 |
| Total | £551 | 17 | 3 |
| Still to charge— |  |  |  |
| Ditchingham | 4 | 6 | 6 |
| Gillingham | 15 | 19 | 11 |
| Bungay | 0 | 18 | 0 |
|  | £573 | 1 | 8 |

There were several other sessions of sewers held under this commission at Lowestoft, Beccles and Loddon, before the business was finally settled. (After the isthmus was formed, the breakwater became useless.)

But as all communications between the sea and the river has ceased for upwards of sixty years, consequently, the apprehensions which the adjoining country were exposed to, have long subsided. The last irruption of the sea which happened at this place was on the 14th December, 1717, occasioned by a violent storm of wind and high tide, when the sea forced its way over the beach, which separated it from the river, with such irresistible violence as to carry away Mutford Bridge, at a mile-and-a-half distance from the sea-shore; and all the fish which were in the eastern part of the river were destroyed by the salt water. (Possibly Mutford Bridge before this event was only a dam of earth, formed across the river. The bridge that was built afterwards consisted chiefly of earth, arranged in the same manner, with a small passage through it for the current of water to pass through, consisting of planks, about three feet wide and two in height, and called the sluice. In the year 1760 a new bridge was built of brick materials consisting of one spacious arch, large enough to admit small craft through the same; and thereby rendered the river navigable to its utmost eastern limits.) Lothingland, most probably, ceased to be an island and became a peninsula about the year 1712; for at that time there was only a small communication with the sea at the part between Lowestoft and Kirkley, which now forms the isthmus. (It was customary about this time, on Pakefield fair day, for a man to stand near this channel, with boots on, to carry children through the water who went from Lowestoft to the fair.) Soon after that period the sea entirely withdrew itself, and the eastern point of the river, through a deficiency of water, gradually receded to the west. The tract of land between the ocean and the river, which forms this isthmus, is about a quarter of a mile in breadth, and is able to resist the most sudden and violent attacks of the boisterous ocean.

I shall conclude these remarks on the island of Lothingland, with subjoining a few observations on the place of the greatest antiquity therein, viz. the ancient Garianonum of the Romans, now called Burgh Castle.

In the celebrated Notitia Imperii, (this work, intitled Notitia Imperii, is supposed to have been written in the reign of Valentinian III, and Theodosius II, but by some, in the very beginning, by others at the latter end of the reign of Theodosius. It contains a succinct account of the state of the Roman empire in those times; to wit, of the provinces, and their governors; of the other magistrates, both civil and military, their titles and officers; of their land and sea forces; of their foot and horse; of their troops, both Roman and foreign; and the places where they were quartered, etc. It was published by Guidus Pancirollus, 1593, under the the title of "Notitia Utraque," etc., that is a General Survey of the Dignities, both of the East and West, since the times of Arcadius and Honorius. Ives.) or Survey of the Roman Empire, it appears that the troops who garrisoned this station, were a body of cavalry, called the Stablesian Horse. (Designed as a watch for this part of the coast, and under the command of the honorable the count of the Saxon Shore, so called from its situation being near, or rather opposite to the country of the Saxons, a warlike people in Germany. The count guarded this shore against the attacks of the Saxons.) They were stationed at this place under the command of a præpositus, who was particularly styled Gariennonensis, signifying the commander at the mouth of Garienis, or river now called the Yare. In ascertaining the number of troops which formed this garrison, we must have recourse to conjecture. A camp so considerable, Garianonum so strongly fortified, and of such great importance must necessarily require a large body of men to defend it. The Roman troops in Britain amounted to about fourteen thousand horse; and seventy-two thousand foot; and these being distributed into near one hundred and forty fortresses, the mean proportion of men to each, is about one hundred horse and four hundred and eighty or five hundred foot: but some stations could not accommodate so many, and others required more, and, also some consisted of horse only, and some wholly of infantry; consequently it is impossible to assert—positively the exact number of troops which composed this garrison.

Sir Henry Spelman, in his Iceni, and also Bishop Gibson, in his Camden, and from them, some writers of inferior note, have placed the Garianonum at Caistor; but Camden himself has fixed its situation at Burgh Castle; and Ives, in his account of this station, has confirmed the opinion of the latter with the greatest appearance of truth.

Upon a stream, whose largeness and rapidity must have rendered it formidable to passing armies; upon a shore, peculiarly exposed to the depredations of lawless pirates; and upon the boundary of a country possessed by a brave and hardy people, Garianonum must have been a station of the utmost importance to the Romans; it gave them weight and consequence in

C

the eyes of the Britons, who were destitute of every idea respecting mural fortifications; it established their influence, extended their territories, and afforded them a secure retreat, and an impregnable defence against the warlike Iceni, who, animated with the spirit of our immortal Boadicea, frequently rose in arms against the invaders of their native soil. In each of these views did the politic Romans consider their new-erected camp; in every respect it answered their designs, and in every particular corresponded with their wishes. From hence they commanded the estuary of the Yare, the German Ocean, and the interior country; and from hence they derived a power and consequence sufficient to awe and intimidate the Britons, and to prevent their making any military attempt against them.

Being destitute of express records, and unable to penetrate the clouds which ignorance and inattention have fabled over our Anglo-Roman antiquities, it is from the tenor of general history alone that we are enabled to fix a time for the building of this fortress; without such a consultation our utmost researches would fail us, and we should have only the miserable alternative of either guessing at the period or passing it by unnoticed.

That portion of Anglo-Roman history which more immediately respects Garianonum is short and limited; it commences with the reign of Claudius, and it extends no further.

This emperor, who assumed the purple at fifty years old, had neither the spirit, courage, nor perseverance of his great predecessor; yet, ambitious of following the steps of Julius, he formed the design of completing what Cæsar had begun, and of reducing Britain to a Roman province. In pursuance of this plan, he arrived here about the year of Christ, 45, having previously sent Aulus Plautius with troops sufficient to effect his intention. After the emperor had continued here six months he returned to Rome, and triumphed for conquests never obtained and for victories never won. (This is confirmed by an inscription in the Barberini Palace at Rome).

After the emperor's departure, Plautius remained here near four years, and carried on the Britannic war with spirit and success.

Next in command was the proprætor, Publius Ostorius Scapula, an experienced officer, in whom conduct and courage were equally united. To him the Romans were indebted for the subjection of the Iceni, to him they were obliged for the retention of their conquests, and to him we owe the foundation of Garianonum.

No part of the policy of this General claims our attention so much as the erecting this fortress: it was the most effectual method of curbing the high spirit of liberty inherent in the native Britons, of dissolving their alliances, breaking their power, and dividing their resources; and without these mural encampments, neither conquest nor security could have attended the Roman banner in Britain. From this period, therefore, we date the rise of Garianonum, built by the command and by the soldiers of Ostorius, and garrisoned by a cohort of veteran troops lately returned victorious from a battle with the Iceni.

Round our now well-cultivated fields, then cold, bleak, and woody, the Romans diverted themselves with the pleasures of the chase; and cross our now green and fertile meadows, they navigated their vessels and caught their fish.

Upon a rising hill, near the confluence of the rivers Yare and Waveney, and overlooking a large extent of Marshes which once formed the estuary it commanded, stands Burgh Castle, the ancient Garianonum of the Romans. In the construction of this camp the Romans pursued their usual method of security in building, and practised their favourite military architecture. It formed an irregular parallelogram, the parallel sides of which were equally right lines, and equally long, but the corners were rounded. Those camps, which were one-third longer than they were broad, were esteemed the most beautiful, but here the proportion is as two to one.

The principal wall of this station, in which is placed the Porta Prætoria, is that to the east, 14 feet high, 214 yards long, and 9 feet broad; the north and southern walls are just the same height and breadth, and just half the length; the western side has no remains of any wall, nor can we determine, with certainty, whether it ever had any; the sea might possibly be considered as a sufficient barrier on that side, and the steepness of the hill, as a collateral security.

Four massive round towers defend the eastern wall; the northern has one; and another, now thrown down, stood opposite on the southern. These towers were added after building the walls, and served not only to ornament and strengthen them, but as *turres exploratorii*, each having on the top a round hole two feet deep, and as many in diameter, evidently designed both for the erection of standards and signals, and for the admission of light temporary watch-towers, under the care and for the use of the spectators. The south-west corner of the station forms the pretorium, raised by the earth taken out of a vallum which surrounds and secures it, and which is sunk eight feet lower than the common surface of the area.

Near this was placed the south tower, which, being undermined a few years since by the force of the water running down the vallum after some very heavy rains, is fallen on one side near its former situation, but remains perfectly entire. The north tower having met with a similar accident is reclined from the wall at the top about six feet, has drawn a part of it, and caused a breach near it. The whole area of the station contains four acres and two roods, and, including the walls, five acres, two roods and twenty perches.

The mortar made use of by the Romans in this work was composed of lime and sand, unrefined by the sieve, and incorporated with common gravel and small pebbles. It was used two different ways; one cold, in the common manner now in use; the other, rendered fluid by fire and applied boiling hot. From the artful mixture of both in the same building, and from the coarse materials of the composition, this cement is extremely hard and durable, very difficult to break, and for several days indissoluble in water. The Romans, raising the wall to a convenient height with the former sort, at the end of every day's work poured the latter upon it, which immediately filled up the interstices, and when cold, proved a most powerful adhesive. The Roman bricks made use of at Burgh are of a fine red colour and very close texture; they are about one foot and a half long, one foot broad, and an inch and a half thick. It does not, however, appear that the Romans had any exact standard for the size of their bricks: in different stations their dimensions are considerably varied. We ought, however, to observe that either in the choice of their materials, or in their method of preparing them, they far excel those of later days, being much harder and less porous than ours, and for durableness more resembling stone, for which they were undoubtedly substituted.

In the area of this camp, and in many of the fields around it, vast numbers of Roman coins have been, and are still, found; but none of them rise higher than the reign of Domitian, (Ives, whom I have chiefly followed in this account of Garianonum, is somewhat mistaken here; for I have seen a coin, found in this place, of Romulus and Remus sucking the wolf), and the generality of them are much later. Few are found of any other metal than copper, and they are seldom curious, either for design or execution.

The fields adjoining to the eastern wall of Garianonum was the place allotted for depositing the ashes of the dead, and for the performance of the funeral rites. Here great numbers of Roman urns have been found, and innumerable pieces of them are everywhere spread over it: but neither the workmanship nor the materials of these urns have anything to recommend them: they are made of a coarse blue clay, brought from the neighbouring village of Bradwell, ill-formed, brittle, and porous. One of these urns, when the pieces were united, contained more than a peck and a half of corn, and had a large thick stone operculum on the top of it; within was a considerable number of bones and ashes, several fair pieces of Constantine and the head of a Roman spear. Here also was found a cockleare, or Roman spoon: it was of silver, and had a long handle very sharp at the point, that being used to pick fish out of the shell, as the bowl, or other end, served to take up liquids and small meat. Rings, keys, buckles, sibulæ, and various other reliquiæ of the Romans, are continually ploughed up in the fields adjoining to the station.

The intestine feuds of Italy called the Romans from their Britannic conquests between the years 418 and 427. They gathered all the treasures which could be found in Britain, some part of which they hid, perhaps in hopes of returning again in better days, and of recovering their effects from whence they had deposited them; or it might proceed from an ambitious design of informing posterity, that the Romans were once masters of this place. (In the year 1781, as some labourers were digging in the fields at Eye, in Suffolk, they discovered a leaden box, which contained several hundred Roman coins and medals; they were all of the purest gold, extremely well executed, and in the highest preservation; they were chiefly of the Emperors Arcadius and Honorius, the last who governed Britain; they were of about 11s. in value each, and near them were found some human bones. Whether they were buried with some eminent Roman, to defray his charges over Styx, or to inform posterity that the Romans once possessed this island, I leave the ingenious to determine. And in 1786 as the workmen were making a new turnpike road at Benacre, in this county, one of them struck his pick-axe against a stone bottle, which contained about 920 pieces of silver coin of Julius Cæsar, supposed by the date to have been hid there 1500 years. The coins were in general in good preservation, and included a large series, some few before Domitian; they were all about the size of sixpence, nine of them weighing an ounce. Sir Thomas Gooch purchased near 700, some were bought by different persons, and the remainder sold to a Jew, who retailed them at a low price in the neighbourhood. Some impressions of Aurelian, Germanicus, and Nerva Trajanus, were amongst them). The Britons, forsaken by their Roman guards, and exposed to the ravages of their merciless northern neighbours, frequently hid their money when threatened with fresh invasions; and if death or exile was the fate of the owners the secret was lost, and the treasure remained till an accidental plough or pick-axe once more brought it to light. Thus both Romans and Britons may have contributed to the great number of ancient coins discovered in the eastern parts of this county.

A Roman spur, which belonged to the Stablesain Horse, was found some years ago, in the area of this station; and is now in the possession of Mr. John Jex, Lowestoft, (son of John Jex, Esq.; late eminent merchant at Lowestoft, and one of his majesty's justices of the peace for the county of Suffolk: to whose kindness the author of this work is much indebted for many papers relative to the herring fishery at Lowestoft.) Sigebert, one of the heptarchial kings, and fifth monarch of the East Angles, ascended the East Anglian throne in the year 636. The Christian faith had made some faint progress in his dominions during the reign of his father, Redwald. To reinstate some of his subjects in their belief, and to convert others, was the great object of Sigebert's ambition: and to assist him in this design, he brought over from France a priest of Burgundy, named Felix, whom he procured to be consecrated bishop of the East Angles, and fixed the episcopal see at Dunwich. (Probably Flixton; a small village near Lowestoft, derived its name from this Felix, the first bishop of the East Angles. This parish is now consolidated with Blundeston, and valued, in Queen Anne's time at £14. There was formerly a small chapel in this parish, which is now in ruins, and appears to have been so ever since the year 1704; for in that year George Burrows, chapelwarden, delivered to his successor Henry Green the following things belonging to this chapel, viz. two books, a surplice, a cup, a cloth, a cushion, and an anchor and two pieces of iron belonging to the chancel window: therefore we may conclude from this, that after this time the chapel was become unfit for religious uses. Possibly so small a parish might be unable to keep it in repair, or possibly it might have received very great damage from the great November storm in the preceding year. This chapel is dedicated to St. Andrew, and is now made use of for the vile purpose of a farmer's out-house; the walls are demolished for the reparation of stables, and the font is split asunder to support the two ends of a hog's trough, to the great offence of common decency. Thomas Skeete was rector of this parish in 1704, and was the last rector; and William Fiske, in the year 1717, was the last chapelwarden. James Smith was rector in 1684 and 1685; John Burrell in 1697, and continued till 1701; and Robert Barrow was curate in 1703. Richard Newman was buried here January 14th, 1682; Elizabeth Bugg was buried May 23rd, 1683; William, son of William Fiske, husbandman, and Mary, his wife, was baptised, November 12th, 1702; John Wallis, of Great Yarmouth, single man, and Mary

Hollis, of Gorleston, single woman, were married December 21st, 1697; John Davey, of Raydon, single man, and Elizabeth Shinglers, of South town, single woman, were married July 4th, 1699; William Dawson, of Cromer, in the county of Norfolk, single man, and Ann Richardson, single woman, were married February 4th, 1695.)

Whilst Felix, under the patronage of the king, was spreading the gospel among the East Angles, Furseus, an Irish Monk, came over to his assistance; and collecting a company of religious persons, under the monastic rule, placed them at Burgh Castle, then called Cnobersburgh. (Cnobersburgh, that is Cunoberi-Urbs, from a Saxon Chief who had formerly resided here.)

Sigebert may be considered as the founder of this early monastery; but being afterwards slain in a battle with Penda, king of Mercia, the walls of the Roman camp afforded to Furseus and his monks a comfortable asylum; and like the Roman soldiers, they lived in tents or huts within the area. At this early period, regular edifices for the service of religion were unknown: churches were erected with hurdles, and covered with straw; and such buildings were fully sufficient for the devotion of a people, who in compliment to their next prince, might return to Paganism. The death of Sigebert deprived Furseus of a great and zealous patron; and to avoid the troubles which succeeded it, he left his monastery at Burgh, and retired into France.

The monks, however, appeared to have been endued with more constancy and resolution; for by the favours granted to this religious society, by some of the latter kings of the East Angles, we find they remained there for several years: but how long they continued at Burgh, or when they left it, is uncertain.

It appears that in the reign of Edward I. the prior of Bromeholme held the manor of Burgh, of our lord the king, in capite; and the prior and monks of Bromeholme continued lords of this manor till the dissolution of their house, 26 Henry VIII.; when, with their revenues, it again reverted to the crown, who possessed it till Queen Mary sold it to William Roberts, town-clerk of Yarmouth.

Roger de Burgh gave the advowson of this church to the priory of St. Olave, at Herringfleet for perpetual alms; and King Henry III, confirmed the donation to them. The prior presented to the rectory, and had a reserved pension of four marks out of it, which is still paid to the owner of St. Olave's. After the dissolution of the priory the patronage of the church came to the crown. (St. Olaves, in Herringfleet, was a priory of black Canons, founded by Roger Fitz-Osbert, of Somerley the last of that family, to the honour of the St. Mary and St. Olave, the King and martyr, in the beginning of the reign of Henry III. Herein were, about the time of the dissolution, five or six religious, who were endowed with £49 11s. 7d. per annum. The site of this house, with great part of the lands, were granted to Henry Jerningham, Esq., patron, 26th January, 38 Henry VIII. The site of this house, together with a considerable estate, comprehending almost the whole of the parish of Herringfleet, about half a century ago, passed from the Bacon family to Hill Mussendon, Esq., who bequeathed it to his elder brother Carteret, who had taken the name of Leathes; from him it descended to John Leathes, Esq., his son, a very worthy gentlemen. and much respected. and is now in the possession of his widow, Mrs. Elizabeth Leathes. Camden says that Sir James Hobart, attorney general and privy councellor to Henry VII., built Loddon Church from the ground, St. Olaves Bridge, and the causeway thereby; but it appears from an inscription in Loddon church, that Sir James built only the former; and that the bridge and causeway were built by dame Hobart, his wife. In the reign of Edward I. there was a ferry near the priory of St. Olave, to carry passengers across the river in a boat. This ferry was then, and for several years before, kept by one Sireck, a fisherman, who received for his trouble, bread, herrings, and such like things, to the value of 20s. a year. After his decease, William, his son, did the like, and made it worth 30s. per year; Ralph, his son, also did the same, and had of his neighbours bread and corn, and of strangers money. And because the prior of Toft hindered passengers from going through his marsh, the said Ralph purchased a passage through the prior's marsh, paying 12d. a year; and of the commoners of Herringfleet, he purchased a way through their common, and was to carry the mover at all times free for it, and then it became worth £10 per year; after Ralph's decease, John, his brother, had it, and it was valued at £12 per year; John sold it to Robert de Ludham, who made it worth £15 per year; and he gave it to Roger de Ludham, who held it till the 25th of Edward I. 1296, the time when that king sent out a writ to William de Kerdeston, sheriff of Norfolk and Suffolk, to enquire, to what detriment it would be to any person, for him to grant leave to Jeffery Pollerin, of Yarmouth, to build a bridge over the river at St. Olave's priory; and a jury being empannelled, etc., returned, that the building of a bridge there would be to the detriment of Roger de Ludham and the prior of Toft; but it would be to the great benefit of the country. Whereupon leave was given, and a bridge began, at least, as it is supposed, but perhaps, not finished in a durable manner; for amongst the patents of the 9th of Henry V. anno domino, 1420, one is for building a bridge over the water between Norfolk and Suffolk, at Seint Tholowe's ferry. What was then done doth not appear, but probably not much; for it was not till the reign of Henry VII.—it is generally believed—that the late bridge was built by dame Hobart. This bridge was found to be so much in decay about 1770 that a new one was forced to be built in its place. The remains of the priory at Herringfleet were chiefly taken down in 1784, but some parts of it are still left. John Jernegan, of Somerley, Esq., and Agnes, his wife, were buried in St. Mary's chapel, in the priory of St. Olave, at Herringfleet, about the year 1470. He left Somerley on his son's marriage, and went and resided at Cove, near Beccles. The Jernegans became owners of St. Olave's, also Herringfleet and the Somerley estates, by marriage with the Fitz-Osberts: for Sir Walter Jernegan marrying Isabel, daughter, and at length heir of Sir Peter Fitz-Osbert, of Somerley, and her brother, Roger Fitz-Osbert, leaving no issue, Somerley came to the Jernegans about 1230, and became the capital seat of that family. The Jernegans came from Horham. The Jernegans of Cossey are a younger branch of the family late of Somerley.)

The church is a small building, consisting of a nave, chancel, and round tower, and is dedicated to St. Peter. It is a rectory, anciently valued at ten marks; in the king's books at £6 13s. 4d.; and being of the sworn value of £44 6s. 1d., is discharged of first-fruits and tenths. The parsonage house adjoins to the north-west corner of the churchyard, and has thirty-nine acres of glebe belonging to it.

The present rector is the Rev. John Bellward, to whom the author here acknowledges himself much indebted for his kindness to him many years since.

## SECTION II.

### OF THE ORIGIN OF LOWESTOFT.

LESTOFFE, Laystoft, Laistoe, or, as it was more anciently called Lothnwistoft, is supposed by some to have derived its name from Lothbroch, the noble Dane, on his arriving in this island about the year 861, and from wista (wista was a measure of land in use among the ancient Saxons, and was equivalent to half a hide, or sixty acres), a half-hide of land; but I apprehend, erroneously, as it is doubtful whether these several appellations be of any earlier date than the reign of Queen Elizabeth. In the charter granted by Edward III. for uniting Kirkley road to the haven of Yarmouth, we find it expressed Loystoft and Lowystofte; probably, therefore, the present mode of expression, Lowestoft, may be only the former ones modernized by subsequent writers. Perhaps, at this distant period, it may be difficult to ascertain with certainty, the true etymology of its name, though possibly it may be no improbable conjecture to suppose its being derived, in some measure, from the fairs and market being held formerly below the cliff, and from the town being situated upon the most eastern point of land in England.

In the preceding section an ample description is given of the numerous revolutions which the northern part of the island of Lothingland experienced from the various incursions of the sea, from the earliest period which history can furnish us with, down to the present time; and it is equally evident that the more southern part of it, particularly that whereon Lowestoft is situated, has been subject to as large a share of the same vicissitudes.

In those early ages, when the Romans were in possession of Britain, it is highly probable that the sea, by its frequent irruptions had not only approached, but actually formed those cliffs, upon whose summits the town of Lowestoft is situated.

During those early periods, when the rivers which form the northern and southern boundaries of the island discharged themselves into the ocean with an extensive and rapid current, it appears that the incursions of that boisterous element upon the extremities of the island had made its utmost progress; but with respect to the intermediate parts of it, the case was somewhat different; for it is evident from the ancient maps of the coast and from authentic records which we find interspersed in topographical history, that those intermediate parts of the island protruded themselves much farther towards the east than either the northern or southern boundaries of it did, or either as they do at this present time.

As a corroborating circumstance of what is here asserted, we shall observe that some centuries since there was situated on that part of the coast which lies between Yarmouth and Lowestoft, a village called Newton, which has long since been entirely swallowed up by the ocean without leaving any other vestiges of it remaining than a small piece of land called Newton Green. Since that period the sea on that part of the island appears to have receded again; as formerly we find there was sufficient space between the bottom of the cliffs and the sea for the neck of the Yare to extend itself south as far as Corton before it discharged itself into the sea; although at this present time the ocean on the same part of the island approaches very near the cliffs.

That the basis of the cliff on whose summit the town of Lowestoft is situated was washed by the German Ocean during that era when the Romans resided in Britain, will evidently appear from an attentive investigation of the coast contiguous to the town, where it is very conspicuous how the cliff inclines to the west as it advances towards the river which lies to the south of Lowestoft, occasioned, probably, by the violence of the current, which in those early ages united that river with the ocean; and also the gradual descent of the cliff from the northern part of Lowestoft to the river on the south part of it, where it becomes a perfect level with the adjacent country is still evident, and points out the ancient state of the river and the parts adjoining to the same. These circumstances, undoubtedly rendered this spot extremely convenient for fishermen resorting to the coast, and probably were those which gave birth to the origin of Lowestoft, as similar circumstances did afterwards to the origin of Yarmouth.

In succeeding ages, when the mouth of the Yare, from being obstructed by sand-banks, was reduced to the more contracted limits of a narrow channel; and when every communication between the ocean and the Waveney, had either totally ceased, or become an insignificant stream, it is evident, that the sea at that time receded from the extremities of the island, and made considerable encroachments on the intermediate parts of it. This is evident, not only from the above-mentioned circumstance respecting the village of Newton, but also from those which follow: for we find (Lowestoft town-book) that in the beginning of the reign of Henry VIII a block-house, which had been erected for the defence of the town, was then standing to the east of Lowestoft, about four furlongs distant from the present boundaries of the sea; so that the place where Lowestoft roads are now situated, was at that time firm land, interspersed with houses, and defended by a fortress; which continued until the 25th of Henry VIII when they were either taken down or destroyed by the encroachments of the sea. And it also appears, about the 30th of Queen Elizabeth, that the sea had made such great alterations in the roads, and in the sands and shores bordering upon Lowestoft, that the roads before the town, which, in the reign of Henry VIII were dry land, had not then less than three fathoms water at the lowest ebb. This was the state of the coast near Lowestoft in the reigns of Henry VIII and Queen Elizabeth, and since that time the sea has kept encroaching near the town; for about sixty or seventy years ago, upon every gale of wind at north-west, especially if it happened at a spring tide, the sea will oftentimes force its way over the beach with great violence, and with so large a body of water, as not only to overflow the Denes, the yards of the fish-houses, and approach even to the bottom of the gardens formed upon the declivity of the cliff, but would also endanger the foundations of the fish-houses themselves. We had a remarkable instance of these formidable irruptions of the sea, in the year 1712; when a fish-house, in the southern part of the town, was entirely washed away, and another fish-house and barn were so exceedingly damaged, as to make it necessary to have them taken down. And, again, in the year 1717, the sea, in one of those raging tides, forced its way over the isthmus which separates the peninsula from the adjacent country, with such irresistable fury, as to carry away Mutford Bridge, which cost the county £200 to repair the damages. But these irruptions have for some time ceased, and the apprehensions which they excited have, consequently, long since subsided: but so fluctuating in her operations is this inconstant element, that upon that part of the coast which lies opposite to Lowestoft, the sea has lately much receded, and is making proportionable encroachments on the parts which lie to the north of it. From all these circumstances we may form this general observation, that whenever the sea obtrudes upon the coast near Lowestoft, it retires from the intermediate parts or coast to the north of it; and when it recedes at Lowestoft, it gains upon the more nothern part.

Being almost destitute of express records (the greater part of them being destroyed by fire in the year 1606) relative to the town of Lowestoft, it is chiefly from selecting circumstances which we find interspersed in history, that we are able to form any conjectures respecting its origin.

The principal evidence which now remains respecting the antiquity of Lowestoft, is that of "The Narrative of the Proceedings between Yarmouth and Lowestoft during the contest respecting the Herring Fishery." (A sand, similar to that whereon Yarmouth was founded, appears at this time to be forming a little to the north of the point bearing east from Lowestoft. It begins to be dry even at high water, and at low water is of considerable length and firmness; so that, probably, in another century, it may become [as Yarmouth was originally] a convenient situation for fishermen to dry their nets, etc.; and who may be induced afterwards to erect the necessary buildings for the purposes of a sea-fearing life; and from thence may give birth to the origin of a new town, which may, with propriety, be called New Lowestoft; as should that ever be the case, it must prove extremely prejudicial to the old town.) Wherein it appears that Lowestoft is a more ancient town than Yarmouth. But notwithstanding the proof which arises from this evidence, it may be necessary for us to guard ourselves against an error which otherwise might mislead us, concerning the origin of Yarmouth; and, therefore, it may be proper to extend our enquiries to this circumstance, and to endeavour to place it in a true point of light. What endangers our mistake respecting Yarmouth, is as follows:—In the tables of records, hanging in the common hall of Yarmouth, it is expressed that in the days of Canutus there was a sand in the sea, which began to be dry land from Anno 1040 to 1090. And in a manuscript book, containing the originality or antiquity of Yarmouth, it is asserted, that in Edward the Confessor's time, the same sand began to appear at low water; and that in the days of King Harold and William the Conqueror the same grew so dry, and not overflown, that they then began to build tents, and fishermen did then begin to repair thither, about killing of herrings. These records—for want of better, which have since been published—have embarrassed the world with difficulties, and involved them in error; and the more so, as these records have been regarded as authentic: but if we compare them with those which are known to be genuine, we may easily detect the imposition, and prove them to be erroneous. It plainly appears, from what has been already observed, that the sand on which Yarmouth was founded was dry in the year 495, when Cerdick the Saxon first landed there; and that shortly after, Yarmouth began to be erected by the Saxons, first on a sand a little to the west of that whereon it now stands, and then shortly after, the inhabitants removed to this latter or Cerdick Sand, upon account of the unhealthy situation of the former. And it is also further recorded that in the time of Edward the Confessor, Yarmouth was become so opulent, that there flourished in it seventy burgesses. From hence it is evident that the former account above mentioned, concerning Yarmouth being founded about the year 1040, is evidently an error; and, consequently, to date the origin of Lowestoft only prior to that year, would be making it, in fact, of less antiquity than Yarmouth

About the year 420, when the Romans had left Britain, the river Yare, at that time very capacious, was found so extremely commodious for the reception of a fleet of armed vessels meditating a descent on this coast, that the Saxons made choice of this place for that purpose, and soon after landed here; and about the beginning of the sixth century began to lay the foundation of Yarmouth, which proved afterwards the most formidable fortress on this part of the coast; and became a place of such perfect security for the foreign invaders, as to resemble, in some measure, the famous Gariononum of the ancient Romans. Prior to this time the ground whereon Yarmouth was afterwards built was only a barren sand, just emerging from its watery element; and if we extend our investigation but a little farther back we shall be unable to distinguish it above the surface of the pathless ocean; and, when it did appear, and also for some time after—previous to the building of Yarmouth—the principal use that was made of it was to serve the temporary conveniences of fishermen resorting to the coast, and the other purposes of a maritime life.

But with respect to Lowestoft the case is quite otherwise. The cliffs, indeed, whereon it is situated, might be formed during that period when the Romans resided in Britain; but the ground itself is of the same origin with the other parts of the island. How long the town had begun to be erected before the sea approached so far as to form these cliffs is now uncertain; we, therefore, can only say that as its situation was found to be extremely convenient for every purpose respecting the herring-fishery, that probably it was the general rendezvous of the fishermen resorting to this coast; and, consequently, not only gave birth to the town, but also to the establishing of a fishery, which has been its chief support from time

D

immemorial, and has continued to be so till this present time. From hence we may conclude that prior to the founding of Yarmouth, Lowestoft was the principal place of resort for all the fishermen employed in the herring fishery on this coast; and furnished with provisions and other necessaries, not only such vessels as were fitted out from our own part of the coast, but those also which resorted hither from the northern and western parts of England; and, therefore, we may reasonably conclude that Lowestoft is a more ancient town than Yarmouth, as we are able to trace its origin previous to the fourth century, and, consequently, before the ground was formed whereon Yarmouth was afterwards erected.

Lowestoft, as we observed before, is situated upon the most eastern point of land in England; it stands upon a lofty eminence, and commands an extensive prospect of the German Ocean, and when beheld from the sea has the noblest and most beautiful appearance of any town upon the coast between Newcastle and London; it chiefly consists of an extensive arrangement of houses, whose line of direction is nearly north and south, and, consequently, faces the sea; it stands upon a dry soil, upon the summit of a cliff, and enjoys a most salubrious air, keen but bracing; and not being exposed to any of those unwholesome damps and vapours which generally arise from low grounds and marshes, it is rendered not only a very pleasant, but a very healthy situation.

The declivity of this cliff, which formerly was one continued slope of barren sand, is now converted by modern improvements into very beautiful hanging gardens, descending from the dwelling-houses above, to the fish houses at the bottom of the hill; and being interspersed with alcoves and summer houses, are not only extremely pleasant and convenient to the inhabitants, but exhibit a very pleasing appearance when beheld from the sea.

At the bottom of these gardens is a long arrangement of fish houses which extend the whole length of the town, and are so numerous, that had they been placed in a more compact form, would have been sufficient of themselves to have formed a considerable town.

Lowestoft derives many conveniences from the fish houses being detached from the other buildings of the town, and placed at the bottom of the hill; such as the easy conveyance of herrings from the boats; also the avoiding those very offensive smells arising from the smoke and drainage of the fish, which otherwise it would be subject to, if the houses wherein the herring are cured had been intermixed with the dwelling-houses; and, consequently, the town is thereby exempted from those disagreeable nuisances, so much and so justly complained of in other places. Between the fish houses and the top of the beach stand the boats employed in the herring fishery, which are arranged before the town to a considerable length; also the lower light-house, conveniences for boat building and the bathing machines. (Bathing in salt water is much in use at this time in many parts of the kingdom, particularly at Southampton, Brighthelmston, Margate, Scarborough, Yarmouth, Lowestoft, and at other places. It was recommended originally for medicinal purposes only, it being pronounced by the faculty to be useful in the cure of many diseases; and, probably, in many cases it has been productive of very happy effects. The first bathing machine in Lowestoft was erected in Lowestoft in 1768, by Mr. Scrivener, from a model procured from Margate, in Kent. It met with that success, that a second machine was soon after set up, and afterwards a third. The bathing season commences about the month of August, and continues about six weeks. During this part of the summer season, the resort of genteel and fashionable company to the town is very considerable, and is of great utility to many of the inhabitants, respecting lodgings and other accommodations. Among many other improvements which the town has lately received, may be included a fine new turnpike road which runs through Lowestoft to Yarmouth; a mail cart under the direction of the general post-office, passes through the town twice a day, with letters to and from London; and the London stage coach once every day.)

The shore opposite Lowestoft is bold and steep consisting of a hard sand intermixed with shingle and perfectly free from ouze and those beds of mud too frequently met with on other shores.

Lowestoft is about a mile in length; and consists chiefly of one principal street, running in a gradual descent from north to south, which is intersected by several smaller streets or lanes from the west; it is well paved, particularly High Street, and consists of about 445 houses—exclusive of the fish houses—which are chiefly built with brick; several of the houses have been lately re-built in the modern style, and make a handsome appearance. (It is probable that the town consists of much the same number of houses now, as it did many years ago; there being very few houses erected upon new foundations, but only re-built upon the old ones. The town is much admired for its fine air, and its remarkably pleasant and healthy situation which much contributes to the longevity of its inhabitants. In 1755, died here, Thomas Cockrum, aged 103 years; in 1784, Silvester Manclarke, aged 107; and in 1788, John Wilkerson aged 96). Lowestoft contains about 2231 inhabitants. An extract from the parish register of Lowestoft shews the number of marriages, christenings, and burials from the year 1561 to 1713, marriages 2539, christenings 10,548, burials 10,056.

During the civil war and to the restoration of Charles II., no entries were made in the parish register. The Rev. Jacob Rous, then vicar, says, that on the 14th March, 1643, himself with many others were carried away prisoners, by Colonel Cromwell, to Cambridge; so that for some time following there was neither minister or clerk in this town; but the inhabitants were obliged to procure one another to baptize their children, by which means there was no register kept; only a few were by myself baptised in those intervals when I enjoyed my freedom. Parish register, 7th June 1646, Jacob Rous. There are many entries in this register of people being married by a justice of the peace, as was usual at this time. Thomas Pacy, widower, and Mary Arnold, widow were married first by a justice and then by a minister, 20th August, 1655. By an Act passed in 1653, those who were in the commission of the peace were empowered to perform the office of matrimony; previous to the marriage of the parties, the bands were to be published three times, either in the church or chapel, on Sundays after morning exercise, or on the market days in some neighbouring town.

Lowestoft is bounded on the north by Gunton, on the east by the German Ocean, on the south by Kirkley, and on the west by Oulton. The soil next the east is light and sandy, but in the adjacent fields it is considerably heavier, being in many places intermixed with clay. There is a market here on Wednesdays, and also two fairs are held in this town, one on the twelfth of May, the other on the tenth of October. (When you pass out of the present Market Place into the lane called Fair Lane—so called from its leading to the place where the fairs were formerly held—and pass directly westward, till you have passed the four cross-ways, you then enter the place where the said fairs were kept some years ago; but upon an application of the town to the Rev. Sir Ashurst Allen, Bart., Lord of the Manor of Lowestoft, in the year 1768, the fairs were removed from thence, and were afterwards held in the market place, and have been kept there ever since.)

In 1735 the number of inhabitants in this town were computed to be 2,200: but by an acutal survey, taken by the minister and churchwardens on the 7th and 8th of August, 1775, the number of inhabitants in Lowestoft was found to be 2231, including lodgers; the number of dwelling-houses 445, of which 438 were occupied; and the number of public-houses, 24; the principal of which is the Crown, kept by Mr. Capon, and is a very good inn. It appears from an actual survey of the houses and lands in this parish, as taken in 1642, that the yearly value of the former was £412 6s. 8d.; and of the latter, £447 11s. 8d.: total value, £859 18s. 4d. But in the year 1649 they appear to have decreased in value considerably, as is evident from the following return of their value, taken that year, in consequence of an order of Parliament.

"Lowestoft, in Suffolk, within the half hundred of Lothingland, the 16th of June, 1649.

"We whose names are hereunto subscribed, inhabitants there, being appointed Surveyors by virtue of a warrant from the commissioners, authorised by an Act of the present Parliament, to return the true value of all the lands and tenements within the said town; have, in obedience thereunto, considered thereof; and in **our judgment we do** return the yearly value **to be about** £655 per annum.

(Signed),<br>
ROBERT ALLIN, HENRY WARD, FRANCIS KINGSLEY,<br>
JAMES WILDE, EDWARD BROWNE."

(The decrease was occasioned, probably, by the civil war).

After you have ascended Rant's score, and crossed High street, **the** first turn out of the Blue Anchor Lane to the left will bring you into a large area, where was formerly kept the market, and is now called the Old Market.

In the year 1698, the Corn Cross, the Town Chamber that is over it, and the adjoining chapel were built by subscription. They are situated about the middle of the town, on the west side of the High street, and formed originally a handsome building. This structure is entered by three large folding pallisade doors or gates. In the upper part **of** it is a clock, and on the top of it a cupola, in which is a bell to summon **the inhabitants** to attend divine service at the chapel, and for other necessary **purposes of the** parish. (The clock was made by Mr. Isaac Blowers, of Beccles, **and cost** £20; the expense of the frame, and other necessary work in fixing it, £2 13s. 6d.—total, £22 13s. 6d. In defraying these charges was collected a subscription **of** £15 16s. 6d.; the remaining money was advanced by the Rev. Mr. Tanner, vicar, who was repaid again in three years by the churchwardens). The chamber over the Cross is the place where the parish usually assemble to consult about town business; it is also fitted up as a schoolroom, and has been used for that purpose ever since the building was first erected, till within a few years past. In the year 1768 the north door of the Cross was closed up, and that part of the Cross was converted into a vestry for the chapel. In the **year** 1698, when this building was first erected, and the front part of it reserved for the purposes of a Market Cross, the market was removed from the place now called the Old Market, to that part of the High street contiguous to the building; but the spot being afterwards found an inconvenient situation for the market to be held in, it was resolved by the parish, in 1703, to take down an inn—called the White Horse—which stood on the ground where the market is now kept—the whole front was parallel with that of the adjoining houses—and re-build it further backwards; which resolution being carried into execution, the market was removed from the Cross to the spot of ground where that inn formerly stood, and has continued there ever since. It is now the sign of the Queen's Head, from Queen Anne, in whose reign it was re-built.

How long the market and fairs have been held at Lowestoft will appear from the following account of the grant, taken from Bishop Tanner's Collections, in the registry at Norwich, wherein it is said, that in the reign of King Henry IV. the king granted to William de la Pole, marquis and earl of Suffolk, one market and two fairs, below the village of Lowestoft—in the reign of Henry IV. the fairs and markets were held below the cliff—which is in the ancient demesne of the Crown of England; and also appoints him his steward, **to** hold his courts of market and fair; and ordains that no justice, viscount, escheator, inquisitor, bailiff, steward of hospital, or clerk of market, tax **the** said village in any manner. And that all people holding of, and residing in the said village, be free from all custom and toll of their goods and vendable wares throughout the whole kingdom. This last-mentioned privilege, how trifling soever it may appear now was deemed an important one at the time it was granted; and was so far accounted valuable in the reign of Queen Elizabeth, as to be renewed in the writ of exemption granted to the town by that princess.

The original design of the Cross of Lowestoft was the providing a convenient shelter for the farmers to stand in when they brought their corn to market; and was always used for that purpose till the year 1768, when part of it was inclosed for a vestry to the chapel, and the remaining part is now made use of merely as a passage to that place of worship.

I should now proceed to give an account of the several benefactions which have been given to this parish by charitable and well-disposed persons, such as a large donation in land, for repairing and ornamenting the church and assisting the poor; an alms house for the residence of four poor people;

and also the very liberal donations for instituting two grammar schools in this town, exclusive of several other benefactions of lesser importance, which I shall pass over in this place, referring the reader to Section V., where they are more particularly enumerated and described.

Lowestoft being part of the ancient demesne of the Crown, has, in consequence thereof, been entitled to many privileges; though many of them, through the various vicissitudes which all human affairs are subject to, are now become useless, and almost forgotten; such as paying toll, stallage, frontage, etc., and an exemption from contributing to the charges of the knights of the shire during their attendance in Parliament; which privileges, with several others which are particularly mentioned in the following writ of exemption, were, some centuries since, esteemed as valuable ones, however they may be regarded now. But there is one privilege which the town is entitled to by virtue of this writ, which is of too advantageous a nature to be passed over unnoticed, namely, that of being exempted from serving on juries, either at the assizes or quarter sessions, being subject to those juries only as are empanelled by the lord of the manor, coroner, etc. This privilege the town enjoys to this day, and is the only one out of the many specified in the writ, from which the town at this present time receives any real benefit; though, possibly, were they duly attended to, they might not at this distant period be found altogether unprofitable.

The above-mentioned privileges, which were granted to the town of Lowestoft, as part of the Crown, appear, by the said writ, to have been confirmed in the fifteenth year of the reign of Queen Elizabeth; and were again renewed in the fourth year of Charles I.—and is now allowed by the sheriff of this county—as is evident from the writ itself.

A writ of exemption granted to the town of Lowestoft, the 15th of Queen Elizabeth, 1573, and renewed the 4th Charles I., 1604:—

"CHARLES, by the grace of God, of England Scotland, France, and Ireland, King, Defender of the Faith, to all to whom these presents shall come, greeting.—We have seen the enrollments of certain letters executory, bearing date the twenty-seventh day of May, in the fifteenth year of the reign of our dearly beloved sister, the lady Elizabeth, late Queen of England, made and granted to the men and tenants of the town of Lothnwistoft, in the half-hundred of Ludingland, in the county of Suffolk, enrolled in the rolls of chancery, and remaining there on record, in these words: 'The Queen, to all sheriffs, mayors, bailiffs, constables, officers, and others, her liege people, as well within liberties as without, to whom these presents shall come, greeting.—Whereas, according to the custom in our kingdom of England, hitherto obtained and approved, the men and tenants in ancient demesne of the crown of England, should and ought to be free from toll, stollage, chiminage, pontage, pannage piccage, murrage, lastage, and passage, throughout the whole kingdom aforesaid, according to the custom aforesaid, concerning men and tenants in ancient demesne of the crown of England, who always hitherto, time out of mind, have been wont to be free from contributing towards the expenses of the knights coming to the Parliament of our ancestors, formerly kings of England, for the community of the county; also, according to the same custom, the men and tenants of the manors which are in ancient demesne of the Crown aforesaid, upon account of the lands and tenements which they hold in the same demesne, ought not to be returned to the assizes upon juries or any recognizances, except only in such cases as are to be transacted in the courts of such manors (a court-leet has been held by the lord of the manor of Lowestoft from time immemorial. A jury used to be empanelled at Lowestoft, which was obliged to attend at the adjoining parish of Corton, the Thursday after Ash-Wednesday, to be sworn. On the Friday they took a survey of the town of Lowestoft, in order to present such nuisances as came under their jurisdiction; and on the Saturday they dined at an inn in the town, where they appointed constables, ale-founders, etc., for the said town, for the year ensuing. After the decade of Sir Thomas Allen, in 1765, this custom was discontinued): and forasmuch as the town of Lothnwistoft, in the half-hundred of Ludingland, is in ancient demesne of the Crown, as it appears by a certificate sent to us by the treasurer, chancellor of our exchequer, from thence into our court of chancery aforesaid. We enjoin and command you, and every one of you, to permit all the men and tenants in the town aforesaid, to be free from toll, and the rest of the premises, and every one of them, throughout our whole kingdom aforesaid, from the expense of the knights of the shire aforesaid; and, also, not to return the men and tenants of the said town to the assizes, upon juries or any recognizances, except only in such cases as are to be transacted in the courts of such towns. In testimony whereof, etc., witness the Queen, at Westminster, the twenty-seventh day of May, in the fifteenth year of her reign.' And we though' fit, by these presents, to exemplify the tenor of the enrollments of the premises aforesaid, at the request of Robert Mellinge, Esq., in witness whereof we have caused these our letters to be made patent. Witness Ourself, at Westminster, the twenty-sixth day of February, in the fourth year of our reign.

The town of Lowestoft appears to have experienced, at different times, a large proportion of the many miseries and distresses arising from those dreadful calamities, pestilence, fire, war, storms, and tempests, which mankind are frequently exposed to.

The great plague which made such dreadful ravages in Europe in 1346, was brought into England in 1348. In the following year it raged with great fury at Yarmouth, where there died in one year 7000 persons; and, most probably, Lowestoft had its share of the calamity, as it was so general, that not above the tenth part of the inhabitants escaped.

In 1547 the plague raged with such violence in this town, that it cost in some weeks, for distressed people, three pounds per week, exclusive of the weekly collections, amounting in the whole to fifty pounds at the least. This weekly collection was a voluntary contribution of the humane and charitable; for the poor were not provided for by Act of Parliament till the reign of Queen Elizabeth. The town did not receive, on this occasion, any assistance of consequence, either from the country, or from the town lands. It was customary in these times, when there was no poors' rates, and a town was distressed with any grievous calamity, for the neighbouring towns to give their assistance.

In 1579, the plague raged so violently in this part of England, that at Yarmouth there died, between the month of May and the Michaelmas following, above 2,000 persons. In consequence whereof, the Mayor of Newcastle, on the 22nd September, in that year, sent a letter to the bailiffs of Yarmouth, forbidding their going to that place for coals; and, probably, the plague at this time was at Lowestoft. In 1579 twice the number of people died in Lowestoft, than in 1578. In 1585 there was a great sickness in this town; for it appears by the register, that in the month of August only, in that year, there were buried 36 persons; and in the whole year, the number amounted to 134. The burials, on an average, for the preceding seven years, were annually about 44.

But the greatest sickness which the town ever experienced, was that in the year 1603; in which year 280 persons were buried in this parish during only the space of five months; and in the whole year, 316.

There died in May, 21; in June, 79; in July, 100; in August, 55; in September 25; Total 280.

In the year 1635 there was another great sickness in this town; in which year, 46 persons were buried in August only; and the number of burials in the whole year, amounted to 170. Probably it was the plague.

Another calamity, by which this town has greatly suffered, is war. If we recollect the many injuries it sustained in Kett's rebellion; the money it was obliged to raise, when threatened with an invasion from the Spanish Armada; the frequent plunderings and other depredations it was exposed to, from its attachment to the cause, during the usurpation of Oliver Cromwell; the distress which it laboured under, when deprived of its principal inhabitants and the greater part of its most useful sailors, to serve in the navy, during our wars with the Dutch; and the heavy expenses it has been subjected to in succeeding wars with the French, in erecting fortresses for the defence of the town. During our wars with the Dutch, the British navy was furnished by the town of Lowestoft with three admirals, viz., Sir John Ashby, Sir Thomas Allen, and Richard Utber, Esq.; also with four captains, viz., Robert and John Utber, sons of the admiral; Captain Canham, and Captain Whiting; exclusive of a great number of excellent seamen. All these circumstances being duly attended to, we shall find too much reason for including this calamity, not only among the many, but even among the greatest misfortunes which the town ever laboured under.

To the above calamities of pestilence and war, may be added that of fire. In the year 1606 the Vicarage-house belonging to this town was burnt down, and never re-built; so that there has not been any Vicarage-house belonging to the parish ever since. This house was situated upon a small piece of glebe land near the Church, which, a few years ago, was taken into the church-yard, and lies at the north-west corner. The Vicarage, when burnt, was occupied by John Glesson, vicar; at which time the old parish register and many of the ancient records belonging to the town, in his possession, were destroyed.

On the 10th March, 1644—5, there happened in this town a great and terrible fire, which consumed dwelling-houses, fish-houses, and goods, as much property as was estimated at £10,297 2s. 4d.

The General Account of each man's particular loss, in dwelling-houses, fish-houses, goods, wares, etc., which happened the 10th day of March, 1644—5, by a lamentable fire at Lowestoft, in the county of Suffolk, as it was surveyed, and viewed, and given into the committee appointed for the same, at Lowestoft, the 25th day of April, 1645; namely:—

John Arnold, dwelling house £143, goods £40—total £183. Thomas Smiter dwelling-houses, £43 10s; goods £15 8s. 4d.—total £58 18s. 4d. William Greenwood, dwelling-house £590. Thomas Webb, dwelling-house £544; fish-houses £450; goods £77 3s.—£1071 3s. Thomas Arnold, dwelling-house £167 10s.; fish-house, £81; goods £127 3s.—total £375 13s. Thomas Mighells, dwelling-house £353; fish-office £21—total £374. Mr. Rivit, dwelling-house, £269; fish-houses £195; goods £240—total £704. Robert Ashby, dwelling house £308 10s.; goods £250—total £558 10s. James Smiter, dwelling house £102. Nicholas Pattin, dwelling-house £34 10s.; goods £23—total £57 10s. Mr. Simonds, dwelling-house £435. Thomas Barrett, dwelling-house £5. Oliver Ashby, dwelling-house £27 10s.; goods £6—total £33 10s. Samuel Fisher, dwelling-house £71 10s.; goods £30—total £101 10s. John Fisher, dwelling-house £215. Robert Ferney, dwelling-house £91 10s.; goods £14—£150 10. Richard Rooke, goods £6. Robert Bits, dwelling-house £162; goods £370—total £532. Mr. Abertson, dwelling-house £200; fish-house £163—total £363. Thomas Harvey, dwelling-house £383; fish-house £108; goods £40—total £531. Mr. Smith, fish-house £230; goods £100—total £330. James Munds, fish-house £145; goods £113 10s.—total £258 10s. Josiah Wilde, fish-house £400; goods £280—total £680. John Barker, fish-house £25; goods £85—total £110. James Wilde, fish-house, £120; goods, £40—total £160. Robert Brissingham, fish-house £94. John Brissingham, fish-house £10. Mr. Allen, fish-house £140; goods £40—total £180. Thomas Guler, fish-house £5. Robert Tooley, fish-house £146; goods £8 8s.—total £154 8s. Mr. Reeve, fish house £102. Thomas Fulwood, fish house £240; goods £32—total £272. Robert Coe, fish-house £156; goods £49—total £205. John Page, fish-house £54; goods £12—total £66. William Cauliam, fish-house £210; goods £15—total £225. John Muese, sen., goods £100. John Meuse, jun., goods £50. William Muese, goods £150. Thomas Muese, goods £20. Henry Geury, goods £35. Henry Ward, jun., goods £97. William Underwood, goods £80. John Dennis, goods £55. James Mendham, goods £2. Richard Mighells, goods, £190. Michael Bently, goods £112. George Woodgate, goods £200. Daniel Sterry, goods £2. Stephen Trip, goods £5. John Jerhenson, goods £7. —The totals are—dwelling-houses, £4145 10s.; fishhouses, £3085; goods £3066 12s. 4d.—grand total, £10,297 2s. 4d.

On Sunday the 14th August, 1670, there happened another terrible fire in this town, which consumed six dwelling-houses and two barns filled with corn; which loss amounted to three hundred and fifty pounds. (In consequence of this misfortune, the following petition, signed by five of his Majesty's justices of the peace, the ministers of Lowestoft, and the most respectable parishioners there, was addressed to the principal inhabitants of the adjoining towns soliciting their assistance for the relief of the sufferers by the said fire.)

"LOWESTOFT IN SUFFOLK."

"Whereas, upon the 14th of August, 1670, being the Lord's day, about twelve o'clock at night, the wind being very high, there happened a sudden, dreadful and lamentable fire in this town, which consumed six dwelling houses with their goods, and two barns with corn, which loss, upon examination, and in the judgment of workmen, amounted at least, to three hundred and fifty pounds; to the utter ruin of six poor families, whose wives and children are left in great distress in testimony of the truth thereof, we, the ministers, his Majesty's justices of peace, and principal parishioners of Lowestoft, have hereunto subscribed our names; and do humbly recommend their condition to the christian charity of your town, and beg the favour that you would promote it by such way and means as in your wisdom shall be thought well, either by recommending it to your minister or otherways; so that a speedy collection may be made answerable to their present distress. That they beholding God's goodness handed to them by you, may bless and praise his holy name for the same. And what monies shall be collected and conveyed to our hands, we shall distribute it to those who are truly the objects of charity; and thankfully remain, etc.,

"SIR JOHN ROUS, JOHN YOUELL, vicar; SIR JOHN PETTUS, SIR ROBERT KEMPE, JOHN BEDDINGFIELD, ESQ., EDWARD NORTH, Esq., and several inhabitants."

There was collected on this occasion, in Lowestoft, £18 11s. 3d.; a, Beccles, £6 1s. 6d.; at Pakefield and Kirkley, £4 1s. 7d.; by Sir John Pettust at different towns, £7 16s. 3d.—total £36 10s. 7d.

And on the 12th of November, 1717, about four in the morning, another sudden and terrible fire broke out in this town, in the fish houses belonging to the co-heirs of Captain Josiah Mighels, then in the occupation of Joseph Smithson, which in a short space of time, entirely consumed the said houses; together with part of those houses belonging to William Mewse, which laid to the south, and part of those belonging to Mr. John Barker and Mr. Thomas Mighels, on the north. The wind blew pretty fresh at south east, so that the sparks flew over the town, and once actually fired the thatch of a house in the Swan Lane: but men and water being ready for that purpose, it was immediately stopped; and it pleasing God of his mercy both to damp the wind and to bring it more to the southward, the town escaped as a brand plucked out of the fire. The damage sustained by the fish houses was estimated at £1000.

And also on Sunday, July 30th, 1780, at one o'clock in the morning, the east Mill, at the north end of the town, by some cause unknown, took fire; which fire being communicated by a strong wind to another wind mill, situate about forty roods distance to the westward, they were both totally consumed.

The other misfortune to which the town of Lowestoft is peculiarly liable, and from which it has greatly suffered, is that of a dangerous coast, when exposed to violent storms. This is, in a great measure, owing to the singular nature of this coast, arising from its numerous sands and shoals, and not having any harbour, or other place of security, to protect the shipping from the violence of a storm; consequently they have been too often sacrificed to the fury of the relentless ocean.

It is impossible to describe every dreadful shipwreck and melancholy scene of distress which have happened on this dangerous coast, they being too numerous to be recounted, as well as painful to be related; it shall suffice, therefore, only to mention a few of the most remarkable ones, such as were attended with the most distressing circumstances, and exposed the unhappy seamen to the most alarming situations.

At the end of the annals of Norwich, a manuscript in the chapter archives, an account is given, that in the year of Christ 1530, in the night immediately following the 4th of November, a violent storm, as it were, all over England, happened; and the next day following, namely, the 5th day of the said month, about one in the afternoon, the lord cardinal Thomas Wolsey was seized in his own house, at Cahowe, within his diocese of York; and afterwards, in his journey towards London, in the vigil St. Andrew next following he died at Leicester, upon which day a storm, *as if from Hell*—(a remarkable instance of the prejudice of the times; and shews how much better Christianity is understood in this more liberal and enlightened age)—again happened almost all over England, by the fury of which at Lowestoft, within the diocese of Norwich, and elsewhere in divers places within the realm of England, many ships were lost.

On the 30th July, 1730, happened in this town and neighbourhood, a most remarkable storm, accompanied with a dreadful tempest of thunder, lightning, and hail; the hailstones were of such prodigious magnitude as to measure from six to nine inches in circumference, and descended with such violence, as to break all the glass windows on the west side of the town, which cost the inhabitants £300 to repair the damage. All the corn was beat down and spoiled, for about a mile in breadth and three in length.

On December 24th, 1739, that severe frost called the hard winter, commenced with a violent gale of wind; when sixteen sail of ships were driven ashore on the coast between Yarmouth and Lowestoft, and were all totally lost, after their respective crews had undergone the severest hardships from the inclemency of the weather.

And in another storm, which happened on the 15th of December, 1757, twenty two sail of ships were driven ashore on the coast between Yarmouth and Kessingland, the greater part of which were lost. A particular account of the damage each ship sustained was soon after published in the *London Gazette*.

But the most dreadful storm that ever happened on this coast in the memory of man, was that of the 11th of December, 1770. The following account of which was written by Mr. Robert Reeve, attorney-at-law, and merchant at Lowestoft, who was a spectator of this dreadful scene, and was published in the *Ipswich Journal* of the 29th December, as follows:

"The dreadful storm on Wednesday the 19th instant, began about one o'clock in the morning, and continued with increasing violence till five; when the wind suddenly changed from south-west to the north-west, and for two hours raged with fury that was hardly ever equalled. Anchors and cables proved too feeble a security for the ships, which instantly parting from them, and running on board each other, produced a confusion neither to be described nor conceived; not a few immediately foundered, others were dismasted, and none escaped unhurt. At day-light a scene of the most tragic distress was exhibited; those who first beheld it assert, no less than eighteen ships were upon the sand before this place at one and the same time, and many others were seen to sink; of those upon the sand, one half were entirely demolished, with their crews, before nine o'clock; the rest were preserved a few hours longer but this dreadful pause served only to aggravate the destruction of the unhappy men who belonged to them, who betook themselves to the masts and rigging; these continually breaking, eight or ten were not unfrequently seen to perish at a time, without the possibility of being assisted. Fifteen only, about two in the afternoon, were taken off one of the wrecks, and about as many more were saved by taking to their boats, or getting on board other ships when they boarded each other. It is impossible to collect with certainty how many lives, or how many ships were lost in this terrible hurricane. Twenty-five at least, perhaps thirty ships, and two hundred men, do not seem to be an exaggerated account. This, indeed, is too small a calculation, it credit is to be given to one of the seamen, who declares he saw six vessels sink not far without the Stanford, among which was a large ship bound for Lisbon, with sixty or seventy passengers on board. One or two of the ships which were lost belong to Yarmouth, and one to Plymouth, but the generality are colliers and belong to Sunderland, Shields and other places in the north. The concern this destructive scene occasioned to the spectators of it was increased by the following circumstance: when the masts of one of the ships, on which were eight or nine men, fell, two of them were some time afterwards seen struggling among the wreck, and at length, after unremitted efforts, got upon the hull. In the afternoon, the pilot boat ventured from the shore, but it was found impracticable to administer any relief to the unfortunate sufferers, whom they were compelled to leave in their forlorn state; an approaching dark, cold, stormy night, heightening the horrors of their situation. The next day to the astonishment of everybody, one of the men was observed to be alive, and about noon the boat again attempted to save him, and approached so near as to ask the poor fellow several questions; but the

E

hull, on which he was, being surrounded with wreck, and the sea running high, it was impossible to rescue from the impending danger. He was at the stern of the ship; towards her head the sailors conceived it barely possible to board her with safety: this they told the unhappy man and bid him walk to the place, but replying he was too weak to change his situation, they were again obliged to leave him, making signs of his inconceivable distress. The ensuing night put an end to his misfortunes and life. (Mr. Aldous Arnold, an eminent merchant in this town, very humanely offered ten pounds to any person who would take this man off the wreck).—If such calamities as these, which are the dispensations of Providence, occasion any painful reflections, how great must our emotions be to consider the thousands of lives wantonly butchered in wars, killed merely to gratify the whim of princes, to feed the ambition of aspiring men, or to furnish men of dissipation with the means of indulging their excesses? To a dispassionate mind it seems equally wicked and absurd, that great civilized nations should sacrifice the property, the repose and the lives of their subjects to determine which of them has the best right to a desert, as truly worthless to them as if it was placed in the satellites of Jupiter."

I cannot conclude this section without recommending to the consideration of the inhabitants of Lowestoft, and all other sea-port towns, the possibility of constructing a vessel, or some other machine, on such principles as should not be liable to overset, but should be capable of approaching any vessel in distress, during the most violent storms, and when surrounded with the most tumultuous waves. The wretched situation of so many distressed mariners as are wrecked on this coast, must be a sufficient excitement to the undertaking; and the pleasure of saving so many valuable lives, will be an ample recompense for any expense or trouble that may attend its execution.

That a scheme of this nature is not totally impracticable will be evident from the following description of a new-invented vessel in France, something similar to that recommended above; and of an experiment that was lately made at Paris to discover its utility:

Monsieur Bernieres, director of the bridges and causeways in France, has contrived and constructed a boat, or sloop, fit for inland navigation, coasting voyages, and short passages by sea, which is not like ordinary vessels, liable to be overset or sunk by winds, waves, water spouts, or too heavy a load.

Some trials were made on one of these vessels on the first of August, 1776, at the gate of the invalids, in Paris, in the presence of a numerous concourse of spectators of all conditions.

A boat of the same sort had been tried, October 11th, 1771, at Choisy, before Louis XV., and his present majesty, then dauphin. During the experiments it was shewn, though eight men were in one of these boats, and the boat filled brim full with water, yet, instead of sinking, it bore being rowed about the river without any danger to the people in it.

M. Bernieres carried his trial still farther. He ordered a mast to be erected in the same boat, when filled with water, and to the top of the mast had a rope fastened, and drawn till the end of the mast touched the surface of the water; yet, as soon as the men who had hauled her into this situation let go the rope, the boat and mast recovered themselves perfectly, in less than a quarter of a second; a convincing proof that the boat could neither be sunk nor overset, and that it afforded the greatest possible security in every way.

In consequence of the above trials, the provost of the merchants and the corporation of Paris gave the sieur Bernieres permission to establish his boats on the river Seine, at the port near Pont Royal; and, moreover, promised him all the protection and encouragement in their power: and the sieur Bernieres, on his side proposed to supply the public with a certain number of these boats before the end of the next year; but whether he fulfilled his engagement, or whether he has been as successful in the subsequent trials of this useful invention as he was in the former, I have not been able to learn.

It is much to be lamented that the general principles on which this ingenious mechanic constructed his vessel, were not communicated to the public. However, it is some satisfaction to know that such an invention has been discovered, and where the author of it resides. And it is hoped that the known humanity which the sieur Bernieres possesses will surmount every illiberal restriction, and that he will generously impart to the public the principles of an invention that may be of such universal utility, and the means of rescuing many valuable members of society from those distressful situations which they are so very often exposed to whenever they frequent this very difficult **and dangerous coast.**

(The **most** probable method of rescuing seamen from those unfortunate situations, **that I can** think of, is that of a kite. When the storm is so far abated **that a boat is** able to approach pretty near the wreck let a line—which **may soon** after easily convey a strong rope—be carried by the kite over the **vessel,** and then let it fall. Thus a communication may be obtained **between** the wreck and the boat, and by that means the seamen, by fastening themselves to a float, may be drawn through the water from the ship to the boat. Or a rope may be conveyed from the boat to the wreck by means of a small cask, sent from the former in the direction of the tide, or waves of the sea; and when a communication is obtained a float may be applied as above-mentioned. And, again, if ships which frequent this coast were to furnish themselves with a floating machine it might be the means of saving the lives of many passengers and seamen, when they happened to be in those distressing situations, by sending them off to the boats which usually attend the wreck. Many lives and much valuable property might thus be saved. Should every one of the above methods be deemed impracticable, yet I should think myself extremely happy, was I only to suggest a hint to some ingenious artist, for the invention of a more successful scheme that might afford relief in such inconceiveable distress.—When the author received the honour of being elected a member of that very respectable body at Norwich, "The Society for the Participation of Useful Knowledge," he communicated to them a proposal of this nature, to be submitted to their consideration). Thus, **it** too plainly appears, that from the many grievous calamities above-mentioned, such as the plague and other sicknesses; the civil war in the reign of Charles I.; the great fire in 1644; the Dutch **war in the** reign of Charles II.; the many losses from storms and tempests; to **which may** be added the great law-suit with Yarmouth, which continued from **1659** to 1664; the town of Lowestoft must have been reduced many times **to** the **greatest** distress; and it evidently appears that it really was so from the many petitions presented to Government during the above suit with Yarmouth, wherein these misfortunes are frequently alluded to.

On an elevated point of land near the edge of the cliff on which Lowestoft is situated, and a little to the north of the town, stands the upper light-house.

(It was from this hill that the royal yacht was first discovered, which brought to England her serene highness, the princess Charlotte, of Mecklenburgh Strelitz, the intended queen of his present majesty, King George III. Lord Anson, vice-admiral of Great Britain, was appointed to convey her **highness,** with a squadron of men-of-war to the British shore. After a voyage **of** ten **days,** occasioned by boisterous and contrary winds, Lord Anson, with his squadron—which was damaged—and the royal yacht, appeared off this place, on Saturday, the 5th September, 1761, about two o'clock in the afternoon, and **anchored** in Harwich road about three in the afternoon the day following. Her **highness landed** at Harwich on the 7th., in the afternoon, and from thence **was** escorted **to** London. Had not the wind suddenly changed, her highness would have landed at Lowestoft, as was the case of his majesty, King George II. who landed at this town on his return from Hanover, January 14th, 1736-7. His majesty had been a considerable time **on** his voyage from Helvoetfluys to England, occasioned by stormy and con**trary** winds, and had been also exposed to the most imminent danger. **When** the royal barge, with his majesty, the countess of Yarmouth, and his **lords,** approached the shore, a body of sailors belonging to Lowestoft, uniformly dressed in seamen's jackets, waded into the sea, and meeting the barge took it on their shoulders, with the king and all the nobility, and carried it to the beach, without suffering it to strike the ground. His majesty was met at the sea-shore by John Jex, Esq., of this town, with his carriage, who conducted his majesty to his house; himself having the honour of being coachman. His Majesty landed about twelve at noon, and about two hours after set off for London. His majesty died in 1760, and his present majesty, George III. was proclaimed at Lowestoft by Mr. Robert Reeve to whom the author acknowledges himself much indebted for many favours, and particularly for his great assiduity in promoting the publishing of this work. John Adams, Esq., the first ambassador from America to England, landed at Lowestoft, the 6th August, 1784).

When the high light-house is in the same direction with the light-house which stands below the cliff, it directs the vessels which are either coming in or going out of Lowestoft roads, to the Stanford channel, which lies between the Holme and Barnard sands. This channel is about a quarter of a mile broad, and three quarters of a mile distant from that part of the shore that is opposite to it; and though it has existed from time immemorial to parts contiguous to its present situation, yet, from the effects of storms and currents, and other causes, beyond perhaps, the reach of human investigation, it is of such a fluctuating nature, that it never continues long in the same situation. Of late years its motion has been northerly, as is evident from the several changes which have been made in the situation of the lower light-house—which is a movable one—to bring it in a line with the upper light-house and the channel; which removals have always been towards the north. About a century ago this channel was situated more distant to the south-west from where it is at present: for on the spot of ground whereon the upper light-house stands, there stood, about a hundred years ago, a beacon; and there was also at the same time, another beacon standing on the north side of the passage going down the Swan score, as guides to the Stanford; and therefore to bring these two beacons on a line with the Stanford channel, that channel must necessarily, at that time, lie more to the south-west than where it does now.

In the year 1676 the beacon at the north end of the town was taken down, and on the place where it stood was erected, the upper light-house. This building is a round-built tower, consisting of brick and stone materials, is about 40 feet in height, and twenty in diameter. About two-thirds of the upper part of it next the sea—and about thirty feet from the ground—was originally sashed, that the fire might be visible to the spectators on the sea. In this part was placed a hearth, whereon a coal fire was continually kept burning every night; and was always conducted in this manner until the alteration in this light-house, in the year 1778, was made.

In the year 1735, when the Stanford channel had proceeded so far to the north that the beacon near the Swan score became useless, from its being brought on a line with the upper light-house,—(this light-house is composed of timber, and hangings in a frame of the same materials; the upper part of it next the sea is sashed, and the light is produced from three lamps placed inside. In the year 1779, the timber was found to be in so decayed a state, that the building was obliged to be wholly taken down, and replaced by another, made of the same materials, and upon the same construction)—a moveable light-house, framed of timber, was erected on the beach below the cliff, whose construction was such as to admit of its being removed according as the channel should happen to change its situation. (In the year 1778, the Stanford channel bore S.S.E. from the upper light-house. The depth of water in the middle of the roads opposite to the Ness, was between seven and eight fathoms at low water. In the middle of the roads opposite to the south part of the town, and about 120 fathoms from the shore, is a shoal, where there is not above nine feet of water at ebb tide; and another shoal lies about three quarters of a mile from the shore, on which is about sixteen feet at low water. In 1788 the roads appeared to grow narrower, from the sea losing against the town, especially at the ness, where the distance from the Holm sand was not more than a mile and a quarter from the shore; this sand still continues to increase, which with the sea receding from the shore, accounts for the roads growing narrower. "Trinity House, London, January 19th, 1782. This corporation having lately caused a survey to be taken of the Stanford, in which was found only three fathoms, in the best of the channel, at high water; it is recommended to all masters and pilots to be very cautious in navigating ships of a great draught through that channel." To give one instance of the fluctuating nature of the sands off Lowestoft; it is observed, that that part of the sands where the church and chapel bore on each other the fishing boats, a few years ago, used to sail over, at their going out to sea and returning again into the roads: this part of the sand is now become perfectly dry; and at low water, when the weather is fine, extends to a considerable distance; and may, possibly, afterwards become the foundation of a new town.)

On the western side of the upper lighthouse, underneath the arms of Trinity House are the arms of Samuel Pepys, Esq., beneath which is this inscription.—

"Erected by the Brotherhood of the
Trinity House of Deptford Strond, in
The Mastership of Samuel Pepys, Esq.,
Secretary to the Admiralty of England,
Anno Dom. 1676.

In the year 1777, when the upper part of this lighthouse became so much decayed that it was necessary to have it repaired in a short time, it was resolved by the brethren of the Trinity House, to take the top wholly off, and to erect in its place one of the new-invented reflecting cylinders. Accordingly in the month of June, 1778, the Trinity yacht, with several of the elder brethren, arrived at Lowestoft, and brought one of these curious inventions with them, in order to observe what effect it would produce. In consequence of this design, a temporary scaffold was erected on an eminence a little to the north of the lighthouse, and the cylinder was hoisted upon it; and in the evening the Trinity yacht sailed off to sea, to a considerable distance, in order to discover what appearance it would have: when it was found to answer beyond expectation. When the yacht returned, the cylinder was ordered to be immediately taken down, and to be shipped on board the yacht, with a view of sending it to the Isle of Scilly, which was then in immediate want of it, and a new one was ordered to be sent to Lowestoft presently after, which was accordingly sent, and erected upon the remaining part of the old lighthouse. The following account of this reflecting cylinder, with an engraving of the same, was published by the author of this work, in the *Town and Country Magazine*, for April, 1788:

"This curious machine consists of a glass lanthorn about seven feet high, and six in diameter, glazed with the best plate glass; the frame of which is copper, and covered with a roof of the same metal. In the centre of the lanthorn is set upon a frame a large hexagonal reflecting cylinder, four feet in height, and three feet in diameter. This cylinder is made of copper, the outside of which is covered with cement, upon which are placed nearly 4,000 small mirrors, each mirror about an inch square. In the centre of this cylinder is fixed a reservoir of oil, which, by fixed pipes passing through hexagonal divisions of the cylinder, support and convey the oil to a large circular tube, which is placed about eighteen inches from the surface of the cylinder, and upon this tube are fixed 126 lamps. One of these lighthouses was made by an order of the elder brethren of the Trinity House, sent on board their yacht, with several of the brethren, and sailed for Lowestoft, in Suffolk, to make a trial of its utility. Accordingly in the night of the 23rd of June, a temporary scaffold being erected for that purpose, the machine was hoisted and the lamps lighted; when it was found to answer beyond conception, exhibiting a globe of fire of a steady and most vivid brightness. This experiment was made at a small distance from the lighthouse commonly made use of, the light of which is supported by a coal fire, and was exerted to the utmost on this occasion, to maintain its superiority; and was appointed to be the criterion by which the difference was to be determined. The yacht accompanied by some boats, sailed off to sea the preceding day, so as to be out of sight of land before sunset—the time appointed for lighting it. They sailed in for the land, and discovered the new light-house as soon as the convexity of the sea would permit, it being at least twenty miles from the shore, and sailed five or six miles nearer before they could perceive the fire of the old light-house.

"The brethren of the Trinity House being thus convinced of the great utility of this invention, gave orders the next day to have it taken down and sent to the Island of Scilly."

## SECTION III.

## OF THE FISHERIES AND MANUFACTORY AT LOWESTOFT.

THE principal commerce subsisting at Lowestoft is derived from its herring-fishery. The town most probably, received its very existence from the convenient situation of its coast for fishermen to exercise the several occupations of a life dependent on those employments; which in the more early ages, extended, very likely, to every kind of fish that the coast afforded; though now, in these more recent times, it is chiefly confined to the herring fishery.

The herrings appear on the coast of Shetland in the month of June, and from thence they proceed to the coast of Scotland; but being interrupted in their passage by the Island of Great Britain, they separate into two divisions, one of which divisions, after steering west, or south west, and leaving the Isles of Orkney and Shetland on the north, pass by the western isles, and proceed to Ireland; and there receiving a second retardation, they subdivide, and one part keeps the coast and shore of Britain and passing down St. George's Channel as far as the mouth of the Severn, where they unite again with their former friends, etc., the second part of the same division, who had edged off to the west and south-west, and sheering along the western shore of the coast of Ireland, and then proceeding south and south-east, were also entered into St. George's Channel. The second part of the first division, which was separated off the north part of Scotland having directed their course to the south and south-east, entered the German ocean; and continuing their progress along the coast of Scotland, they proceed to the south, and rounding the high shore of Berwick and St. Abb's, are not seen any more till they arrive upon the Yorkshire coast, and not in any great quantities till they appear off Yarmouth and Lowestoft; where, after continuing a few weeks, and leaving an immense quantity of spawn, they pass through the German ocean, and entering the straights of Dover continue to proceed along the coasts of Sussex, Hampshire, etc., to the Land's End, where the two divisions forming a junction, they enter the vast Atlantic ocean.

Herrings have been seen on the shores of North America, though not in such large quantities as have appeared on the coasts of Britain; neither are they seen in America any farther south than South Carolina. But whether these herrings be part of that enormous shoal which first approach the north of Scotland, and instead of confining their progress to the British Isles, extend it to the coast of America; or whether they be part of that vast collection, who, after forming a junction on the coast of Cornwall, launch into the Atlantic ocean, is difficult to determine with certainty. It may, perhaps, be no improbable conjecture to suppose, that the herrings which appear on the American coast are only such as have deserted from the main body of the fish during their continuance in the western ocean. And as it is evident that these fish are never seen in any considerable quantity upon the coast of the more southern parts of Europe, such as Spain, or Portugal, or the southern parts of France, neither in the Mediterranean, or coast of Africa; but, after they have entered the Atlantic ocean, are seen no more till the succeeding summer, on the coast of Shetland. We may conclude, that after the herrings have appeared early in the summer on the northern coasts, and proceeded on the eastern and western sides of the British Isles, discharging their roes, and having formed a conjunction at their general rendezvous near the Land's End, and launched into the Atlantic ocean, and continued there the remainder of the winter, that they afterwards proceed to the north; and assembling together near the coasts of Greenland, in the Spring they continued their progress from those parts to the south, and in the summer appear again on the north of Shetland and Scotland, thereby performing, in the course of a year, one entire revolution round the islands of Great Britain and Ireland; so that the herring may, without impropriety, be termed a fish of passage.

The convenient situation of the eastern parts of this kingdom for the advantageous prosecution of the herring fishery, and the great benefit which the nation derives in consequence thereof, have much excited the envy of our maritime neighbours, the Dutch; and have frequently induced them to infringe on the liberties which this kingdom is indisputably entitled to, by approaching too near the British coasts, in view either to usurp the whole of this fishery to themselves, or to monopolise a considerable share of it: but the policy of these rivals has hitherto been such, that whenever they perceived that their illegal proceedings were complained of, and threatened to be opposed, they always endeavoured to pacify our resentment, either by compounding for the trespass, or by relinquishing their pretensions, and afterwards having recourse to a more legal mode of conducting their fishery. (In the reign of James I. the Dutch paid an acknowledgement for leave of fishing on our coasts, which being withdrawn, his son, Charles I. in the year 1636, issued a proclamation, declaring that he should maintain such a fleet at sea as would protect his coasts from the insults of the Dutch. And soon after sent a fleet, under the command of the Earl of Northumberland, to disperse them, and obliged them to pay 30,000 florins for leave to continue their fishing that season. And thus it has frequently happened since; the Dutch, by infringing on our liberties, and having had complaints alledged against them, have paid considerable sums to appease our resentment; and sometimes, when they have proved unsuccessful in these methods, have been severely chastised: but all to no purpose; for to this day they continue practising the same depredations on our coasts and we every year experience the usual inconveniences which attend them. About the year 1636 great progress was made in this fishery by the Dutch; and the wealth procured it to the republic, caused, as I have just observed, much jealousy in the English nation. In 1601, eighty thousand tons of herrings were caught, which being worth eight hundred gilders per ton, brought to the republic sixty-four millions of gilders. It increased so much from that time that Sir Walter Raleigh assures us, that in 1610 the inhabitants of the united provinces employed in this fishery, upon the coasts of England, three thousand busses, manned with fifty thousand hands. Such a prodigious gain occasioned the English that year to renew their ancient pretensions to the property of the seas which surround their island, and to exact of the Dutch fishermen the tenth herring as a sort of duty. About the year 1600 the Dutch, the French, the citizens of Embden, Hamburgh, and Bremen, got out of our seas, upon a medium, to the value of between six and seven millions sterling annually. Another inconvenience which the British nation experienced from foreigners being permitted to usurp so large a share of the herring fishery, was the great increase of their seamen. This was very evident from the wars with the Dutch which happened in the reign of Charles II., when they were able to supply with able seamen a fleet of upwards of one hundred sail of line of battle ships. It may be worth observing, that the ground work of the regulations pursued by the Dutch in their herring fishery, is taken from the sagacious institutions laid down by Edward III., in the famous statute of herrings passed in that reign.)

It is highly probable, that the herring fishery on this part of the coast originated at Lowestoft, and, in some measure, afterwards transferred itself to Yarmouth: for in the early ages, before Yarmouth was founded, Lowestoft appears to have been the general rendezvous of the northern and western fishers employed in the herring fishery: but when the sand upon which Yarmouth was afterwards built, appeared above the surface of the water, and became dry land, it was then that the fishermen from different parts of England, especially the cinque ports— who were antiently the principal fishermen of England—resorted thither annually to catch herrings; where, finding this sand to be unoccupied, and its situation extremely convenient both for drying their nets, manufacturing their fish, and exhibiting it to sale, they began to erect temporary booths or tents, as their several circumstances required, either to secure themselves from the irruptions of an enemy, or as a shelter from the inclemency of the weather.

And for the better keeping the peace and securing to every owner his respective property, the barons of the cinque ports deputed several officers, called bailiffs, to attend this fishery the space of forty days, viz., from Michaelmas to Martinmas, the principal time of the herring season; as it would have been dangerous both to private interest as well as public tranquility, to have permitted such a mixed multitude of natives and foreigners to have assembled in one place without having a person with proper authority to preside over them, in order to preserve subordination and regularity; and in this manner the herring fishery continued for some time after its commencement at this place, which, probably, happened soon after the landing of Cerdick, the Saxon, in the year 495, as above related; and from which circumstance it was called the Cerdick sand. (It is probable, that Lowestoft, as a fishing town, was in a flourishing state some ages before this period: for though the herring is a northern fish, and but few of them are seen in the Mediterranean; yet it is a fish that was known to the Romans, who, probably, acquired the knowledge of it from their having a station in the vicinity of Lowestoft, viz., Burgh Castle.)

Some years after, as soon as it appeared that the **herring fishery was** established upon a permanent foundation, and the sand became safe **and commodious** to reside upon, some of the inhabitants on the western **shore, and** others from different parts of the kingdom, began to build houses thereon, and for their mutual support and defence founded a town there, from whence arose the origin of Yarmouth; whereby it appears that the founders of Great Yarmouth were chiefly portsmen, or natives of the cinque ports. These portsmen continued to frequent the place for several centuries afterwards, and many of them chose to reside here, and became seized of lands and tenements, some portion whereof, at their deaths they would bequeath to their countrymen of the cinque ports, in order to signify to posterity from whence they came. But as soon as the burgesses of Yarmouth had a charter of liberties granted them by King John, and the barons of the cinque ports having also certain liberties granted them at Yarmouth by the same king, or rather confirmed what they held before by prescriptive right,—("Prescription is a title acquired by use and time, and allowed by law: as when a man claims anything because he, his ancestors, or they whose estate he hath, have had or used it all the time whereof no memory is to the contrary.")—the liberties which were granted to the cinque ports, by interfering with those newly granted to the burgesses of Yarmouth gave rise to the most violent disputes and animosities, such as are not to be paralleled, perhaps, between any other two places in the British dominions; for the riots and depredations which arose from these disputes became at last so very outrageous as to be not only extremely injurious to the contending parties, but even to alarm the whole kingdom.

These violent quarrels and commotions continued to agitate the respective parties, with little permission, until the reign of Queen Elizabeth, when a proposal **was** made for compromising their differences and establishing a durable reconciliation, by making Yarmouth a member of the cinque ports; but this attempt, however laudable in its intention, proved wholly ineffectual **in its** execution: nevertheless, we find, that in the year 1576, every circumstance which had afforded matter of dispute was amicably adjusted, and finally settled to the mutual satisfaction of the respective parties: and accordingly **an award** was published, which contained the following article, namely, "That **whereas for** every fishing vessel coming to the said free fair, in ancient times, fourpence **for** toll or custom was paid to the bailiffs of the cinque ports, which afterwards, by composition was reduced to a certain sum of six pounds yearly: but for the sake of restoring peace and quiet it was hereby agreed that the bailiffs of Yarmouth should pay to the bailiffs of the barons of the cinque ports, at their departure from Yarmouth, three pounds and ten shillings only, in recompense and full satisfaction for the said toll."

After the conclusion of this agreement, the several parties maintained a more peaceable and friendly correspondence with each other than had subsisted for many years before; and persevered in this amicable intercourse until the year 1662, when the annual composition of three pounds and ten shilling being either refused or neglected to be paid by the burgesses of Yarmouth to the bailiffs of the ports, the said bailiffs never repaired to

Yarmouth any more in a public capacity. (But, notwithstanding, the bailiffs of the cinque ports, in consequence of the composition not being paid by the burgesses of Yarmouth, discontinued to frequent, as usual, the Yarmouth herring fair. Yet those fishermen called the west countrymen still continued coming to these parts till the year 1756, but after that time they declined coming any longer. These vessels from the western part of England, as it was called, *i.e.* from the coast of Kent, etc., used to frequent these coasts during the herring season, and sell the fish which they caught to the merchants of Lowestoft and Yarmouth. Also vessels called north country cobles used to attend and dispose of their fish in the same manner. These vessels used to engage themselves to some owner here for the fishing season, which was called being bosted; but this mode of practice is also now almost wholly discontinued. It was not the custom formerly for the merchants of Lowestoft to catch all the fish they wanted with their own boats, but were supplied with a considerable part of it from the vessels above mentioned: but now the merchants from increasing the number of their own boats, are able to furnish themselves with a sufficient quantity of herrings without the assistance of either of the west country boats, or those from the north. This new mode will appear very evident, if we compare the number of boats employed by Lowestoft in the year 1670, with the number employed in the year 1775; in the former they were only twenty-five, in the latter they amounted to forty-eight.)

The town of Yarmouth having thus driven away the bailiffs of the cinque ports, that place became the general rendezvous of all such vessels as were employed in the herring fishery; and thereby monopolised, in a great measure, the whole fishery to themselves, by confining to the narrow limits of their own haven, the purchasing of all such herrings as were not caught by the boats belonging to the neighbouring towns, and where they were compelled to pay the custom demanded by the town of Yarmouth: for the town of Lowestoft, and all other towns on the coast, an indisputable right to fit out what number of vessels they pleased from their own towns, for the purpose of catching herrings, without being subject to any customs payable to Yarmouth, and also to purchase herrings at sea from certain vessels called ketchmen; but if they could not be sufficiently supplied with herrings by these means, they were then under the necessity of repairing to Kirkley road or Yarmouth haven, where they became subject to the customs due to the town of Yarmouth; for the right of the burgesses of Yarmouth to levy these customs was confined solely to the haven and Kirkley road; and therefore the ketchmen, who sold herrings at sea, thereby evaded the customs and injured the town of Yarmouth; which formerly had occasioned many disputes, particularly in the reign of queen Elizabeth, and probably was the principal motive which induced the burgesses of Yarmouth to force away the portsmen.

The town of Yarmouth, not being satisfied with their late acquisitions, began to extend their views much farther, even so far as to endeavour to exclude the town of Lowestoft from having any share in the herring fishery; and in order to give their designs the greater appearance of justice, they pleaded the Charter, 46 Edward III., for uniting Kirkley road to Yarmouth haven; and pretended that the seven leuks, inserted in that charter as the boundary of their liberties, were not miles, but leagues; and also, that the said leuks were not to be measured from the key of Yarmouth, but from the mouth of the haven which at this time had extended far to the south, and formerly as far as Corton; thereby expecting to extend their liberties beyond the roads of Lowestoft, and consequently wholly to exclude the merchants of that place from a privilege which they had enjoyed from time immemorial, viz., that of purchasing herrings near their own town.

Corton is situated about a mile to the north of Lowestoft, and comprehends upwards of a thousand acres, chiefly cultivated, and prettily diversified with rising grounds and some woods; and contains about thirty-eight dwelling houses, mostly situated in a street, tolerably compact, on a high cliff that commands an extensive prospect of the sea. This parish is a vicarage, and the impropriation, before the dissolution of the monasteries, belonged to the abbey of Leystone, in Suffolk. (This abbey was of the Premonstratensian order. It was founded by Randulph de Glanvill, A.D. 1182. At the dissolution, the annual revenues were estimated at the sum of £180 17s. 1d.,

F

and the site, with the greatest part of the manors, rectories, and lands, were granted 28 Henry VIII. to the above Duke of Suffolk; afterwards it became the property of Daniel Hervey; next it was vested in the honourable Elizabeth, relict of Killand Courtney, Esq., daughter of the Vicountess Hinchinbroke, and grand-daughter of the right-honourable lady, Ann Harvey; afterwards it belonged to Sir Joshua Van Neck, of Putney, in Surrey, Bart.; and now to Sir Gerrard Van Neck, of Hevingham, in this county). It was granted by Henry VIII. to Charles Brandon, duke of Suffolk, and has passed through various hands since to the present owner, John Ives, of Yarmouth, Esq. The advowson of this vicarage formerly belonged to the proprietors of the impropriation; but, by some neglect or other, has been suffered to lapse to the Crown.

The body of the Church is now dilapidated, and the chancel is the only part of it appropriated to divine service. The ruins which are now remaining give evident proof that the building was of considerable dimensions; and the handsome tower, which is still perfect, strongly denotes its original elegance.

Tradition informs us that when the church became ruinous, the parishioners, finding themselves unequal to the task of repairing it, and at the same time thinking it unnecessary, petitioned the bishop of the diocese for his license to suffer it to remain as it was, on condition that, at their own charge, they would fit up and maintain the chancel as a place of public worship, which was granted them, and the chancel was made very adequate to the purpose. But in a long series of years, either by means of the inability, or through the inattention of the people, this too was suffered to fall into decay, insomuch, that in the year 1776, the lead admitted the rain in various places, and pulpit, the desk, gallery, etc., were rotten, and ready to fall down. Under these circumstances, the Rev. Francis Bowness, then vicar, thought it expedient to coincide with the wishes of the generality of the parishioners, to apply to the diocesan for a faculty to dispose of the lead, and lay out the money arising from the sale of it, in the reparation of the building; and notwithstanding much opposition, the perseverance of the vicar prevailed, and he obtained, from the candour of Bishop Younge, a full power to sell not only the lead, but also, if it should be necessary, a large bell, which hung in the porch of the old church. He availed himself of no more than the former part of the license; and with a very small rate added to the produce of the lead, the chancel was again put into complete good order, and divine service is now regularly performed there, and decently attended.

In justice to the merits of the worthy vicar, I hope it will not be thought impertinent to add, that he has been an equal benefactor to the church and the living; that he lives in great harmony with his parishioners, and receives from them that respect, which a constant endeavour to be useful seldom fails to inspire. He was instituted in 1758. The church is dedicated to St. Bartholomew. The vicarage, though of late years much improved by the increased cultivation of the parish, is yet inconsiderable.

The same difficulty which we have to encounter with respecting the origin of Lowestoft Church, presents itself in our enquiry concerning this at Corton, viz: How so small and inconvenient a village as this seems always to have been, should ever have been able, from any resources of its own, to erect so stately a structure; and if unable of itself, from what other sources did it derive its assistances? In solving this difficulty we must have recourse to the same mode of reasoning as we shall urge hereafter respecting Lowestoft Church, which is, that as the church at Corton was part of the endowment of Leystone Abbey, it is highly probable that this church was first erected and afterwards kept in repair through the assistance of the Abbey, as Lowestoft Church was by the priory of St. Bartholomew, in London.

After the dissolution of the monasteries, when no further assistance could be received from those institutions, and the parish being unable of itself to keep such structure in repair, the building fell to ruin. And the case would have been the same with respect to Lowestoft Church, notwithstanding it was a much larger parish, had not a benefaction of lands, expressly given for repairing and ornamenting the same, been happily recovered at the dissolution of the priory, and prevented the like misfortune.

It is supposed that the village of Corton, in former times, was much larger than it is at present. It is certain there were two churches in the parish, or, at least, a chapel of ease to the mother church; the small remains, still visible at a place called the Gate, tend to confirm the latter opinion, as the old foundations of houses discovered in different parts of the parish, lead to evince the former. Probably the parish had arrived at its most opulent state about the 13th century, when the mouth of Yarmouth haven had extended almost to this place; which added to the adjoining situation of Kirkley road, must occasion a great resort of fishermen, from different parts of the kingdom, to this village.

Some centuries ago there was, contiguous to Corton, another parish called Newton, of which scarce any other vestiges are now remaining, than a stone which supported a cross, called Newton cross, and a small piece of ground, called Newton green; almost every other part of this parish being swallowed up by the sea.

It appears, that in the year 1408, 10th of Henry IV., Yarmouth haven made near Newton Cross; and Swinden informs us, "that the charges and monies bestowed and spente in and aboute repairenge of the haven of the towne of Yarmouthe, and of the fortfienge the same with two greate mayne peeres, which at the firste was cutte a-newe and digged out, into the sea right over agenst the parsonage of Gorleston, and the same haven then runninge alongeste the cliffe as farr as Newton Crosse, was agenst the parsonage stopped up, and there forced to runne into the sea; which was done in the yere of our Saviour 1559. After which tyme, in few yeres, the said haven, for want of two peeres, did eate, and seeke towardes the south, for preventenge of whose olde evell and accustomed course, the towne did begenne this charge, by the advice of a verrye conninge workman, sent for from beyond the sea."

In 1306 John de Herling, a family of great antiquity in the parish of East Herling, in Norfolk, had free warren allowed him in the manors of Newton and Corton, and died seized of these manors and many others; and left them to his eldest son and heir, Sir John de Herling, Knight, whose brother Robert a great warrior who followed Henry V. into France, and was killed in 1436—had an estate in Newton and Newton and Corton, as had also Thomas, another brother, at Lounde. The manors of Corton, Newton, Lounde, and Blundeston, together with Lounde advowson, and some others, were in the Herling family, and possessed by lady Anne, daughter and sole heiress of the above Sir Robert, 1408. Soon after she married her third husband, lord Scroop, of Bolton, and was afterwards a great benefactress to Gonvile (afterwards Caius) college, Cambridge; her mother being the heiress of the Gonvile family.

The Yarmouth men attempted also further to prove that that part of the sea called Kirkley Road was opposite to the parish of Kirkley, which is situated about a mile to the south of Lowestoft, notwithstanding the real name of the sea at that place is Pakefield bay.

Kirkley parish lies so contiguous to Pakefield (being separated from it only by the common highway) that it forms a considerable part of what is generally understood by that town. It is situated to the west of Pakefield and on the north side of it lies the lake of Lothing, from whence runs a small inlet, called Kirkley Ham; which, probably, was made use of formerly as a haven for the fishing craft employed by this parish, at the time when the communication between this lake and the sea retained such a sufficient depth of water as to admit vessels of small draught. The chief support of this village, as well as that of Pakefield, arises principally from their fisheries, which formerly were considerable, but are now much declined. It appeared, from an account of the inhabitants of this parish, taken in the year 1676, in pursuance of the penal laws then in force against religious dissenters, that the number amounted to 103, from sixteen years of age and upwards; of which number, 18 were dissenters. Since that time the number of inhabitants has rather increased, whilst that of dissenters has decreased; the former may be owing to the herring fishery being a little revived there; the latter to the toleration which they have since enjoyed; it being evident that the exercise of rigorous measures against religious sects, instead of exterminating them, tends to increase them; probably therefore the relaxing those severities may be the cause of the number decreasing. The church is dedicated to St. Peter, and valued in the King's books £15 10s.; and till the year 1749 was dilapidated: but this misfortune was in some measure compensated by the minister of Kirkley having permission to make use of the church at Pakefield one part of the Sunday, and the minister of Pakefield to use it on the other part. In this manner both these parishes were supplied for many years, but at length they were parted again. After this separation the incumbent of Kirkley not only declined performing divine service in Pakefield church any longer, but also refused to allow anything to the incumbent of Pakefield for officiating on both parts of the Lord's day; alledging that he could not legally be compelled to it. The Rev. Mr. Tanner, vicar of Lowestoft, was at that time commissary and official in the archdeaconry of Suffolk; and he failed not to use all the mild persuasive arguments in his power, to prevail on the incumbent of Kirkley to make an allowance, but to no purpose; so that finding him inflexible in his resolution he left him with this threat :—"Sir, if you will not officiate in Pakefield Church I will build you a church at Kirkley, and in that you shall officiate." Mr. Tanner was as good as his word; for partly at his own expense, and partly with the assistance of his friends and acquaintance, he shortly erected the present church at Kirkley; and divine service has accordingly been performed there ever since. Mr. Tanner collected money from house to house at Lowestoft, and contributed himself twenty guineas. He also preached the first sermon there in the summer, 1750. The old church consisted of two aisles; the north aisle still continues in ruins, and it is only the aisle which constitutes the new church. The steeple is about 72 feet in height, is a good tower, and an excellent sea-mark; but is now somewhat in decay. It contains only one bell. December 5th, 1749, when they began to clear away the rubbish from the ruins of the old church, they discovered (eighteen feet from the east wall, and six from the north) a stone with a brass label containing the following inscription :—" Orate, Pana Thome Melle Clarisi, nup. Rectore, deKerkley, q' obijit XVI° die augustij A° do m° V°XXVI cui (ane ppinet des) ame." That is, " Pray for the soul of Thomas Melle, clerk, late rector of Kirkley, who died 16th day of August, anno. dom. 1526. For whose soul may God provide. Amen."

An on another label, found in the north isle, a like inscription for one, John Boodherd, who died in August, 1486.

There were several other brass-plated stones taken out of the body of the church and north isle; but were all disrobed, and laid promiscuously under the pews, etc., of the new building.

The old font was broken to pieces, probably by accident, and was left amongst the ruins of the north isle. The font now used in the new church, was brought from the church of Saint ———, lately taken down at Gillingham.

Kirkele, Suff, Edmundus de Wymundhale Clamat habere liberam Warennam in Dominicis terris Suis in Kirkele, etc. Et profert Curtam Dri Henrici Regis, patris Dri Regis Nunc, que hoc testatur, etc. Plita Corone, A°. 14° E. I R 4°. Vide Wymundhale.

Kirkele 33 E I Inter Robertum Rist de North Jernemuth Quer. et Godefr le Ludham de Mag. Jernemuth, et Constantiam Ux : ejus Imped. de I Mess. 45 acr. terr et v acr turbar in Kirkele. Pagefelde south Carlton, Mutford Jus Roberti. Fin : Suff : A°. 33. E. I. Lig 3. N°. 151.

Kirkele 1560. Henricus Hobart de Loddon in Com Norf : Arm : Cond : Testam 17 Oct : 1560 etc. Habuit inter Alia Maneriu de Kirkly, voc : K. Hall. Terras & Tenemta in K. et alibi in Hundredo de Mutford perquisit de Antonio Rouse Armigo cum Advoc : Ecclie de Kirkley pred : etc, probat, 3 May 1561. Ex libro Bircham Regr : Norwic. (Le Neve, from T, Martin's Suffolk papers.)

The ascertaining the true situation of Kirkley road, and determining whether the seven miles which terminated the liberties of Yarmouth, were to be measured from the key or the haven's mouth, occasioned the great law suit between that burgh and Lowestoft.

Pakefield is a considerable large parish about a mile to the south of Lowestoft. Under the general name Pakefield is commonly comprehended not only what is properly called by that name, but also the adjoining parish of Kirkley ; and though to a common observer they appear as only one town, yet, in reality, they are distinct parishes, and under different regulations respecting all the branches of parochial government. The town is situated to the east of Kirkley, and extends to the very summit of the cliffs which form its eastern boundary. The German ocean by frequently dashing against the bases of these cliffs, has often received large portions of those ponderous masses, together with the buildings they supported into its voracious bosom. When a raging tide has occasioned an extraordinary fall of the cliffs either here, or at Corton, or Kessingland, the curiosity of the antiquarian is frequently gratified by the discovery of many ancient coins, etc.

There is scarce any trade carried on in this town; what little there is is chiefly in piloting ships to London, catching cods, sprats, etc., and a small part of the herring fishery.

According to Ecton, the church is dedicated to All Saints; but it seems, by the inscription on the communion-cup, to be dedicated to St. Margaret. It is valued in the king's books at £29 1s. 1d. (Probably one mediety of the church was dedicated to All Saints; the other to St. Margaret).

It consists of two isles, built nearly uniform; the steeple stands at the west end of the south isle, and contains five bells.

At the east end of the south isle stands the altar; it is elevated on three steps of considerable height, and underneath is a charnel house.

A new pulpit was erected a few years since by the late rector, the Rev. Dr. Leman: the old one was a very ancient piece of architecture; on several parts of it was the figure of a man in a devout posture, with a label issuing from his mouth, containing this inscription:—

Misericordia diu in eternu Cantabo.

That is

I will celebrate the divine mercy for ever.

At the upper end of the south isle, on a fair brass-plated stone, is the following inscription, in Anglo-Saxon characters:—

Here lies master Richard Folcard, formerly rector of a mediety of this church to the south, who died on St. Martin's day, in the year of our Lord, one thousand four hundred.

To whose soul be merciful O God. Amen.

On a brass plate of a man and his wife, with eleven children, in the north isle, is another inscription, in old Anglo-Saxon characters, to the memory of one John Bowf or Bowfe, who died anno millo 6666, XVII.

On a flat marble in the north isle is an inscription to the memory of Philip Richardson, who was rector of Pakefield fifty-one years, and died October 8th 1748, aged 82.

On the north side of the church is a very ancient parsonage-house, built with stone.

On a small silver communion cup is the following inscription:—

✕ PAKEFELDE - SANTE - MARGARET, 1367.

On a silver paten,

PACKEFELDE.

And on a fine Holland communion cloth,

III III · 1640.

This church was lately much repaired and beautified at the expense of its late rector, the Rev. Dr. Leman; who not only new laid the floor, erected a new pulpit and desk, and placed over a curious old font, a handsome model of the tower and spire of Norwich Cathedral, but also embellished it with many other useful ornaments. He was endued with many excellent qualities particularly charity and beneficense, which he constantly exercised with the greatest liberality, both with respect to his parishioners and to mankind in general; and, consequently, was justly entitled to the following character, which was given of him at his decease:—"He was an admired preacher, a strenuous assertor of the rites and ceremonies of the church of which he was so bright an ornament, and indefatigable in every other part of the pastoral office."

There is also a meeting house in this parish for the people called Quakers, who have held meetings here for 130 years past, though their number is but small.

Int Rogeru Townesend & Henricum Spilman Quer et Tho: Aslack et Eliz ux ejus Deforc, Manerij de Elgh als dict Willingham All Saint set Advoc:

Ecclie ejusd: Et Ecclie de Pakefield: Jus Rogeri. Fines Suff. A.º 10 E. 4 Lig. 1, Nº.24.

Edmund Jenney Miles, Cond: Test die Veneris ante fm **Nat S. Marr**: Virg. 1522. Habuit int al: Advoc: Ecclie de Pakefield. P.bat 21º Dec. 1522 'ᴇ libro. (Briggs Regr. Norw. 35 vid. plus in Knodeshall.)

These injuries, and, in a great measure, illegal attempts to exclude the town of Lowestoft from having any share in the herring fishery occasioned a most violent rupture between the towns, and who carried their resentment so far as to fit out armed vessels, to commence hostilities on each others property, and even to commit bloodshed; the one party insisting upon the privileges they pretended to be entitled to by their charter, and the other party as strenuously defending those rights which for many centuries they had enjoyed, without any other interruption than paying the custom due to Yarmouth for the purchase of herrings in Kirkley road. But now it evidently appeared, that an utter exclusion of the Lowestoft men from the benefit of the herring fishery, was the determined resolution of the town of Yarmouth; and, therefore it occasioned the most violent struggles between liberty and oppression that can be well imagined; which continued so long as to make both the parties, most probably, weary of the contention, and agreed at last (in order for settling the dispute) to lay this long-contested affair before the Privy Council; from thence it was referred to the judges, and at last to a hearing before the house of Lords, where the case was finally determined in favour of the town of Lowestoft, as will be more fully shewn in the following section.

Upon an inquiry into the state of the herring fishery, after this contest was decided, it was found that the fishery at Lowestoft, and also at the adjoining towns, was greatly on the decline, occasioned partly by the disputes with Yarmouth, by the civil war in the reign of Charles I, the great fire at Lowestoft in 1644, and the war the nation was then engaged with the Dutch.

In consequence of these distresses, the town of Lowestoft and the neighbouring towns of Pakefield and Kirkley, presented a petition to both Houses of Parliament, requesting their lordships to take the unfortunate state of these towns into consideration, and to grant them relief; and particularly with respect to enforcing the old statutes relative to the consumption of fish in this Kingdom, and also by adding such new ones for that purpose as their lordships might think necessary.

"To the right honourable the lords and commons in the high courts of Parliament now assembled,

"The humble petition of the fishing adventurers and fishermen of the townes of Lowestoft, Pakefield, and Kirtlye, in the countye of Suffolk,

"Humbly sheweth,

"That your petitioners have ever chieflye subsisted by the fishing trade, in catching lingg, codds, and herrings, the staple fish of this Kingdom; and have, before the unhappye difference fell in this Kingdom, (the civil wars of Charles I) uttered and soulde greate quantitye of the said fish, which tendered to the welfare and mainteyneing of these townes, in regard of the sale they found for the same, (but nowe so it is.) May in please your honours that our townes are become very poore, and these adventurers in fishing affaires so undone, that one half of them are taken off, our fishermen lamentablye impoverished, and if better encouragement be not given they will fall to nothing; and these fishermen, the nurserye of seamen, will be enforced to undertake other employments, which will prove a greate prejudice to the nation; and for want of expense of the fish, through our adventures therein are soe much declined, yet that fish which we have cannot be soulde for twoe thirde of the price it have formerlye yielded, when twice as much fish have been taken, whereby manye poore faimilyes are utterly decayed, and these poore townes will be undone; they wholye depending upon the fishing trade.

"Your petitioners therefore, humblye pray your honours will be pleased to take the premises into consideration, and in your greate wisdomes make provision for the reveiveing of the ould good lawes, and making such additional lawes, that from henceforth fish may be more expended in this Kingdome. That soe your petitioners may be inabled to adventure in the fisherye as formerlye, and thereby support themselves, the fishermen, and theire faimilyes.

"And your petitioners, as in dutye bound, shall ever pray."

| | | |
|---|---|---|
| John Youell, vicar, | Thomas Tye, | John Landifield, |
| Samuel Pacy, | James Reeve, | James Sprat, |
| Peter Durrant, | Robert Bell, | Simond Spicer, |
| John Durrant, | Thomas Harvey, | Richard Drake, |
| John Wilde, | Ar. Jermey, | John Drake. |
| Tho. Uttinge, | Thomas Ashby, | Robert Bray, |
| John Gardinar, | William Pearson, | William Fowler, sen., |
| Richard Spedlove, | Thomas Felton, | John Colby, |
| Robert Daines, | Edward Long. | Thomas Fowler, |
| Robert Ashby, | John Longe, | William Thurrkettle, |
| John Gardinar, | Robert Botson, | William Wood, |
| Robert Hawes, | Francis Botson, | William Church, |
| Thomas Bolton, | Cornelles Landifield, | Obed Haulsworth, |
| Francis Mewse, | Henry Ward, | George Wooden, |
| Thomas Newton, | John Fowler, | William Browne, |
| William Shorting, | Thomas Batchelor, | John Barber, |
| Stephen Corfin, | James Spicer, | John Munds, |
| John Uttinge, | Simon Mewse, | William Seagoe, |
| Thomas Harrould, | William Harrould, | William Richman, |
| Matthew Reeve, | John Postle, | Thomas Church. |
| John Soane, | John Kittrige, | |
| Thomas Mighells, | John Bootey, | |

To this petition were annexed several proposals tending to the improvement of the herring fishery; and both together were transmitted to Sir John Pettus, to be by him presented to the committee appointed by Parliament for drawing up an Act for the further support and advancement of the herring fisheries, these complaints were so far attended to by Parliament that the petitioners obtained for the further increase of their fisheries; and also seamen and shipping; together with other privileges of considerable importance.

"A trewe copy of the severall proposalls sent to London this 24th of February, to Sir John Pettus, to be offered to the courtte of Parliament, 1670.

IMPROVEMENTS FOR ADVANCING THE FISHING TRADE.

"1st. That the fishers be free from payeing costome or excyse for any materralls to build, finish, victuall, repayre, and fitt to sea, their vessells, on their respective voyadges for herring, codd, ling, or any other fish.

"2nd. That the fishers be free to dispose of their fish at all tymes, in all places for their most advantage, within his majesty's dominions and countries, without restraint of corporation, or any other place or places whatever. And that noe person or persons be excluded that trade.

"3rd. That one year's assessment for the pore may be advanced in the respective parishes in England, to be employed in building convenient houses in the chefist of their townes; and for stocke for hempe, to sett the pore and idle persons oute of imployment to work to spinn twine and make netts.

"4th. That when one yeare after such housis be built, stocke of hemp provided and the pore sett on work to make netts; that all forryne nets be exhebated, upon payne of forfeiture of the same.

"AND FOR THE EXPENCE OF FISH, TO SUPPORT THE FISHERS.

"1st. That all persons of abilitie may have a small quantitie of fish and herrings imposed on them, at the common rate, according to their qualitie.

"2nd. That tooe fish days in the weke be duly observed, and no flesh spent unless for good reason they be lysensed by the mynister of the parish.

"A BILL FOR CARRYING ON THE FISHING TRADE, AND FOR INCREASE OF SEAMEN AND SHIPPING.

"Whereas the sovereignty of the British seas hath been ever (tyme out of mind) a flower inherent in the crown of England; and whereas the principall supporte thereof, as alsoe of the safetye and welfare of the English nations depend upon multidudes of shipping and seamen. And whereas the fishing trade doth above all others breede and increase seamen and shipping; and alsoe employes greate nombers of all sortes of impotent and aged people, as well women as children, above any other trade, in spinning, making and tanning netts, and in making roapes and sailes; and alsoe in curing, dressing and drying herrings, pilchards, ling, cod, salmon, and other sortes of fish, and otherwise. And whereas this soe advantagious and beneficiable trade, wherein the crowne, strength, and safetye of England is soe much concerned, and whereby innumerable people of all sorts might be maintayned, is of late years become neglected, and in hazard to be wholly lost, to the indangering not onlye the soveraignty of the British seas, but also of the safetye of these three nations, if not timelye prevented. And whereas it is impo-sible for the people of England to attaine unto a share in the taking of herrings, ling, cod, or other fish, to be pickled or otherwise cured and vented in forreigne countryes, unless they be in all respects enabled to builde, furnish and victuall busses and other fishing vessels, to catch them as cheape as other nations; and that the returnes of the said fish, more than shall be found usefull for England, may be brought into England and shipped out againe into any forreigne parts with as little charge and trouble as merchants, fishermen and others, in like cases, are put unto other countryes. Be it therefore enacted by the King's most excellent maiestie, and by and with the advice and concern of the lords spirrittuall and temporall and commons in Parliament assembled, that all materialls and provisions for building, furnishing, victualling, or repayring of busses or other fishing vessels, or otherwise, to be imployed or spent in and about the fishing trade upon certificate of the trueth thereof, shall be freed from paying the duty of costomes and excise. And be it further enacted, by the authority aforesaid, that all victuallers, inns, alehowses, ordinaries, chaundlers, vintners, and coffeehowses, according as they are better accustomed one then another, be and are hereby obliged to take of such merchaunt or other person as shall first tender the same in such porte or other convenient towne or cittye, upon a river neare unto theire respective habitations (as his maiestie, by advice of his right honourable privye council shall appoint) and cause notice thereof, by letters or otherwise in writing to be left here, and a copy thereof to be left with the cheife magistrate or chiefe officer, of such cittye, porte, or towne, or with theire respective officers or servants in that behalfe, one, two, three, four, or more good and merchantable barrells of herrings of herrings yearly, at such tymes and prise as his maiestie, by advice of his right honourable privye councill shall appoint dureing the term of seven years, to commence immediately after the end of this present sessions of Parliament, upon penalty of double the said prise unto the owners of the said herrings soe tendered by due course of lawe in any of his maiestie's courts of justice, etc."

The town of Lowestoft soon after presented another petition to the lords spirtual and temporal, praying to be relieved from paying a duty of two shillings and sixpence per barrel upon all such beer as should be used in the herring fishery; which petition was also accordingly granted.

"To the right honourable the lords and Commons now assembled
  in the high Court of Parliament,
"The humble petition of the inhabitants of the towne of
  Lowestoft, in the countye of Suffolke,
"Sheweth

"That your petitioners have ever cheifliest subsisted by the fishing trade, which for many yeares have much decayed, and your petitioners greatly impoverished by reason of the late wars and dearness of tacklin. (During the civil war in the reign of Charles I, Lowestoft took an active part against the Parliament.)

"That notwithstanding the officers for the excise have required the duty of twoe shillings and sixpence per barrell upon all fishing beer, which in noe tyme past have ever bene demanded; and for non-payment thereoff, have taken some of your petitioners goods, which doth much add to the decaye of youre poore petitioners trade, and discurridgement in the pursuite of theire calling; good bread and beer being theire cheifest comfort.

"Wherefore they most humbly pray that your honours would be graciously pleased to take into your considerations, that the excise uppon fishing beere, may wholly be taken off, as in your grave wisdomes shall be thought fitt; that youre poore petitioners may be incorridged comfortably to followe theire calling.

"And your petitioners, as in duty bound, shall ever pray, etc."

It is evident, from the above petitions, that Pakefield and Kirkley, etc., were involved in a considerable share of the misfortunes which distressed Lowestoft; and that in petitioning for relief under the hardship respecting the fishing beer, the towns mutually concurred, as appears by the following letter:—

"TO MR. JAMES WILDE, AT LOWESTOFT.

Sir,—By order of Henry Trott, from yourself, these are to certifye you, that here is belonging unto these townes of Pakefield and Kirkley, 14 fisher boats; which in their several voyages of one year, by estimation of us whose names are under-written, may expend nine tunns of beer each boate, which in the whole, is 126 tunnes, which is all at present from them that are

Yours at command,
JO. FOWLER and others."

Pakefield, this 9th of January, 1670.

The state of the herring fishery at Lowestoft and the adjoining towns, in the year 1670, will appear from the following account; together with what beer they respectively expended that year:—

LOWESTOFT.

| | |
|---|---|
| Thomas Mighells | 3 boats |
| Thomas Wilde | 1 ,, |
| Robert Barber | 1 ,, |
| John Wilde | 2 ,, |
| Margaret Munds | 1 ,, |
| Richard Church | 1 ,, |
| Richard Jex | 1 ,, |
| Thomas Ashby | 2 ,, |
| William Rising | 1 ,, |
| Joe Wilde | 2 ,, |
| Nicholas Utting | 1 ,, |
| Samuel Pacy | 2 ,, |
| John Landifield | 3 ,, |
| John Utting | 1 ,, |
| Thomas Hayles | 1 ,, |
| Henry Ward | 1 ,, |
| Joe Pacy | 1 ,, |
| Total | 25 boats |

Twenty-five at nine tuns each, is two hundred and twenty-five tuns.

| | |
|---|---|
| Pakefield and Kirkley | 14 boats. |
| Southwold, 8 herring boats and 3 Iceland boats | 11 ,, |
| Alborough, 2 herring boats and 3 Iceland boats | 5 ,, |
| Corton | 2 ,, |
| Dunwich | 1 ,, |
| Total | 33 boats |

These 33 boats from Pakefield and Kirkley, etc., together with 25 boats from Lowestoft (the towns which joined in the petition), expending nine tuns each boat, make the consumption of beer, in the whole, to be 522 tuns.

A few years after, the merchants of Lowestoft presented a petition to the lord-treasurer, praying that they might have the further privilege of importing coals, and exporting corn and other goods, for the benefit of the said town; which petition his lordship reported to the lords of the privy council, who granted the request.

## "THE ORDER FOR IMPORTING COALS, AND EXPORTING CORN, ETC., AT LOWESTOFT.

"After our hearty commendations—Wee have received your report of the 12th instant upon the petition of the inhabitants of Lowestoft; praying that corne and coles may be exported and emported there as well as other goods mentioned in a report by you to the late lord-treasurer of the 15th of October last. In which report of the 12th instant you gave us your opinion that the petitioners may have liberty to export corn from Lowestoft, due entryes being first made at Yarmouth. But not to emport it thither from beyond the seas. Also that they may emport sea coles thither due entreyes being first made at Yarmouth; but not to export them from thence to parts beyond the seas. And that, when the officers at Yarmouth shall see it necessary, an officer be sent over to Lowestoffe, the petitioners paying the officer such allowance per diem for his paines as shall be reasonable. These are therefore to pray and require you to give the necessary orders and directions for permitting and suffering corne to be exported, and sea coales to be imported at Lowestoft aforesaid, provided that due entreyes be made at Yarmouth; and that when the officer at Yarmouth see it necessary, an officer be sent over to Lowestoft, and gain for his pains according to the said Regulation by you proposed. And for soe doing this shall be your warrant.

"Whitehall Treasury Chamber, the 24th May, 1679.

To our very loving friends ) ESSEX. J. ERULE<br>
the Commissioners } ED. DERING<br>
of his majesties customs. ) S. GODOLPHIN."

Their lordships also at the same time issued another order to the commissioners of the customs informing them, that the merchants at Lowestoft should have liberty to import salt for curing fish, and also to import all such materials as are generally used for fishing vessels, as tackling, etc.

"After our hearty commendations—Whereas upon a petition presented to the late lord treasurer, by the inhabitants of Lowestoft, praying that an officer might be settled in the saide towne for receiving their entreys with his maiesties customes, and for granting coequetts for exportation of goods, or that the chiefe officer of his maiesties customes in Yarmouth, upon the petitioners making honest and just entreys, may permit the landing theire goods at Lowestoffe. And upon reference made of the said petition unto you, you did in a report made to the said late lord-treasurer of the 15th October last, set forth,—That the petitioners alledge theire having beene of late denyed to land theire goods at Lowestoft, notwithstanding they have entered them, and paid his maiesties dutyes at Yarmouth, and profered to be at the charge of an officer to see the delivery of them, but are forced to deliver them at Yarmouth, where the towne dutyes are great, and the charges (in regard of theire distance from the port of Yarmouth), also greate, especially upon salt for the fishery, which they cannot carry without greate and apparent loss; for which cause they were compelled to send their ships last yeare beyond the seas with theire goods, whereof his maiestie lost his customes, and the petitioners were much damnified. They likewise alledge that to land the grosser sort of goods at Yarmouth, it would consume almost a quarter part of their profitt to get them home. That the said towne of Lowestoffe is increased in shipping to the number of sixty vessells which is more considerable than both the townes of Southwold and Aldeborough, at each of which townes is an officer to receive entreyes and to grant coequetts. On the other side you set forth, that Southwold and Aldeborough are members of the port of Yarmouth, where antiently there hath been established a collector, and the patent officers of that port are required by law to keep theire deputyes in the said members; but that Lowestoffe is but a creeke in the said porte, where the patent officers are not required by law to have theire deputyes to attend, although it be much increased in shipping. And that it would be a great charge to his maiestie, and the patent officers, to make it a port of receipt, and a member annexed to the said port. That you have also received the report of Mr. Dumsteir, one of the general surveyors, and the patent officers and surveyors of the port of Yarmouth upon the said petitions. Wee are of opinion that it would be to the prejudice of his maiesties customes, besides a charge to his maiestie, to settle a

## HISTORY OF LOWESTOFT.

collector there. That great frauds have been formerly practised in the Port of Yarmouth, where with much difficulty things are brought in some good order. That you are of opinion, that by giving the general liberty desired by the petitioners, the same frauds would be practised at Lowestoffe. But as to the importing gross goods, **viz.,** salt, timber, deale boards, pitch, tarr, rozine, iron, hemp, ropes, **cordage, and** pantiles; and as to the exporting butter, cheese, and fish, **you think** they may be laden and unladen at Lowestoffe, entreyes **being first** duly made at Yarmouth, and an officer being sent over to Lowestoffe, **when** the officer at Yarmouth shall see it necessary, they at Lowestoffe **payeing the** officer such allowance per diem for his paines as shall be **reasonable.** Wee have considered what you have set forth and proposed as aforesaid in your said report and do accordingly order and direct that you permitt and suffer the gross goods before enumerated to be respectively imported and exported at Lowestoffe in such manner and under such regulations, as you advise in your report above received, and that you give such directions to the officers whom it concerns as may be necessary in this behalf; and for see doing this shall be your warrant.

Whitehall Treasury Chamber, June 6th, 1679.

To our very loving friends  
the commissioners of  
His Maisties customes.  
} L. HYDE,  
E. D. DERING,  
S. GODOLPHIN,  
J. ERULE."

The herring season begins on the eastern coast of England about a fortnight before Michaelmas, and continues till Martinmas. The number of boats annually employed at Lowestoft in this fishery, upon an average from the year 1772 to 1781, was about 33; and the quantity of herrings caught in each of those years, was about 714. lasts, or 21 lasts to a boat, which makes the quantity of herrings caught by the Lowestoft boats during that period to be 7140 lasts. These herrings were sold, upon an average, at about £12 10s. per last, which makes the whole produce arising from the sale of the said fish to be £89,250. After the year 1781, the number of boats employed in this fishery were rather less, occasioned by the war with the Dutch and other powers. (In the year 1737, one boat only, belonging to Joshua Marshall, caught 72 lasts of herrings. A last is 10,000.)

At the beginning of the season, the boats sail off to sea about thirteen leagues north-east from Lowestoft, in order to meet the shoals, or second part of the first division of the herrings (mentioned in the beginning of this section), which separated off the north part of Scotland. Being arrived on the fishing ground, in the evening (the proper time for fishing) they shoot their nets, extending about 2,200 yards in length, and eight in depth, which, by the help of small casks, called bowls, fastened on one side, at the distance of 44 yards, from each other, cause the nets to swim in a position perpendicular to the surface **of the** water. If the quantity of fish caught in one night amounts only to **a few thousands,** they are salted, and the vessels, if they have no better success, continue **on the** fishing ground two or three nights longer, salting the fish as they are caught, **till they** have obtained a considerable quantity, when they bring them into the roads, **where** they **are** landed, and lodged in the fish houses. Sometimes when the quantity of fish is very small, they will continue on the fishing ground a week or ten days; but in general they bring in the fish every two or three days, and sometimes oftener, especially when the quantity amounts to six or seven lasts, which frequently happens, and instances have been known, when a single boat **has** brought into the roads, at one time, twelve or fourteen lasts.

As soon as the herrings are brought on shore, they are carried to the fish houses, where they are salted, and laid on the floors in heaps, about two feet deep; after they have continued in this situation about fifty hours, the salt is washed from them by putting them into baskets and plunging them into water; from thence they are carried into an adjoining fish house, where, after being pierced through the gills by small wooden spits about four feet long, they are handed to the men in the upper part of the house, who place them at proper distances as high as the top of the roof, where they are cured and made red.

The upper part of the house being thus filled with herrings, many small wood fires are kindled underneath, upon the floor, whose number is in proportion to the size of the room, and the smoke which ascends from these fires is what dries or cures the herrings. After the fish have hung in this manner about seven days, the fires are extinguished, that the oil and fat may drip from them and in about two days after the fires are re-kindled and after two more such drippings, the fires are kept continually burning until the herrings are perfectly cured, which requires a longer or shorter time, according as they are designed either for a foreign or home consumption. After the herrings have hung a proper time, they are taken down (which is called "striking"), and are packed in barrels containing 800 or 1000 herrings each.

From the many frauds which have been formerly practised in this part of the fishing branch the packing of herrings, a complaint was made to the government, in the reign of Charles II. praying that this grievance might be redressed, and accordingly an Act of Parliament was obtained, 15 Charles II, to the following purpose :—

"That from and after the first day of August, 1664, no white or red herrings of English catching shall be put up to sale in England, Wales, or towne of Berwick upon Tweed, but what shall be packed in lawful barrels or vessels, and what shall be well, truly, and justly laid and packed; and shall be of one time of taking, salting, saveing, or drying, and equally well packed in the midst, and every part of the barrel or vessel: and by a sworn packer, with a mark or brand denoting the gage of the barrel or vessel, and quantity, quality and condition of the herrings packed therein, and the towne or place where they are packed. And the bayliffs of Great Yarmouth for the time being, and the mayor, bayliffs, or other head officer for the time being, of every port, haven, or creek, out of which any vessell or ships do proceed to fish for herrings are hereby authorised and required before the the first day of July in the year 1664. And before the first day of July every year after, to appoint for their respective haven, port, or creek, a competent number of able and experienced packers to view and pack all white and red herrings of English catching as shall be brought into their port, haven, or creek; and well and truly to mark and brand the barrels or vessels into which such herrings are put, with such mark or brand as is above directed. And to administer to them yearly an oath, (which oath they are hereby authorised and appointed to give them) for the well and true doing thereof according to this Act. And in case the said bayliffs of Great Yarmouth, or the mayor, bayliffs, or other head officer for the time being of any such port, haven, or creek, shall not appoint and swear such packers before him in every year, as is by this Act required they shall for every default, forfeit the sum of one hundred pounds of lawful money of England. One moiety to his maiestie, his hiers and succesors and the other moiety to him or them that shall informe or sue for the same in any court of record, by bill, plaint, or other action, wherein no essoyn, protection, or wager in law shall be allowed.

### THE OATH.

"You shall well and truly doe, execute, and perform, the office and duty of packer of herrings; according to the tenour of an Act of Parliament in that case made and provided. So help you God."

The herrings are shipped off for market, which formerly was chiefly confined to foreign ports especially those belonging to Roman Catholic countries, and only a small quantity reserved for home consumption; but of late years the home consumption has greatly increased, and the commissions from foreign parts have neither been so numerous nor so large as in former years. The great increase of inhabitants in London appears to be the cause of the former, as the less rigorous observance of Lent, and other fish days, in Popish countries, is the reason assigned for the latter.

These reasons will receive farther confirmation from the following account of the demand for herrings for foreign consumption, in 1755. In that year there were cured in Lowestoft and Yarmouth 70,000 barrels, which were consigned to the following ports :—

|                |              |           |
|----------------|--------------|-----------|
| To Leghorn     | 13,000       | barrels   |
| Naples         | 7,500        | ,,        |
| Venice         | 5,700        | ,,        |
| Genoa          | 5,500        | ,,        |
| Ancona         | 4,500        | ,,        |
| Cadiz          | 900          | ,,        |
| Trieste        | 700          | ,,        |
| Civita Vecchia | 700          | ,,        |
| Bordeaux       | 500          | ,,        |
|                | 39,000       | ,,        |
| To Holland     | 13,000       | ,,        |
| Home Consumption, chiefly in London | 18,000 | ,, |
| Total          | 70,000 barrels |         |

From hence it appears, that out of 70,000 barrels of herrings cured that year, only 18,000 were consumed in England. Since that time the demand for herrings for foreign markets has further declined, and that for home consumption has increased in the same proportion.

The quantity of herrings properly termed a barrel is 1000, though oftentimes 800, as when the fish are picked; the antient method of packing red herrings was in cades, containing 600; but that is a method observed now only in the packing of sprats.

In the year 1776 the herring merchants of Lowestoft were much alarmed with apprehensions of the utter extinction of their fishery, and, consequently, with the total ruin of the town. Some merchants belonging to Liverpool, the Isle of Man, and Dunbar and Caithness, in Scotland, having introduced the method of curing herrings into these parts, and set up a red herring fishery in opposition to Yarmouth and Lowestoft, endeavoured to become their rivals both at the London as well as the foreign markets. But, after repeated attempts, their schemes proved totally abortive, through the superior quality of the Lowestoft herrings; and, consequently, the fishery at Lowestoft was thereby re-established upon a more permanent foundation than before.

The superior quality of the Lowestoft herrings, both in respect of colour and flavour, is evident from this circumstance—their bearing a better price at market than those from any other place.

It has been a long-established rule with the fish-mongers in London, to give ten shillings per last for the Lowestoft herrings more than those of Yarmouth, let the Yarmouth price be what it will. Two reasons may be assigned for the cause of this difference.

In Yarmouth, the merchants entrust the curing of the fish to the care of a head man, called a towher, more than the merchants at Lowestoft do; for at Lowestoft the merchants inspect the curing of the fish chiefly themselves. The other, and more probable cause may be, that in Yarmouth the fish houses are intermixed with the dwelling-houses, and being situated in these narrow passages called rows, are too closely confined, and, consequently, deprived of that free circulation of air so necessary in the proper curing of herrings. At Lowestoft these houses are detached from the other buildings of the town and are arranged at the bottom of the cliff by themselves, where from the benefit of a free and uninterrupted currency of the air, they acquire those excellent qualities which are not to be attained in any other place which has not the same advantages.

Nevertheless, it afterwards appeared, that these new adventurers had a design of this nature in contemplation some time before they attempted to carry it into execution; and in order to the rendering it successful, had sent several persons to Lowestoft, for the purpose of taking dimensions of the fish houses, their manner of construction, etc., and to make every other inquiry respecting the method of curing herrings.

Having by these means obtained every information necessary for their purpose, they began soon after to erect houses, and made every other preparation proper for the curing of herrings, and were able in a short time to furnish the markets with immense quantities of fish; and had not their herrings been so extremely large and fat as to prevent their being properly cured, the undertaking, most probably, would have been successful. The last circumstance which I shall mention concerning the herring fishery at Lowestoft, is the proposal made in 1779, by the French King to the English Court, for a reciprocal neutrality respecting their fisheries, during the war, which met with the approbation of both courts, as appears from the letters below :

COPY OF THE LETTER FROM M. DE SARTINE TO M. D'ANGLEMONT

"Versailles, the 31st May, 1779.

"The benefit, sir, that must result from the reciprocal liberty of fishing between France and England, and above all the desire to preserve the means of subsistence during the war, to the subjects of the two nations, to whom this employment is essential, have determined the King in no respect to interrupt the fishery of the English; his MAJESTY, persuaded that this example of humanity will be followed by the court of London charges me to order you to make it known to all the officers commanding his ships, and to all private commanders, that it is most expressly forbid them to molest in any manner till after new orders, the fishing boats of the English which shall have no offensive arms ; and also such as shall be laden with fresh fish, though such fish should not have been taken by those vessels, unless they should be found making signals to give intelligence to the cruizers of the ships of the enemy.

"I have no doubt that you will carefully observe that the King's commands will be executed.—I am, very truly sir, your very humble and very obedient servant,  *(Signed)*  DE SARTINE."

A Copy of this letter was sent by M. D'Anglemont to the officers of the chamber of commerce at Dunkirk, who had it printed, that they may the better conform to the views of the minister of the marine.

THE FOLLOWING LETTER WAS ALSO SENT FROM THE FRENCH KING TO HIS SERENE HIGHNESS THE ADMIRAL OF FRANCE :—

"Cousin,

"The desire I have always had of softening, as much as in my power lies, the calamities of war, has induced me to direct my attention to that part of my subjects, who employ themselves in the fisheries, and who derive their sole subsistence from those resources. I suppose that the example which I shall now give to my enemies, and which can have no other views than what arise from sentiments of humanity, will induce them to grant the same liberty to our fisheries, which I readily grant them. In consequence whereof, I send you this letter to acquaint you, that I have given orders to all the commanders of my vessels, armed ships, and captains of privateers, not to molest (until further orders) the English fishery, nor to stop their vessels, whether they be laden with fresh fish, or not having taken in their freight ; provided, however, that they do not carry offensive arms, and that they are not found to have given signals, which might indicate their holding an intelligence with the enemy's ships of war. You will make known these my intentions to the officers of the admiralty, and to all who are under your orders. Such being the purposes of these presents, I pray God, my cousin, that he will grant you His Holy protection,

"Given at Versailles, the 5th day of June, in the year, 1779.

"*(Signed)*  LOUIS.
"*(Countersigned)*  DE SARTINE."

Two gentlemen were sent from France to the English Court, to solicit our concurrence in this proposal ; they came first to Lowestoft and the other towns on the coast, to request these places to join with them in the solicitation. It appeared that the English Court refused to accede formally to the overture, though they tacitly complied with it, and gave such orders to their commanders that no act of hostility was committed on the fisheries by either side during the war.

Another fishery subsisting at Lowestoft, is that called the mackarel fair. The principal advantages which the merchants receive from this fishery, is that of employing the fishermen, and keeping them at home for the herring season, more than any emolument to themselves ; as the benefits which they receive are very inadequate to the expense of fitting out the vessels, the dangers they are liable to from the sea, and in time of war from the enemy.

The mackarel season begins about the middle of May, and continues to the end of June. The number of boats annually employed at Lowestoft in this fishery are about 23; and the money arising from the sale of the fish caught by these boats, amount upon an average to about £2,309. At the beginning of this season (as in the herring season) the boats sail into the north-east, in order to meet the fish at the beginning of their annual revolution around the British Isles. The mackarel being naturally a slothful fish, never rises to the surface of the water in any large quantities in calm weather, so that the success of the voyage almost entirely depends upon a blustering, stormy season, which rouses the fish from the lower parts of the ocean, and brings them within reach of the fishing nets. The quantity caught at the beginning of the season is generally small; afterwards it so far increases, that 500 or 1,800 fish will be caught by one boat in a night, if the weather be turbulent; otherwise, if it be calm and serene, the quantity is inconsiderable. As the mackarel is never salted, but requires an immediate consumption, the boats employed in catching them are under the necessity of returning every day to their respective towns, to deliver the fish which they caught in the preceding night; but when the quantity of fish is small, the weather calm, or the wind contrary, they will sometimes continue upon the fishing ground a second night.

An ACCOUNT of the MACKAREL FISHERY at LOWESTOFT, from 1770 to 1785 INCLUSIVE; CONTAINING THE NUMBER OF BOATS EMPLOYED EACH YEAR, AND THE ANNUAL AMOUNT OF THE MONEY ARISING FROM THE SALE OF THE FISH.

| Year. | Boats. | £ | s. | d. |
|---|---|---|---|---|
| 1770 | 26 | 2401 | 2 | 2½ |
| 1771 | 26 | 3080 | 15 | 6¼ |
| 1772 | 33 | 3179 | 5 | 1 |
| 1773 | 36 | 3374 | 15 | 6 |
| 1774 | 35 | 2012 | 13 | 0 |
| 1775 | 32 | 2441 | 5 | 2 |
| 1776 | 30 | 1595 | 17 | 8½ |
| 1777 | 20 | 1698 | 15 | 0 |
| 1778 | 21 | 1295 | 19 | 1¼ |
| 1779 | 21 | 1618 | 4 | 6 |
| 1780 | 20 | 1559 | 3 | 10 |

In 1781, sixteen boats averaged £173 15s. 3½d. per boat.
In 1782, sixteen boats averaged £136 1s. 2d, per boat.
In 1783, sixteen boats averaged £189 1s. per boat.
In 1784, twenty boats averaged £119 5s. 11½d. per boat.
In 1785, twenty boats averaged £249 8s. 8½d. per boat. (Supposed to be the greatest mackarel season ever known at Lowestoft).
In 1786, twenty-four boats averaged £146 7s. 9½d. **per boat.**
In 1787, twenty boats averaged £105 5s. per boat.
In 1788, twenty boats averaged £93 6s. 6d. per boat.
In 1789, twenty-six boats averaged £98 16s. 2¼d. per boat.

Total amount from 1770 to 1789 inclusive, £49,769 4s. 3¼d. (On the 29th May, 1781, fifteen boats, belonging to Lowestoft, caught 24,600½ of mackarels, being the greatest number ever remembered to have been taken in one day. The sale of these fish amounted to £295 7s. 9d., and were sold by the late Mr. John Spicer, who usually sold the mackarels. (Mr. Spicer was clerk of this parish about fifty years; he died about the year 1776, and was succeeded by Mr. Bolchin).

As soon as the mackarels are brought on shore they are poured upon the beach in heaps, each boat's by itself. The beach being the place where the fair for the fish is held; here it is that the padders and other purchasers assemble for the purpose of buying them. The fish being thus exposed for sale, are generally sold by private contract, though some times by public auction; formerly by a man appointed by the merchants for that purpose, but now many of the merchants sell their own fish.

The common markets for vending the mackarel are London, and the principal towns in Norfolk and Suffolk, and the adjoining counties; they are sent to the former place in small vessels, called cutters, employed by the fishmongers in London; and to the latter places by carriers, called padders who are employed by the fishmongers belonging to the several towns to which the fish are sent.

There were formerly in this town two other fisheries, called the North Sea and Iceland fisheries. These fisheries were in a flourishing state about the middle of the last century, both here and at Yarmouth. According to Swinden, the number of vessels employed in these fisheries in the year 1644, by the town of Yarmouth only, numbered 205; in the North Sea fishery, 182; in the Iceland fishery, 23; and it was at this time that these fisheries appeared to be in the most flourishing state. Afterwards they gradually declined; for the merchants proving unsuccessful in their voyages, the number of adventurers decreased, and some years after, the fisheries totally ceased. In the year 1740 there was only one boat sent to Iceland from Yarmouth, which appeared to be the last employed in this fishery. At Lowestoft there were about 30 boats sent annually to the North Sea and Iceland; in the year 1720 they were reduced to only five; and in 1748, Mr. Copping, an eminent merchant in this town, was the last person who sent a boat from Lowestoft to the North Seas, which proving unsuccessful, put a final period to these fisheries, they being never attempted afterwards.

The first voyage to these seas was called the Spring voyage; after that was finished they went a second voyage, but returned home again time enough for the herring fishery; but those who were not engaged in the herring fishery, attempted a third voyage. Cod and ling were the principal objects of this fishery, and in a good season would catch about 400 each vessel.

The method of curing these fish was by pickling them in casks, and some dry-salted; which, upon their return home, were exported to foreign parts. The livers of these fish were a considerable article; these they carefully preserved in casks, and the oil they extracted from them was sold to a considerable amount. There is a trench still visible upon the Dênes, a little to the north of Lowestoft, in which stood the blubber coppers, where they used to boil the livers of the fish when they returned home from the voyage. They also traded with the natives of Iceland, Shetland, Farra, etc., and imported from hence stockings, blankets, caps, and other articles of the woollen manufactory.

The first decline of these fisheries may be attributed, in a great measure, to the political animosities which subsisted between Yarmouth and Lowestoft, towards the conclusion of the reign of Charles I; for as Yarmouth, during the civil war, took an active part on the side of Parliament, so Lowestoft was as much distinguished for its attachment to the King. In the years 1643 and 1644 the inhabitants of Yarmouth suffered so very much from losses at sea, in having their ships and vessels taken and carried off by armed ships acting in hostility against the parliament, that the town was greatly impoverished, and the fisheries to the North Sea and Iceland much injured. From these circumstances, and the great indulgence allowed the Roman Catholics in foreign parts, in the observance of Lent and other times of abstinence, so prejudicial to fisheries depending on a foreign consumption, the North Sea and Iceland fisheries received so much discouragement, as never to recover it afterwards.

A ship, laden with soldiers and ammunition, sent by the queen from Holland, for the use of the King, springing a leak at sea was obliged to put into Yarmouth, where she was seized for the Parliament and given to the town, who equipped her and sent her to sea in 1645 as a man-of-war, to take any vessels, etc., that were in hostility against the Parliament. Amongst the prizes which she made was the Pink, Captain Allen (afterwards Admiral Allen), of Lowestoft, who, it was said, was in rebellion against the Parliament, of which ship he was the owner of one half part, and which part was seized, and sold to Mr. James Wilde, of Lowestoft, for £35.

Captain Allen and some others who had suffered the like oppressions appear to have entered into a confederacy against Yarmouth, to retaliate the injuries they had received from that town; and for that purpose retired beyond sea, with the design of fitting out vessels to distress the trade at Yarmouth; and, accordingly, we find that in the year 1644, out of the twenty-three vessels employed by Yarmouth in the Iceland fishery, only three of them escaped being taken.

The Yarmouth men being thus distressed, applied to Parliament for a convoy to protect their trade; in consequence whereof, in 1645, three men-of-war were sent, by order of the lord admiral, to convoy their fishers and guard their coasts; who took several of their enemies who were engaged in the confederacy, amongst whom were some Lowestoft men.

As soon as the parties concerned in this confederacy (who had retired beyond sea) were informed of these proceedings on the part of Yarmouth, they sent the town the following letter:

"To THE BAILIFFS OF GREAT YARMOUTH, IN NORFOLK.

"Right Worshipful,

"We hereby give you to understand that those seamen of ours, which your men-of-war have lately taken, or may hereafter take in prizes of ours, be not imprisoned. And that you set at liberty all those that are confined, otherwise you shall not have that usuage you formerly had from us. Without delay let this be observed, else you will have cause to repent. We have given you thousands of prisoners which we might have endungeoned, nay hanged, but that rebellious ignorance have pleaded their escape. Now we can, if you compel us, make a hundred suffer for one. Our pleasures are commended to you, by just and due observation, not to make the innocent suffer for the nocent. Therefore we do daily set at liberty yours, supposing, that upon receipt of these, you will do the same by ours; otherwise we shall soon make known to you our intentions.

THOMAS ALLEN, WILLIAM COPE, GEORGE BOWDEN, JOHN DASSET, RICHARD WHITING, PETER CLIFF, FRANCIS FOURTHER, JONATHAN BANTER, BROWNE BUSHELL, JO. MERRITT, DAN. WILKINSON, FRANCIS COLMAN.

"Ostend, June 22nd, 1645."

The Yarmouth historian, speaking of this transaction, says, "Probably all these (who had subscribed the above letter) were Englishmen, who had fled for protection into foreign parts, and lived by plundering the Yarmouth fisheries and others upon the high seas, under pretence of loyalty, and serving their king and country."

How far this censure is consistent with candour, I shall leave the impartial reader to determine; the only observation I shall make on it is this: that the town of Yarmouth having taken an active part in behalf of Parliament, and the town of Lowestoft, being as warmly interested on the part of the king; and the towns having also acted, for many years, as rivals to each other in the herring fishery, we may consider them, in a great measure, as inveterate enemies; whether we regard them in a political or commercial point of view; and, consequently, may easily account for their animosities, without having recourse either to censures or misrepresentations.

Captain Allen, a few years after, greatly alarmed the town of Yarmouth with the apprehension of an immediate retaliation of the injuries which he and his associates had sustained; for on Sunday, January 13th, 1648-9, he came into Yarmouth roads in one of the prince's ships, and threatened an immediate revenge on the town: but it appears, notwithstanding these threats, that his humanity conquered his resentment; for neither history, nor tradition informs us, that the town of Yarmouth ever received any injury from him.

The only manufactory carried on at Lowestoft is that of making porcelain, or china-ware; where the proprietors have brought this ingenious art to a great degree of perfection; and from the prospect it affords, promises to be attended with much success. The origin of this manufactory is as follows:—

In the year 1756, Hewlin Luson, Esq., of Gunton Hall, near Lowestoft, having discovered some fine clay, or earth, on his estate in that parish, sent a small quantity of it to one of the china manufactories near London, in view of discovering what kind of ware it was capable of producing; which, upon trial, proved to be somewhat finer than that called the Delft ware. Mr. Luson

H

was so far encouraged by this success as to resolve upon making another experiment of the goodness of its quality upon his own premises; accordingly, he immediately procured some workmen from London, and erected upon his estate at Gunton, a kiln and furnace, and all the other apparatus necessary for the undertaking: but the manufacturers in London being apprised of his intentions, and of the excellent quality of the earth, and apprehending also, that if Mr. Luson succeeded, he might rival them in their manufactory, it induced them to exercise every art in their power to render his scheme abortive; and so far tampered with the workmen he had procured, that they spoiled the ware, and thereby frustrated Mr. Luson's design.

But, notwithstanding this unhandsome treatment, the resolution of establishing a china manufactory at Lowestoft was not relinquished, but was revived again in the succeeding year by Messrs. Walker, Brown, Aldred, and Richman, who, having purchased some houses on the south side of the Bell lane, converted the same to the uses of the manufactory, by erecting a kiln and other conveniences necessary for the purpose: but, in carrying their designs into execution, they also were liable to the same inconveniences as the proprietor of the original undertaking at Gunton was; for being under the necessity of applying to the manufactories in London for workmen to conduct the business, this second attempt experienced the same misfortune as the former one, and very near totally ruined their designs; but the proprietors happening to discover these practices of the workmen before it was too late, they took such precautions as rendered every future attempt of this nature wholly ineffectual, and have now established the factory upon such a permanent foundation as promises great success. They have now enlarged their original plan, and by purchasing several adjoining houses, and erecting additional buildings, have made every necessary alteration requisite for the various purposes of the manufactory. They employ a considerable number of workmen; and supply with ware many of the principal towns in the adjacent counties, and keep a warehouse in London to execute the orders they receive both from the city and the adjoining towns; and have brought the manufactory to such a degree of perfection as promises to be a credit to the town, useful to the inhabitants, and beneficial to themselves.

## SECTION IV.

### THE CONTEST BETWEEN YARMOUTH AND LOWESTOFT RESPECTING KIRKLEY ROAD AND THE HERRING FISHERY.

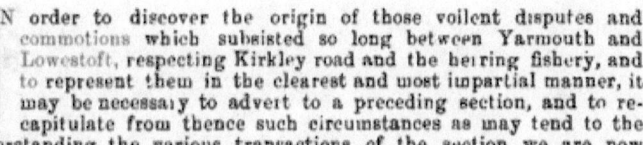

IN order to discover the origin of those voilent disputes and commotions which subsisted so long between Yarmouth and Lowestoft, respecting Kirkley road and the herring fishery, and to represent them in the clearest and most impartial manner, it may be necessary to advert to a preceding section, and to recapitulate from thence such circumstances as may tend to the better understanding the various transactions of the section we are now engaged in.

It was there observed, that in early ages, even before Yarmouth was founded, it is probable, that Lowestoft was the general rendezvous of both the northern and western fishers employed in the herring fishery; because, until the sand whereon Yarmouth was afterwards built appeared above the surface of the water and became firm land the fishermen that resorted to these coasts for herrings must necessarily have a place more southerly to assemble at. That as soon as the sand called Cerdick sand had made its appearance, (the Saxons came first; afterwards the portsmen), they found its situation so extremely convenient for drying of nets, and the other necessary occupations of a seafaring life, that they began soon after to erect temporary booths or tents there, as their several circumstances would admit as well for the accommodation of their persons as the security of their property. Soon after they had officers, called bailiffs, deputed by the barons of the cinque ports, to superintend the fishery for the space of forty days; afterwards they began to erect houses, and at last was founded the burgh called Great Yarmouth.

The burgesses of Yarmouth had a charter of liberties granted them by King John; and the barons of the cinque ports had also certain liberties at Yarmouth granted them by the same king or rather confirmed what they held before by prescriptive right only: but these several liberties interfering with each other gave rise to the most violent disputes and depredations upon each others' property, which continued, with some intermissions, until the reign of queen Elizabeth, when a proposal for conciliating these differences was offered, by making Yarmouth a member of the cinque ports, but it failed of success: but in the year 1576 all matters in dispute being adjusted to their mutual satisfaction it was at the same time finally agreed, "That as every fishing vessel frequenting this fair in antient times paid four pence, as a toll or custom, to the bailiffs of the cinque ports; and that afterwards the said bailiffs accepted from the bailiffs, of Great Yarmouth, in lieu thereof, the annual sum of six pounds: Yet now, for the sake of restoring peace and tranquility, it was further agreed by the said bailiffs of the cinque ports to receive only three pounds ten shillings from the bailiffs of Yarmouth, in full satisfaction for the above-mentioned toll." Thus their disputes being amicably adjusted, the contending parties preserved afterwards a more friendly intercourse with each other, which continued for some years, when the Yarmouth men refusing to pay the bailiffs of the cinque ports the above-stipulated sum of three pounds ten shillings any longer, the said bailiffs preferring peace to contention, and wishing to avoid any farther disputes, discontinued coming to the fair at Yarmouth in a public capacity any longer,

(The disputes arising from the privileges granted to the burgesses of Yarmouth and the barons of the cinque ports clashing with each other, gave birth to the most violent outrages and domestic wars that were ever known before between any two places in this kingdom; they even proceeded to such lengths as to alarm the whole kingdom with their mutual depredations.

By a special pardon granted to the men of Yarmouth, 10 Edward I. it appears, that they were fined £1000 for damages which they had done upon the western coast as far as Shoreham and Portsmouth. And in the 31st of that king it appears, that Yarmouth had sustained damages by the portsmen to the amount of £20.13s, an enormous sum at that time. This, probably, is what Hollingshed alludes to in his Chronicle, where it is recorded, that in the 25th of Edward I, "That king passing into Flanders, to the assistance of the earl thereof, being no sooner on land, but the men of the ports and Yarmouth, through an old grudge long depending between them, fell together and fought on the sea with such fury, that, notwithstanding the king's commandment to the contrary, twenty-five ships of Yarmouth and their partakers were burnt, etc." But Manship observes, "That in the town's Record of that year he did not find that so many were burnt; but by a complaint and presentment made to his majesty it appears, that thirty-seven ships were greatly damaged by the portsmen, 171 men killed, and goods to the value of £15,356 were spoiled and taken from them; of which (says he) a grevious requital was not long after made by the men of Yarmouth against portsmen. The late disputes seem to have originated from the mistaken idea which each of the parties had conceived of their own importance from their newly-acquired grants, and for want of having their respective privileges more clearly ascertained.)

The town of Yarmouth having now engrossed the whole of the herring fishery usually carried on near their own town to themselves, it became, in consequence thereof, the general rendezvous of all the vessels employed in buying and selling those fish, of whom they demanded a toll or custom; and having also obtained a charter, 46 Edward III for uniting Kirkley road to the port of Yarmouth, and for extending their liberties seven miles from the said port, were legally authorised to levy their customs upon all such herrings as were bought and sold in the above-mentioned road and within the said seven miles.

But the Yarmouth men, so far from being satisfied with the additional emoluments arising from these acquisitions, envolved themselves in fresh disputes with the men of Lowestoft, in the reign of Henry IV. respecting their customs, which were revived again in the reign of queen Elizabeth, (exclusive of the above-mentioned dispute with the portsmen in 1576), and again about the year 1659, when they attempted to extend their liberties beyond their legal bounds, and endeavoured to hinder the Lowestoft men from purchasing any herrings either at or near their own town, unless they paid the usual customs to Yarmouth; and grounded their claim on a pretence, that the grant of the 46th of Edward III. which extended their liberties seven leuks or miles from Yarmouth, was not to be measured from the key of Yarmouth, but from the mouth of the haven; and consequently would thereby wholly exclude the town of Lowestoft from buying herrings even in the roads belonging to their own town, unless they first submitted to pay such customs as should be claimed by the burgesses of Yarmouth. They also endeavoured farther to show, that that part of the sea called Kirkley road was opposite the parish of Kirkley, a town situated about a mile to the south of Lowestoft, notwithstanding the real name of that part of the sea is Pakefield bay; and that the seven leuks prescribed in their charter as the boundary of their liberties, were not miles but leagues.

These unreasonable and ill-grounded claims on the part of Yarmouth were productive of a most violent rupture between the two towns; they even proceeded so far (in order to defend what each of them thought to be their just and legal privileges) as to fit out armed vessels, in consequence of which many sharp engagements ensued, and much blood was shed on both sides. At last the respective parties, being weary of contention, agreed to lay the affair before the privy council, from whence it was referred to the judges, and lastly to a hearing before the house of lords where it was finally determined in favour of the town of Lowestoft, as will be more fully shewn in the subsequent part of this section.

The above circumstances being premised, I shall now proceed to make some inquiries concerning the several charters granted to Yarmouth respecting the herring fishery, how far the liberties contained in those charters extended; and particularly, whether the charter which annexed Kirkley road to Yarmouth haven tended to exclude the town of Lowestoft from the privilege, which it had enjoyed from time immemorial, of buying and selling herrings in the roads belonging to their own town.

I have observed before, that the great charter of liberties granted to the town of Yarmouth, was that granted by King John, in the 9th year of his reign. This king being distressed in fitting out a fleet of ships for the recovery of his Norman dominions, lately lost, indulged them with a charter, on condition, "that they should provide for him fifty-seven ships for forty days, at their own charge, as often as the wars he was engaged in should give him occasion to demand them. (In the reign of Edward III. Yarmouth had more ships than any city or town in England.) By this charter Yarmouth was created a free burgh, and the burgesses thereof were invested with many immunities and privileges, to be held in fee-farm, paying to him and his heirs, an annual rent of £55 for ever; for payment thereof they were allowed only the customs arising out of the port; not being authorised to receive any custom of goods bought or sold in the market upon land at the time of the year. (Upon uniting Kirkley road to Yarmouth haven by letters patent, 46 Edward III. the fee-farm rent of £55 per annum was augmented to £60.

In the reign of Henry III, when that prince exchanged the fee-farm of Yarmouth and Lothingland with John de Baliol, for other lands in Cheshire, which was very detrimental to the town of Yarmouth, on account that ships with victuals might unlade on Lothingland side, and particularly so, as fish was one of the principal articles from whence their greatest profits arose; and, therefore, they petitioned the King in the fortieth year of his reign, to grant them a new charter, whereby all merchandise and wares, as well fish as other commodities, should be sold at Yarmouth by the hands of the importers of them into the haven of Yarmouth, whether found in the ships or without, etc.; which charter was accordingly granted. But the Baliols (father and son) still continued to take tolls and customs belonging to the port of Yarmouth, notwithstanding its charters to the contrary, to the great prejudice of the burgesses, who were either unable or unwilling to contest the matter with so powerful an enemy as the King of Scots. But upon the said King renouncing his homage to Edward I, all his English estates became forfeited and, consequently, the said fee-farm of Yarmouth and Lothingland, reverted again to the British monarch. The town Yamouth embraced this favourable opportunity of making an application to Edward I. for a confirmation of the privileges granted to them by the charter of Henry III, in which they were so fortunate as to succeed. Yet, notwithstanding this charter of Edward I, it appears, by sundry records, that their adversaries still persisted in their claims, and continued to take customs, contrary to the liberties of the burgesses. The above privileges were afterwards confirmed by Edward II, and also again by the 1st of Edward III; and in the 6th of Edward III. they were again confirmed by a special charter, after a long and tedious suit with the Earl of Richmond (the proprietor of the fee-farm of Lothingland, given to him by Edward I) about levying the customs, etc., in the haven of Yarmouth.

During these litigious disputes respecting the privileges of Yarmouth and the customs to be levied on vessels frequenting that port, the haven belonging to that town became so obstructed by sand-banks, formed at its entrance by the easterly winds, that the mouth of it extended to the south of Corton before it discharged itself into the ocean; and so many shelves were formed therein, especially between the 10th and 20th of Edward III., as rendered the navigation so very dangerous, that no ships of any considerable burthen could enter it with safety; and therefore the inhabitants of Yarmouth, in the 20th year of the reign of Edward III were under the necessity of petitioning that King, viz., for liberty to cut a newmouth to the haven nearer to Yarmouth, opposite to Corton, which petition was immediately granted. This haven at a considerable expense, continued the space of twenty-six years, viz., till the

46th of Edward III, when it again began to be obstructed with sand banks that no ships could enter therein, but were obliged to unlade their goods and merchandise in an adjoining place called Kirkley road.

It was a matter of much controversy, during this contest, to ascertain with certainity where the place called Kirkley road was situated. The Yarmouth men insisting that it was opposite the village of Kirkley, about a mile to the south of Lowestoft; and the Lowestoft men as strenuously asserting, that the real name of that part of the sea near Kirkley was Pakefield bay; that in consequence of the town of Kirkley having been formerly a town of considerable trade in the herring fishery, it gave to all the sea thereabouts, even as far as Yarmouth, the general name of Kirkley seas; part of which, namely, that which was situated a little to the south of where the haven's mouth then was, was called Kirkley road, and was then annexed to Yarmouth haven.

In the old manuscript view of Lowestoft referred to in a former section (late in the possession of Thomas Martin, of Palgrave, in Suffolk) Kirkley road is placed between Lowestoft and Corton; and in the old map of the coast, given in Garianonum, the situation of Kirkley road is the same.

It was also alleged by the Yarmouth men, that the seven miles, the boundary of their liberties, granted by this new charter, was to be measured, not from the key, but from the haven's mouth, which would exclude the town of Lowestoft from buying herrings, unless they paid the customs to Yarmouth; the Lowestoft men insisting, that the seven miles should be measured from the key at Yarmouth, and not from the haven's mouth.

These declarations on the part of Lowestoft will receive further confirmation from the following extract from the town book, taken from Cawden

"About the year of our Lord 1100, about 500 years past, it pleased God to lay the first foundation of the east town of Yarmouth into firm land, even out of the main sea. Which place was then called and known by the name of Sardike sand, and Sardike shore; and in a short time it proved to be a fit and commodious place for a town to be built, meet for seafaring men to inhabit in. And by the permission of many noble kings in this land, his majesties progenitors, many did resort thither, and began to build the same, and to enclose it with a stone wall on the east side of the town (the haven being on the west side) inasmuch that within a short time the same grew populous.

"And long before Yarmouth town was incorporated, the barons of the five ports did yearly hold a free fair in the three towns of Yarmouth (that is to say) Easton, Westen, and Southton, beginning the said fair on the feast of St. Michael and so continued forty days together.

"And by the authority of the King, they did then use to make their repair thither on purpose for the governing of the said fair. And in those days was yearly sent from the brotherhood of the five ports, and the antient towns, nine or ten bailiffs who governed the fair. And it is to be noted, that long before any liberties were granted to Yarmouth, the towns of Lowestoft and Kirkley in the county of Suffolk, were built, and populously inhabited; and the then town of Kirkley being the greatest town of account, and the most antient upon the coast, and being a haven town, (the place now called Kirkley haven was the antient haven), before that Yarmouth was Yarmouth, and thereupon the whole fishing seas upon the confines of Suffolk and Norfolk, take the name of Kirkley seas.

"And to this day the seas upon those coasts are called or known by the French fishermen coming there to fish, by the name of Kirkley seas. And long since, before Yarmouth was incorporated there was such trading and merchandising of herrings at Lowestoft, and the same was by the Yarmouth men so much envied that civil wars subsisted for a long time between them, with much bloodshed, until it pleased God to take the matter into his own hands, who ended the strife with such a great mortality of people, that there died of the plague in Yarmouth 7,000 persons, and then the wars ceased."

The dreadful pestilence here alluded to, first began in the northern parts of Asia in 1346; from whence it passed into Greece, from thence into Italy and France, and in the beginning of August 1348, broke out in Dorsetshire: many who were well in the morning died before noon. About the feast of All Saints it reached London, making dreadful destruction; and about Christmas, Yarmouth and the neighbouring parts felt its direful effects. It immediately spread itself over the nation, and raged so violently in 1348 and 1349, that there scarcely remained the tenth part of the people alive in most places.

His Majesty, Edward III. after being duly informed of the circumstance relative to the affair of the Kirkley road, was pleased, after an application of six years continuance, and after the greatest opposition being made thereto from Lowestoft **and** other neighbouring towns, who reaped great advantages from vessels **discharging** their goods in Kirkley road, and were hitherto exempted from **paying the** customs to Yarmouth, to unite the said road of Kirkley into the **town and** port of Yarmouth (Kirkley road united to Yarmouth haven, 46 Edward III), upon paying him and his successors one hundred shillings **yearly;** and to grant use to the burgesses full power to receive the like duties **there as at** Yarmouth for ever. (Exclusive of the above mentioned rent of £55, **which** made the whole fee-farm £60 annually.)

It may be necessary here to inform the reader, that there are two remarkable circumstances in this charter; the one is, that Kirkley is there represented as a certain place in the high seas near the entrance of the haven of the town; the other that the seven leuks to which the liberties were then extended, are described as issuing from the town of Yarmouth, and not from the haven's mouth. It is proper to mention these particulars because towards the end of this section it will appear that there was much altercation between Yarmouth and Lowestoft respecting the true situation of Kirkley road; and also, whether the seven leuks or miles were to be measured from the key, or from the haven's mouth.

The form observed by government, previous to their granting this charter, was, first to issue a writ of *ad quod dampnum*, directed to the escheator of Norfolk and Suffolk; then followed a mandate to the sheriff; afterwards inquisitions were taken to examine the premises; and lastly the charter itself was granted. Subjoin are the writ, the mandate, the inquisitions, and the charter.

## THE WRIT OF AD QUOD DAMPNUM.

"Edward, by the grace of God, king of England and France, and lord of Ireland, to his beloved and faithful John de Rockewode, his escheator in the counties of Norfolk and Suffolk, Reginald de Eccles, and Edmund Gurnay, greeting. Know ye, that we have assigned you, and two of you, to enquire by the oath of good and lawful men of the counties aforesaid, as well within the liberties as without, by whom the truth of the matter may be better known, if it be to the damage or prejudice of us or others if we grant to our beloved the burgesses and good men of the town of Great Yarmouth, a certain place in the sea, near the entrance of the haven of the same town, called Kirkley road; so that after such our grant, that place to the said haven they may annex and unite, and if so annexed and united, to hold and to have of us and our heirs, as parcel of the same haven, together with the haven aforesaid, to them and their successors, burgesses of the same town, for relief of the town aforesaid, and **for an aid** of the farm which to us and our heirs, **they** are holden, for the same **town** and haven annually to pay, by the same services by which the town and haven aforesaid were before holden of **us;** and that all ships and boats to the same place of Kirkley road **coming** or to **come, and from** thence going or to go, may there as freely lade **or unlade, and the customs** and all other profits thereof receive and have, as **before in the said port they** have done, had and received, or have been used or **ought to do, have and receive**, without hindrance or impediment of us or our **heirs, or** others **whomsoever for** ever. And **also** if it be to the loss or prejudice **of** us or others, **then to** what loss, or what **prejudice** of others, and of whom, and in what manner, **how** and of whom the **aforesaid** place called Kirkley road **is** holden, and by **what** service, and in what manner, and how; and how much it is worth by the year in all issues and profits, according to the real value of the same; and how far distant from the entrance of the haven aforesaid; and who occupies or occupy that place, and receives and receive, the issues and profits thereof; by what right, title, how, and in what manner. And therefore we command you, that at certain days and places which you or two **of** you shall appoint for this business, you may make diligent enquiry, upon all and singular the premises in what manner soever; and it distinctly and openly make to us, into our chancery, under the seals of you, or two of you distinctly, and openly send without delay, and this writ.

"For we have commanded our sheriff of the same counties, that at certain days and places which you shall make known to him, he cause to come before you, so many, and so good and lawful men of his bailiwick, as well within the liberties as without, by whom the truth of the matter in the premises may be better known and examined into."

### THE MANDATE TO THE SHERIFF.

"Edward, by the grace of God, King of England and France, and lord of Ireland, to the Sheriff of Norfolk and Suffolk, greeting,—Whereas we have assigned our beloved and faithful John de Rokewode, our escheator in the counties aforesaid, Reginald de Eccles, and Edmund de Gurnay, and two of them to enquire by the oath of good and lawful men of the counties aforesaid, as well within the liberties as without, by whom the truth of the matter shall be better known, if it be to the loss or prejudice of us or others, if we grant to our beloved the burgesses and good men of our town of Great Yarmouth, that they, a certain place in the sea, near the entrance to the haven of the town aforesaid, may annex and unite the same to the haven, and, it so annexed and united, as parcel of the same haven, hold and have to them and their successors, of us and our heirs for ever. And also to do and accomplish some other things contained in our commission to them thereof made, as in the same our commission it is more fully contained. We command you, that at certain days and places which the same John, Reginald, and Edmund, or two of them, shall make known to you, you cause to come before them, or two of them, so many, and such good and lawful men of the counties aforesaid, as well within the liberties as without, by whom the truth of the matter shall be better known, and inquired into, and have this writ. Witness myself at Westminster, the 14th day of February, in the 44th year of our reign of England, and of France the 31st.

### THE FIRST INQUISITION.

"An inquisition taken at Waybrede, in the county of Suffolk, on Thursday next after the feast of St. James the Apostle, in the 46th year of the reign of King Edward the Third, after the conquest before Reginald de Eccles, and Edmund Gurnay, justices of the lord the king, assigned by commission of the lord the king, to inquire if it be to the damage or prejudice of the lord the king or others, that the lord the king should grant to the burgesses and good men of the town of Great Yarmouth, a certain place in the seas near the entrance of the haven of the same town, called Kirkley road; by the oath of Theobald Osborn, John Pynn, Thomas Crane, Bennett de Reading, Thomas Attie Wood, William Child, William Nicholas, John de Ireland, Robert Barker, William Danes, Richard Sallern, and Richard Allred, who say upon their oath that it is not to the damage nor prejudice of the lord the king nor others: that the lord the king should grant to the aforesaid burgesses and good men of the town aforesaid, the aforesaid place in the sea near the entrance of the haven of that town, called Kirkley road, and that place to the said town and haven to be annexed and united, and so annexed and united, to the haven aforesaid, to have and to hold to them and their successors, burgesses of the same town for ever; for the relief and support of the aforesaid town, and aid of the farm of the same town which they have paid, and still do pay, to the lords the king and his heirs annually. They say also, that the said place is main sea, and nothing distant from the entrance of the haven aforesaid, and so has been, from time immemorial. And they say, that the said place is not holden of any man, but has been the property of the lord the king, as main sea; nor is there any profit thence to the lord the king or others annually rendered.

"And further they say, that it is not to the damage nor prejudice of the lord the king, nor others, that all ships and boats to the same place coming, or to come, or from thence, going, or to go, may there as freely in every case, lade and unlade; and the customs and other profits of the aforesaid burgh thence may receive and have, as formerly in the said haven they have received and had; and to make executions touching their liberties as freely as in the said haven they have done, and used to do. And they say, that it is worth nothing a year, since nobody has received, nor ever occupied any customs or profits thereto, because it is in the high sea."

"Being asked why it is not to the damage of the lord the king or others, if the lord the king grant the place aforesaid in the manner aforesaid? they answer, that the entrance of the haven aforesaid is of late so dry that no ship laden there near the haven aforesaid can enter, unless first in the place aforesaid, called Kirkley road, it be unladed; nor will it there pay any customs to the lord the king or others. And they say, that the said town of Great Yarmouth cannot be supported, nor pay the farm to the lord the king, unless by the aid of a grant of the lord the king, to receive customs of the ships and boats in the said place, coming, entering, and going out, in the manner wherein they have received them in the haven aforesaid. In witness whereof the aforesaid jurors to these presents have put their seals."

### THE SECOND INQUISITION.

"An inquisition taken at Attlebridge, in the county of Norfolk, on Monday next after the feast of St. Peter in chains, in the 46th year of the reign of king Edward the Third, after the conquest, before Reginald de Eccles and Edmund Gurnay, justices by commission of the lord the king, assigned to inquire, whether it be to the damage or prejudice of the lord the king or others, that the lord the king should grant the burgesses and good men of the town of Great Yarmouth, a certain place in the sea, near the entrance of the havan of the same town, called Kirkley road, by the oaths of Richard de Martham, John de Westly, George Seafowl, John de Berking, Ralph Noreman, William Arnold, Nicholas Bannok, John Baxter, James Atte Church, Richard de Kent, John Dawys, and Edmund Cooke; who say, ect."

### THE CHARTER FOR UNITING KIRKLEY ROAD TO THE HAVEN OF YARMOUTH.

"Edward, by the grace of God, king of England and France, and lord of Ireland, and Duke of Aqitain, etc.—Know ye, that we, willing for the aid and relief of the town of Great Yarmouth, to shew more abundant grace to the burgesses and good men of the same town, have given and granted for us and our heirs to the same burgesses and good men, for an aid and relief of the same town, and for 100s. which they and their successors, at the terms of St. Michael and Easter, by equal portions (for an increment and augmentation of the farm of £55 which the same burgesses and good men are holden annually to pay us and our heirs, into the same exchequer, for a certain place in the high sea, near the entrance of the haven of the town aforesaid, should pay every year to us and our heirs, into the same exchequer, for a certain place in the high sea near the entrance of the haven of the town aforesaid called Kirkley road; and have annexed and united that place to the said town and haven; to have and to hold unto the same burgesses and good men and their sucessors, of us and our heirs, that place, annexed to the said town and haven for ever. Willing and granting, for us and our heirs, to the same burgesses and good men, that they and their successors for ever may have in the said place of Kirkley road, all and every the liberties and quittances by the charters of our progenitors and confirmation of us to them formerly granted, as they the same liberties and quittances in the said town, by virtue of the charters and confirmation aforesaid, ought to have; and may have and receive of all ships and boats which shall happen to come to the said place of Kirkey road, and in part or wholly unlade, the same customs which they, according to the liberties aforesaid, should have, if they at the said town should arrive, and there in part or wholly unlade. We have also granted, for us and our heirs, to the said burgesses and good men, and for ever confirmed to the same and their successors, that no ship, nor any boat, should be laden or unladen at any town or place upon the sea coast, within seven leuks distant from the said town of Great Yarmouth, by any person whomsoever, of herrings or any other merchandises, unless the ship, boat, or herrings, and also the merchandises, were that person's proper goods only and not any other's, except at the said town of Great Yarmouth, or in the haven of the same, or at the place of Kirkley road abovesaid. And also, that in the time of the fishing and fair of herrings, no fair should be holden, nor any selling or buying, on account of merchandising be made in any place within the space of seven leuks about the town aforesaid, but only at the same town of Great Yarmouth, or in the haven of the same town, of herrings or other merchandise whatsoever. And we strictly prohibit, for us and our heirs, that no one within the space aforesaid of seven leuks, presume to lade or unlade any other ship or boat than his proper **own,** and of his own proper herrings, and other merchandises, anywhere, but only at the same town of Great Yarmouth, or in the haven of the same, or at the place of Kirkley road, or in the time aforesaid, to hold any fair, or to sell or buy any herrings or other wares, on account of merchandising, but only at the said town of Great Yarmouth, or in the haven of the same upon forfeiture of the ships and boats so to be laded or unladed, or from that time to be put to sale in such fairs or elsewhere, by way of merchandising, contrary to the said prohibition, to be applied to the uses of us and our heirs. Of which forfeitures aforesaid we will, and have granted, for us and our heirs, that the bailiffs of the said, **town of** Great Yarmouth, for the time being, may and shall enquire from time **to time, and** take them into custody, and cause them to be kept for our use, **and** answer to us and our heirs, thereupon into the exchequer aforesaid, every year, at the term of St. Michael and Easter.

"And all our letters whatsoever, to the town of Lowestoft or to the men of the same, contrary to any of these premises, made by us, as to such contrariety, we do revoke.

"Witness myself, at Westminster the 22nd day of August, **in the 46th** year of our reign of England."

By virtue of this charter, the Yarmouth men not only obtained the privilege of having Kirkley road united to the town and haven of Yarmouth, but also to receive the same customs there which had usually been collected before in the **port** of Yarmouth, and were also farther empowered to seize the ships, goods, etc., of such as bought or sold within seven leuks of it, under certain restrictions mentioned in the said charter.

The word leuk, leuga, or leuca, is liable to various definitions. Blomefield says, that he has often rendered the word league, but must inform his readers, that he does not mean by it our league of three miles, nor agree with Mr. Bailey in making the distance one mile only (though he says it is so used in Domesday), being almost certain, the leuga in Domesday signifies two miles, or thereabouts, for that answers to the generality of places that I have examined, as to the extent, which to me seems the best way of judging such a point; and upon looking into the various glossaries, I find that several of them concur in the same opinion; for which reason, wherever the word occurs I mean by it two miles and no more. Nevertheless, in the continuation of Blomefield, by Parkin, vol. V. it is said, "In the rolls of the King's Bench it appears that the Bishop of Norwich had a fair at East Dereham, and that the town was sixteen leuca distant from that city; by which it is plain that a leuca was then (in 1277) accounted only one mile, Dereham being exactly sixteen measured miles from Norwich." But whatever may be the opinion of Blomefield on this word, Swinden confines the admeasurement of a leuk to be one mile only; probably upon the authority of Domesday and other antient records. At the annual proclaiming of Yarmouth fair, the seven leuks **are** denominated to be seven miles. And in the statute of the 13th of Richard **II. for** the extent of the King's Government, the word implies a single mile. Also, in the patent of the Knight marshal, for the extent of the government of the king's household within the verge, the word leuca stands adjudged **to** be miles, eight furlongs to every mile, and to begin at the funnel of **the** chimney in the king's lodging.

As the privilege which the town of Lowestoft and other places had long enjoyed, of being exempt from the customs demanded for the herrings bought and sold in Kirkley road (which would have been due had they merchandised in Yarmouth haven), was now lost, they consequently suffered much inconvenience from the granting of this charter, as they now became liable to all the customs due to Yarmouth for buying and selling herrings in Kirkley road, the same as though they were bought and sold in the haven. The granting of this charter, therefore, excited much animosity, and occasioned many disputes between Yarmouth and Lowestoft, as the latter was unwilling to relinquish their antient privilege; and accordingly, soon after, we find several men belonging to Lowestoft indicted at Yarmouth for not complying with the charter. The Lowestoft men, for trial of the premises, removed the suit, by writ of certiorari, into the Court of Chancery, where the affair was finally determined in favour of the burgesses of Yarmouth. The case was as follows:—

"An indictment was brought by the burgesses of Yarmouth against John Botile and others, of Lowestoft, for that they, on Friday next after the feast of St. Luke the Evangelist, in the 46th year of the reign of Edward III. bought of John Trample, of Ostend, an alien, in the said place called Kirkley road, which is within seven leuks of Great Yarmouth, twenty-five lasts of new herrings value fifty pounds."

Against this charge the defendants returned only evasive answers, pretending that they knew not that the aforesaid place of Kirkley road was annexed to the port of Great Yarmouth, nor that there was a fair kept there, nor that the said place was in the county of Norfolk. However, these were pleas which had too little the appearance of truth to be admitted in their favour, and therefore they were found guilty of acting contrary to the above charter, and of infringing on the liberties of Yarmouth. Whereupon the said John Botile and others being convinced of their error, in refusing or evading the payment of the legal customs due to the town of Yarmouth, prayed the favour of the court, that the affair might be ended; and putting themselves upon the grace of the lord the king, they accordingly were fined and discharged.

In the year 1368, one John Lawes was hanged for exporting seven sacks of wool out of Kirkley road without paying the custom to Yarmouth.

As soon as this contentious business was decided, the inhabitants of Lowestoft, in the 50th year of Edward III., together with other commons, petitioned the parliament then holden to have the said grant or charter repealed; alleging that it opposed the common interest of the kingdom. For this and other reasons specified in the said petition, the Parliament repealed the charter for uniting Kirkley road to Yarmouth haven.

The grant of Kirkley road repealed the 50th of Edward III.

In the Parliament roll of the 50th year of Edward III amongst the petitions of the commonalty of England, is the following:—

"Also be it remembered, that, as well, at the request of the commons of England, as at the suit of certain people of the town of Lowestoft, in the county of Suffolk, made in this Parliament, the charter of our lord the king, whereby he has lately granted to his burgesses of the town of Great Yarmouth, that a place in the sea, called Kirkley road, should be united and annexed to the port of the said town of Great Yarmouth for ever, be totally repealed and revoked, in respect to that new grant, as the thing was done contrary to the common profit of the kingdom; always saving entirely to the said burgesses, and to their successors, all their other privileges, franchises, and customs, granted and confirmed to them by the same our lord the king, or any other of his progenitors, with the clause of licet to them, granted by the same our lord the king."

Out of the roll of the parliament holden at Westminister, on Monday next after the feast of St. George, in the 50th year of the reign of King Edward III. is the following:

"Also the commons of the counties of Suffolk, Essex, Cambridge, Lincoln, Northampton, Bedford, Bucks, Leicester, and other of the commons, pray, That whereas a greater scarcity and want of herrings have been in the said counties, and elsewhere throughout the whole kingdom, since your charter was granted to the burgesses of Yarmouth, that no herrings, nor other merchandise whatever, should be sold within seven leuks of the said town of Yarmouth, during the fair of the said town, in the time of the fishery, than ever was before; and because no herrings might be made and sold elsewhere but at the said town, to which no cart nor horse can approach without passage twice by water, (at this time there was no bridge over the Yarmouth haven), to the great hindrance of carriage; and the greatest part of herrings has been taken by strange fishers, in the time of the fishery, who would not come to the said town; because they could not sell their merchandises but at the will of the said burgesses, and that at a certain price and quantity. That it would please your highness to command that the said charter be repealed; and that herrings may be bought, made, and sold in places where it was wont before the grant of the said charter; for having a better price in time to come, and for common profit of the whole kingdom."

Whereupon the said charter was repealed, as appears by the following letters patent:—

"Edward, by the grace of God, King of England, etc.—Know ye, that we, the liberties and privileges to the burgesses and good men of the town of Great Yarmouth, lately so by us given and granted, at the suit and voluntary clamour of certain people, alledging that those liberties and privileges have been and are contrary to the profit of the republic, and to us and our people prejudicial and hurtful, in our parliament holden at Westminister, on the morrow of St. George, in the 50th year of our reign, with the assent of the prelates, earls, barons, nobles, and other great men, in the same parliament being, have revoked, and totally made void.

"Witness myself, at Westminster, etc."

Soon after the repeal of this charter, Edward III. died; and a commission of *ad quod dampnum* was sued out by the burgesses of Yarmouth, concerning the said road, and directed to William de Ufford, earl of Suffolk; John Cavendish, William de Witchingham, William de Elmham, John de Sutton, Roger de Boys, and William Sibilys; dated 12th day of April, in the 1st of Richard II. alledging, that they were unable to pay the fee-farm rent tenths, and fifteenths, and to support the navy which they maintained in time of war, etc., unless they enjoyed the liberties granted to the burgesses by Edward, the late king of England. By virtue of this commission, and in consequence thereof, an inquisition was taken at Yarmouth, on Friday next after St. Faith, in the 2nd of Richard II. which certified that Yarmouth was a place of defence, and able to resist the enemies, if it be supplied with a sufficient number of forces; that it is a good port for supplying vessels with provisions and necessaries during the fishing season; and that the said town of Yarmouth hath a certain port, the entrance of which is much in decay. There was also another inquisition taken at Lowestoft the day following, which declared that Lowestoft is situated upon dry land, by the sea, and is not enclosed, nor has strength of itself to resist the enemies; but that the uniting of Kirkley road to the port of Yarmouth was to the damage of the men of Lowestoft. The result of these inquisitions was that a survey of both the towns being taken by the commissioners, and laid before the parliament held at Gloucester, the Wednesday before St. Luke, 1738, it was presented, that, upon the whole, the uniting of Kirkley road to the port of Yarmouth might be prejudicial to the neighbouring towns, yet it would be advantageous to the community at large; and thereupon the former grant which had been repealed was again re-granted to Yarmouth, by a private act or ordinance of his parliament, and confirmed by a charter dated the 25th of November, in the 2nd of Richard II.

Upon proclaiming of this charter, by the under-sheriff of the county, at Lowestoft, a riot was made by the inhabitants of that town; and in consequence thereof, an inquisition was ordered to be taken, to enquire into the causes of this disturbance, but it does not appear what ensued thereupon.

Before the invention of printing, charters, statutes, etc., were proclaimed by the sheriff in every county by the king's writ.

An inquisition taken before John Harsyk, sheriff of Norfolk, on Monday next after the nativity of the blessed virgin Mary, at Little Yarmouth, in the second year of the reign of King Richard the second, after the conquest by the oath of Roger de Hakenham, Walter Read, William Barker, and other juors, etc.

"Who say upon their oath, that whereas the aforesaid sheriff had sent certain liberties, granted by the aforesaid lord the king, to the bailiffs and commonalty of the town of Great Yarmouth, by John de Foxley, his under sheriff, by virtue of a certain order of the lord the king, to him directed on that account, to cause them to be proclaimed, viz., on the feast of the apostles Philip and James last past: (commonly called May day, on which a fair at Lowestoft was held, as it is also now); on which day the aforesaid under sheriff, at Lowestoft intended to proclaim the aforesaid liberties according to the form thereof, and there openly shewed the letters patent of the lord the king; on that account came Martin Terry, Stephen Shelford, Andrew de Lound, Robert Shincale. J. Cote, Roger Caley, Richard Gall, Thomas Smyth, John Smyth, Thomas Murring, Thomas Stoneman, and William his brother, Henry Freberne, and Emma his wife, J. Keene, Henry Boocher, of Lowestoft; also John de Rookesburgh, John Spencer, and Alice his wife, with a greater company of men and women of the town aforesaid, of whose names they are ignorant, who, by the abetment and procurement of William Hammell, John Blower, Thomas de Wade, Richard Skinner, William Lacye, etc., they violently resisted and hindered him; some saying to the same sheriff, they would not suffer him to depart; others forcing his letters from him, and so with dangerous and reproachful words, etc., saying that if he dared to come there for any execution of the lord the king, he should not escape. That for fear of death he durst not execute the writ aforesaid. And they drove him then and there with a multitude of rioters, with hue and cry, out of the town, casting stones at the heads of his men and servants, to the pernicious example and contempt of the lord the king and against his peace. "In witness whereof, etc."

It appears, that in the 4th of Richard II. the commons of Suffolk and Norfolk, and all the other counties of England, petitioned parliament, that whereas it had been formerly ordained by statute that every subject of the realm might buy and sell without disturbance in city, burgh, sea-port, and elsewhere, throughout all the kingdom; and if any charters or patents were granted to the contrary, they should be holden null, which statute was confirmed at the last parliament holden at Gloucester; and notwithstanding the said statute, a charter in the same parliament was granted to the people of Yarmouth, that none should buy or sell round the said town by seven leuks, etc. These petitions had their desired effect; for we find, that during the sittings of this parliament, the inquisitions taken in the first and second of Richard II. were so far reprehended, that an order was then given for a new commission, and that it should be more uprightly conducted; and the burgesses of Yarmouth had a penal command to make no disturbance in the mean time. Accordingly, in the 5th of Richard II. a commission was solemnly awarded with a quorum, and was set upon the Monday next after St. Matthew, the apostle, the same year, in Suffolk and the Thursday after in Norfolk, by the then lord chief justice of England and other great commissioners, who viewed the place, and did take their inquisitions, the one held at Lowestoft, the other at Norwich, before Robert Trisilian, John Argentium, and John Holcome, on the oaths of divers, knights, and other special gentlemen of both counties, whose presentment was certified in chancery, and afterwards laid before the parliament held in November following; and an act was made, that the new grants should be repealed for ever, and shall never be re-granted; that the charter should be called in and cancelled, and should also remain in the tower under special causes thereupon written, why it was so cancelled. (The charter for uniting Kirkley road to Yarmouth haven repealed the second time, the 5th of Richard II.) Notwithstanding this Act, the burgesses renewed their petitions to have their charter re-granted: insomuch, that Richard II. in the sixth year of his reign, in order to form a new judgment of the affair, came to Yarmouth, and viewed the premises himself; and soon after, namely, in the eight year of his reign, the burgesses obtained a new grant, dated the 20th February, of all their former privileges till the meeting of the next parliament.

As these inquisitions tend to cast considerable light on this complicated affair, they are inserted hereunder:

The determinations of all the Inquisitions taken before Robert Trisilian, (Sir Robert Trisilian was chief justice of England in the time of Richard II. He was adviser of many illegal acts in that reign, for which he was impeached, with several other judges and some noblemen in Parliament. Being convicted of the offences he was charged with, he was executed, February 19, 1388) John Argentium, and John Holcome, the one at the town of Lowestoft, in Suffolk, and the other at Norwich, by the oaths of divers, knights, and other great gentlemen of both counties.

## THE FIRST INQUISITION,

TAKEN AT LOWESTOFT, THE MONDAY AFTER THE FEAST OF ST. MATTHEW THE APOSTLE, 5 RICHARD II.

"That the new liberties and privileges to the burgesses of Yarmouth in a certain place called Kirkley road, is prejudicial and hurtful to the commonalty of the counties of Norfolk and Suffolk, and all other counties, etc.

"1st. For that the liberties and privileges aforesaid be contrary to common right, and also to the statute made for the common profit of the realm of England; that is to say, that every one of the realm of England may buy and sell without let in city, burgh, port of the sea, and elsewhere, through all the realm of England: and if deeds or patents be granted to the contrary, they shall be of no force; which statute was confirmed in the last Parliament at Gloucester, holden in in the time of our lord the king that now is.

"2nd. And also, that the ships anchoring in the said place of Kirkley road, as often as a contrary wind come, they can by no means enter into the port of Great Yarmouth; but are compelled to cast their herrings into the sea.

"3rd. And also for that the said burgesses of the town of Great Yarmouth, by force of the said liberties and privileges to them of new so given and granted, will not suffer the said commonalty of the realm of England to buy or sell any victuals or merchandise, at any time of the year in the said place of Kirkley road.

"4th. And also the said commonalty do sustain and support great griefs and hinderances by color of the liberties and privileges aforesaid in this behalf.

"5th. Also they say, that there is a great space of the high sea between the said place called Kirkley road, and the entry of the said port of Yarmouth, by reason of which space many ships may come from the main sea into the said port of Great Yarmouth at their liberty, and also go out; which place called Kirkley road, is in the county of Suffolk, and before the grant of the liberties and privileges aforesaid, was, and yet is, parcel of the same manor, etc.; and by all the time aforesaid have, used to have, and of right ought to have, all the wreck of the sea happening in the said place called Kirkley road. Also they say, that the ships loaden with herrings can return twice from Kirkley road into the sea to fish, whilst the ships loaden with herrings going to the town of Yarmouth can but one in the same time unload an return into the sea to fish.

"6th. Also they say, that before the new grant of the liberties and privileges aforesaid, all the ships and boats loaden with herrings, and other victuals and merchandise, have used at their pleasure to come as well to the port of the town of Great Yarmouth, as to the said place called Kirkley road, without any manner of let, and to unload their herrings, victuals, and other merchandise, as well in one place as in the other; and have sold the same unto any man of the realm of England willing to buy freely without any let or challenge of any man.

"7th. And at the same time it was the common profit, as well of the commonalty of the realm of England, as of the said town of Yarmouth."

"8th. Also they say, that the greatest commodity should be to all the commonalty of the realm of England; that all ships and boats laden with any victuals and merchandise might come as well to the port of the town of Yarmouth, as to the said place of Kirkley road, freely at their wills; and their victuals and merchandise might unload as well in the one place as in the other; and the same without let of any person, might sell to any of the realm of England that would buy the same.

"9th. And they further understand, that the men of Great Yarmouth may sustain and bear towards our lord the king all charges which they did sustain and bear before the granting of the liberties and privileges aforesaid, and maintain the said town, although the same liberties and privileges shall be revoked.

"In witness, etc."

## THE SECOND INQUISITION,

TAKEN AT NORWICH THE **THURSDAY** BEFORE THE **FEAST OF** ST. MICHAEL, 5 RICHARD II.

"That it should be to the commodity of the commonalty of the counties of Norfolk and Suffolk, and all other counties of the realm of England:

"1st. That all the ships and boats laden with herrings, and other victuals and merchandise, coming to the parts of Norfolk and Suffolk, upon the sea coast might unload their herrings, victuals and merchandise, wheresoever they please, and the same without let of any person, to sell to any of the realm of England that will buy the same.

"2nd. And that all the realm might lawfully buy the herrings, victuals, and merchandise aforesaid, wheresoever within the counties aforesaid. Also they say, that the burgesses of the town of Great Yarmouth, by force of the liberties and privileges aforesaid, to them of new so given and granted, do not suffer the said commonalty of the realm of England, at any time of the year, to buy or se l any victuals or merchandise in the said place of Kirkley road.

"3rd. And that whensoever any ships or boats apply themselves into Kirkley road, laden with herrings, they may twice unlade again and return to fish; whereas the ships or boats applying into the port of the town of Yarmouth, they can but once in the same time unload and again return to sea to fish.

"4th. Also they say that the commonalty do sustain and bear very great griefs, damages, and hindrances, by colour of the liberties and privileges aforesaid.

"5th. Also they say, that the said place of Kirkley road lyeth in the main sea over against the town of Lowestoft, in Suffolk, and is distant from the town of Yarmouth ten miles.

"6th. Also they say, that all the ships and boats laden or unladen, often, and when they come into the sea between the entry of the port of Yarmouth and the place of Kirkley road, if the wind be not contrary, they may at their wills enter into the port and also the said place of Kirkley road.

"7th. Also they understand, that the men of Yarmouth may sustain and bear all charges towards our lord the king, which before the granting of the liberties of the new charter aforesaid they did bear, and maintain their town, besides that charge that they render yearly for the said charter to them newly granted, although the said charter be revoked and made void.

"8th. Also they say, that if the wind do serve for the ships, that they cannot come to the said town of Great Yarmouth, sometime it happeneth that they must cast their herrings into the sea for oldness, if that they may not lawfully deliver their herrings at the place of Kirkley road.

"In Witness, etc."

The charter for uniting Kirkley road to Yarmouth Haven repealed the second time, the 5th of Richard II. The grant restored again till the meeting of Parliament to consider of it, the eighth of Richard II.

At the meeting of parliament, which was in the ninth of Richard II. the last grant of the eighth of Richard II. was, by an ordinance of that Parliament, dated the 18h day of December, in the ninth of Richard II. annulled, and the act of repeal, in the fifth of Richard II. continued in force.

The last grant annulled the ninth of Richard II. and the repeal of the fifth Richard II continued in force.

But notwithstanding all the allegations, statutes, etc., to the contrary, the burgesses of Yarmouth, by their petitions, etc., in the subsequent Parliament, holden at Westminster, in the tenth of Richard II, recovered all their former liberties and grants, by an act or ordinance of Parliament, which privileges, etc., were confirmed by a charter under the great seal of England, which charter has never since been repealed, but continues in force to this day.

After the re-granting of the said liberties and customs to the town of Yarmouth, by parliament, and confirmation of the same by charter, under the great seal of England, the burgesses collected the same customs in Kirkley road that had been usually paid in the port and haven of Yarmouth, without any molestation or interruption whatever. For after this legal decision of this litigious and long-contested dispute, the Lowestoft men were compelled peaceably to submit to any inconvenience it might subject them to and, consequently, were under the necessity of farming of the town of Yarmouth the customs belonging to Kirkley road, at a certain annual rent, as the safest and most advantageous mode of proceeding.

## FARMERS OF KIRKLEY ROAD.

| | Rent per Annum. |
|---|---|
| | £. s. d. |
| 1393. In the 17th of Richard II. the men of Lowestoft paid ... ... ... ... | 23 0 0 |
| 1394. In the 18th of Richard II. the farmer not recorded paid ... ... ... | 26 0 0 |

|   |   | £ | s. | d. |
|---|---|---|---|---|
| 1396. | In the 20th of Richard II. William Spencer paid | 26 | 0 | 0 |
| 1408. | In the 20th of Richard II. a fisher of Flanders paid for a forfeiture in Kirkley road | 1 | 0 | 0 |
| 1410. | In the 10th of Henry IV. the farm of Kirkley road was paid weekly by Simon Thirkeld, bailiff of Kirkley road | 8 | 0 | 0 |
| 1414, | In the 2nd of Henry V. John Waller paid | 8 | 0 | 0 |
| 1417. | In the 5th of Henry V. the men of Lowestoft paid | 8 | 0 | 0 |
| 1420. | In the 8th of Henry V. Thomas Couehithe's hosts, for a trespass and rescue committed in Kirkley road paid | 4 | 0 | 0 |
| 1433. | In the 12th of Henry VI. the farmer's name not recorded paid | 4 | 0 | 0 |
| 1434. | In the 13th of Henry VI. the farmer's name not recorded paid | 3 | 16 | 8 |
| 1438. | In the 17th of Henry VI. John Davy, merchant, paid | 3 | 0 | 0 |
| 1442 | In the 21st of Henry VI. John Folvile, of Lowestoft, paid | 7 | 6 | 8 |
| 1445, | In the 24th of Henry VI. farmer's name not recorded paid... | 4 | 13 | 4 |

Sometimes the water-bailiff collected the rents, but it does not appear that Kirkley road was ever farmed during the reign of Queen Elizabeth, or afterwards.

Nevertheless, about the beginning of the reign of Henry IV fresh disputes arose between the said towns, respecting the manner of collecting the said customs; the Lowestoft men endeavouring to deprive the burgesses of Yarmouth of their just and legal dues; and also indicted several officers and others belonging to Yarmouth, and carried the suit into the Court of Chancery, where it continued till an agreement between the contending parties was made by the King and his council, in the second year of his reign. And in the following year another order was issued by the kings' council, whereby an accord or composition, and final decision was settled and agreed upon between Yarmouth and Lowestoft, that the latter might buy herrings in Kirkley road under certain conditions therein specified. And these decisions, the Yarmouth men were once more restored to their usual privileges, and for some time were permitted peaceably to collect their lawful customs in Kirkley road, and to proclaim their free fair there as usual as well as at the other stated places in the town and haven.

But, notwithstanding this seeming amicable adjustment, many fresh disputes arose soon after between the towns, which occasioned many interruptions, and at last frequent depredations on each other's property; for the Yarmouth men would frequently make seizures of boats, etc., belonging to Lowestoft, under pretence of non-compliance with the last-granted charter; and not only continued to do so till the year 1595, the 37th of Elizabeth, but endeavoured also further at that time to extend the boundary of their liberties beyond the limits by the prescribed charter, which gave but too much reason for fresh complaints being exhibited against them.

Before proceeding any further in investigating the causes which produced the various disputes between Yarmouth and Lowestoft, concerning the herring fishery, it may be observed that the burgh of Yarmouth held its charter upon paying the fee-farm rent of £55 per annum, to King John and his successors; which rent they were empowered to raise by levying a toll or custom upon vessels bringing herrings and other merchandise into the port of Yarmouth, to be bought and sold there; but as the entrance into the haven leading to the port of Yarmouth having, in consequence of the sand banks that were formed there, extended itself as far as Corton, and was also so choaked up that vessels could not enter therein, but were obliged to sell their goods in an adjoining place called Kirkley road, by which means the burgesses of Yarmouth lost their customs, and were rendered incapable of paying their fee-farm rent; they therefore petitioned to have the said road united to their haven, which accordingly was granted, upon condition that the above annual rent of

£55 was advanced to £30. Thus for the proceedings on the part of Yarmouth were just and reasonable; and the riotous and illegal behaviour of the Lowestoft men, by refusing or evading the payment of the customs belonging to the port of Yarmouth, was very unjustifiable and reprehensible. The point, therefore, which rendered the burgesses of Yarmouth so very blameable in this affair, was their attempting under the pretence of claiming their just rights and liberties granted them by their charter, to extend them much further than they were authorised to do; for they pretended that Kirkley road was situate to the *south* of Lowestoft; that the seven leuks or miles, the boundary of their liberties, was to be measured from the mouth of the haven and not from the key or port of Yarmouth: and also, that the said leuks were leagues and not miles; and, consequently, had they succeeded in their designs, the town of Lowestoft must either have been wholly excluded from the fishery, or become tributary to the port of Yarmouth, from being liable to the above customs. These proceedings on the part of Yarmouth were illegal, and therefore justly opposed by the town of Lowestoft. The methods made use of in those early times by the merchants at Lowestoft to supply themselves with herrings, were very different from what it is at present; for now they are furnished with herrings by their own boats; but then, in general, they were obliged to repair to the port of Yarmouth whilst it was open, and afterwards to Kirkley road (as the place of general rendezvous for buying and selling herrings), in order to supply themselves with fish, they having but few, if any boats of their own at that time. Whilst the Lowestoft men repaired to the port of Yarmouth to buy herrings, they had a just right to pay the customs that were due there, and also the same in Kirkley road, when it was united to the haven, and therefore were blameable in either refusing or evading them; what, therefore, rendered the burgesses of Yarmouth so very culpable was, their unjust and illegal attempts above mentioned (about the 37th of Elizabeth, and again in 1659) wholly to exclude the town of Lowestoft from the herring fishery, and to monopolize it to themselves. The proceedings relative to these designs will appear in the subsequent part of this section.

The first complaint against the Yarmouth men was that made to the lords of the privy council, in the year 1595, by the bailiffs and other inhabitants belonging to the several towns of Ipswich, Colchester, Dunwich, Orford, Aldborough, Southwold, and Manningtree, in behalf of the ketchmen, who resorted to Kirkley road and parts adjacent to buy herrings; signifying the many hardships and inconveniences which they laboured under from being deprived by the burgesses of Yarmouth of the ancient privilege they enjoyed, and the great injury they were liable to, in consequence thereof.

The ketchmen were those vessels which frequented these coasts in the fishing season for the purpose of buying and selling herrings, which they transacted in the open sea; but now Yarmouth men were for compelling them to resort to Kirkley road, in order that they might receive the customs, grounding their claim upon a grant of Queen Elizabeth.

## THE COMPLAINT OF THE KETCHMEN AGAINST YARMOUTH.

"Whereas there is a certain grant passed from her majesty to the township of Great Yarmouth, in the county of Norfolk, as we are credibly informed, and as the township of Yarmouth aforesaid have given out speech and reported, That no fishermen, after the feast of St. Michael, by the space of forty days, should utter or sell any herrings within the compass or limit of seven miles of the said town, to any person or persons; but that the said fishermen should be constrained and urged to utter and sell all such herrings as should be by them taken within the time before limited at the town of Yarmouth aforesaid, and there to take and abide their market and utterance of the same herrings, and not elsewhere. We, therefore, which hereunder have subscribed, having had due consideration of the premises, and seeing and proving not only the great damage and inconvenience that the same will bring to the whole commonwealth of this realm, but also the utter ruin and destruction that will fall upon a number of poor ketchmen which be in trade with the said fishermen, whereby the said ketchmen, their wives and families, as also a great number of others who are thereby supported, sustained, and upholden, do think the said grant to be very unprofitable and inconvenient. The reasons that do move us thereto are these; that is to say, If the fishermen, after the taking of the said herrings, shall be constrained to repair, abide, and make their market and sales at Yarmouth aforesaid, they shall within that time lose the benefit of the taken twice so many herrings or more, as they shall utter and sell, and not the half part of the herrings taken that might be taken if they might abide and make their market at sea. And also, if the said ketchmen shall be dismayed from buying of herrings of the said fishermen, the most parts of the realm during that time shall be unserved and unprovided for, and the queen's highnesses, poor distressed people and others would be unrelieved, which were a most pityful and lamentable th ng. And finding also, as we are credibly informed, and some of us of our own knowledge do know, that the bailiffs of the said town of Yarmouth have taken seven men's goods, which they have brought thither to be sold, and have committed the owners thereof to prison, and constrained them to buy their own goods again. (All which inconveniences, discommodities, and hard dealings being considered.) We doubt not but that their godly wisdoms to whom these presents shall be committed, will have due regard and consideration thereof, as well for the benefit and maintenance of the common wealth of this realm, as also for the maintenance and relief of the poor distressed therein. And thus thinking it our duties to certify our knowledge therein, we most humbly take our leaves, the seventh day of August, 1595.

Signed at IPSWICH—EDWARD GOODYNGE, WILLIAM MYTUAL, Bailiffs and 46 inhabitants. SOUTHWOLD—27 ditto. MANNINGTREE—10 ditto. DUNWICH—ROBERT SWOTCHETT, JOHN ALLEYN, bailiffs and 20 ditto. COLCHESTER—22 ditto. ALDBOROUGH—FRANCIS JOHNSON, JOHN JEAMES, bailiffs and 25 ditto. ORFORD—5 ditto.

The only grant made to Yarmouth in the reign of Queen Elizabeth, was a charter, in the first year of her reign, which empowered them to hold a court of admiralty, to try all maritime causes whatsoever, piracy only excepted; and wherein the boundaries of their liberties were restrained within the limits of seven leuks of the town, haven, or Yarmouth roads, and not from the haven's mouth, or Kirkley road; without adding any additional privilege tending to justify this encroachment on the liberties of the ketchmen.

Another complaint made also at the same time against the burgesses of Yarmouth was one from the town of Lowestoft; for the town of Yarmouth pretended that the seven leuks or miles which bounded their liberties was not to be measured from the key or port of Yarmouth but from the haven's mouth; whereas the Lowestoft men affirmed that the said admeasurement ought to be made from the key or port of that town; otherwise the fishermen of Lowestoft would be excluded the indisputable privilege of buying herrings in the open road before their own town, which hitherto they had always enjoyed.

In consequence of these complaints, their lordships after hearing what each party had to alledge in its own defence; referred the further consideration thereof to three judge of the realm, viz., the right honourable Sir John Fortescue, knight, one of Her Majesty's privy council; Mr. Justice Clench, and Mr. Justice Gawdye, in order that they might certify to their lordships in what manner the dispute between the said towns might be fairly and equitably adjusted to the reasonable satisfaction and advantages of both parties.

A LETTER of REFERENCE to SIR JOHN FORTESCUE, Knight, MR. JUSTICE CLENCH, and MR. JUSTICE GAWDIE.

"After our hearty commendations.—The inhabitants of the town of Lowestoft, in the county of Suffolk, have exhibited a complaint unto us against the towne of Great Yarmouth, in the county of Norfolk, shewing, that by some unlawful courses held by the townsmen of Yarmouth, they are deprived of their antient trade of buying of herrings of fishermen in an open road before the town of Lowestoft; whereupon we have called before us of each town some two or three, with intention to make order in the controversie between them. And because the affair do consist of many points and proofs by charters, and by special statutes we have thought good to be assisted therein with the opinions of some learned in the laws, and therefore have thought good to join with you Mr. Chancellor of the Exchequer, you Mr. Justice Gawdie—(Sir Francis

Gawdie, of Wallington Norfolk, was son of Thomas Gawdie Esq., of Harleston. In 1582, he was appointed sergeant-at-law and queen's sergeant; in 1589, a judge; and in 1605, lord chief justice of the common pleas, being then a knight. He died after a fit of apoplexy at Sergeant's Inn, London, before he had sat a year in that station, leaving no male issue)—and you Mr. Justice Clench. And do hereby heartily pray and request you, at some convenient time this term, to call the parties before you, and effectually to appease the griefs of the plaintiff, and the answers to the other, and to hear and consider their allegations and proofs, to be delivered either by the parties themselves, or by their learned council thereupon; we pray you to certify unto us what you shall find, and with your opinions prove their differences may in equity be duly and orderly ended and compromised to the reasonable benefit of either; which we earnestly recommend unto you, and so bid you each heartily well to fare. From the Star-Chamber the second of July, 1595.

Your very loving friends,<br>
L. Archbishop, L. Admiral,<br>
L. Keeper, L. Cobham,<br>
L. Treasurer, L. Buckhust,<br>
Mr. Vice Chamberlain.

Con cordat cum origine,

Thos. Wilkes."

Accordingly, soon after it was certified to their lordships by the judges, that after due consideration of the premises, and hearing the several allegations advanced by both the said towns, and their learned council, they were of opinion, that by a statute of 31st of Edward III, no persons were legally authorised to hang herrings within seven miles of the haven of Yarmouth, viz., South Town; East Town; and West Town, unless the said herrings were of their own catching.

A CERTIFICATE from Sir John Fortescue, Justice Clench, and Justice Gawdie, concerning the CONTROVERSY betwixt the Town of YARMOUTH and the Town of LOWESTOFT.

"Whereas your lordships did direct unto us your letter dated the second of July last past, to examine and understand the griefs and controversies between the inhabitants of the town of Great Yarmouth, in the county of Norfolk, touching the trade of buying herrings; and to certify unto you our opinions how their differences might in equity be duly and orderly ended and compounded; we have accordingly called before us divers of the inhabitants of either of the said towns, and heard their allegations alleged by themselves, and their council learned on both sides. And it doth appear unto us, that this condition between the said towns hath depended of very long time; and divers statutes hath been made in this case by parliament for the town of Yarmouth, and repealed again for the town of Lowestoft. And divers ordinances and inquisitions have been made by the king's commission, directed to men of great authority, and afterwards revoked, and altered again by the same authority. But there was one statute made in the 31st year of Edward III, whereby, amongst other things, it is provided, that none shall hang herrings about the haven of Yarmouth by seven miles, but in the three towns of Yarmouth, except the said herrings be of their own fishing. And another Act, made in the 10th of Richard II. for revising of divers former repealed charters made to Yarmouth, in which, amongst other things, a certain place in the main sea, then by the mouth of the haven of the said town of Yarmouth, called Kirkley road, was united to the said town of Yarmouth, and by which it is provided, that none shall buy or sell herrings by way of merchandize in time of their fair, within seven miles of the said town, but only in the said haven and road. Which said two statutes we do think by the law stand still in force at this day, not repealed, nor avoided touching these points. But for unity to be made between the said towns, and for the good and common wealth of her majesty's subjects in the counties of Norfolk, Suffolk, Essex, and the city of London, We do think in our opinions, it were good and convenient (if it may so seem good to your lordships), that orders might be given to have the said seven miles measured, to begin at some such place in Yarmouth town as your lordships shall think meet; which we think, for our parts, to be the key, where the fair of herrings is kept, and so to go towards Lowestoft; and where the said seven miles do end, to set up some apparent thing to make it known. And this being done we think it would make some quietness, because there is great contention now in this point. Also we do think it fit, that all pikers and ketches, being English, might buy upon the main sea, or coasts thereof, and also in Kirkley road, of the fishermen, fresh herrings at their pleasure, to be by them carried to what place of the realm they think good, without any let or disturbance of Yarmouth men, according to the true meaning of the statute of the 31st of Edward III, which we think would be very profitable for the fishermen, and very beneficial for her majesty's subjects. Also we think it would make great quietness in this contention, if, by some commission or other, (as it shall seem to your honourable lordships), it might be certainly set down where Kirkley road is, and how far it doth extend. November 28th, 1595.

Concordat cum Registro Exor.

JOHN WOLLEY,
Keeper of the Records of the Councell Chamber."

THE OPINION OF THE LOWESTOFT COUNSEL TOUCHING THE CONTROVERSY BETWEEN YARMOUTH AND THE SAID TOWN.

"A brief being made upon the allegations of the Yarmouth men, and delivered to the judges in writing (which such allegations, in truth, were not under the hands of their councel, though they proceeded from their councel), shewing that the judges should have delivered a certificate of their opinions to the Council-Table before the Yarmouth men were gone out of London, although the judges had not sufficient time for that purpose, the Yarmouth men not presenting their allegations till the last day of term, and then deferred it till the judges were going to supper; therefore the Lowestoft men have retained Mr. Sergeant Drewe and Mr. Bargrave, her majesty's attorney, together with Mr. Councellor Bacon, to consider the whole state of the matter, and that their opinion might be shewed as occasion should require, they have subscribed to to the same as followeth: "That by the statutes and charters aforesaid, any man may sell and buy herrings in the road called Kirkley road, or elsewhere, without the lawful let or hindrance of the town of Yarmouth; and if any proclamation be made by the said men of Yarmouth, or any other of the subjects of this realm, to the contrary, the same, in our opinion, is unlawful, whether it be within or without the time of the fair.

CHAR DREW, JA. BARGRAVE, FR. BACON."

In order to form the better judgment of this intricate and much disputed affair, it may be necessary to observe, that by the statute of the 9th of Edward III it was enacted, "That every subject of the realm might buy and sell herrings without disturbance in city, burgh, sea-port, or elsewhere throughout the kingdom; and if any charters and patents were granted to the contrary they should be holden null; which statute was confirmed in a subsequent parliament." Probably from some abuse of this privilege, it might become necessary afterwards to lay it under some restrictions, in view of preventing those infringements which interested persons, from lucrative motives, had made on the rights and privilege of others; and therefore to redress this grievance, the following statute of the 31st of Edward III was granted, on which the Yarmouth men grounded part of their claim, and is the statute referred to in the certificate of the judges.

### STATUTE OF THE 31ST OF EDWARD III.

"Edward, by the grace of God, king of England and France, and lord of Ireland—To our bailiffs of the cinque ports, and the burgesses of our town of Yarmouth, keepers of the said town, greeting, etc.

"A certain concord by us and our council, made within the time of the present fair of the said town, we will have kept, etc.

"That none shall go by boat nor bridge into the sea, nor unto the road of Kirkley, for to meet the fishers, to compel them, or to capture them to sell them herrings in the road of Kirkley, to the disturbance of the said fair, upon the same pain, etc.

"But if the said fishers be disposed and willing to sell their herrings in the said road after that they be anchored there, it shall be lawful to the merchants of Lowestoft and Winterton, to buy any herrings in Kirkley road and Winterton, of ships so anchored there, as freely as the pycards do load their carts and horses there, which come thither from divers counties, and to hang there, provided that they sell no herrings therefore towards the sea, upon pain aforesaid, etc.

"And in case that any fishers ships charged with one last and a half of herrings, or less, come into the road of St. Nicholas, and will not come into the haven for the charge thereof, and will sell the same herrings in the road that it shall be lawful for him to set up his sign, and sell the said herrings there to the merchants that will buy them."

When the judges delivered their opinions, that by this statute none should hang herrings about the haven of Yarmouth, by seven miles, etc., they meant that port of the haven near the key where the fair was kept, and not the mouth of the haven. The Yarmouth men on the contrary, insisted that the words in this statute, "and to hang there," implied, not to hang anywhere else but near the said haven, thereby endeavouring to exclude the town of Lowestoft from the privilege of curing herrings. But the opinion delivered by the judges being found just and reasonable it was confirmed by an order of council as will be afterwards more clearly shewn. Nevertheless, it may be observed that the disputes which these statutes principally refer to, and are alluded to by the judges are those which relate to the extent of the liberties of Yarmouth. For the charter which united Kirkley road to Yarmouth haven was not granted until the 46th of Edward III. which was fifteen years after the passing of the preceding statutes.

And by an Act passed in the tenth year of the reign of Richard II (which confirmed the Act of the 46th of Edward III) it was enacted, that a certain place in the main sea, called Kirkley Road, should be united with the said town of Yarmouth; and by which Act it was provided, that none should buy or sell herrings, by way of merchandise, in time of their fair, within seven miles of the said town, but only in the said haven or road. Which two statutes they thought were still in force, and unrepealed; but yet for the sake of restoring peace and harmony between the said town, and promoting the common benefit of the kingdom in general, they recommended it to their lordships, that the said seven miles which circumscribed the liberties of Yarmouth, should be measured from the key of the said town where the herring fair is always held, towards Lowestoft; and at the termination thereof some apparent mark should be placed, in order to ascertain the exact boundaries of their liberties, and to prevent any farther disputes. And also, that they were of opinion, that by virtue of the statutes of the 31st of Edward III all English vessels were entitled to the privilege of buying fresh herrings in the middle of the sea, or coasts thereof, and also in Kirkley road, without any let or hinderance from the men of Yarmouth. And lastly, that they thought it very advisable, that a commission might be appointed to consider the premises, and to ascertain with precision the true situation of Kirkley road, in order to adjust the present differences, and to prevent any future contentions between the said towns.

This opinion of the judges was no sooner delivered, than it was opposed by the burgesses of Yarmouth with the utmost vehemence, and every method was made use of to conceal its reasonableness, and to divert its consequences, the Yarmouth men still persisting that the seven miles which terminated the boundaries of their privileges, were to be measured upon the sea, and not to be contracted by the numerous windings that would necessarily attend an admeasurement taken upon land

Upon the starting of these objections by the burgesses of Yarmouth, their lordships were pleased to issue orders for a re-hearing of the case, which was appointed to be held before Sir John Fortescue and the other judges; who after hearing and examining what the learned counsel employed by each party had to advance in support of the demands of their respective clients, and duly considering how far their several pretensions were just and reasonable, they certified to their lordships, that they were unable to discover any legal or equitable reason why they should depart from their former opinion.

A SECOND CERTIFICATE FROM SIR JOHN FORTESCUE, JUSTICE CLENCH, AND JUSTICE GAWDY, CONCERNING THE CONTROVERSY BETWEEN THE TOWN OF YARMOUTH AND THE TOWN OF LOWESTOFT.

"Whereas, upon the return of our first certificate, the men of Yarmouth opposed it, as discontented with some things therein specified: whereupon it pleased your lordships to re-commit to us the hearing of both parties; and having accordingly heard both they themselves and their learned council, at Serjeants Inn, in Chancery Lane, we do further certify, that we find no cause to alter the said certificate.

"CONCORDAT CUM REGISTRO
" EXOR
" JOHN WHOLLEY,
" Keeper of the Records of the Council Chamber, April 30th, 1596."

In consequence of this second certificate of the judges, their lordships, on the 16th day of May, 1596, issued an order that an actual admeasurement of the said seven miles should be immediately carried into execution, and at the termination thereof towards Lowestoft, some apparent mark should be affixed, to point out the boundaries of the liberties of Yarmouth; and that the same admeasurement should commence at Yarmouth key, the place where the herring fair is usually held; and also further to ascertain the true situation of the place called Kirkley road; and accordingly a commission was granted to Sir Arthur Heneningham, Sir Henry Woodhouse, Knight, and Henry Gawdy, Esq., on the part of Yarmouth; and to Sir Robert Jermyn, Sir John Higham, Knight, and Anthony Wingfield, Esq., on the part of Lowestoft, or any five or four of them, to superintend the said admeasurement, to affix the said mark, and to point out the precise situation of Kirkley road, where it beginneth, and how far it extendeth. (Henry Gawdy, of Claxton, Norfolk, Esq., afterwards Sir Henry Gawdy, Knight, who was a judge of the Common Pleas; he died in 1588 and was buried in the chancel of the church at Redenhall. The above Sir Henry Gawdy was created Knight of the Bath at the coronation of James I. and served the office of sheriff, for the counties of Norfolk and Suffolk about the sixth of that King's reign. Another branch of the Gawdy's flourished for many years at West Herling, near Thetford. Sir Thomas Gawdy, Knight, of Gawdy Hall, in Redenhall, a judge in the reign of Charles II. was employed in all the public business transacted in this neighbourhood about that time. He was one of the commissioners respecting the sea-breach at Lowestoft in 1661.)

AT THE COURT AT GREENWICH, the 16th of May, 1596.
Present,
LORD ARCHBISHOP, LORD CHAMBERLAIN, LORD BUCKHURST.
LORD KEEPER, LORD COBHAM, SIR JOHN FORTESCUE.

"This day John Felton and Thomas Dannett, burgesses of the town of Yarmouth, and William Wild and Thomas Ward, inhabitants of the town of Lowestoft, having been before the lords of the council, and presented to them the certificate sent down by Sir John Fortescue, Justice Clench, and Justice Gawdy, signed with their own hands, concerning the controversy before referred to them by their lordships, between the towns of Yarmouth and Lowestoft, concerning the trade of buying herrings. Their lordships having perused the said certificate, and deliberately considered of it, have approved of it in these two points: first, for the privilege of seven miles; and secondly, for a commission to be granted for finding of the right place of Kirkley road (leaving the other matter of the pikers and catchers, mentioned in the said certificate, by consent of both parties themselves). And because the question between them is concerning the measuring of seven miles where the same ought to begin (the one part saying that it should begin at the haven's mouth, the other at the key, where and about which place, the fair is usually kept), their lordships do approve of the judgment and certificate of the said judges, that it ought to be taken from the said key, or place of their fair, in Yarmouth town; and have therefore ordered, that letters should be written and directed from their lordships unto Sir Arthur Heneningham, Knt., Sir Henry Woodhouse,

Knt., and Henry Gawdy, Esq., for the town of Yarmouth; and for the town of Lowestoft Sir Robert Jermyn, Knt., Sir John Higham, Knt., and Anthony Wingfield, Esq., or any five or four of them, to undertake the measuring of the seven miles from the town of Yarmouth, according to the intention of the privilege claimed by the town of Yarmouth by their charter; and at the end of the said seven miles so measured, to affix and set down an apparent mark; and upon good examination and enquiry, to set down and define the place where Kirkley road is, which the charters of Yarmouth mentioneth; where it beginneth, and how far it extendeth.

Ex. Sipe. THO. SMITH.

"FROM THE COURT AT GREENWICH, the 16th day of May, 1596.

Present,

| JOHN CANTERBURY, | WM. CRICELL, | THO. BUCKHURST. |
| THO. EGERTON, | WM. COBHAM, | J. FORTESCUE. |

"To our very loving friends, Sir Arthur Heneningham, Sir Henry Woodhouse, Sir Robert Jermyn, Sir John Higham, Knts., Henry Gawdy and Anthony Wingfield, Esqs., or to any five or four of them.

"After our hearty commendations.—Whereas, upon some controversy between the towns of Yarmouth and Lowestoft, concerning the trade of buying herrings, we have referred the consideration thereof to our very loving friends Sir John Fostescue, Knt., Justice Clench, and Justice Gawdy, who have accordingly returned certificates of their opinions of the matter, which herewith we send unto you; we have now, by the consent of both parties, made choice of you, as fit persons to execute the determination of the said certificates and do therefore pray and request you, or any five or four of you, with all convenient expedition to undertake the pains of measuring the seven miles from the town of Yarmouth sideway (i.e. southerly) according to the intention of the privilege claimed by the town of Yarmouth, by their charters; and at the end of the said seven miles so measured, to fix and set down apparent marks; and also upon good examination and inquiry to set down and define certainly where Kirkley road is which the charter of Yarmouth mentioneth; where it beginneth, and how far it doth extend. And of these two material points, and to certify your opinion and proceedings there upon such further orders shall be given therein as we shall think requisite. And so we bid you heartly farewell.

From your loving friends, etc.,

But the burgesses of Yarmouth being conscious that they were prosecuting a claim for which they had neither a legal nor equitable pretension; and being also apprehensive, that if the affair was carried before the said commissioners, and submitted to a strict and impartial investigation, it would terminate greatly to their disadvantage; therefore they resolved as there was but little prospect of being successful in the enquiry, they would exert every effort in their power to retard and embarrass it; and that the most effectual mode for accomplishing their designs would be to counteract the commission; and accordingly, in a subsequent application to the Privy Council for redress of grievances, they transmitted such a partial representation of the case, as to obtain from their Lordships an order for a new commission. In this second commission we find, that an alteration was made in the appointment of commissioners; for in the place of Anthony Wingfield, Esq., one of the commissioners nominated in the first commission on the part of Lowestoft, William Rowse, Esq., was appointed in this second commission, a person partially attached to the interest of Yarmouth. And whereas, by the first commission, any four or five of the commissioners had a power of deciding any point relative to the dispute; but by the second commission it was ordered, that they should be unanimous: and also it was further directed by the first commission, that the inquiry should determine the two principal points in dispute, viz., the admeasurement of the seven miles and the true situation of Kirkley road; whereas the burgesses of Yarmouth, by this second commission so ordered the business, that when the parties appeared before the commissioners, they confined the inquiry solely to the situation of Kirkley road, and withheld from them every information that related to the admeasurement of the seven miles; and also had given previous directions for Mr. Rowse to be absent from the meeting, which consequently rendered every resolution of the Commissioners void, as by the commission they were directed to be unanimous.

"To Sir Arthur Heneningham and Sir Henry Woodhouse, Knts., and Henry Gawdy, Esq., and to Sir Robert Jermyn, and Sir John Higham, Knts., and William Rowse, Esq.

"Whereas, we gave orders and directions unto you, for the appeasing of the controversy between the town of Yarmouth and Lowestoft, concerning their liberties, to measure the seven miles claimed by them of Yarmouth for their jurisdiction, from the key of Yarmouth; whereby they pretend the same will be very prejudicial to their charter, antient liberties, and other rights. And they also alledge, that by a statute of the 31st of Edward III, the said seven miles ought to be accounted from the uttermost bounds of the haven (i.e. from the mouth), which hath been extended, in memory of man, a mile further towards the south than it is now. These, therefore, shall be to require you, that according to your former directions you will cause seven miles to be measured from the key at Yarmouth, and likewise seven miles to be measured from the uppermost bounds of their haven; and to be unanimous in your opinion, and to certify unto us how far each admeasurement doth extend; and in the mean season to forbear setting up any marks or bounds until we shall consider of the same, and give such further orders therein as shall be agreeable to reason and equity, and satisfaction of both parties.

LORD KEEPER, LORD TREASURER, LORD COBBHAM, LORD BUCKHURST, MR. SECRETARY, MR. CHANCELLOR OF THE EXCHEQUER.

Concordat cum Registro Exor.

JOHN WOOLEY.
Keeper of the Records of the Councell Chamber.   8th July, 1596."

On the 4th day of August, 1596, all the Commissioners nominated in the first commission, together with the bailiffs and principal inhabitants of Yarmouth assembled at Lowestoft; and the Commissioners, as directed by their commission, intended to have made the admeasurement of the seven miles the first object of their inquiry; but the Yarmouth men objected against this mode of proceeding, and insisted upon inverting the order of the enquiry, and that the ascertaining of the true situation of Kirkley road ought to be the first business that engaged their attention. The Commissioners so far acquiesced in this unreasonable demand, as to employ about four hours in investigating the exact situation of Kirkley road, and limiting its boundaries; but when the Yarmouth men began to discover that the result of the inquiry would be prejudicial to their interests, as well as contrary to their expectations, they then produced the new commission, which effectually answered all the purposes they had been aiming at; and notwithstanding the Commissioners made a proposal of sending for Mr. Rowse, the absent Commissioner, and also of suspending any further proceedings till he should arrive and concur with them in their deliberations, yet all these offers proved wholly unavailable, and nothing would satisfy the desires of the Yarmouth men but an acquiescence on the part of Lowestoft in such a decision respecting the situation of Kirkley road and the extent of its boundaries, as the bailiffs themselves thought proper.

In consequence of these illegal and unreasonable proceedings on the part of Yarmouth, the commission was dissolved. Nevertheless the Commissioners on the part of Lowestoft were so perfectly convinced of the oppressive designs of the Yarmouth men, as well as apprehensions of the inevitable ruin that would ensue to the inhabitants of Lowestoft, that before they broke up, they unanimously resolved to present a certificate of their proceedings to the Lords of the Privy Council, both for remonstrating against the unjust and unlawful proceedings of the Yarmouth men, as also to represent to their lordships, the apparent poverty and distress which threatened the town of Lowestoft.

THE CERTIFICATE OF SIR ROBERT JERMYN AND SIR JOHN HIGHAM, KNTS., AND ANTHONY WINGFIELD, ESQ., ON THE PART OF LOWESTOFT; SHEWING THE UNNECESSARY SHIFTS, DELAYS, AND HARD DEALINGS OF THE YARMOUTH MEN AND THE NECESSITY OF ENDING THE CONTROVERSY:

"Our humble duties to your honours remembered.—May it please the same to be advertised, That by authority of your lordships' letters to us and others directed, concerning the deciding of the controversies arisen between the township of Yarmouth, and the inhabitants of Lowestoft, proceeding from the certificate of the Honourable Sir John Fortescue, knt., Justice Clench and Justice Gawdy, we met together at the town of Lowestoft, whither the Commissioners named for Yarmouth, together with the bailiffs and chief inhabitants of Yarmouth, did also make their repair; and upon our meeting we desired that we might employ ourselves about the measuring of seven miles from Yarmouth to Lowestoft; but that would not be allowed of, but only to search and try out where, and how far Kirkley road did extend, upon which two points the whole of your honours' commandment did consist, in which, after hearing the learned councell on both sides, we had spent at the least four hours about the extent of Kirkley road only, and had heard the effect of sundry affidavits taken and returned upon several writs of ad quad damnum, mentioning the said Kirkley road: at length the bailiffs of Yarmouth delivered to us and the other Commissioners, a letter of your honours, which they had kept in their hands at the least five days, and had suffered some of us not only to travel almost fifty miles, but also to spend so many hours as we have before expressed, about a question, which upon the receipt of this your honours' second letter, we had no authority to deal in; namely, the second point, or to describe the situation of Kirkley road.  Also, in the proceeding of that letter, they omitted the name of Anthony Wingfield, Esq., who was then absent and had caused the name of William Rouse, Esq., to be put in; and also had gotten the letter so indited, as that the whole number of the said six commissioners must need agree to the measure of the said seven miles, and which could not be done by reason Mr. Rowse was absent; and although an offer was made to send for Mr. Rowse, and so to proceed to the admeasurement, yet in the end they would not proceed to it, except the Lowestoft men would confess that Kirkley road extended as far as the Yarmouth men would have it. All which proceedings we are bold to signify to your honours to prove the unnecessary delays, and hard and unjust proceedings of the Yarmouth men, and the desire they have to enjoy their private gain in the herring fishing shortly approaching, to the utter impoverishing and undoing of the poor inhabitants of Lowestoft, if by your honours' favours they be not relieved; and whose lamentable estate, arising from the hard measure and unjust delays of the said Yarmouth men, do move us, in consideration of them, to be bold to offer to your lordships' view, the hard dealings in this cause; and in their behalfs humbly to entreat your most honourable and speedy relief in this their grievous distress.  And thus very humbly we take our leaves of your good lordships.

ROBERT JERMYN,<br>JOHN HIGHAM<br>ANTH. WINGFIELD."

From Somerleyton, the 4th August, 1596.

The Lowestoft men were so far from being dispirited by these illegal proceedings of the burgesses of Yarmouth, that, on the contrary, from the favourable representation of their case, made to the Privy Council by the Commissioners, they received so much encouragement as to renew their application to their Lordships for relief; and petitioned that they might be indulged with re-hearing of their cause.

(Whoever impartially considers the tendency of the second commission, and the manner of introducing it, will perceive but too much reason to suspect its being obtained by some improper means.)

In consequence of their application, their lordships immediately sent letters to the several Commissioners nominated in the first Commission, informing them that as the differences subsisting between Yarmouth and Lowestoft were become a matter of great difficulty, and that some certain points of law were so connected therewith as to require explanation, they were under the necessity of referring it to the judges for their opinion thereon; and in the mean time requesting that the herring fishery and fair at Yarmouth might be conducted as usual and without any interruption, until the said judges had certified their opinion.

L

To Sir Robert Jermyn, Sir John Higham, Sir Arthur Heneningham and Sir Henry Woodhouse, Knts., and Anthony Wingfield, and Henry Gawdy, Esqs.

"After our hearty commendations.—We have received the letters severally sent unto us from you that were appointed to be the Commissioners on both sides for certain controversies between the towns of Yarmouth and Lowestoft. And because we find by your several reports, that it will be a matter of great difficulty for you to set in order those differences, some proceedings depending upon matter of law, and are to be decided by certificate from the judges, we have thought good to respite the same until next term; and in the mean season to request you, that those of Yarmouth may not be interrupted in their fair and herring fishing this season, but that they may use the same in such sort as the same has usually been, until there shall be a final end made in those matters now depending between them. So praying you to take thorough hearing accordingly we bid you farewell.

John Canterbury, Lord Keeper, Lord Buckhurst, Lord Treasurer, Lord Chamberlain, Lord Buckhurst, Mr. Secretary, Mr. Chancellor of the Exchquer."

From the Court at Greenwich, the 17th August, 1596."

Thus was this long-contested affair brought the third time before the judges, who, after duly weighing every circumstance respecting the same delivered their opinion, "That as the matter in dispute was become so exceedingly intricate and perplexed, and entangled with such numerous difficulties as to make them despair of accommodating the differences to the mutual satisfaction of both parties, they therefore have thought it more advisable to refer the decision thereof to the determination of parliament."

"Whereas it hath pleased the right honourable the lords of her majesty's most honourable privy council, upon the humble petition of the inhabitants of Lowestoft, in the county of Suffolk, to remit to us now this third time the controversy now depending before their lordships, between the bailiffs, burgesses, and community of the town of Great Yarmouth, in the county of Norfolk, of the one party, and the said town of Lowestoft of the other party, touching the trade of hanging and making of red herrings, and also the procuring of white herrings, for victuals of store, to be merchandised: we see no decisive course therein can be taken by us, to compound their controversies and adjust their differences, whereby to bind both parties, as is most necessary and convenient (their differences being of such great difficulty); and therefore we think it fit that the cause be respited, and referred unto the next parliament; at which time, upon supplication and complaint of those that shall find themselves aggrieved, the cause may receive hearing and due remedy. J. CLENCH, FRANCIS GAWDY."

Given this 29th day of April, 1597."

But notwithstanding the judges declined passing a final decision upon this long-contested affair, but referred it to parliament, yet the Yarmouth men still continued to pursue the inhabitants of Lowestoft with the utmost rancour, and came shortly after into Lowestoft roads with two armed vessels, and under a pretence of being within the liberties granted by their charter, demanded anchorage; in consequence whereof a battle ensued, and much blood was shed on both sides; and though a complaint was lodged by the Yarmouth men in the star Chamber, against Lowestoft, yet their accusations appeared so frivolous and ill-grounded, that their cause was dismissed, and instead of recovering any damages, were fined twenty marks.

In consequence of this reference, an Act of parliament was passed in the year 1597, directing that an actual admeasurement of the said seven miles (eight furlongs to every mile) should immediately take place, and begin to be measured from the crane key in Yarmouth, and to proceed the directest way towards the roading place, near the sea shore, where the fishermen usually anchor for the sale of their herrings; and at the end of the said seven miles, a post or some other apparent mark, should be erected near the sea shore, to signify to all persons whom it may concern the termination of the said seven miles, prescribing the boundary of the liberties of Yarmouth. (That a post was erected is evident, from the order in 1662, for a *new* post to be set up.)

In this defence of their rights and liberties, the town of Lowestoft expended £120 which was collected from a voluntary subscription of the inhabitants; some subscribing £10, some £6, some £4, and others lesser sums, according as their abilities enabled them. But exclusive of the above expenditure, the inhabitants were under the necessity of contracting a debt of upwards of £50 which, by reason of their distressed situation they were utterly unable to discharge any other way than by appropriating a part of the rents and profits of the town lands; for it had always been an established maxim of the town to support and maintain the free trade of buying and selling herrings in Lowestoft roads; therefore, at a general meeting of the inhabitants, it was resolved that as a large sum had already been expended in support of this right, that out of 200 persons who reaped advantages from this fishery, many were unable to contribute towards the above expense; and that if the fishery was not supported, the town would be inevitably ruined. Therefore, the state of the town being thus considered, and the affair regarded as a case of necessity and charity, and of the utmost utility to the inhabitants; they agreed, That it was a very justifiable application of the rents of the town lands, in the present emergency, in discharging the said debt.

An Act of the 39th of Elizabeth, for the measuring of seven miles from the town and haven of Great Yarmouth, in the county of Norfolk, mentioned in the statute made in the 31st year of King Edward III, and certain letters patent, granted by the same king unto the bailiff and burgesses of the said town of Yarmouth.

"Whereas, King Edward the Third, at the parliament holden at Westminister the Monday after the week of Easter, in the 31st year of his reign, amongst other things, ordained, that none hang herrings in no place about the haven of Yarmouth, by seven miles, except in the three towns of Yarmouth, that is to say, Easton, Weston and Southton, unless it be the herrings of their own fishing. And whereas, the said King, by his letters patent, in the 46th year of his reign, among other things did grant unto the bailiffs, burgesses, and good men of Great Yarmouth, in the county of Norfolk, in the time of herring fishing, no fair should be kept, nor buying nor selling by way of merchandise, should be had anywhere within the space of seven miles about the said town, of herrings or other merchandise. The which letters patent and grant were afterwards revived and confirmed by act of parliament in the 10th of Richard II. And by colour and pretence of the aforesaid statute and letters patent the aforesaid bailiffs and burgesses of the said town of Yarmouth, have of late years, practised, in the principal time of herring fishing viz., from the feast of St. Michael the Archangel, forty days then next following, to restrain buying and selling of herrings, and making of white and red herrings, in other towns and places on the sea cost of Suffolk and Norfolk, above seven miles from the said town, and the place where the fair of herrings is yearly kept, contrary to the true meaning of the statute and letters patent above mentioned; by means whereof great debates and controversies have been moved, the trade of taking herrings greatly decayed in the coast of Suffolk and Norfolk, and likewise the trade of making of red herrings, which was more proper to that part of the realm than to any part of the world else, is now transferred into the parts beyond the seas, to the great hurt and undoing of the inhabitants of divers coast towns in the said counties, and to the general hurt of all fishermen using the trade of herring fishing; for that by means of this restraint there is nothing so many herrings taken as otherwise might be; and of these that be taken, the fishermen, to avoid this restraint, endeavour themselves to utter some greater quantities of herrings unto Hollanders, Zealanders, and Frenchmen, than they were wont to do, whereby the price of herring, red and white, is more than double increased, to the hurt of all the commonalty of the realm of England. Now, therefore, for the avoiding of the above mentioned and other inconvenience that in time to come may ensue, if remedy be not herein provided, be it enacted, by the queen's most excellent majesty, the lords spiritual and temporal, and the commons in this present parliament assembled and by authority of the same, that the aforesaid seven miles, mentioned in the aforesaid statute, shall be measured from that part of the said town of Yarmouth whereabout the fair of herrings is kept, which is the crane key, within the said town; from thence the usual ways sou'hwards and northwards by the sea shore; and at the end of either of the said seven miles, apparant marks shall be fixed, such as may be seen as well upon the sea as upon the land, as a manifest declaration how far the liberties claimed by bailiffs and burgesses of Yarmouth shall extend upon the sea coast of Suffolk and Norfolk, either by sea or by land, concerning the buying, selling and hanging of herrings; and that either of the said seven miles shall be accounted to contain eight furlongs, and every furlong to contain in length, forty poles or perches, and every pole or perch to contain sixteen feet and a half; and that the high sheriffs of the counties of Norfolk and Suffolk, or their deputies, shall before the feast of St. Batholomew the apos'le, now next coming, measure seven miles, in manner and form aforesaid from the said crane key, over the haven, thence southwards, and at the end of the said seven miles six apparent marks as aforesaid; and so before the said feast of St. Batholomew, measure seven miles in manner and form aforesaid, from the said crane key and at the end of the said seven miles six apparent marks as aforesaid; and that either of the said sheriffs of the said counties of Suffolk and Norfolk, for the time being, shall take such orders from time to time in their several counties, that the said marks shall be continued for ever. And the aforesaid bailiffs, burgesses, and community of the said town of Yarmouth, o· the barons of the five ports, or any of them, shall not, at any time hereafter by colour of any manner of liberties, jurisdictions or privilege, claimed to belong to them or any of them, by reason of the aforesaid statute or letters patent, or any other statute, charter, usage, or rescription, restrain or inhibite any pe son whatsoever, buying, selling, changing, or discharging of herrings, in any place or places whatsoever, being without the compass of the said seven miles."

Thus was this litigious and long-disputed difference, which had subsisted between Yarmouth and Lowestoft for a great many years, and had been prosecuted with the utmost vehemence, at length happily concluded. Nevertheless it afterwards appeared, that during these dissensions the seeds of animosity had been so profusely scattered and became so deeply rooted in the breasts of the contending parties, that it was impossible to eradicate them even by the most lenient and conciliating measures; and, consequently, he apparent reconciliation proved, in reality, little better than a truce, in order that the parties might be enabled to renew their differences with greater vigour.

In the year 1659 we find, that the former disputes between Yarmouth and Lowestoft respecting Kirkley road and the admeasurement of the seven miles, the boundary of the liberties of Yarmouth, were again revived. During the further prosecution of this affair, the burgesses of Yarmouth traversed the same ground as they had done before; and insisted that Kirkley road, which was united to their haven by the statute of the 46th of Edward III. was opposite to the town of Kirkley, and consequently to the south of Lowestoft; and that the seven miles which circumscribed their liberties were not to be measured from the Crane quay, but from the haven's mouth; and the better to obviate every objection that might be alleged against them, and that their new pretensions might carry the greater appearance of justice, they had provided, that in the recital of the statute of the 46th of Edward III, in the renewal of their charter in the reign of James I. to have the situation of Kirkley road described as opposite to the town of Kirkley, notwithstanding it is represented in the original statute as being contiguous to the haven's mouth; and having thus removed the greatest obstacle to a successful renewal of their pretensions, they only waited for a favourable opportunity of carrying their designs into execution. In the year 1659, this desirable and much-wished-for opportunity presented itself. A time when the inhabitants of Lowestoft were overwhelmed with the greatest misfortunes; when their unshaken loyalty, during the late rebellion, had exposed them to all the distresses which soldiers living in free quarters could involve them in; when their principal inhabitants (whom they wanted to defend their rights) were employed as commanders of the royal navy, and their sailors were absent in manning the fleet; when they were reduced to the greatest poverty and distress by a terrible fire, which consumed in the town, houses and merchandise to the amount of £10,000; whilst they were thus struggling under the accumulated miseries of war, fire, and oppression, and sinking under the insupportable burden of those grievous calamities, then it was that the Yarmouth men, imagining that the happy period had arrived when they might renew their pretensions without opposition, and pursue them with success, contrary to all legal authority, renewed their unjust and unreasonable claims, and attacked the almost-ruined and defenceless town of Lowestoft with an armed vessel, which was termed a man-of-war.

In this unhappy situation, when almost every avenue to redress was shut against them, and nothing but the ghastly spectres of poverty and ruin were continually presenting themselves to their alarmed imaginations, no other remedy was left but to implore the assistance of the legislative powers of their country, and to lay before them a true representation of their unfortunate state, which was done in the following complaint, shortly after presented to the lords of the privy council.

A COMPLAINT OF THE TOWN OF LOWESTOFT IN THE COUNTY OF SUFFOLK, TO THE LORDS OF THE PRIVY COUNCIL.

"Whereas the Yarmouth men under pretence of a privilege granted them in their charter, that no fishers should deliver any herrings within seven miles of their town during the time of their free fair, which beginneth at Michaelmas, and continues till Martinmas, have, on one day of the year, come rowing in small boats into the roads before Lowestoft, and there have exacted anchorage, although eight or nine miles distant from Yarmouth; and if they refuse to pay it they violently take their goods, cruelly beat the fishermen and their assistants, confiscate their vessels and set grievous fines on them, on purpose to prevent their delivering any herrings at Lowestoft to the great damage of the poor fishers and injury of the said town; who, if compelled to deliver all their herrings at Yarmouth, must lose at least one third part of their time; and when they do proceed to Yarmouth, by an ordinance of that town, the first freeman that comes on board must be his host, and will set the price of the fisher's herrings without their knowledge or consent, which commonly is 20s. to 50s. a last cheaper than they give to their own townsmen, which the fishers are ready to make app ar by certificates, or other ways; whilst at this town they are free to sell to whom they please, and are furnished with such necessaries as they want; and if they like not this market, they are free to sell their fish to any other, and return to sea again at their own pleasures."

OBSERVATIONS ON THE ADMEASUREMENT OF THE SEVEN MILES AND THE PLACE CALLED KIRKLEY ROAD.

The Yarmouth men alleged that Lowestoft south road was within the compass of seven miles from the town and herring fair of Yarmouth, although upon an admeasurement it was found, that only Corton road and part of Lowestoft north road were within the limits of the said seven miles and that the greatest part of even Lowestoft north road is beyond the said seven miles, the boundary of the liberties of Yarmouth, yearly proclaimed. Yet, notwithstanding, the Yarmouth men have made a practice of coming one day in the year, in the time of their fair, only into Corton and Lowestoft north road, but also into Lowestoft south road and have there unjustly extorted anchorage under the colour of a grant of Kirkley road being united unto their town and haven, and was situated off the town of Kirkley, which place so granted was found (before the granting), by two inquisitions of record, to be at the mouth of the haven of Yarmouth, and nothing distant; which inquisitions agreed with no other place but that now called Yarmouth road; and there they have enjoyed all those things mentioned in the said inquisitions, and grant of the 10th of Richard II. until the first of Queen Elizabeth, and then they obtained a new grant of Yarmouth road which until that time they held by the name of Kirkley road, and by no other name or grant; and though they have come wrongfully into the roads of Lowestoft one day in the year, exacting anchorage, they leave all other profits, jurisdictions, and government, all other parts of the year, unto the Vice-Admiral of Suffolk; for admiralty causes, and concerning wreck of the sea, things found in the roads, flotsom and jotsom, and all other casualties in the said roads and shores of the same, all that they leave to the lord of the manor of Lothingland, Lowestoft, and Mutford all along the shores as far as Kessingland, which is three miles southward of

Lowestoft; but they never had any part of the same in use or possession but as before mentioned. It appears by copies of letters patent in the 9th of Richard II. and by an edict of the extent of the manor of Lowestoft, taken the 10th of Richard II. and returned into the Exchequer in the term of St. Michael, that the lords of the manor of Lowestoft have had and enjoyed from time to time in the roads before Lowestoft, and all shores of the same; and also had, and still have, all petty customs of all goods there landed, (which was much in those days), and all casualties happening in the said roads, and upon the shores thereof; and the trade of merchandising herrings and other merchandise have continued ever since; as the great number of herring houses, warehouses, and other buildings do now remain, as monuments, to prove the use of the said trades at Lowestoft. And likewise there have been of antient time, and still continue, officers for the collecting such customs as should be due to the lord, etc., and a deputy searcher for the king's customs; and although the aforesaid trade of merchandising, loading, and unloading of ships and boats continued there, and never any of the customs claimed by the town of Yarmouth were either taken or demanded for such loading or unloading; and although the statute of the 31st of Edward III. concerning the prohibition of discharging any more herrings in the roads of any more herrings in the road of Kirkley, but for the charge of the pickers, was never in use etc., yet, under the pretence of the grant (46th Edward III.) of a place in the sea, then called Kirkley road, which no ways agreeth to be Lowestoft roads, they have of late used to come into the said roads before Lowestoft, which is above seven miles from the town of Yarmouth, and fair of herrings kept in the said town; and have compelled the fishers to sail to Yarmouth and sell their herrings, etc.; and likewise have exacted anchorage, tending greatly to the breach of the peace, and without any material profit to Yarmouth, and which tends only to the disturbing and diminishing of the trade of merchandising herrings at Lowestoft.

But now the Yarmouth men, as if all their former injuries were not sufficient, have sent a vessel, a man-of-war ship as they term it, with a flag on the main-top-mast head, having 25 men aboard, armed with swords, halfpikes, muskets, and great store of stones, which sail into the roads of Corton, Lowestoft and Kirkley, to ride there at anchor, and to act as above by virtue of a commission under the hands of the bailiffs and three justices of the Peace, and the seal of the said town, so that the fishers may not deliver any herrings at all, which before they never practised.

THE AFFIDAVIT OF JAMES MUNDS, OF LOWESTOFT.

"James Munds, of Lowestoft, Suffolk, fisherman, aged sixty years and upwards, maketh oath, that he has used the trade of fishing forty-five years and upwards, last past, upon the coasts of Norfolk and Suffolk; and that the western fishermen and strangers have constantly, during the time of the free fair kept at Yarmouth, delivered herrings in the roads of Lowestoft aforesaid, to several merchants inhabiting in the said town, without any disturbance or molestation, till this last year the men of Yarmouth sent out a vessel, which they called a man-of-war, furnished with five and twenty men, and several weapons of war, which anchored in the roads of Lowestoft the chiefest part of the season, daily chasing the fishermen, so that none durst deliver any herrings, to their great damage, and, if not timely prevented, to their utter ruin and undoing. JAMES MUNDS."

Prob. 30th die Januarii, A.D. 1660, Corum me in Cancell. Magistro,
THOMAS ESCOWTR.

THE AFFIDAVIT OF ROGER HOOPER, OF RAMSGATE.

"Roger Hooper, of Ramsgate, Kent, aged forty-six, or thereabouts, maketh oath that he hath used the trade of herring fishing four and thirty years, last past, upon the coasts of Norfolk and Suffolk; and that the western fishermen, his neighbours, and others, and also strangers, have constantly, during the time of the free fair kept at Yarmouth, delivered herrings in the road of Lowestoft aforesaid, to several merchants, inhabitants there, without any molestation, until this last year, when the Yarmouth men sent out a vessel, which they called a 'man-of-war,' to ride in the roads of Lowestoft the chiefest part of the season; which man-of-war threatened him, that if he delivered any herrings at Lowestoft, they would seize him. So that none dare deliver any herrings, to their great damage, and, if not timely prevented, to the utter undoing of their voyage. ROGER HOOPER."

Prob. Febrn. 1660. Coram me in Cancell. Magistro.

BYRED.

Having been grievous sufferers for our constant fidelity to his sacred Majesty; several times plundered, grievously burthened with taxes above the neighbouring towns, soldiers living at free quarters, great losses by sea, depopulated of our principal inhabitants by their being engaged in his majesty's service, as Captains Allen, Utber, Canham and Whiting, besides a great number of our common seamen, and many who have lost their lives in contending with these oppressors, and also a most lamentable fire in this town, which consumed 140 houses, together with tackling and goods to the amount of ten thousand pounds and upwards, for which we never had any favour. And now having made large provisions for the fishery of all sorts, as also for the receiving, salting, and drying such herrings as they should bring in being able to ang in this town about 700 lasts, which time out of mind, have been the sole subsistance of this town, are now bespoiled at once, and like to perish, if speedy remedy be not obtained, being no ways able to wage war with them, for reasons above.

We therefore humbly pray, etc.

THE SECOND ORDER OF THE TOWN OF GREAT YARMOUTH TO THOMAS ALLEN TO ENTER CORTON ROAD, LOWESTOFT ROAD, AND KIRKLEY ROAD, TO PROTECT THE LIBERTIES OF THE SAID TOWN OF GREAT YARMOUTH.

"Whereas Thomas Allen was late ordered by us, the bailiffs and justices of the burgh and town of Great Yarmouth, in the county of Norfolk, her under named, to go into Corton road, Lowestoft road, and Kirkley road, Suffolk, with a vessel and a convenient company, to take notice of such persons, strangers and others, as shall there deliver any herrings or other merchandise, during the time of the free fair here at Great Yarmouth, contrary to our liberties and charters; and to seize such vessels and merchandise, as forfeited to the king's majesty, and to bring the same into the haven of this town. And we did also order the said Thomas Allen, with his company, to demand and take in the said several roads such duties as were or should be due to this town of Great Yarmouth for anchorage of ships and vessels in these roads, or for any other cause, which said orders by us so given unto the said Thomas Allen, were done by virtue of an act or ordinance of common council of the said town of Great Yarmouth. And whereas the said Thomas Allen, by virtue of our said order unto him given, did go into the said road of Lowestoft, with a convenient vessel and competent number of men, to execute the orders by us given unto him; and was there opposed by the chief men of the said town of Lowestoft, who came upon the said Thomas Allen and his company in the road of that town, violently and riotously in boats, and with force of arms, etc., drave him and them out of that road, threatening them otherwise to fire their vessel; whereby the said Thomas Allen, with his vessel and company, was enforced to come away without doing anything. Now, therefore, we the said bailiffs and justices, do again order, authorise, and appoint the said Thomas Allen to go with a competent vessel and company of men, and with convenient weapons for their defence into the said roads of Corton, Lowestoft, and Kirkley, from time to time, during the time of the free fair here at Great Yarmouth, and there to do and execute all things, specified in our former order given unto him. In witness whereof we the said bailiffs and justices have hereunto set our hands and seals this fifth day of October, in the year of our Lord, one thousand, six hundred and sixty.

NICHO. CUTTINGE,    JAMES SYMONDS,
                                                         (*Bailiffs*.)
JOHN CARTER,    GEORGE ENGLAND,
JO. WODROFFE."

The adjoining towns of Pakefield and Kirkley also lodged complaints before the Privy Council, against the Yarmouth men, similar to those from Lowestoft, so did likewise Hastings, Dover, Rye, and other towns of the western coast; and afterwards some private adventurers in those parts of England did not scruple, on this important occasion, to petition the throne to protect them from the despotic designs of the Yarmouth men.

"To THE RIGHT HONOURABLE THE LORDS OF HIS MAJESTY'S MOST HONOURABLE PRIVY COUNCIL.

"THE CERTIFICATE OF THE SEA COAST TOWNS OF PAKEFIELD AND KIRKLEY, IN THE COUNTY OF SUFFOLK.

"Humbly certifying,

"That the said towns are joining upon the sea, and divided by one street, subsisting chiefly by the fishing trade. And that we never knew, or heard our forefathers speak of any roads lying against or near the said town, called by the name of Kirkley road, but Pakefield bay or hithe, and Lowestoft roads; nor was there ever any road near our said town so called, but by the men of Yarmouth, on purpose to engross the whole of the fishery; and monopolise the whole trade to themselves; whilst, in truth, our town of Kirkley is near three miles southwards of the pole set up to the northward of Lowestoft, always accounted the boundary of the seven miles granted to the town of Yarmouth, measured from their crane key, and to be the uttermost extent of their privileges. Nevertheless, in the year 1657, two or three days after Michaelmas, as Thomas Fowler the elder, and Thomas Fowler the younger, of our said towns, were, for delivering of herrings betwixt our town of Kirkley and Lowestoft, at their next going to Yarmouth, had before the bailiff, who set a fine upon each of them, of £40 a-piece, which they were commanded to pay, or else their boats and tackling would be confiscated. But after alleging their poor condition, they mitigated it to £30, and at last to £20 a man, which they were compelled to lay down upon the table; and large writings were produced for them to sign and seal, to indemnify the said bailiff, which if they would do, they would take but £5 a man; but one of the Fowlers desiring to understand the contents of the writings, and beginning to read, Mr. Bailiff England interrupted him, and said that if he would not seal it, he should pay the whole £20; so that they were obliged to seal they knew not what, and were dismissed by each of them paying £5. Such is the great bondage of the poor fishermen. In testimony of the truth, we the inhabitants of the said towns have hereunto subscribed our names this 14th day of January, 1660; and are ready to aver the same upon oath when we shall be thereunto required.

| ROBERT BRONSEY, | WILLIAM RICHMAN, | WILLIAM GOGGE, |
| THOMAS COLBY, | WILLIAM THURKITTLE, | THOMAS FOWLER, |
| MICHAEL FOWLER, | WILLIAM WOODS, | THOMAS ERTIS, |
| JOHN COLBY, | JOHN SWATT, | JOHN SETTAVAYE, |
| FRANCIS DURRAND, | WILLIAM ERTIS, | WILLIAM ROUSE, |
| ABELL HOULSWORTE, | THOMAS MASON, | JOHN MASON." |
| HENRY CROSS, | WILLIAM BROWN, | |

"To THE RIGHT HONOURABLE THE LORDS OF HIS MAJESTY'S MOST HONOURABLE PRIVY COUNCIL.

"THE CERTIFICATE OF THE FISHERMEN OF THE TOWNS OF BRIGHTHELMSTONE, HASTINGS, RYE, DOVER, RAMSGATE, AND THE REST OF THE WESTERN FISHERY.

"Upon perusal of a petition presented unto the king's most excellent majesty by the town of Lowestoft, in Suffolk, representing the injurious proceedings of the town of Yarmouth to them, and also the whole Western Fishery; and his majesty's gracious reference thereupon unto the right honourable the Lords and others of his Majesty's most honourable Privy Council for satisfaction and relief therein,

"We do humbly certify unto your Lordships,

"That the Western Fishery, has time out of mind, sold and delivered herrings in the roads of Lowestoft, until this last year, when the Yarmouth men sent forth a man-of-war (as they term her) not only to affright them and others from delivering herrings in the said roads, but also to prevent any that should offer to deliver herrings there. And in case they should presume to deliver any, to seize upon them, and bring them into their haven, to be dealt with accordingly (as by the commission granted to the commander or captain of the said man-of-war may appear) : which they have done, not only to the great loss of some particular men, imposing great fines upon them, which they were forced to pay, but also the great discouragement, (and if not in time prevented) the ruin of the whole Western fishery. For if we be forced to deliver our herrings only at Yarmouth, we shall lose at least one-third part of our time, the winds falling so as that sometimes we lye through three or four days before we can get to sea again. Besides, having that advantage, they will give only what they please, which will amount to the loss of near half our time and profit, and will be much to the disadvantage of his Majesty's subjects in trading, both at home and abroad. Whereas at Lowestoft we have the privilege to make the best of our market, and can go to sea when we please, furnished with all necessaries as plentifully as we can at Yarmouth. The truth of all which we do attest under our hands, humbly praying relief therein.

Signed at Bradstow, Foulstone, Hastings, Ramsgate, Hyde, Dover, Rye, Brighthelmstone, by 469 Western fishers, and others."

Lowestoft answereth, That the said statute of 31 Edward III. is repealed by the statute of 2 Richard II., cap. i.: which grants a free trade for all persons to buy and sell at any place within the realm, notwithstanding any statute, grant or usage to the contrary; and by 46, Edward III., which united Kirkley road to Yarmouth Haven.

Yarmouth alleges, That the anchoring place opposite the town of Kirkley, and the road before the town of Lowestoft, is that Kirkley road mentioned in the grant of 46 Edward III., which united Kirkley road to Yarmouth haven.

Lowestoft answers, That the town of Lowestoft is situated eight or nine miles to the south of Yarmouth; and that a mile further to the south is a village called Kirkley, joining to the head town called Pakefield; before which towns the anchoring places have always been called Pakefield bay or hithe, as by a certificate under the hands of the principal inhabitants of both those said towns doth appear.

Yarmouth says, That the seven miles, which bound their liberties, begin at the haven's mouth.

Lowestoft answereth, That by the charter of 46 Edward III. the seven miles were confined to the town of Yarmouth.

Yarmouth declareth, That Kirkley road lies at a considerable distance from the haven's mouth.

Lowestoft answereth, That the situation of it was contiguous to the mouth of the haven at the time when the haven discharged itself into the sea to the south of Corton, 46, Edward III., when the charter was granted for uniting Kirkley road to Yarmouth haven.

Yarmouth affirms, That the power and authority derived to them by extending their liberties to the distance of seven miles, were not detrimental to the nation in general, nor to Lowestoft in particular.

Lowestoft answereth, That it is prejudicial to both of them; and grounded their reasons on the two inquisitions held during 5 Richard II.

Yarmouth denieth, That the statute 31 Edward III. was repealed by the general statute 2 Richard II., and also insists, that by the charter 46 Edward III, for uniting Kirkley road to Yarmouth haven, their liberties were to extend seven miles from the said haven.

Lowestoft answereth, That the said charter 46 Edward III was repealed by an act 50 Edward III (though the judges declared that the statute 31 Edward III was not repealed) and that the statute 2 Richard II was prejudicial to the kingdom in general: and therefore a complaint was made thereof, in the parliament holden 4 Richard II, and an inquisition was taken by three judges of the realm, who surveyed the premises, and declared, that to extend the liberties of Yarmouth seven miles from the haven's mouth, was against common right, and that the said statute 2 Richard II was hurtful to the commonwealth; and, consequently, by the statute 5 Richard III, the statute 2 Richard II was repealed.

Yarmouth declareth, that by the statute 10 Richard II all their privileges were confirmed to them, and again by statute 1 queen Elizabeth.

M

Lowestoft alloweth, that the liberties granted to Yarmouth, 46 Edward III were confirmed by statute 10 Richard II; but concerning the statute 1 Queen Elizabeth that did not relate to the herring fishery, except confining their liberties to seven miles from the town, but to the establishing a court of admiralty at Yarmouth; and, therefore, though the town of Yarmouth, under a pretence of being authorised by that grant, made considerable encroachments on the privileges of Lowestoft, and insisted that their privilege of seven miles was to be measured from the haven's mouth, and not from the key of Yarmouth, thereby attempting to exclude the town of Lowestoft from the fishery; yet, on complaint thereof being made to her majesty's privy council, who referred it to the judges, Sir John Fortescue, Justice Clench, and Justice Gawdy, they certified, that it was their opinion, that the seven miles should be measured from the crane key in Yarmouth, towards Lowestoft, and at the termination thereof a post, or some other mark should be erected to denote the same. Whereupon the Lords of the Council, on the 16th May, 1596, after referring the case again to the judges, laid it before the Parliament, who issued an order, in 1597, to Sir Arthur Heneningham, Sir Henry Woodhouse, and Henry Gawdy, Esq., on the part of Yarmouth, and to Sir Robert Jermyn, Sir John Higham, and Anthony Wingfield, Esq., on the part of Lowestoft, to undertake the admeasurement of the said seven miles; accordingly the said admeasurement was actually made, and a great post, denoting the boundary of the liberties of Yarmouth, was erected, which remained unto that day.

Yarmouth insisteth, That a Charter of confirmation, granted to them in the reign of James I., Kirkley road is expressly described as opposite to the town of Kirkley; and that their jurisdiction shall extend from Winterton Ness in Norfolk, to Easton Ness in Suffolk, which is twenty-four miles, and includes the town of Lowestoft, which is only eight or nine miles from Yarmouth; and that by virtue of this jurisdiction, they justify their interruption of the herring fishery at Lowestoft, and all other trades within the extent of their said liberties.

Lowestoft answereth, That such a charter as the Yarmouth men pretend to have obtained, would be a monopoly, and contrary to the common rights fo the Kingdom in general. That such a charter, if it was really granted, was obtained privately; that no writs of ad quod dampnum were issued, so that it is evident that they had imposed upon his majesty. That it would be prejudicial to the commonwealth, and the utter ruin of the western fishery, as is testified by above 3000 fishermen, who have subscribed a petition which certifies the truth of this assertion, and prays for relief. That it relates chiefly to the jurisdiction belonging to their court of admiralty, as is evident by their coming with a boat into Lowestoft roads, and demanding sixpence for anchorage. And lastly, That the artifice of having Kirkley road represented in this charter as situated opposite to the town of Kirkley, merely with a design of furnishing themselves with a plausible pretence for extending their liberties beyond the town of Lowestoft, towards the south, and thereby to exclude them from the herring-fishery, was a fraudulent imposition, and a manifest perversion of the Charter 46 Edward III, which represents it as situate near the entrance of Yarmouth haven.

Previous to the report of the attorney-general, a certificate was presented to him from James Wild and Samuel Pacy, two eminent merchants at Lowestoft (the persons who had the principal management of this suit, which was conducted with the most indefatigable industry and scrupulous integrity, as appears from the account of their expenses, which is preserved and will be given further on) asserting the reasons why the seven miles, the boundary of the liberties of Yarmouth, ought to be measured from the crane key belonging to the said town of Yarmouth, where the herring fair is usually held, and not from the haven's mouth.

"To the Honourable Mr. ATTORNEY GENERAL

"The humble CERTIFICATE of the INHABITANTS of the town of LOWESTOFT, in SUFFOLK, shewing the reasons why the seven miles, the extent of the liberties of Yarmouth, in Norfolk, ought to be measured from the crane Key, and not from the haven's mouth.

1st.—"That their fore-fathers being obstructed in their fishing by the Yarmouth men (which time out of mind they had enjoyed), had appealed to her late majesty, queen Elizabeth, to her parliament, and privy council, and obtained an order for setting bounds to the seven miles granted to Yarmouth.

2nd.—"In consequence whereof an order was also obtained from the lords of the council, directed to several men of authority in both counties, to make due enquiry concerning the controversy, and survey the premises, in order to ascertain the place from whence the admeasurement ought to begin, which was certified to be from the crane Key in Yarmouth, where the herring fair was usually held. And though the Yarmouth men, thinking themselves aggrieved obtained a second survey to be made, yet was it certified by the inquiries a second time, that they found no reason to depart from their former opinion. The reasons which they assigned, were that it was beneficial to her majesty's good subjects in general, and the encouragement of the herring fishery in particular.

3rd.—"That the order from the council, for the admeasurement of the seven miles, was never revoked, as the Yarmouth men falsely suggested, but only suspended, as by the copy of their letters appears, and though by indirect means they occasioned a delay, and endeavoured to weary the commissioner appointed to settle the controversy with frivolous evasions, yet it was agreed, that the seven miles should be measured from the crane Key, in Yarmouth, directly towards Lowestoft, and a great post should be set up at the end thereof, to denote the same, which remaineth to this day.

4th.—"That ever since that time (which was in the year 1595 and 1596) the fishers have freely delivered their herrings in Lowestoft roads, in the time of the free fair at Yarmouth, without any molestation, until this last year, 1660, when they were interrupted by a vessel, called a man-of-war, employed by the Yarmouth men for that purpose."

"May it therefore please your honour, "That as this controversy has been for so long standing, and it plainly appearing that no remedy can be obtained but by another admeasurement; that your honour will give credit to the orders and certificates lately pleaded before his majesty in council, as also to the certificates of several thousand fishermen belonging to the western fishery, then produced, shewing the inevitable ruin and destruction both to them and their families, that would immediately ensue, if prevented from delivering their herrings at Lowestoft, as from time immemorial they have been accustomed to do, which certificates have been since confirmed by a petition from Captain Tattersell, to his sacred majesty; and that your honour would be graciously pleased to report your sense of this difference concerning the admeasurement as soon as possible; for that the Yarmouth men will continue to claim the same privileges, or greater, than they did in the year 1595; and exercise the same ruin to our poor town, as in the last year (1660), with their armed vessel called a man-of-war. Neither do the Yarmouth men desire that the controversy should be brought before the parliament, but to weary us out with delays and expense, well knowing how unable we are to wage law with them, and that unless they persist in opposing us, it will end in an admeasurement. We therefore humbly pray your honour, that you will be pleased to consider the equity of our case; the great expense, travail and loss of time we have been at; and with due regard to our poor condition, speedily to report the state of the whole matter to his majesty in council, that so we may be no longer delayed, but repair home to follow our lawful callings; and we shall, as in duty bound, for ever pray, and remain, your honours most humble and grateful servants, JAMES WILD,
SAMUEL PACY."

The attorney-general, in pursuance of the order of council, paid due attention to the allegations of both parties; and after hearing what each of them had to advance in support of their several pretensions, together with the opinion of their learned council, delivered a report to his majesty; wherein, after reciting the many charters which had been granted to the town of Yarmouth, and afterwards repealed; and the various ordinances and inquisitions issued and taken by the King's commission in preceding reigns, and revoked by the same authority; declared that he had considered the statute 31 Edward

III, the different opinions of the several judges thereupon, and the orders of her late majesty queen Elizabeth and her privy council, in consequence thereof, which were, that seven miles should be measured **from the Key of** Yarmouth, and also from the utmost bounds of their haven, and that a certificate should be presented, declaring how far each of the said admeasurements extended ; and that during the interval, they should forbear to erect any marks or bounds, pointing out the termination of the said admeasurements, until further orders were issued; but that it did not appear to him that the said seven miles were actually measured by any order for that purpose. It is evident that the attorney-general had not perfectly informed himself of all the circumstances of this dispute, or else they were misrepresented to him; for in **1596** an order in Council was given for seven miles to be measured from the key of Yarmouth towards Lowestoft, and at the end thereof to set up some apparent mark; and in that remarkable commission, which had all the appearance of being fraudently obtained, is contained directions for the two admeasurements, and the suspension of the order for erecting a mark pointing out the extent of the liberties of Yarmouth. Nevertheless the inhabitants of Lowestoft did affirm, and it was certified by great **numbers of** the **Western** fishermen, that the said Western fishery had ever **since the recited order** (as they did before), sold and delivered herrings in the roads **of Lowestoft till** this last summer, without any disturbance or molestation from **the town of** Yarmouth.

### THE ATTORNEY GENERAL'S FIRST REPORT.

"May it please your most excellent Majesty.

"In obedience to your Majesty's order in council, of the 25th January last, I have heard the inhabitants of the town of Lowestoft, in the county of Suffolk, and also the inhabitants of Great Yarmouth, in the county of Norfolk, and their learned counsel on both sides; and do find, that the contention between the said towns concerning the herring fishery, hath depended for a very long time. And that divers statutes have been made in this case by parliaments, and again afterwards repealed. And also divers ordinances and inquisitions have anciently been made and taken, by the king's commission directed to men of great quality, and afterwards altered and revoked again by the like authority. But there was one statute made in the 31st Edward III, whereby amongst other things it is provided, that none shall sell herrings in any place about the haven of Yarmouth, by seven miles, but in the three towns of Yarmouth, except the said herrings be of 'their own fishing.' And I have likewise seen the opinions of several learned judges, some of them conceiving, that the said statute, 31 Edward III is repealed ; and others, that the said statute, and also one other Act made in the tenth year of Richard II, for reviving divers former repealed charters, made to Yarmouth, stand still in force by law, and are not repealed. And those judges who were of opinion that the same were not repealed, did think it good and convenient to have the seven miles measured, and to begin at the crane key in Yarmouth, where **the** said fair of herrings is kept (to which place the fishers who sell their fish at Yarmouth must first come, and their cable draw to land, before they deliver their herrings), and so go towards Lowestoft, and where the seven miles do end, to set up some apparent mark to make it known; and did certify the same accordingly to the lords of Queen Elizabeth's privy council; But the inhabitants of Yarmouth being discontented with the first certificate of the said judges, did procure a rehearing of their cause before them, who having accordingly heard them and their learned counsel, did certify that they did find **no** cause to alter their former certificate; yet the admeasurement was suspended by reason of the Yarmouth **men** alledging, that the admeasurement of the seven miles from the **key of Yarmouth would** be prejudicial to their charters and **liberties;** and **that by** the said statute, 31 Edward III, the seven miles ought **to be accounted** from the utmost bounds of the haven, which they affirmed **to** havebeen extended, in the memory of man, a mile beyond where it was **then ;** so that it was directed by the lords of her said late majesty's most honourable privy council, that there should be seven miles measured from the key at Yarmouth and from the utmost bounds of their haven, **where** the five ports begin their jurisdiction, and that it should be certified **unto** them how far each admeasurement **did** extend; and that in the mean time they should forbear to set up any marks or bounds, until such further orders should be issued therein as might be just and reasonable, and to the mutual satisfaction of both parties. But there is nothing appears to me, that the said seven miles were measured as the said last-recited order did direct. Yet, notwithstanding, the inhabitants of Lowestoft do affirm, and it is certified by great numbers of fishermen, that the western fishery has been ever since the said recited order (as they did before) sold and delivered herrings in the roads of Lowestoft, till this last summer without the disturbance of the Yarmouth men.

"All which I humbly submit to your Majesty's great wisdom."

It also appears that the Attorney-General, upon further consideration of this contested difference, presented an additional report to his majesty, wherein he represented, that since his former report he had seen the certificate of the two learned judges, dated April 29, 1597, subsequent to the certificates mentioned in his first report, in which they declared that they could not see how any method could be taken for compromising the differences between the two towns, but by referring them to Parliament.

### THE ATTORNEY-GENERAL'S SECOND REPORT.

"May it please your most excellent Majesty."

"In obedience to your Majesty's order of council of the 25th of January last, concerning the matter of difference between the inhabitants of the town of Lowestoft, and the inhabitants of the town of Great Yarmouth, I lately made certificate to your majesty according to the truth of what was then produced before me. But since that time there hath been produced to me a certificate under the hands of the learned judges, dated the 29th of April, 1597, subsequent to those mentioned in my former certificate, wherein they did declare, that they did see no other course could be taken by them, in order to compound their controversies and decide the differences between the said towns, and whereby they could bind both parties in such a manner as was most fit and convenient (their differences being of such great difficulty), and therefore they thought it fit, that the cause should be respited, and referred to the next parliament. At which time, upon supplication and complaint of those that should find themselves aggrieved, the cause might receive hearing and due remedy.

"And I humbly crave liberty to certify to your Majesty, that by the word "crane" key, in my former certificate, I did intend the key of Yarmouth, that is known by that name, without any the least prejudice to either party thereby, in relation to the admeasurement mentioned in the same certificate, further or otherwise than the truth of the cause would bear.

"All which I humbly submit to your Majesty's great wisdom."

At a council held at Whitehall the 10th of April, 1661, at which were present his Majesty, and the Duke of York, and many of the first nobility, these reports of the attorney-general were presented and read; and it was accordingly ordered by the council, that by reason of his Majesty's approaching coronation, they were unable to pay such proper attention to the complaints of the respective parties, as their cases required; therefore the affair must necessarily be suspended a short time longer; and that both parties do attend the Board on Friday three weeks, the third of May next ensuing, at three in the afternoon, for the further hearing and determining of this matter.

Upon the issuing of the order for deferring the hearing of the cause to a subsequent council, the Lowestoft men presented another petition to His Majesty, beseeching him that as it was the opinion of the judges, and also of the Attorney-general, that the only method which could be taken for compromising the differences so long subsisting between these two towns, would be to consider seven miles to be measured from the key of Yarmouth, towards Lowestoft, in order to ascertain the boundary of the liberties of the former place, and secure the privilege of a free fishery to the latter, and at the end thereof to have some apparent mark erected, to denote the same; that his Majesty would be pleased to order the said admeasurement to be immediately carried into execution; or otherwise, by reason of their many misfortunes and losses, they must be involved in inevitable ruin.

"To the KING'S MOST EXCELLENT MAJESTY, the humble PETITION OF THE INHABITANTS OF THE TOWN OF LOWESTOFT, IN THE COUNTY OF SUFFOLK,

"Sheweth,

"That your majesty having been graciously pleased, at the humble suit and prayer of your petitioners, to hear the complaint of your poor petitioners, against the rich inhabitants of the town of Great Yarmouth, in the county of Norfolk, before the right honourable the lords of Your majesty's privy council, touching the free trade of herring fishery, which hath of long time been in controversy between them; and upon a full hearing, did order both parties to attend your majesty's attorney-general, that he, upon due consideration and hearing of all parties, should report to your majesty the true state of the whole matter of fact accordingly: whereby it appears, that the opinion of all the reverend judges, and such other worthy gentlemen of quality to whom the matter hath been formerly referred, is, 'That there is no other visible way to end their controversies, and to procure unity between the said towns, but by an admeasurement of seven miles from the crane key of Yarmouth towards the town of Lowestoft.' And whereas your petitioners are exceeeingly impoverished by reason of their said controvorsy, and their sufferings during the late troubles, their affections to your majesty's late royal father, of ever blessed memory, having been plundered by Oliver Cromwell and the said inhabitants of Yarmouth, who were instrumental with, and assisting him in the same; and since that time have been almost ruined by a sad and lamentable fire which happened in their said town, whereupon inevitable destruction will follow, except a speedy and effectual end be put to their differences, and that they may have free liberty to use their trade of herring fishery.

"Your petitioners therefore humbly pray, That your majesty would be graciously pleased, upon the report of Mr. Attorney-General, as also the reports and certificates of former learned judges and justices of the peace of both counties, by your royal command to declare and publish, that seven miles may be measured from the crane key of Yarmouth aforesaid, towards the town of Lowestoft, and not from their pretended utmost bounds of their haven, which is uncertain, and by which means they would destroy your petitioners said fishing trade. And that a post, or some other apparent mark, may be set up at the end thereof, so that the trade of herring fishing may be used during the time of their free fair at any place without the said post or mark, without the molestation of the said inhabitants of Yarmouth, whereby your petitioners, and many thousands of your majesty's poor western fishermen, may live and subsist by their said trade of herring fishing, as time out of mind they have done; which otherwise will be their utter ruin and undoing, as appears by their humble certificate and remonstrance to your sacred majesty.

"And your petitioners as in all duty bound, shall ever pray, etc."

**Petitions** were also at the same time presented by the Lowestoft men to Lord **Chancellor** Hyde and the Duke of Albemarle, entreating their interest and authority at the privy council intended shortly to be held for the further discussion of this litigious contest; also that an order might be obtained for the admeasurement of the said seven miles from the crane key at Yarmouth, and that the same admeasurement should not be made from the haven's mouth, as thereby the town of Lowestoft would be excluded from their indisputable claim to the privileges belonging to the herring fishery.

A petition was also presented to his majesty, praying that his majesty would graciously please to be present in his royal person at the council appointed to be held on Friday the third of May next ensuing, for deciding this long-controverted difference.

In consequence of this appointment a privy council was held at Whitehall on the third of May, 1661, at which were present his majesty, the duke of York, many of the great officers of state, and others of the nobility; when, after hearing the learned counsel on both sides, and after full debate on the several complaints and allegations advanced by the respective parties, it was ordered by his majesty in council, that as the determination of the differences between the said towns of Yarmouth and Lowestoft depended upon the validity of several charters, acts of parliament, and orders of council, that the inhabitants of the the town of Lowestoft should make application to the right honourable the House of Lords, shortly to be assembled in Parliament, who would consider their complaints and afford them such redress as their lordships, upon due examination of the whole matter, should think just and reasonable.

The Lowestoft people having conceived the highest expectations of an amicable adjustment of their differences with Yarmouth at the late hearing of their cause before the privy council, were extremely chagrined and disappointed at its being referred to the House of Lords; especially as their inability (from their late misfortunes) to continue the contest, and the continual interruptions and depredations of the Yarmouth men, had rendered a final decision of the affair absolutely necessary. In this critical situation of their affairs, they thought it necessary, as preparatory to the introduction of their cause before the House of Lords, to present a petition to their lordships informing them, that whereas, from time immemorial, they had enjoyed the free trade of buying herrings of the western fishers in the roads of Lowestoft; but that the Yarmouth men, taking advantage of their late misfortunes by fire and civil wars, had greatly interrupted and annoyed them, and threatened them with the total destruction of their fishery, and, consequently, with the utter ruin of their town. That they had laid their case before his majestly and the privy council; that it had been referred by them to the attorney-general, that the opinion of the attorney-general had been laid before his majesty and the privy council; who, after due examination of the premises, were pleased to refer a further investigation thereof to their lordships, recommending such redress of the grievances complained of as they should think just and equitable. Therefore the said petitioners humbly besought their lordships, that they would be pleased to take the matter into consideration, and afford them such immediate relief as would prevent the annihilation of the fishery, the ruin of the town, and the great loss and inconvenience of the nation in general.

On reading of the above petition before the house of lords, their lordships ordered, that the cause so long depending between the said towns should be heard at the bar of that house by such counsel as should be retained on each side, on the seventh of June, 1661; and that the said petitioners should give timely notice thereof to the inhabitants of Yarmouth, and that both parties do attend the same hearing.

"DIE SABBATHI, 25° MAIJ, 1661.

"On reading the petition of the inhabitants of the town of Lowestoft, in the county of Suffolk, this day in the house, concerning a free trade of fishing, which the petitioners complain they are molested in by the inhabitants of Great Yarmouth, it is ordered, by the lords in parliament assembled, that the cause shall be heard at this bar, by counsel on both sides, on the seventh day of June next. And that the petitioners, or some of them, shall give the said inhabitants of the town of Yarmouth, timely notice thereof, and that both the said parties do attend the said hearing accordingly

JOHN BROWNE, Cleric. Parliamenti."

The state of the town of Lowestoft, and the herring fishery, on which it solely depended, were now become truly alarming; the towns of Ipswich, Orford, Alborough, and Dunwich apprehended also their being involved in a share of the calamity; and the company of fishmongers in London, as well as the numerous body of fishermen on the coasts of Sussex and Kent, evidently foresaw the distress and inconveniences which must inevitably ensue should the town of Yarmouth be permitted to monopolise the whole trade of the herring fishery to themselves. Alarmed with these apprehensions, and stimulated with the desire of independence, they united their utmost efforts in one common interest, in guarding themselves against the oppressions of the Yarmouth men, which, it was too evident, they were most industriously endeavouring to burden them withal.

The first who offered their assistance to the Lowestoft men in this difficult but necessary undertaking, were the fishmongers of London. They presented a certificate to the house of Lords; wherein after premising that several petitions had been presented to his majesty and the privy council, from the town of Lowestoft, representing the injurious proceedings of the town of Yarmouth; and also his majesty's reference of the case to their lordships they further certified, to the house of Lords; wherein, after premising that several petitions had been presented to his majesty and the privy council, from the town of Lowestoft, representing the injurious proceedings of the town of Yarmouth; and also his majesty's reference of the case to their lordships; they further certified, that Lowestoft was a very antient town; had always subsisted chiefly by the herring fishery; that they had, from time immemorial, enjoyed the privilege of having herrings delivered in the roads off that town until the last year, when they where interrupted by the Yarmouth men, under a pretence, that by virtue of a charter they had granted to them, no fishers were authorised to deliver any herrings during the continuance of their herring fair, or from Michaelmas to Martinmas, within the distance of seven miles from the mouth of their haven; that were the Yarmouth men permitted to persevere in these injurious proceedings, it would be attended not only with great prejudice to the town of Lowestoft, but the utter ruin of the western fishery, and would also be extremely detrimental to the nation in general, exclusive of many other inconveniences.—Seventy-eight of the London fishmongers attested the truth of the premises under their own hands and prayed for relief.

A petition was also presented at the same time from the towns of Ipswich, Orford, Alborough, and Dunwich, similar in general to the above petition from the fishmongers of London; entreating their lordships, that the town of Lowestoft may not only enjoy their ancient freedom of buying and selling herrings on every occasion, but also be protected for the future against the interruptions of the town of Yarmouth; and that each town might enjoy the common right of the nation without any restraint or limitation from each other, as the most effectual means of preventing a monopoly, and rendering the herring fishery of more general utility.

"To THE HONOURABLE THE PEERS OF ENGLAND ASSEMBLED IN PARLIAMENT.

"THE HUMBLE PETITION OF THE BURGESSES ETC., FOR THE TOWNS OF IPSWICH, AND DUNWICH IN THE COUNTY OF SUFFOLK,

"Humbly shewing,

"That your petitioners being informed, that his majesty, together with his council have recommended the case between the towns of Lowestoft and Yarmouth, concerning the free trade of herring fishing, to your lordships' care and determination; your petitioners do think fit to recommend some particulars to your lordships' consideration.

"1st. That the town of Lowestoft is more antient than the town of Yarmouth.

"2nd. That Lowestoft is in the county of Suffolk, and Yarmouth in the county of Norfolk.

3rd. So that it seems unreasonable to us, that the town of Yarmouth should infringe upon the town of Lowestoft, which is a more antient town than Yarmouth, and in a distinct county, and full nine miles distant, and thereby not only bring a prejudice to Lowestoft, but to the whole coast of Suffolk, and consequently to the whole trade of herring-fishing, by their destroying the common right which the western fishermen and the city of London have enjoyed by trading with our coast rather than Yarmouth, to the great advantage of the whole nation; whereas such a monopoly as the town of Yarmouth pretends to, would be destructive both to us and the town of Lowestoft.

"Your petitioners therefore humbly pray, That the town of Lowestoft may not only enjoy their antient freedom of buying and selling herrings at all times, but that there may not be any encroachments by the town of Yarmouth upon the town of Lowestoft, but that each town may enjoy the common right of this nation without circumscription to each other; whereby monopolies will be prevented, and the trade of herring fishing become more advantageous to the nation.

"And your petitioners, as in duty bound, shall ever pray, etc."

JOHN ROUS, RICHARD COOKE, for Dulwich. JOHN HOLLAND, ROBERT BROOKS, for Alborough. WALTER DEVERRIX.

Probably Sir John Holland, Bart; who died in 1700, aged 98; who was the son of Sir Thomas Holland, of Quidenham and Wortwell, in Norfolk, Knt. The Hollands were a very ancient family, and flourished before the conquest. They came out of Lancashire, and a branch of the family settled at Wortwell Hall, near Harleston, about the year 1500; and from thence they removed to Quidenham about the year 1600. The estate at Wortwell then belonged to Mr. Aldous Arnold, of Lowestoft.

Another petition was also presented by Captain Tettersall, a commander in the British navy, a person firmly attached to the interests of the western fishermen. This petition was addressed to the Knights and burgesses of the counties of Sussex and Kent: wherein, after recapitulating the oppressions of the Yarmouth men, and that this long-contested difference had been referred by his majesty to the decision of the house of lords, he informed them that many hundreds of his friends, neighbours, and acquaintance, western fishermen of the said counties, and who were greatly interested in the prosperity of the herring fishery, had concurred with the town of Lowestoft in presenting a certificate and petition to the lords of the privy council, respecting the illegal proceedings of the Yarmouth men, and had requested their said petitioner to appear in behalf of the said towns before the council, and deliver the same, which office he had undertaken and executed. And also further informed them, that an order had been issued by the House of Lords, summoning both parties, with their counsel, to appear at the bar of that house on the seventh of June next ensuing, being the day appointed for hearing and determining their cause; and that their petitioner being unable to attend the said hearing (he being a commander in the navy), the decision whereof being pregnant with the most important consequences both to the town of Lowestoft and the whole western fishery: therefore, he humbly petitioned the knights and burgesses of the counties of Sussex and Kent to unite their interests with those of the county of Suffolk, in procuring a redress of those grievances which the town of Lowestoft, and the said western fishermen were then labouring under; such as the exigency of their situation required, and the wisdom of their lordships should think just and reasonable.

"To the Right Honourable the KNIGHT and BURGESSES of the Counties of ESSEX and KENT.

"The Humble PETITION of Captian NICHOLAS TETTERSALL.

"Sheweth,

"That the town of Lowestoft, in the county of Suffolk, having been interrupted this last year in their free trade of herring fishing, by the inhabitants of Great Yarmouth in the county of Norfolk, tending not only to the ruin of the said town of Lowestoft, but of the whole western fishery; and seeking for remedy by their humble petition to the king's most excellent majesty, who referring it to the right honourable the lords and others of his privy council, for satisfaction and relief, many hundreds of his neighbours, friends, and acquaintance, the western fishermen of both your said counties, whom it so highly concern, did join with the said town of Lowestoft, by their humble certificate and petition subscribed by them, and requested your petitioner to appear on their behalfs before the said lords, to affirm the said petition, which accordingly he hath done; and several hearings have been before his majesty in council, held on the third of this instant May, it was ordered, in regard that the determination of the difference depended upon the validity of several charters, acts of parliament, and orders of council, that the complainants should apply themselves to the right honourable the house of lords, speedily to be assembled in parliament, to consider their complaint, and afford them such relief as their lordships shall, on examination and consideration of the whole matter, find to be just and fit. Whereupon, on the twenty-fifth of this instant May, 1661, the said complainants, on their humble petition to the right honourable the lords assembled in parliament, obtained an order, summoning both parties to appear at the bar of that house on the seventh day of June next ensuing, together with their learned counsel, in order for the hearing of their cause. And your petitioner being in no capacity of serving his countrymen any longer therein, by reason of his command in his majesty's service at sea; and because that apparent ruin must necessarily attend the said fishermen, which of his own knowledge he doth affirm; and as by the copy of their remonstrance and petition, hereunto annexed, and read twice before his majesty and the privy council, doth plainly appear.

"Your petitioner doth therefore, in their behalf, most humbly pray your honours to join with the knights and burgesses for the county of Suffolk, and as true patrons for your country's good, be instrumental that the poor complainants be no longer interrupted and distressed by the rich inhabitants of Great Yarmouth; but that they may be heard at the time appointed, in order to the adjusting of their differences, and settling them by an act of Parliament, as the right honourable the lords and commons in their grave wisdoms shall think to be just and right.

"And your petitioner, as in duty bound, shall ever pray, etc.

N. TETTERSALL."

In pursuance of the appointment of the House of Lords, for the hearing of the cause depending between the towns of Lowestoft and Yarmouth, at the bar of that house, on the seventh of June next following, notice thereof was delivered to the bailiffs of Yarmouth, on the 30th May preceding, requiring their attendance; but the inhabitants of Yarmouth pleading the want of sufficient time to collect the necessary evidence upon such short notice, petitioned the house, that the hearing of the case might be deferred a short time longer; and accordingly their lordships gave orders, that the said hearing should be postponed to the 20th of June next ensuing; at which time all the parties concerned were to attend with their counsel and witnesses, and to be otherwise duly prepared.

"Die Mercurii, 5th Junij, 1661.

"Upon the petition of the bailiffs of the town of Great Yarmouth, read this day in the House, shewing that they were served with an order of this Court, on the 30th of May last, for a hearing at this Bar on the 7th of this instant June, concerning a free trade of fishing between the inhabitants of the town of Lowestoft, in Suffolk, and the town of Yarmouth; it is ordered by the Lords in Parliament assembled, That the said cause is hereby put off unto the 20th of this instant June, peremptorily. And that then all parties concerned are to attend, with their counsel and witnesses, and come fully prepared for a hearing at this bar accordingly.

· JNO. BROWNE, Cleric Parliamenti."

Accordingly, on the 20th June, the House of Lords being assembled, the council for the respective towns was heard at the bar of that house; and all the claims and privileges of the contending parties were carefully scrutinised and debated, in order to terminate the dispute, and to establish harmony and friendship between the said towns on a permanent and lasting foundation; but at the conclusion of the hearing it appeared, that as the principal point on which the whole controversy seemed to turn, was whether the statute 31 Edward III, upon which the Yarmouth men grounded their claim, was repealed by the statute 2 Richard II, as the Lowestoft men affirmed, and being a point of law, their lordships were unable to decide upon, therefore they referred it to the judges; and ordered that the counsel belonging to both parties should attend the judges at such time as they should appoint, who were to deliver their opinion concerning this point as soon as conveniently they could; and also ordered that the witnesses should be sworn and examined at the bar of the house, on Thursday next, the 27th of this instant June, 1661, respecting such matters of fact as related to the present dispute; and also it was further ordered on the 22nd instant, that John Humphrey, Richard Gillam, Sidrich Seager, William Fox, and such other necessary witnesses as the inhabitants of Lowestoft should have occasion to produce in the cause now depending between them and the bailiffs of Yarmouth, and to be heard in that house on Thursday the 26th June, 1661, do appear at the bar of that house; and that the witnesses not therein named, have their names delivered in writing to the clerk of the parliament before the commencement of the said hearing.

The first step taken by the Lowestoft men after their cause was referred by the House of Lords to the opinion of the judges, was to present a petition to

Sir Robert Foster, Lord Chief Justice of England; and also to Sir Orlando Bridgeman, Lord Chief Justice of the Court of Common Pleas; wherein they represented, that the House of Lords having referred to their Lordships for their opinion, whether the statute of the 31st of Edward III be repealed by the statute of the 2nd of Richard II, or by any other statute; and that their poor petitioners having attended upon this business for six months, were not able to support the expense thereof, or to contend any longer with such powerful adversaries as the rich inhabitants of Yarmouth, who endeavour to weary them out by delays, to ruin their poor petitioners and the whole western fishery, and monopolise the whole trade of herring fishing to themselves, to the great prejudice of the kingdom in general, and of their petitioners in particular. Therefore they humbly prayed that their Lordships would be graciously pleased to appoint a day, in order to meet the rest of the judges, that the counsel on both sides might attend their lordships, and a report of their opinion be delivered to the parliament as soon as possible.

"TO THE RIGHT HONOURABLE SIR ROBERT FOSTER, KNT., LORD CHIEF JUSTICE OF ENGLAND; AND SIR ORLANDO BRIDGEMAN, BART., LORD CHIEF JUSTICE OF THE COMMON PLEAS,

"THE HUMBLE PETITION OF THE INHABITANTS OF LOWESTOFT IN THE COUNTY OF SUFFOLK,

"Sheweth,

"That your poor petitioners having had several hearings before his Majesty in council, concerning the differences between them and the rich inhabitants of Yarmouth, respecting the free trade of herring fishery; who thereupon was pleased to refer the same to the right honourable the Lords assembled in Parliament, who, upon a full hearing thereof, were pleased to refer the matter of law to the reverend judges, to consider whether the statute of 31 Edward III, ch. i and ii be repealed by the statute 2 Richard II, ch. vii., or by any other statute, and to report their opinion to the house accordingly. And your petitioners having awaited six months for relief, and being quite worn out with expense and attendance, and are not able any longer to contend with such powerful adversaries, who, by delays and all other possible means, strive to ruin your poor petitioners and the whole western fishery, and to monopolise the whole trade of herring fishing, to the great prejudice of the kingdom in general, as appears by the certificate of many hundreds of the western fishermen, the certificate of the fishmongers in London, and a remonstrance of the burgesses of parliament for the sea coast towns in the county of Suffolk.

"They therefore most humbly pray, That your lordships would be graciously pleased to appoint a day of meeting, with the rest of the reverend judges; and that the counsel on both sides may attend your lordships, so that in a convenient time you may report your sense to their lordships in parliament, as is desired in their orders of the 20th of this present June.

"And your petitioners, as in duty bound, shall ever pray."

A petition was also presented from the town of Lowestoft to the House of Peers, wherein, after reciting the order of reference to the judges, they doubted not but that their Lorships would evidently for see the ruin which threatened the town of Lowestoft, the western and northern fishery, and the great damage that would accrue to the city of London and the nation in general; as appears from the certificates of many hundreds of fishermen, and the remonstrance of the fishmongers in London, and the burgesses of the sea-coast towns in Suffolk, if the Yarmouth men were suffered to persevere in the cruel depredations which they had lately practiced; for, exclusive of distressing them in late unhappy wars, assisting Oliver Cromwell in taking and plundering the town, imprisoning many of their principal inhabitants, and causing others to fly beyond the sea, they now distressed them again by sending a vessel, called a man of war to ride in the roads before the town of Lowestoft during the whole herring season, and not suffering the fishers to deliver any herrings in those roads, but compelling them to go to Yarmouth, whereby their petitioners and the western and northern fishermen were greatly injured, and a thousand last of herrings were thereby prevented from being caught. Therefore they humbly beseech their lordships to afford them such relief as they in their great wisdom should deem meet and reasonable; that so they might follow the trade of herring-fishing as usual, and prevent their becoming the most miserable people in his Majesty's dominions.

"To THE RIGHT HONOURABLE THE LORDS SPIRITUAL AND TEMPORAL IN PARLIAMENT ASSEMBLED,

"THE HUMBLE PETITION OF THE INHABITANTS OF THE TOWN OF LOWESTOFT, IN THE COUNTY OF SUFFOLK.

"Sheweth, That your Lordships having been graciously pleased, after several hearings before his sacred Majesty in Council and your lordships in Parliament to recommend the difference between your poor petitioners and the rich inhabitants of Yarmouth unto the reverend judges, to report to your Lordships their sense therein; we doubt not but your Lordships will further understand the threatening ruin which attends both, them and the western and northern fishery the damage to the city of London and to the kingdom in general, as appears by the certificate of many hundreds of fishermen, the remonstrance of the fishmongers in London, and the burgesses of this present Parliament for the sea-coasts towns of the county of Suffolk, if the Yarmouth men persevere in their cruel practices, as of late these have done, by spoiling your poor petitioners, as in the late unhappy wars, assisting Oliver Cromwell in taking and plundering the town, imprisoning many of the chief inhabitants, and others, who left their relations, fled beyond the sea into his Majesty's maritime service; and as if that were not sufficient, when upon his majesty's most happy restoration, your petitioners hope for a happy and comfortable issue of all their calamaties, even then the men of Yarmouth, taking advantage of your petitioners' poverty, most cruelly practiced their utter ruin, by sending a man of war as they called her, to ride in the roads before the town the whole season of the herring-fishing, not suffering the fishers to deliver any herrings in the said roads, but forced them to carry them all to Yarmouth; whereby your petitioners and the poor fishermen were despoiled of their trade, and fewer herrings were taken that year by at least one thousand lasts, than otherwise would have been.

"And whereas his most excellent majesty, with the advice of his privy council, hath been graciously pleased, by his royal proclamation, to promote and encourage the trade of herring-fishery, as his royal progenitors have done; and also sent forth a fleet of burses, which must necessarily suffer proportionably with the other fishery, if the Yarmouth men be suffered to continue such oppressive courses.

"They therefore most humbly pray. That your lordships would be graciously pleased, out of your great wisdom and pious regard to your poor petitioners and the fishermen, to afford them such relief in this their sad condition as in your grave wisdom shall seem just and fit. That after their so great sufferings expense and delays, they may not be rendered the most miserable people in all his majesty's dominions, but encouraged to follow their trade of herring-fishing (which time out of mind, they have used as their sole subsistence, and whereby many thousands of families may live and be maintained) the fishery being the nursery of seamen, may be preserved, navigation increased, to the great benefit of the kingdom in general, and the freedom of your poor petitioners from inevitable ruin, and who are no longer able to contend with such powerful adversaries.

"And your poor petitioners, as in duty bound, shall ever pray, etc."

The House of Lords being assembled on the 27th of June, the witnesses which were subpœned by the respective parties were called to the bar, to make their several depositions.

THE DEPOSITIONS OF THE LOWESTOFT WITNESSES, JAMES MUNDES, RICHARD GILLAM, SIDRICH SEAGER, JOHN GILL, WILLIAM FOX, AND JOHN HUMPHREY DEPOSED,

"1st. That the western fishers and others have frequently delivered herrings in Lowestoft roads in the time of the free fair held at Yarmouth, until this last year, when they were prevented by a man of war.

2nd, That the fishers, if they be compelled to carry all their herrings at Yarmouth, will lose a third part of their time, as well as ruin their voyage; because Yarmouth is to the north of Lowestoft, and the choicest sea for herrings is off Lowestoft, and to the southwards twenty miles, so that of necessity the fishermen must come first to Lowestoft, which they can oftentimes gain when it is impossible to get Yarmouth, when the wind is against their course, and may thereby save their night's drift; but if compelled to go to Yarmouth, must lose sometimes three or four nights, and lose the taking a great quantity of herrings.

"3rd. That the fishermen may have quicker dispatch at Lowestoft than at Yarmouth, and herrings may be brought fresher to land, and better to furnish the country; and also the ketches and pikers that frequently lay for London, Colchester, Ipswich, and other places, will meet with quicker dispatch than they had lately done.

4th. That although the fishers freely sell at Lowestoft, yet Yarmouth may be sufficiently, and as plentifully served with herrings as formerly they have been; and the whole coast may be well supplied, to the great advantage of the nation, the benefit of the country, and the supply of the city of London with fresh victuals. (The above witnesses also proved the inconveniences which would attend the fishermen in particular, as well as the kingdom in general, if there be not free liberty to sell herrings in Lowestoft roads.)

"5th. That when the fishers come first to Yarmouth, they must sell to none but their hosts, who give them what price they please."

Mr. PALGRAVE deposed, "That the Yarmouth men frequently discharge herrings out of the fishers before they come to the place where the fair is kept."

Mr. PALGRAVE and Mr. SAMUEL WILD proved the place where the fair is held, and at what place proclaimed first.

Mr. LOCKINGTON, Mr. NOY, Mr. GREEN, and the Fishmongers' certificate also proved the general damage which the fishmongers in London, as well as several other places, and also the kingdom in general would sustain, from their not being privileged to buy herrings at Lowestoft as well as at Yarmouth, as they could not be had so good nor so cheap at the latter place as at the former.

The fishermen's and the fishmongers' certificate do testify all the aforesaid matters, and the burgesses in Parliament for the county of Suffolk, do certify the same also.

After hearing the above evidence, their Lordships still declined passing a final determination upon the affair, until the judges, to whom they had referred for their opinion, concerning a point of law, had made their report; and therefore a second order to the judges was issued by their Lordships; wherein, after informing them that the witnesses belonging to both parties in the cause between Lowestoft and Yarmouth having been heard that day at the bar of that House, and being desirous to hear the opinion of the judges, concerning the point of law referred to them, before any resolution was formed, it was ordered, that the judges should be as expeditious as possible in hearing the counsel on both sides relative to the matter in reference, and make their report accordingly, that so their Lordships might speedily terminate the business so long depending before them.

"DIE JOVIS, 27° Junij, 1661.

"This day the witnesses on both sides, in the controversy between the inhabitants of Lowestoft and the bailiffs of Great Yarmouth, were heard at the bar, concerning the usage and custom of fishing and selling of fish, and the House being desirous to hear the judges opinions before any resolution be given between them; it is ordered by the Lords in Parliament assembled, That the judges be desired to expedite the hearing of the counsel on both sides upon the matter of reference mentioned in the order of the 20th of this **instant** June, and to make their report unto this House, with what convenient speed they can; that so their Lordships may put an end to the business now depending before them.

JO. BROWNE, Cleric. Parliamenti.

The judges returned for answer to their Lordships, that their attention being wholly engaged with the great and important affairs of the nation, and also that upon account of the approaching assizes, they were under the necessity of setting off very shortly upon their circuit; therefore they begged to inform their Lordships, that they were unable to deliver their opinion concerning the matter of reference mentioned in the order of the 20th instant, until the months of October or December next. Thus the final decision of this long-contested difference was further protracted, and the herring season being now nearly approaching, wherein the Lowestoft men and also the northern and west country fishermen would be exposed to the usual insults and depredations of the Yarmouth men they were seized with the most alarming apprehensions that the moment was now hastily approaching wherein they were to be sacrificed to the malice and revenge of their inveterate enemies. In order, therefore, to divert the impending ruin, and to guard against the danger which threatened them, they once more made application to their former and only protectors, the House of Lords; to whom they addressed themselves in a petition, representing to their Lordships, that they had presented an address to the judges, beseeching them to appoint a day for the counsel belonging to the respective parties to attend them, but by reason of the great and weighty affairs of the nation, and the approaching assizes, they could not deliver their report before the months of October or December next; but that lest, during the interval, their petitioners and the northern and western fishermen should be interrupted in the free exercise of their trade of herring-fishing, which was now approaching, as they were the last year, by the outrageous violences of the Yarmouth men; they implored their lordships, that they might be protected from the oppressions of the enemies during the ensuing herring season, and also until such time as the judges shall have made a report to their Lordships concerning the point of law referred to them in the order of the 20th June last.

"To the Right Honourable the PEERS of ENGLAND, assembled in Parliament.

"The Humble PETITION of the INHABITANTS of the Town of LOWESTOFT in the County of Suffolk,

"Sheweth,

"That your Lordships having been graciously pleased, upon the humble suit and prayer of your poor petitioners, to hear the difference between them and the rich inhabitants of Yarmouth, concerning the herring fishing, and to refer to the judges for their consideration, a matter of law, whether the statute of 31 Edward III, ch. i and ii be repealed by the statute of 2 Richard II, ch. vii, or by any other statute. And your petitioners having accordingly made their humble address to their Lordships to appoint a day for the counsel on both sides to attend them, who, by reason of the great and weighty affairs of the nation, and the approaching assizes, could not answer your Lordships' desires therein before the months of October or December next. And lest, in the meantime, your petitioners and the poor fishermen should be disturbed in the free exercise of their trade of herring-fishing now nearly approaching, to the threatening ruin of them and their families, as the men of Yarmouth practised the last year by force and violence.

"They therefore most humbly pray, That your Lordships would be pleased, out of your great wisdom and pious regard to your poor petitioners, to afford them relief in this their so great sufferings in the late war, a lamentable fire, and great expenses in this unhappy contest, that they be not rendered the most miserable people in his Majesty's dominions; but that they may, by your Lordships' protection, be encouraged to exercise their trade of herring-fishing, without molestation from the Yarmouth men, the purchasing a present subsistence for themselves and families, until the judges shall deliver their opinion to your Lordships, in pursuance of your orders.

"And your petitioners, as in duty bound, shall ever pray, etc."

In consequence of this petition, an order was immediately issued by the Lordships, directing that town of Lowestoft, and also the northern and west country fishermen, should be permitted to carry on the said fishery as usual, without any interruption or molestation from the Yarmouth men, until such time as the judges had delivered their report concerning the statutes of 31 Edward III, and 2 Richard II.

DIE LUNÆ, 22° July, 1661.

"Ordered by the Lords in Parliament assembled, that the northern and western fishermen are hereby empowered to fish this season of the herring fishery about the town of Yarmouth, as formerly they have done, for three years before the last year, with a salvo to the said town of Yarmouth and the town of Lowestoft; the right of which fishing now depends before the Lords in Parliament.

JOHN BROWNE, Cleric Parliamenti."

THE ORDER.

"Whereas there is a controversy depending in the House of Lords assembled in Parliament, between the inhabitants of the town of Lowestoft in the county of Suffolk, and the town of Great Yarmouth, in the county of Norfolk, concerning the right and free trade of herring fishing, and of buying and selling the said fish. And whereas upon hearing of the counsel on both sides, it is ordered, by the said Lords, That it be referred to the judges, to consider whether the statute of 31 Edward III, ch. i and if be repealed by the statute of 2 Richard II, ch. vii, or by any other statute; and that the judges are to deliver their opinion unto the said House of Lords. And in regard much damage may arise, not only to the inhabitants of the aforesaid towns of Lowestoft and Yarmouth, and also to the northern and western fishermen, as well as to his Majesty's kingdom in general, if some course be not taken for the preservation of the said free trade of herring fishing: be it therefore enacted, by the King's most excellent Majesty, with the Lords and Commons assembled in Parliament, that fishermen from henceforth shall and may have free liberty and full power to sell herring at all times, at their pleasure, at the town of Lowestoft, or elsewhere, and shall not be compelled to carry the same to Yarmouth; any statute, custom, or usage to the contrary thereof, in any wise notwithstanding: provided that this Act is only to continue and stand in force until the judges have certified their opinions to the House of Lords as aforesaid, and the said differences be settled, and the rights be established and confirmed to such party as the same by law doth properly appertain."

The judges soon after returned from the circuit; but in consequence of the many important affairs they were engaged in, respecting the nation, they were unable to appoint a day for hearing the allegations of the respective parties before the 4th December; when, at a meeting of their Lordships for that purpose, they appointed the 24th of January next ensuing, at three o'clock in the afternoon, for both parties, with their respective counsel, to appear before them at Sergeants' Inn Hall, in Fleet street, in order to examine the complaints of the several parties, and to hear what each of them had to advance in support of their respective privileges and pretensions.

"DECEMBER 4TH, 1661.

"We do appoint Friday the 24th of January, next ensuing, at three of the clock in the afternoon to hear the matter in difference between the bailiffs of Great Yarmouth in the county of Norfolk, and the inhabitants of Lowestoft, in the county of Suffolk; at which time both parties are desired to attend us, with their counsel, at Serjeant's Inn Hall, Fleet street.

"R. FOSTER, ALAN BRIDGEMAN, MATTHEW HALE, THO. MALET, ROBERT HYDE, EDWD. ATKYNS, THOMAS TWISDEN, THOMAS TYRREL, WM. WYNDHAM, CH. TURNER.

Com. Board."

"In consequence of this appointment of the judges, both the parties, with their counsel, appeared before their Lordships on the 24th of January; who, after hearing what each party had to advance in support of their several pretensions and also duly investigating their respective claims and privileges, they soon after made their report of the same to the House of Lords; and in consequence thereof it was ordered by their Lordships, that the counsel belonging to each party do attend at the bar of that House, on Wednesday, the 26th of that instant February, at nine o'clock in the morning, in order to sum up the evidence, given at a hearing of the cause, before their Lordships, and to state the case to the House, that such a final determination may be passed as their Lordships shall think just and reasonable.

"DIE SABBATHI, 20° FEBRY., 1661.

"Upon the report of the Lord Chief Justice of the Common Pleas, concerning the business relating to the towns of Yarmouth and Lowestoft, concerning their fishing; and a petition of the inhabitants of the said town of Lowestoft, read this day after the report was made; it was ordered by the Lords spiritual and temporal in Parliament assembled, That the Counsel on both sides are to be heard at the bar on Wednesday next, the twenty-sixth of this instant February, at nine of the clock in the morning, to sum up the evidence formerly given at a hearing before their Lordships, and to state the case to the House, that such determination may be given therein as their Lordships shall think fit.

JO. BROWNE, Cleric. Parliamenti.

The House of Lords being assembled on the 26th February, 1661-2, the Council on both sides were called to the bar of the House; when, after a full hearing of their respective evidence, and duly weighing the report of the judges, and after a long and serious debate amongst their Lordships concerning the whole matter; it was resolved, declared, and adjudged, by a vote of the Lords spiritual and temporal, that since the judges, in their report, had given their opinion, that the statute of the 31st of Edward III, chap. i and it hath not been repealed by the statute, but continues in full force and effect; but that concerning the principal point in dispute, viz., From what place the seven miles, the boundary of the liberties of Yarmouth, (and mentioned in the said statute of the 31st of Edward III) was to be measured, had been left by the judges to the determination of their Lordships. Therefore it was ordered by their Lordships that an admeasurement of the said seven miles should actually be made some time between that day and the 24th of June next, by the several and respective sheriffs of the counties of Norfolk and Suffolk, beginning from the *crane key* in the haven of Great Yarmouth aforesaid; and at the end thereof a new post should be erected, to denote the termination of the same; and within which extent the said bailiffs and corporation of Yarmouth were to enjoy their full privileges and immunities as the said statute of the 31st of Edward III and their other charters do afford them, and no farther.

" DIE MERCURII, 26° Feby., 1661-2.

" Upon hearing counsel on the twentieth day of June last, at the bar, on the behalf of the inhabitants of Lowestoft, in the county of Suffolk, plaintiffs; and the counsel for the bailiffs of Great Yarmouth, in the county of Norfolk, on the behalf of themselves and that corporation, defendants; upon their several petitions depending before the Lords in Parliament, concerning the herring-fishing, and buying and selling of herrings in the fair of Great Yarmouth aforesaid; it was then ordered by this house to be referred to the judges to consider whether the statue of the 31st of Edward III. ch. i. and ii., be repealed by the statute of the 2nd of Richard II. ch. vii., or by any other statute. And that the counsel on both sides should attend the said judges in that behalf; and a report having been since made unto this House by the Lord Chief Justice of the Common Pleas, that he and others of the judges had, according to the said order of the twentieth of June, heard the counsel on both sides, and considered of the statutes therein referred to them; and that they all are of opinion, that neither the statute of the 2nd of Richard II. nor any other statute, had repealed the statute of the 31st of Edward III.; but that the said statute of the 31st of Edward III., in that behalf, is in full force and effect. But as for the great matter of the differences between the petitioners, and the town of Yarmouth, concerning from what place the seven miles mentioned in the said statute of the 31st of Edward III., was to be measured, the judges had left that point to the determination of this House. Whereupon the Lords this day heard the counsel on both sides at the bar, in order to sum up the evidence formerly given before their Lordships; who also stated the cause to the House. And after a long and serious debate amongst their Lordships, it is resolved, declared, and adjudged, by the votes of the Lords spiritual and temporal, in Parliament assembled, That there shall be a measurement made between this day and the 24th of June next after the date hereof, by the several and respective sheriffs of the counties of Norfolk and Suffolk, from the *crane key* in the haven of Great Yarmouth aforesaid, to extend seven measured miles from the said crane key, and no farther; at which place a new post is to be set up, to bound the limits aforesaid. Within which extent the said bailiffs and corporation of Yarmouth are to enjoy their full privileges and immunities, as the said statute of the 31st of Edward III. and their charters do afford them, and no farther.

Jo BROWN, Cleric. Parliamenti."

Thus was this great and litigious contest at length finally determined; and therefore the next business necessary to be undertaken on the part of Lowestoft, was to see that the order of the House was carried into execution. In order to this purpose a letter, addressed to the bailiffs of Yarmouth, was sent from the gentlemen concerned for Lowestoft, acquainting them with the decision of the Lords; and also further informing them, that as the time limited by their Lordships for making the admeasurement would expire on the 24th of June next ensuing, they requested that they would resolve upon a certain day, during that interval, on which the men of Lowestoft, together with the sheriffs, might attend them, and make the said admeasurement.

"To the Bailiffs of Great Yarmouth, Norfolk," March 4th, 1661-2.

"Gentlemen,—There having been a controversy depending between the towns of Lowestoft in Suffolk, and Great Yarmouth in Norfolk, for a very long time concerning the herring fishing, which, after several hearings the last year before his Majesty in Council, he was graciously pleased to refer the matter to the Lords in Parliament, who having heard at their bar the learned counsel on both sides, and where the case was also stated; after a long and serious debate among their Lordships, it was resolved, declared and adjudged, by the votes of the Lords spiritual and temporal assembled, that there shall be a a measurement made between this day (the 26th of February) and the 24th of June next after the date thereof, by the several and respective sheriffs of the counties of Norfolk and Suffolk, from the crane key in the haven of Great Yarmouth aforesaid, and to extend seven measured miles and no farther; at which place a new post is to be set up, to bound the limits aforesaid. And in order thereunto, we, whose names are hereunto subscribed, do desire that you will affix a certain time, when and where you will please to meet and make the said admeasurement that accordingly you may be attended by,

"Gentlemen, your Servants,

"John Pellus, Geo. Reeve, Richd. Cooke, John Bayspoole, Henry Felton, John Rous, Robert Brooke, Thos. Waldgrave, Edmund Pooley."

Accordingly the 27th of May was as agreed on by the respective parties to meet and undertake the admeasurement of the said seven miles; but the Yarmouth men being so much disappointed and chagrined at the late decision of the House of Lords in favour of the town of Lowestoft, and also perceiving that all their attempts for carrying into execution their favourite and long-projected scheme of wholly excluding the town of Lowestoft from the herring-fishery, and monopolising it to themselves, totally frustrated, that they had recourse to stratagem, and endeavoured to accomplish by artifice what they were unable to obtain by legal proceedings. In order, therefore, to effect their designs, they endeavoured to evade the order of the House, by attempting to prevent its being carried into execution. For which purpose they not only prevailed upon Sir Richard Bacon, the high sheriff of Norfolk, to be absent at making the admeasurement, but also so far influenced the under sheriff, Mr. Roger Smith, that when the gentlemen appointed to superintend it were assembled at Yarmouth, in order to undertake it, the said under sheriff absolutely refused to concur with them therein, expecting thereby to render every measure that should be then taken, totally void and of none effect. A circumstantial account of the proceedings in this very extraordinary business, as well as the opinion and behaviour of the Lowestoft people concerning the same, will more fully appear from the following narrative of the case, as drawn up soon after by special order and appointment:

## A NARRATIVE

Concerning the proceedings upon an order of the House of Lords, bearing date the 26th of February, 1661-2; wherein the determination of the admeasurement of the seven miles from the crane key in Yarmouth, towards Lowestoft, was referred to the two several and respective sheriffs of Norfolk and Suffolk.

"WE, whose names are underwritten (whereof seven of us are the next adjacent justices of the peace, and of equal regard to the interests of both towns—Sir John Playters, Sir George Woodhouse, Sir Henry Bacon, Sir

John Pettus, Sir William Coke, John Bedingfield, Esq., and Thomas Scrivener, Esq—, besides many other gentlemen of quality in both counties), being solicited by the inhabitants of Lowestoft, and also sensible of the great importance the adjusting of the differences, and the admeasurement of the said seven miles is of, not only to the peace and advantage of the respective parties in particular, but to the fishery of this kingdom in general, did, on the 27th of May, at nine o'clock in the morning, attend the arrival of the sheriffs at the foot of the bridge entering the town of Yarmouth, being the place and day appointed by the sheriffs.

And whereas about eleven o'clock the under sheriff of Norfolk appeared, and made his excuse for the high sheriff, namely, "That he was at his house, about thirty miles distant, and not in health." But that he, the under sheriff, was sufficiently empowered to dispatch the business. Soon after the under sheriff appeared the second time, and informed us that he expected the high sheriff, and desired that his employment in this business might be suspended as long as possible. So that apprehending we should be disappointed of both the high sheriffs, and conceiving the under sheriffs might proceed in the undertaking, the town of Lowestoft desired (because the day was far spent, and lest our journey and trouble might be to no purpose) that the under sheriffs would undertake and begin the admeasurement.

On this proposal, the under sheriff for Norfolk made several cavils concerning the House of Lords, declaring that it was not of sufficient validity to dispose of other people's right; and that there was no certain and legal mode of composing the differences, but by a trial at common law.

On the other hand, the town of Lowestoft insisted on his obedience to their Lordships' order, and pressed him that he would undertake and begin the admeasurement from the crane key, according to order. The under sheriff replied, that the whole river, from the bridge to the haven's mouth, (which extends full two miles) was the crane key, as he had been informed; and that the admeasurement might as properly begin at the haven's mouth as at any other place.

On this assertion, some of us (for better satisfaction) went into the town of Yarmouth, and viewed the place; and found that there was no other crane standing between the bridge and the haven's mouth, but only that which is mentioned in their Lordships' order. And that this key, upon which the crane now standeth, hath ever been called the crane key, and no other; as was testified by several ancient Yarmouth men. It is true that there are several other keys, belonging to private persons, but those keys are maintained at the particular charge of the owners. But this key whereon the crane standeth is town ground, and doth solely belong to the town, and hath been called so time out of mind, and is placed just opposite to their Custom House. And the ground wheron their crane standeth is abutted and bounded by Mr. George England's key towards the south, and Mr. James Johnson's key towards the north, by the haven on the west, and the Custom House on the east. And there is no crane upon any other key; so that we affirmed that there could be no other crane key but this, from whence the admeasurement ought to begin. But the under sheriff told us, that he was not satisfied that he ought to begin at that place, because the name of the key was so general; notwithstanding, for above a mile and a half by the river, there is no key, nor crane, but upon the aforesaid public key.

Whereupon we advised the under sheriff of Norfolk to begin where his own reason dictated, and to certify the place to the House of Lords, and the reasons for their begining there, and to leave the determination thereof to their Lordships. But the under sheriff refused to comply with this proposal, and still persisted to affirm that there Lordships had no legal power to alienate any person's right to another. To which we replied, That their Lordships' order was not giving away another person's right, but an explanation or direction how that right might be enjoyed: and that it was not intended that the least portion should be taken from the seven miles, (which is all that the Yarmouth men have a just claim to), but to point out where the seven miles ought to begin, and where to end, according to their Lordships' order.

But the under sheriff still continuing obstin-ate, retired from us into the town, where he dined with the bailiffs, etc.

On the same day, the 27th of May, about three o'clock in the afternoon, the under sheriff of Norfolk was again requested to concur with the under sheriff of Suffolk, and assist in the said admeasurement; but he not only refused to join with him in the undertaking, but returned many unhandsome answers to some of the justices who made the request. In consequence of the refusal, the Lowestoft people entreated the under sheriff of Suffolk to engage two surveyors, of honest reputation and sufficient abilities, and proceed to the admeasurement. And although it had been more easy and advantageous for the Lowestoft men to begin the admeasurement on the other side of the crane key, or the opposite side of the water (whereby they would then have walked wholly upon Suffolk ground), yet, (that the town of Yarmouth might be privy, if they chose it, to what so nearly concerned them) the said under sheriff for Suffolk and the two surveyors (with some hazard to all our persons) began the said admeasurement from the foundation of the crane, upon the public town key, and continued to measure, in as direct a line as possible, to the place where the boat was to conduct them over to the Suffolk shore; and though they measured the breadth of the water which they crossed over, containing eighteen poles in length, yet they did not compute it in the admeasurement of the said seven miles.

It was near four o'clock when they began the admeasurement; and notwithstanding the under sheriff of Norfolk exerted his utmost efforts, and in the most public manner endeavoured to obstruct their proceedings as far as the gate of the town, where he left us; and afterwards the people of the town continued to pursue us in great multitudes, with much insolence, provoking language, and many disturbances, no magistrate appearing to disperse them, yet the under sheriff at Suffolk, riding by the two surveyors, finished the admeasurement about half-an-hour before sun-set that day; the period of the seven miles falling short eighteen poles of the ancient limits of the said seven miles, exclusive of the breadth of the haven before mentioned, which was not computed in the admeasurement.

During this whole transaction, two of the justices, together with the two surveyors, kept an exact account of the number of the length of every chain: and to prevent any mistakes, on the conclusion of the undertaking, the under sheriff, in the presence of the whole company, with a sealed yard and two feet rule, measured the said chain; which measure contained four poles, every pole being sixteen feet and a half, according to the statute measure of the 35th of Elizabeth, ch. vii. So that ten of those chains' length made a furlong, and eight furlongs a mile; and on the ending of the said seven miles thus measured, the under sheriff hath ordered a post to be set up. In testimony of the proceedings, we have set our hands this 28th day of May, Anno Domi, 1662.

    Jo. Playters, H. Bacon, Wm. Cooke, Jo. Bedingfield, Jo. Hall, Cyriac Cooke, Tho. Leman, Rich. Palgrave, G. Woodhouse, Jo. Peltus, Wm. Crane, Rich. Vyner, Tho. Scrivener, Tho Plumstead, Antho. Jenkinson, Wm. Gooch, Ja. Defebure. Jo. Pulham, Tho. Fulcher, surveyors; Jo. Wythe, sub-surveyor.

### THE TESTIMONY OF THE HIGH SHERIFF FOR SUFFOLK.
"May 28th, 1662.

"Coming the last night to Yarmouth (being evening the of the day appointed, by mutual consent, for making the admeasurement), and from thence this morning to Lowestoft, I found the persons above written remaining there; who were pleased to give me this narrative of my under sheriff's proceedings, as above said. And I do hereby approve of the said admeasurement, as conceiving it to be a means of determining the differences of the said two towns.

ROG. WILLIAMS, High Sheriff for the county of Suffolk."

All the gentlemen who have signed the narrative, together with the other persons of distinction who had attended the admeasurement, and also the high sheriff and under sheriff for the county of Suffolk, were entertained by the town the next day, viz.: the 28th May, at the Swan inn, at Lowestoft. This house, at that time, was the principal inn in the town; and was situated on the east side of the High street, on the south side of the passage leading to the sea, called, from the adjoining inn, the Swan score; as was also the opposite lane called the Swan Lane. In an apartment in this inn Oliver Cromwell was entertained when he came to Lowestoft.

On the evening of the 27th May, the gentlemen who had attended the admeasurement, met the gentlemen of Lowestoft, at the Swan inn in this town, and the next day was spent in great festivity and rejoicing, for having so happily concluded this important undertaking; and on the 20th of June following the post was erected, according to the order of the House of Lords.

The next business which the Lowestoft men proceeded to examine into, was the conduct of the under sheriff of Norfolk, respecting his contemptuous behaviour at the late admeasurement to the order of the House of Lords; and thereupon resolved to present a petition to their lordships, complaining of the under sheriff's conduct in that affair; and also of the insults which they had received from the Yarmouth men during the late herring season, notwithstanding their lordships' orders to the contrary; and therefore prayed their lordships to enforce their said order for the admeasurement, and to issue such further orders for the future security f their petitioners as might protect them against any insults or interruptions of their powerful and malicious enemies.

"To the right honourable the LORDS Spiritual and Temporal, in **Parliament assembled,**

"The humble PETITION of the INHABITANTS of the town of **LOWESTOFT in SUFFOLK,**

Sheweth

"That after several hearings before your lordships in Parliament concerning the herring fishery, between your petitioners and the town of Great Yarmouth, the matter of difference being from what place the seven miles mentioned in the statute of the 31st of Edward III were to be measured, your lordships were pleased, by your vote of the 26th February, 1661-2, 'To resolve, declare, and adjudge, That an admeasurement should be made between that time and the 24th of June following, by the respective sheriffs of Norfolk and Suffolk, from the crane key of Yarmouth, and to extend seven miles towards Lowestoft and no further. At which place a new post was to be set up, to bound the limits aforesaid; and within which extent the Corporation of Yarmouth were to enjoy their full privileges, and no further?' That thereupon your petitioners attended the said sheriffs, who, in pursuance of your lordships said order, appointed the 27th of May then next following, to meet at Yarmouth and make the admeasurement accordingly. At which time their respective under sheriffs did meet; but the under sheriff of Norfolk refused to join to make the admeasurement, declaring that your lordships' order was not of sufficient validity to give away another's right. That your petitioners insisted on his obedience to your lord-ships' order, and requested the under sheriff of Suffolk (in case the other would not join) to begin to measure the seven miles; who taking to him two surveyors, did, in the presence of many justices of the peace and gentlemen of quality, with a chain, measure from the said crane key, seven miles towards Lowestoft; and at the end thereof caused a new pole to be set up, and the high sheriff of Suffolk, under his hand, approved thereof, as by a narrative hereunto **annexed doth more** fully appear That **the town of** Yarmouth (notwithstanding your lordships' order) has since come with **boats,** during this last herring season, and disturbed your petitioners and **divers** fishers, near three miles beyond the said post towards Lowestoft, even in their south roads, chasing the fishermen, and enforcing them to carry all their herrings to Yarmouth; and by reason of the plenty thither carried, the Yarmouth men have set the price of them from 50s. down to 30s. per last, and some under; and some were enforced to throw their herrings away. So that the poor fishers, by reason of the small price, did not get a sufficiency to make good their tackling, to the apparent ruin of the fishers, the great damage to the whole kingdom, and the utter undoing of your petitioners; they being impoverished and wearied **out with** the endless suits of their great and powerful adversaries.

"Wherefore your petitioners humbly pray, that your lordships would be pleased to ratify and confirm the aforesaid admeasurement, made in pursuance of your lordships' order, and that out of your great wisdoms you will be graciously pleased to provide for the future security and quiet of your poor petitioners and fishermen; whereby they may with peace and comfort use and enjoy their trade of herring fishing, as formerly they have done, free from the disturbance of their powerful and malicious adversaries.

"And your petitioners, as in duty bound, shall ever pray,"

In consequence of this petition, the House of Lords, on the 30th of April, 1663, issued a warrant, directed to the Serjeant-at-Arms, to apprehend the body of Robert Smith, late under sheriff of the county of Norfolk, as a delinquent, for acting against the honour and dignity of that house, and to bring him forthwith before the Lords in Parliament assembled to answer for his said great offence.

"DIE LUNÆ, 13° April, 1663.

"The house being this day certainly informed by oath, that Roger Smith, late under sheriff of the county of Norfolk, hath disobeyed a judgment of this House of the 26th of February, 1661-2, concerning the inhabitants of Lowestoft and the town of Great Yarmouth, by forbearing to execute the same as was directed; and using flighting words, in a most contemptuous manner, against the honour and dignity of the House of Peers: It is ordered, by the Lords, Spiritual and Temporal, in Parliament assembled, That the Sergeant at-Arms attending this House, or his deputies, shall take the body of the said Roger Smith, as a delinquent, and forthwith bring him before the Lords in Parliament, to answer the said great offence. And this to be a sufficient warrant in that behalf. JO. BROWNE, Cleric Parliamenti.

"To the Sergeant-at-Arms attending this House, deputy or deputies; and to all Mayors, Justices, and others his Majesty's officers, to be aiding in the execution of his order."

It was further ordered that the admeasurement therein directed to be made and performed, should be executed again by the present Sheriffs of Norfolk and Suffolk, between the 15th of that instant April and the 24th of June then next.

"DIE LUNÆ, 15° April, 1663.

"Upon the oaths of Sir Henry Bacon, baronet, and Sir John Pettus, knight, made this day at the bar; and the reading of a narrative subscribed by several Justices of the Peace, and many other gentlemen of quality of both the counties of Norfolk and Suffolk, on behalf of the townsmen of Lowestoft, in the said county of Suffolk. That on viewing the premises they find, that this key whereon the crane now standeth hath ever been called the crane key, and no other. And a resolution, declaration, and judgment, passed by the vote of the Lords Spiritual and Temporal, in the high court of Parliament assembled, dated the 26th February, 1661-2, between the said inhabitants of Lowestoft, and the bailiffs of Great Yarmouth, in the county of Norfolk, for the measurement of seven miles from the said crane key, in the haven of Yarmouth aforesaid, and to extend seven measured miles from the said key and no further, hath been disobeyed, and contemptuously neglected to be executed, by Roger Smith, the late under sheriff of Norfolk, although he was earnestly pressed to yield obedience, by making an admeasurement of the said seven miles, from the said crane key, as in the said judgement is directed; of which neglect and disobedience this House is very sensible. It is therefore now ordered and declared, by the Lords Spiritual and Temporal, in Parliament assembled, That a punctual obedience shall be yielded unto their former judgment, and that the measurement therein directed to be made and performed by the present sheriffs for the said counties, be made between the date hereof and the four and twenty day of June next ensuing. JO. BROWNE, Cleric Parliamenti."

Pursuant to these orders, letters were immediately sent to the sheriffs of Norfolk and Suffolk, from the gentlemen in the interest of Lowestoft, informing them, that the House of Lords had voted the late under sheriff of Norfolk, a delinquent, for his contempt of their order; and had ordered him to appear at the bar of their House to answer for the same. And that their Lordships insisted on a punctual obedience being paid to their order of the 26th of February, 1661-2, for an admeasurement, and to be carried into execution by the said sheriffs some time between the 13th of that instant April, and the 24th June next ensuing

"TO THE SHERIFFS OF THE COUNTIES OF NORFOLK AND SUFFOLK,
"London, 16th April, 1663.

GENTLEMEN, There having been a controversy depending a long time between the towns of Yarmouth in Norfolk, and Lowestoft in Suffolk, concerning the herring fishery; and after several hearings before his Majesty in Council and their Lordships in Parliament; it was ordered by the vote of the Lords Spiritual and Temporal, the 26th February, 1661-2, That the privileges of the seven miles granted to Yarmouth by the statute of 31 Edward III should be measured from the crane key in Yarmouth, towards Lowestoft, and at the end thereof a new post should be set up, which; accordingly was done. But the under-Sheriff of Norfolk refusing to join and yield obedience to their Lordship's decrees, the under-Sheriff of Suffolk, at the importunity of Lowestoft made the said admeasurement, and drew up a narrative of the whole proceeding, which was subscribed by many gentlemen of quality there present; which, with their petition, was read on the 13th of this instant, April 1663, in the House of Lords; and Sir Henry Bacon, Bart., and Sir John Pellus, knight, being called to the bar, affirmed the same on oath. Whereupon their Lordships debated the matter, and for the contempt of the under sheriff of Norfolk, it was then voted by the Lords Spiritual and Temporal, in Parliament assembled, That the said under sheriff should be sent for as a delinquent; and that a punctual obedience should be given and yielded to their former judgment; and that the admeasurement therein directed to be made and performed by the present sheriffs for the said counties should be made between the date thereof and the 24th of June next ensuing. And in order thereunto, we, whose name are hereunto subscribed, do desire, that you will affix a certain time when and where you will please to meet us, and make the said admeasurement, that accordingly you may be attended by some of us, who are,

"Gentlemen, your servants,
"HEN. BACON, JOHN ROUSE, RICHARD COOKE, EDM. POTRE, E. BACON, GEORGE REEVE.

(Sir George Reeve was judge, and lived at Oulton High House; but was buried at Long Stratton.)

"We desire that you appoint the time about the 21st or 24th of May, and then we will be there to attend you."

But during the interval the said under sheriff presented a petition to the House, informing their Lordships that in consequence of his being taken into custody by the Sergeant-at-Arms, from a complaint being lodged against him by the inhabitants of Lowestoft and divers gentlemen of that neighbourhood, he had sustained great injury and inconvenience in his own private affairs; and also, as receiver of the monthly assessments in the county of Norfolk, and other monies belonging to his Majesty, his confinement was extremely prejudicial to his Majesty's service. Therefore he prayed their Lordships either to discharge him from his confinement or to grant him a speedy hearing, so that he might prove his innocence, and discharge his duty to his Majesty.

"THE HUMBLE PETITION OF ROGER SMITH, OF THE CITY OF NORWICH,

"Sheweth, That upon a misinformation given to your lordships against your petitioner, this honourable House was pleased, on the 13th of this instant April, to order his being taken into custody by the Sergeant-at-Arms; by virtue whereof he is now under restraint, to his exceeding great damage, and the great neglect of the King's Majesty's service; your petitioner having the receipt of the monthly assessments in the county of Norfolk, and of other monies belonging to his Majesty; and to the great prejudice of other your petitioner's weighty affairs.

" Wherefore your petitioner most humbly prays your Lordships, that you will be pleased either to discharge him from his said restraint, or grant him a speedy hearing; whereby your petitioner may clear his innocence, and betake himself to the discharge of his duty on his Majesty's aforesaid service, and the dispatch of other his great employments.

And your petitioner, as in duty bound shall ever pray, etc.,
ROGER SMITH.

On the reading of this petition before this House, on the 29th of April, and also the narrative subscribed by the gentlemen who attended the admeasurement, it was ordered by their Lordships, that as the said under sheriff denies the accusation contained in the said narrative, that he be brought to the bar the next day morning at ten o'clock; and that the persons who presented the said narrative, and attested the same on oath, do also give their attendance at the same time, and make good their charge, as they will answer the contrary thereof to that House.

"Die Mercurii, 29th April, 1663.

"On reading the petition of Roger Smith, late under sheriff of the county of Norfolk, now in the custody of the Serjeant-at-Arms attending this House, for his delinquency in disobeying a judgment of this House, of the 26th Febuary, 1661-2, concerning Lowestoft and Yarmouth; and in reading a narrative subscribed by several justices of the peace ot Norfolk and Suffolk, setting out the said contempt: It is ordered, by the Lords Spiritual and Temporal in Parliament assembled, That the said Roger Smith (who denies the accusation of the said narrative) be brought to the bar to-morrow morning, at ten of the clock; at which time such as have appeared on bringing in the said narrative, and have attested the same on oath, and to give their attendance on this High Court, at the time aforesaid, to make good the said charge. And herein obedience is to be given by such as are concerned therein, as the contrary will be answered to the House. JNO. BROWNE, Cleric. Parliamenti,"

Accordingly, on the day following, the said Roger Smith, Esq., late under sheriff, and his opponents, appeared before the House; when their Lordships, after hearing what his accusers had to alledge against him, and not being satisfied with such defence as he was able to make in answer thereto, were pleased to order, That the said Roger Smith, for refusing to execute a judgment of that House, dated 26th February, 1661-2, and also for uttering scandalous words against the honour and dignity of that high court, should immediately acknowledge his fault, and make submission upon his knees at the bar of that House, before their Lordships, in the words following

"I do humbly beg your Lordships pardon, and express my hearty sorrow for not executing your Lordships' order, and for any unadvised words uttered by me, which might have any reflection upon your Lordships' judgment and order, concerning the matter in difference betwixt the towns of Lowestoft and Yarmouth."

And it was further ordered by their Lordships, that the said Roger Smith should make the like public submission in the face of the country, upon the place, and at the time appointed by that House, for the re-admeasurement to be made between the inhabitants of Lowestoft and the bailiffs of Great Yarmouth, according to a late order of that House of the 15th of that instant April; as he would answer for disobeying the same. And lastly that the said Roger Smith be released from his confinement, paying his fees.

"DIE JOVIS, 30° April, 1663.

"Whereas Roger Smith, late under sheriff of the county of Norfolk, was this day brought to the bar as a delinquent, for refusing to execute a judgment of this House, dated the 26th of February, 1661-2, concerning the inhabitants of Lowestoft and the bailiffs of Yarmouth; which was now confirmed upon oath by Sir Henry Bacon, Bart., and Sir John Pettus, knt., who formerly did swear to the truth of a narrative presented to their Lordships, subscribed by several justices of the peace, and other gentlemen of quality of the counties of Norfolk and Suffolk, relating to the said judgment. As also for scandalous words spoken by the said Roger Smith against the honour and dignity of this high court. It is therefore proposed by the Lords Spiritual and Temporal, in Parliament assembled, That the said Roger Smith do immediately make his submission upon his knees at the bar of this House, before their Lordships, in these words following: "I do humbly beg your Lordships' pardon, and express my hearty sorrow for not executing your Lordships' order, and for any unadvised words uttered by me, which might have any reflection put on your Lordships' judgment and order, concerning the matter in difference betwixt the towns of Lowestoft and Yarmouth." And it is further ordered by the authority aforesaid, That the said Roger Smith shall make the like public submission in the face of the country, upon the place, and at the time appointed by this House for the admeasurement to be made between the inhabitants of Lowestoft and the bailiffs of Yarmouth, according to a late order of this House, dated the 13th of this instant April; and herein obedience is to be given, as the contrary will be answered to this House. And lastly, That the said Roger Smith shall be **released of his present restraint or imprisonment, paying his fees. And this to be a sufficient warrant in that behalf.**

JOHN BROWNE, Cleric. Parliamenti."

All differences being thus far settled and adjusted, the next business which the inhabitants of Lowestoft proceeded upon, was to have the gentlemen in their interest inform the sheriffs of the counties of Norfolk and Suffolk that they appointed the 10th of June next ensuing, about ten o'clock in the morning, for the day whereon ot make the said second admeasurement, and to have the same convenience at Yarmouth.

THE SHERIFFS' ACCESSION TO THE APPOINTMENT FROM LOWESTOFT.

"We do agree to the day and place appointed by mutual consent, between the sheriffs of Norfolk and Suffolk and the inhabitants of Lowestoft, for making the admeasurement between the towns of Yarmouth and Lowestoft, according to the several orders in Parliament and to be on the tenth day of June next, about ten o'clock of the morning, in Yarmouth.

THO. MEADOWS,<br>JOSEPH BRAND.

22nd May, 1663.

In pursuance of this appointment, the order for the admeasurement was, without any difficulty or interruption, immediately carried into execution; and a certificate of the same was presented to the House of Lords on the 19th of June, 1663, by the right honourable Earl Cornwallis, attested by the sheriffs of Norfolk and Suffolk.

THE CERTIFICATE.

DIE 19TH JULY, 1663.

"To the right honourable the LORDS Spiritual and Temporal assembled in the High Court of Parliament.

"We the several and respective sheriffs of the counties of Norfolk and Suffolk, do humbly certify, to your Lordships, That, in obedience to an order of your honourable House, bearing date on Monday the fifteenth day of April last past, and of a former judgment of your honours bearing date the six and twentieth day of February, in the year of our Lord one thousand, six hundred and sixty-two, we have measured from the crane key, in the haven of Great Yarmouth, mentioned in your Lordships said last-mentioned judgement, seven miles, extending towards Lowestoft, there likewise mentioned. And in further pursuance of the said several orders and judgements, have, at the end of the said seven miles, given orders to set up a new post for the bounding of the limits, etc., according to your said orders and judgements, this present Wednesday, being the tenth day of June, in the fifteenth year of his Majesty's reign. JOSEPH BRAND, AND THOS. MEDOWES, Sheriffs.

"Whereas James Wilde did declare, upon oath, at the bar, that the handwritings wherewith the said certificate is subscribed, are the hand-writings of the several sheriffs of the counties of Norfolk and Suffolk, and that he, the said James Wilde, did see them write the same.

Jo. BROWNE, Cleric, Parliamenti."

Thus was this long dispute and sharply-contested law-suit between Yarmouth and Lowestoft, respecting the herring-fishery, and which had been prosecuted by the respective parties for upwards of four years with the utmost vehemence, at length happily terminated by a decisive order of the House of Lords. Too much praise for this important and happy event can never be expressed by the inhabitants of this town on their worthy and indefatigable townsmen Mr. James Wilde, Mr. Samuel Pacey, and Mr. Thomas Mighells, who were the principal managers of this suit, and who so generously exerted themselves, during the whole transaction, in promoting the happiness of the place of their nativity, by defending its indisputable rights and privileges, and rescuing it from the ruin which threatened to overwhelm it. Consequently, their memories deserve to be transmitted to the latest posterity with the highest respect, veneration, and gratitude; and as their services for the interest of the town are too beneficial and important ever to be forgotten, so they who obtained them are deserving of every possible testimony of respect from their grateful townsmen, who, to this day, are enjoying the fruits of their generous and unremitting labours for their benefit and happiness.

Soon after the settling of these differences, the town of Lowestoft sent letters of thanks to the several members of the House of Lords, who, during the debates, had interested themselves in defending and restoring to the town the re-possession of her ancient rights and privileges; namely, to Lord Hollis, the Earl of Anglesay, Earl Cornwallis, Lord Roberts, Lord Privy Seal, Lord Lucas, Lord Devereux, Lord Ashly Cooper, and others, acknowledging the many eminent services they had received from them; and assuring them, that for their great goodness and condescension, their Lordships would receive, as they were justly entitled, the thanks and prayers of many hundreds of the poor inhabitants of Lowestoft The subjoined letter serves as a specimen of the whole.

"To the LORD ROBERTS, Lord Privy Seal.

London, 28th June, 1663.

My good Lord, I being prevented taking my leave of your Lordship at my going into the country, do humbly beg your pardon. And by these presents I presume to return your Lordship the most humble and hearty thanks of the poor town of Lowestoft, and the fishermen thereof, for your great condescension in appearing for them against their rich and powerful adversaries of Yarmouth. For which your lordships will assuredly have the prayers of many hundreds, and God's acceptance of so charitable a work; rendering your name and fame ever deep in the memory of future ages. My Lord, it was my lot to follow the business of that poor town, encouraged by the friends of our cause, amongst whom your Lordship has been one of the most eminent. For which great kindness I cannot express my thankfulness so sufficiently as I would, being, alas!—Yet my good Lord, I shall presume to subscribe myself, your Lordship's ever most humble and grateful servant,

"JAMES WILDE."

The expenses incurred by the town of Lowestoft in this suit with Yarmouth, amounted in the whole to about six hundred pounds. It was observed, in the former part of this section, that the town, in order to defray the charges of the suit with Yarmouth in the reign of Queen Elizabeth, respecting the situation of Kirkley road, had recourse to the rents and profits of the town lands; but on this occasion they made use of other methods, such as were judged the least burthensome to the town in general, and most effectual for the purposes for which they were wanted; such as levying a tax upon the herring fishery, and also upon the brewers and coopers residing in Lowestoft. The first levy was made in 1660, at two shillings a last upon herrings, which raised £67 12s.; the second levy was made in 1661, at five shillings a last upon herrings, which raised £114 9s.; the third levy was made in 1663, in the same manner as in the preceding year, which raised £159 2s. 3d.; the forth levy was made in 1665, which raised £108; and the fifth and last levy was made in 1674 (in order for a final discharge of all debts incurred by the town in the prosecution of this suit), and was made after the rate of two shillings upon every last of herrings, which raised £70. The levy made upon the brewers and coopers raised the sum of £62 10s., and was also applied to the purposes above-mentioned.

But notwithstanding this final decision of the House of Lords, in favour of the town of Lowestoft, it appears that the burgesses of Yarmouth were extremely unwilling to relinquish their former pretentions; and were so attached to their former interest and practices, as shewed but too much inclination to renew the disputes and disturbances which had agitated and distressed the respective towns for many years past. For we find, that about Michaelmas, 1663, (the first herring season after making the second admeasurement) the Yarmouth men, with their boats, came into Lowestoft south roads, and seized two vessels, the one a Dutch yagger, with red herrings for Holland; the other a French fisherman; from the former they took a barrel of red herrings, until he paid 14/- which they claimed as a duty due to Yarmouth, the same as though the vessel had been laden in their haven; from the latter they took their fish kettles, valued at 13s. 4d., under the same pretence. From these arbitrary and illegal proceedings, the fishermen were so alarmed and intimidated, as to be deterred from delivering their herrings at Lowestoft any longer, to the great injury of the fishers, and detriment of the town, which was in danger of being greatly impoverished thereby To remedy this

P

inconvenience, Dr. Lewin, Judge of the Court of Admiralty in the county of Suffolk, for his royal highness the Duke of York, called a court at Lowestoft, in 1654, the jury whereof presented the Yarmouth men for exceeding the bounds which had been lately prescribed them, and fraudulently seizing the property of the fishermen. Shortly after Dr. Lewin called a second court at Lowestoft, and the Yarmouth men were summoned to appear, in order to make answer to the complaint of Lowestoft. The Yarmouth men appeared accordingly, and pretended to vindicate their proceedings upon the privileges of their charters. Dr. Lewin being more inclined to compromise the affair than to involve the parties in any fresh disputes, proposed, that if the Lowestoft men would forbear to prosecute the affair any farther, he would bury in oblivion, every appeal which had been made to that court; and therefore recommended it to each of the parties to pay their respective fees, and to suffer their differences, which only tended to revive their former animosities, totally to subside; and it seems that they agreed to Dr. Lewin's proposal, and the difference was settled to their mutual satisfaction.

ARTICLES of AGREEMENT Between the Respective Parties on Terminating the Dispute.

"1st, That the admeasurement lately made, and the boundary mark that is set up, be ratified and confirmed.

"2ndly, That all fishers be free to sell their herrings in the roads of Lowestoft, or in any other place beyond the said seven miles, without any disturbance or interruption from the Yarmouth men.

3rdly, That if any disturbance or interruption should be made by the Yarmouth men on the fishers or any others beyond the said seven miles, that the said Yarmouth men should forfeit £500, one moiety thereof to his Majesty, and the other moiety to——. Also the offending party to suffer three months' imprisonment, without bail.

"And, lastly, that if the Yarmouth men shall at any time imprison, either at their own town or in any other place, any of the fishermen, for delivering their herrings at Lowestoft, or any other place beyond the said seven miles, that the said Yarmouth men shall forfeit treble damages to the party aggrieved, and be imprisoned three months without bail."

However the Lowestoft men were so exceedingly alarmed at the late infringement on their ancient privileges, and so very apprehensive of being compelled to exhibit fresh complaints against the Yarmouth men, before the House of Lords, that they had renewed their application to the several peers of that House who had espoused their cause during the late debate before that assembly, soliciting their interest, should they be under the necessity of presenting to the House another petition relative to the injurious proceedings of the Yarmouth men.

"TO THE LORD ROBERTS, LORD PRIVY SEAL.

"London, 16th April, 1664.

"My good Lord, Your Lordship having been graciously pleased, from the very first, to appear for the poor town of Lowestoft and the fishermen, against their powerful adversaries of Yarmouth; for which great condescension your Lordship has the prayers of many hundreds depending upon the said fishery, and the most humble and hearty thanks of that poor town, who implore the continuance of your Lordship's favour; humbly beseeching your Lordship to peruse this short brief of the late pleadings before their Lordships in Parliament, and the cause of our present complaint that we are going up with to their Lordships, occasioned by the pride and malice of our potent adversaries, who concluded we were so disabled by the great charge of expense they had put us to, that we should never appear further in this matter, especially as they dared to shew such contempt for their Lordships' order and judgment. But so it is, my Lord, that unless your Lordship shall, upon our petition being read in the House, be graciously pleased to plead for our future peace and security, the poor fishermen and your petitioners must be inevitably ruined. I beg your Lordship's pardon for this presumption, which my necessity enforces me to, and for the favour in having access to your Lordship in this case, especially now in the absence of our highly-honoured friend the Lord Hollis; and that I may subscribe myself, my good Lord,

"Your Lordship's most humble and grateful servant,

"JAMES WILDE."

"To the LORD CORNWALLIS,

"London, 16th April, 1664.

"My good Lord, Your Lordship having been graciously pleased to understand the difference, and to appear for the poor town of Lowestoft and the fishermen, against their rich and powerful adversaries of Yarmouth, before the Lords in Parliament; for which great condescension your Lordship has the prayers of many hundreds depending on the said fishery, and the most humble and hearty thanks of that poor town, who implore the continuance of your Lordship's favour. And although many persons of honour, out of a sense of the equity of our case, have stood up in our defence, yet can we not apply to any so properly, as those of our own county, amongst whom, from an experience of your paternal care, I humbly beseech your Lordship to peruse this short brief of the late proceedings before your Lordship in Parliament, whereby your Lordship may easily discern the pride and malice of our adversaries, who, to the amazement of all our gentry, durst so slight the Lords' late orders and judgments. But their design was to spoil us at once; concluding, that we were so disabled by the charge and great expense of the late suit they have put us to, that we should never be able to stir any further in this matter; as, in truth, they might well suppose, it having cost our poor town, at least, upwards of £500, to the great impoverishment thereof. Yet, so it is, my Lord, that should we desist in our defence, no man of trade can stay to live in the town, except some few to till the ground. So that unless your Lordship shall, upon our petition, at the next sitting of the House, be graciously pleased to afford us relief, and plead for our future peace and security, we shall be inevitably ruined. I shall not dare your Lordship's further trouble at present, but beg pardon for this presumption, which our necessities compel me to; and acknowledge the favour of having access to your Lordship in this case, especially now in the absence of our highly honoured friend Lord Hollis, and that I may subscribe myself, as I am, my good Lord,

"Your Lordship's most humble and grateful servant,

"JAMES WILDE."

A similar letter was sent by the same writer to the EARL of ANGLESAY.

By the constant irruptions of the sea about this time, on that part of the coast whereon the post was erected which bounded the liberties of Yarmouth, the said boundary-mark was washed down. And as the want of some conspicuous object, to denote the boundary of the said liberties, might possibly be attended with some disagreeable consequences, and occasion fresh disputes; it was therefore thought necessary to solicit the attendance of several gentlemen of distinction in the neighbourhood, to superintend the re-placing of the said boundary mark, which was necessary, both for the security of the privileges of Lowestoft, as also for obviating any imputation of infringement on the liberties of Yarmouth. Accordingly, on the seventh of February, 1676, the gentlemen who were requested to be present at the re-placing of the said boundary-mark, assembled for that purpose at Lowestoft, and executed the same; the particulars of which proceeding are contained in the following relation:—

"Whereas, in obedience to an order of the Lords in Parliament, bearing date the six and twentieth day of February, one thousand six hundred and sixty-one, there was an admeasurement made by the Sheriffs of Norfolk and Suffolk, from the crane key in Yarmouth, towards Lowestoft, and no further. At which place a new post was set up, to bound the limits granted by charters to the inhabitants of Yarmouth, and in which extent the bailiffs and corporation are to enjoy their full privileges, as the statute of 31 Edward III, and other charters do empower them.

"And whereas the said post or boundary-mark, by the incursions of the sea upon that part of the coast whereon it stood, was in the late tempestuous weather thrown down, and in great danger of being washed away. Wherefore, at the humble request of the inhabitants of the town of Lowestoft, for the securing of the said post or boundary-mark from the danger of the sea; we, the gentlemen of the counties of Norfolk and Suffolk, who have hereunto subscribed our names, do humbly certify, that we were this day personally present at the place where the post formerly stood, and finding the said post fallen to the ground, being undermined by the sea, and not to be raised again in the same place, to stand any ordinary rage thereof; for at the very instant of time that we were there present, the sea came up to the foot of the said post, as it then laid upon the ground. Wherefore we advised, that a small post should be set up in the place whereon the aforesaid boundary-post formerly stood; and to remove the said boundary-post higher up, out of the danger of the sea, there to affix it, by the help of a compass and line, at the same distance from the crane key of Great Yarmouth as it formerly stood; which we did then see performed accordingly. Dated this seventh day of February, in the nine and twentieth year of the reign of our sovereign Lord Charles the second, by the grace of God, of England, Scotland, France, and Ireland, king defender of the faith, and so forth; and in the year of our Lord one thousand six hundred and seventy-six.

(Signed)—Hen. Bacon, Lionell Playters, Tho. Loud, Jas. Febure, Hen. Wotton, Jas. Catelyn, John Walne, Neville Catebyn, Richd. Bacon, J. Porter, Edwd. Paxton, Tho. Cloumstead, Jas. Reeve, John Playters, Edw. North, Tho. Leman, Richd. Vesy, Phil. Hayward, Robt. Selling.

After these affairs were all fully settled and adjusted, the towns of Yarmouth and Lowestoft appear to have conducted the herring fishery on more amicable terms; and the latter continued the enjoyment of their rights and privileges, without interruption from the former, until the year 1729, when the burgesses of Yarmouth once more attempted to revive their former pretensions to an exclusive right to the herring-fishery; and, as a prelude to their carrying those pretensions into execution, had formed a resolution to seize all such fishing vessels fitted out at Lowestoft (called yaggers) as were employed by the merchants of that town to go out to sea to purchase herrings of the northern and west country fishers. But all these designs of the Yarmouth men were entirely frustrated by the speedy and vigorous exertions of the Lowestoft merchants; who, on the first alarm, immediately opened a subscription for raising a fund, in order to defend their ancient rights and privileges, which so far discouraged their adversaries, that they immediately relinquished every farther proceeding in the affair, and, consequently, were prevented from carrying their designs into execution.

The following is a copy of the ORIGINAL INSTRUMENT drawn up on this occassion, and signed by the principal merchants of the town:

"Whereas we, whose names and seals are hereunto subscribed and set, are all, or most of us, persons concerned in the herring-fishery. And do intend to employ and send out yaggers to sea, to buy herrings for this herring-fishing season, and to all other subsequent herring-fishing seasons, during our respective lives. And whereas the Corporation of Great Yarmouth, in the county of Norfolk, do give out speeches, and threaten, that in case we, or any of us, do so buy herrings at sea, that they will commence and prosecute one or more suit or suits against us, or him, or them of us, who shall so buy herrings at sea. And whereas, in case any suit or suits shall be brought, begun, commenced or prosecuted against us, every, or any of us, for our, every, or any of our buying herrings at sea, during this or any other subsequent herring-fishing season, we are unanimously resolved to defend such suit or suits. And in order to defray the charge and expense of such suit or suits, we, and every of us, whose names and seals are hereunto subscribed and set, do hereby severally and respectively, each one for himself, and for his own heirs, executors, and administrators, and not jointly, or one of us for another, covenant, promise and agree, to, and with, John Tanner, of Lowestoft aforesaid, clerk, his executors, and administrators, in manner and form following, (that is to say), That we, and every of us, shall, and will, within seven days next after any suit or suits shall be brought, begun, or commenced against us, every, or any of us, by the said corporation of Great Yarmouth, or by any person or persons whomsoever, for our, every, or any of our, buying herrings at sea as aforesaid, well and truly pay, or cause to be paid, this several sum and sums of money by us severally subscribed or set down at or near the end of our respective names, into the hands of such person or persons as the majority of us whose names and seals are hereunto subscribed and set, shall, by any writing, to be signed by such majority in the presence of two credible witnesses, direct and appoint. And that such suit and suits shall be defended during the pleasure of the majority of us. And also, that it shall and may be lawful to and for the person or persons into whose hands the majority of us shall so, as aforesaid, direct and appoint the said several sum and sums of money so, as aforesaid, by us severally subscribed to be paid, out of the same moneys, to pay not only such costs and charges and other moneys as may happen to be obtained or recovered against us, every, or any of us, in any such suit or suits. And that we, and every of us, shall and will, out of the same moneys so, as aforesaid, by us subscribed, bear a proportionable part, with respect only to our several subscriptions, as well as of all such costs and charges and other moneys as may happen to be obtained or recovered against us, every, or any of us, in any such suit or suits as aforesaid, as also of the charges in defending such suit or suits. And so, likewise, in case the corporation of Great Yarmouth shall act in any such manner as to make it necessary for us to commence and prosecute any suit or action against them, it is hereby agreed, That the money underneath subscribed shall be liable to be employed as well in bringing and prosecuting any such suit or action as the majority of us shall think necessary to commence and prosecute against them, as in defending any such suit or action as they shall commence and prosecute against us. And likewise to make good to any particular person the loss he may sustain by his vessel being seized and detained by the said corporation, on account of his buying herrings at sea as aforesaid. Provided always, and it is our and every our intents and meanings, that in case any of us shall happen to depart this life before any such suit or suits shall be brought, begun, or commenced against us, or any of us, that then the sum and sums of money subscribed by him and them of us who shall depart this life as aforesaid, shall not be paid. And that then, and in such case, the executors or administrators of him or them of us so dying shall not be any way concerned in any such suit or suits, any thing herein before mentioned or contained to the contrary thereof, in any wise notwithstanding. In witness whereof we have hereunto set our hands and seals, this two and twentieth day of September, in the third year of the reign of our sovereign lord George the second, by the grace of God, of Great Britain, France, and Ireland, King, defender of the faith, and so forth, and in the year of our Lord one thousand seven and twenty-nine.

"John Jex, £50; William Balls, £30; James Reeve, £20; Thomas Manning, £20; Samuel Adams, £20; John Arnold, £5; Robert Hayward, £35; John Fowler, jun., £25; Robert Payne, £15; Samuel Church, £25; Thomas Landifield, £25; Daniel Long, £20; John Ibrooke, £5; John Barker, jun., £30; John Ellis, £20; John Munds, £20; Charles Boyce, £20; Matthew Arnold, £25; Thomas Watson, £5; John Brame, £20; Robert Dixon, £10."

Thus was the last effort of the Yarmouth men to monopolize the herring-fishery totally frustrated, and the Lowestoft people have enjoyed the free exercise thereof, without any interruption ever since.

How far the disputes between Yarmouth and Lowestoft had engaged the attention of the public, will, in some measure, appear from the following circumstance:—

About the beginning of the reign of Charles I, lived Thomas Nash, who was born at Lowestoft, and was a sharp satirist. He wrote a play called "Lenton-Stuffe; or, The Praise of the Red Herring," published in 1599, in 4to. Also another play called "The Isle of Dogs," together with other works. His writings relate chiefly to the disputes between Yarmouth and Lowestoft, the former of which places he attempted much to ridicule. Swinden says, "The facetious Nash designed nothing more in Lenton-Stuffe than a joke upon our staple—red herrings; and being a Lowestoft man, the enmity between the two towns led him to attempt that by humour which more sober reason could not accomplish.

## SECTION V.

## OF THE CHURCH.

LOWESTOFT is a vicarage endowed with great tithes. In the reign of Henry I the impropriation of this parish was given by that king towards augmenting the endowment of the priory of St. Bartholomew, in London, and continued in the possession of that house till the dissolution of the monasteries, in the reign of Henry VIII; when the site of this priory being granted to Sir Richard Rich, afterwards Lord Rich, probably the impropriation of Lowestoft, as part of the endowment of the priory, devolved to Sir Richard and his family. How long it continued there, or into whose hands it came afterwards, is now uncertain; the most material information obtainable concerning it is, that about the year 1719 the impropriation was the property of three grand-daughters of one Mr. Church, at Pakefield, whose names were Fowler, Landifield, and Warwick; and was purchased of them soon after by the Rev. Tanner, vicar of the parish, at the price of £1050, which money was raised by Mr. Tanner by subscription. In gratitude to the memory of those who so generously contributed to the purchase of this impropriation, Mr Tanner caused a list of their names to be entered upon two tables, and affixed to the north side of the chancel, together with the several sums they severally subscribed. Between these tables of impropriation benefactors is a neat marble tablet with the following inscription

A.D. 1720.
Two Hundred Pounds of Queen Anne's Bounty were given
towards purchasing the
Impropriation of Lowestoft, for the benefit of the Vicar.

Mr. Tanner, previous to the subscription for purchasing the impropriation, distributed among his friends, and the neighbouring gentlemen, a printed representation of the vicarial tithes and the state of the living; and wherein it appears that the income was very small.

## THE REPRESENTATION.

"The parish of Lowestoft, in Suffolk, is a large parish, consisting of about three or four and twenty hundred souls; and the living, which is a vicarage only, is but meanly endowed; there being no house, and but one acre of land belonging to it, and out of that piece of land the crown claims a pension of 3s. 4d. per year, and 8d. for an acquittance; the vicarage tithes are not worth above £20 per year, one year with another; and all the rest of the minister's income depends on the offerings, surplice fees, and fisheries, which are very precarious and uncertain. And as the number of the poor increaseth greatly in the said parish (the poor's rate, which about 35 years ago came only to £13 a quarter, cometh now to £63 per quarter, besides a great deal that is paid to the poor out of the town lands), so doth the number of the inhabitants in general increase too (several families coming to us almost every year from other places, and the number of our christenings exceed the number of our burials); so that the duty of the minister is plainly increasing, whilst his revenue must as certainly decrease as the poor increase. But under this melancholy prospect it hath pleased God to order things so that the great tithes of the said parish are to be sold, by a decree in Chancery, to the highest bidder; and to put it into the hearts of several, both in the parish and places adjoining, to contribute according to their abilities, towards purchasing the said tithes for the benefit of the vicar for the time being, for ever. But as all that can be raised hereabouts will go but a little way towards so large a purchase, we are forced to ask the assistance of charitable and well-disposed persons further off, hoping they will not be backward in promoting so good a work.

"It is thought that these tithes will cost £1,800, which being a larger sum than can possibly be raised by benefactions; the method proposed is, to raise as much as we can by benefactions, and to borrow the rest of the money; and to have the tithes conveyed to divers persons, in trust for payment of the money borrowed; and when both principal and interest of that is paid off, then to be for the use and benefit of the minister for the time being, for ever. So that it is uncertain whether the present minister will ever have any benefit of it. And therefore he hopes that all whom he applies himself to on this account will believe that he acts more, in what he herein doth for the good of the church than out of any principle of self-interest."

It is apprehended that the acre of land referred to by Mr. Tanner, (on which formerly was built a messuage or tenement, since decayed) for which the vicar of the parish paid to the crown the annual sum of 3s. 4d, and 8d. for an acquittance, was given by some pious person, to support a light before the image of St. Roche. (St. Roche lived in the 14th century, and was lord of Montpelier; but abandoned his fortunes to turn pilgrim. After curing many persons of the plague, he was himself attacked, but cured by a dog licking him. For this reason he is, in France, invoked, in order to avert that calamity, and is alway represented with a sore thigh and a dog. *Gent. Mag.*, March, 1785.) Where this image was placed, whether in the church or in one of the chapels, is now uncertain; though most probably in the church; as this acre of land lies next the quarter of an acre at the south-west corner of the churchyard, on which the vicarage-house stood that was destroyed by fire in 1546. Probably at the dissolution, the premises came into the hands of Government, and as the vicar enjoyed them, he became subject to the above annual payment. A discharge of the above-mentioned payment was purchased of Government in 1788, by the Rev. John Arrow, late vicar of this parish, at the expense of £5 as appears by the following certificate:

"BY THE COMMISSIONERS OF THE LAND REVENUE.

"These are to certify, that the said commissioners have contracted and agreed with the Reverend John Arrow, vicar of Lowestoft, in the county of Suffolk, clerk, for the sale to him of all that yearly rent of three shillings and fourpence, due and payable to his Majesty by the said John Arrow, as vicar of Lowestoft aforesaid, for or in respect of a certain messuage or tenement and pightle of land, called St. Roch's Light, situate and being at Lowestoft, with the appurtenances thereof, at or for the price or sum of five pounds of lawful money of Great Britain, to be paid by the said John Arrow into the Bank of England, in the name of the said Commissioners. Which said rent, from and immediately after the payment of the said sum, in manner aforesaid, and the inrollment of this certificate with the receipt of the said purchase-money, in the office of the auditor of the land-revenue for the county aforesaid, shall be adjudged, deemed, and taken to be absolutely vested in the said purchaser and his successors, vicar of Lowestoft, for ever by virtue of an Act passed in the twenty-sixth year of the reign of his present Majesty King George the Third, intitled, "An Act for appointing commissioners to inquire into the state and condition of the woods, forests, and land-revenues belonging to the crown, and to sell or nalieate fee-farm and improveable rents."

"Given under the hands of the said Commissioners, the twenty-ninth day of Feburary, one thousand seven hundred and eighty eight.

"CHARLES MIDDLETON, JOHN CALL, JOHN FORDYCE.

Witness to the signing, by the said Commissioners,

WILLIAM HARRISON."

"Received the 6th day of March, 1788, of and from the above-named, the Rev. John Arrow, the sum of five pounds, of lawful money of Great Britain, being the consideration-money expressed in the above certificate.

"Witness my hand, for the governor and company of the Bank of England,

J. PADMAN, cashier.

Inrolled the 6th day of March, 1788, before me,

JOHN HOSIER, dep. aud.

Paid for the conveyance of the premises £0 11s. 8d.; Paid into the Bank of England, for purchase of ditto £5; Paid for inrolling ditto at the Auditor's office, New Palace Yard, Westminister 10s. 0d.; Total £6 1s. 8d.

Mr. Tanner was greatly encouraged in this undertaking by **Mr. Thomas Mighells**, of Lowestoft, merchant (the brother of Admiral Mighells, and father of Thomas Mighells, of Lowestoft surgeon, who died in 1763) and assisted by the Rev. Gregory Clarke, rector of Blundeston.

It appears that there was a suit in chancery respecting the impropriation of Lowestoft, and that it was obliged to be sold by order of a decree of that court. Mr. Tanner alludes to this suit in the following letter addressed to **Mrs. Dorothy Mighells**, Burlington Key, Yorkshire

"Madam, The suit which was begun in chancery two or three years ago, concerning the great tithes of this parish, is now brought so near to an end that 'tis thought they will be sold before harvest; so that we are now making all the interest we can to get them. And to that end Mr. Clarke and I are to ride about the country two or three days every week a-begging; and, God be thanked, we have made a pretty good beginning. As you were pleased to tell me more than once that you would give £5 towards it, I have presumed to put you down so much, for an example and encouragement to others; and also have sent you a copy of the paper which we have printed and sent to such as we cannot well get to.

I am, your most obliged Kinsman,

Lowestoft, 21st May, 1719. J TANNER."

(Mary, the wife of the Rev. John Tanner, was a daughter of Mary Mighells, by Robert, son of Mr. Nicohlas Knight, gent., which Mary Mighells was sister to Captain Josiah Mighells, who married the above Dorothy whose maiden name was Coates, of Burlinton, in Yorkshire. This excellent woman, Mrs. Dorothy Mighells, was a person of the most exemplary piety and charity. Among her many other pious acts she gave two silver flagons, weighing upwards of 146 ounces, for the use of the communion table at Lowestoft.)

The undertaking of the Rev. Tanner proved so successful in the subscription, **as to** enable him to complete the purchase, and consequently endowed the **vicarage** of Lowestoft with the impropriation of the great tithes in the manner **inserted under**:

## IMPROPRIATION OF LOWESTOFT

The impropriation of the parish of Lowestoft, being to be sold in the year 1719, John Tanner, then vicar, being greatly encouraged by Mr. Thomas Mighells, of Lowestoft, merchant, and very much assisted by the Rev. Gregory Clarke, rector of Blundestone, solicited contributions from the tradesmen and gentlemen of the country, and obtained Queen Anne's bounty towards it; and got conveyances thereof to him the said John Tanner, about Christmas, 1719; but several difficulties arising, it could not be finally settled till 1721; when the great tithes of all the lands lying on the north, or right-hand part of the highway leading from the Swan Lane to Mutford Bridge, were settled (in conjunction with the govenors of Queen Anne's bounty, who have all the writings relating to this purchase) on the then vicar immediately, and his successors for ever, without any condition but that of paying thirty shillings per year towards repairing the chancel. And in November, 1721, the said John Tanner conveyed the other moiety, or the great tithes of all those lands lying upon the south, or left-hand part of the aforesaid highway, unto Mr. Thomas Mighells, Mr. Stephen Buxton, Mr. John Barker, jun., Mr. Robert Hayward, and Mr. John Durrant, of Lowestoft; to the Rev. Clarke, of Blundestone; Mr. Burton, of Gisleham; Mr. Richardson, of Pakefield; Mr. Camell, of Bradwell; and Mr. Woolmer, of Carleton; and their heirs for ever. That out of the profits of the same the sum of our hundred and forty pounds (which being wanted to complete the purchase, was kindly lent by the Rev. Dr. Thomas Tanner, a Chancellor of the Diocese of Norwich) might be repaid with interest; and after the said £440 was repaid, then to be for the benefit of the Vicar of Lowestoft for the time being for ever, in the following words:—

"And from and after he the said Dr. Thomas Tanner, his **executors, administrators**, or assigns, shall be fully reimbursed and repaid the **said sum** of £440 of good and lawful money of this nation, and also all interest for the same, to become and grow due; and also all costs, charges and expenses which he or they shall be put unto for or by reason or means as aforesaid. That then the said Thomas Mighells, Stephen Buxton, John Barker, Robert Hayward, John Durrant, George Clarke, Joshua Buxton, Philip Richardson, Robert Camel and Robert Woolmer, and the survivors or survivor of them, and the heirs and assigns of the survivor of them, shall stand be seized of the said tithes of corn and grain, in that part of the said parish above particularly described, to the only use, benefit and behoof of the Vicar of Lowestoft aforesaid for the time being for ever. So as, and upon this express proviso and condition, nevertheless, That such Vicar for the time being, and all and every his successors, vicars of the said parish of Lowestoft, shall, for rightfully qualifying him or themselves to take and enjoy such tithes, or the rents and profits thereof, reside within the said parish of Lowestoft for the space of eight kalendar months, or five and thirty weeks in every year to be computed from Midsummer to Midsummer wherein he shall have or claim such tithes, or the rents and profits thereof. And by himself, or his sufficient curate or curates, read divine service and preach twice every Lord's day, commonly called Sunday, and read prayers every Wednesday and Friday weekly, and also on every holy day; and publicly administer the holy sacrament of the Lord's supper in the said parish church at Lowestoft, in every year at least six times, as now within the said parish is accustomed to be done. And so as such person or persons who shall, by virtue of these presents, become entitled to the said tithes of corn and grain in that part of the said parish of Lowestoft, herein before particularly mentioned or described, or the rents and profits thereof, shall from time to time, and at all times for ever hereafter, maintain, repair, and keep the whole chancel of the church of Lowestoft aforesaid in good and tenantable repair, being yearly and every year allowed towards the doing of the same, the sum of thirty shillings, by or from such person or persons as shall rightfully have claim, receive or take the tithes of corn and grain growing or arising, or to be received in that part of the said parish as lyeth on the north or right-hand side of the said score, lane, way or road, before herein particularly described and distinguished from the other part on the southern part thereof. Provided always, and upon this further condition, that if the said Vicar for the time being, or his successor or successors, vicar or vicars of the said parish of Lowestoft shall, after the first Midsummer after the institution and induction of such vicar or vicars, unto and into the said parish church, be absent from the said parish by the space of four kalender months, or seventeen weeks in any year, to be computed from Midsummer to Midsummer; or shall neglect to perform, or cause the said duties to be performed, in any manner that shall be judged wilful negligence, and not casual, undersigned, or allowable omitance, by the chancellor of the diocese of Norwich, or any other person or persons deputed by him (whose sentence shall be final.) Then for every year the vicar is negligent or absent as aforesaid (after the said sums repaid and re-imbursed unto the said Dr. Tanner, his executors, administrators or assigns), it shall and may be lawful for the churchwardens of the said parish of Lowestoft, and the schoolmaster of the free school of the foundation of Mr. Annott in Lowestoft to take, collect, and receive the said tithes of corn and grain in that part of the said parish of Lowestoft herein particularly mentioned and described, for the use and benefit of the schoolmaster of the said free school; upon this condition nevertheless, that the said schoolmaster shall for every year's profit that shall by this means fall to him, teach six such poor children as shall be sent unto him by the churchwardens of Lowestoft aforesaid for the time being for the space of three years. And whereas it may so happen, that he that is schoolmaster of the said free school, when the vicar is thus absent, may be removed within three years afterwards: it is hereby directed and appointed, that the monies arising by and from the said tithes shall be laid up in the hands of the churchwardens, or one of them, or such other person or persons as the said schoolmaster shall appoint and approve of, who shall give sufficient security to the satisfaction of the said schoolmaster, to pay the sixth part of it every half-year to the schoolmaster of the said free school for the time being, for teaching such six poor children as shall be sent thither as aforesaid; exclusive of such part or parts thereof as shall be for the

Q

repair of the said chancel, having such allowance as aforesaid. And so shall every year that the vicar is absent or negligent, as aforesaid. And when the vicar is resident, and performs, or causes the duties aforesaid to be performed, within the said parish, by the space of eight kalendar months, as aforesaid, then the same is to be for the use of the vicar only, anything herein before mentioned to the contrary thereof, in any wise notwithstanding.

In witness whereof, etc."

That the above £440 and interest was (after a great deal of money laid out about the chancel etc.,) cleared off and discharged about Lady Day, 1742, by the above twenty years care and trouble of the above John Tanner, vicar of the said parish of Lowestoft, who besides his contribution of eighty pounds, given by him when the subscription was first opened, gave likewise afterwards twenty years' profits of that part of the tithes, which was settled on the vicar by the govenors of Queen Anne's bounty, in the year 1721; disclaiming at the same time all merits to himself, and attributing it solely to the bounty and goodness of the Supreme Being, saying

At non nobis, Domine, sed nomini tuo sit Gloria. Amen.
Not unto us, O Lord, but to thy name be the Glory. Amen.

With the impropriation there was likewise purchased a large barn (to lay the tithes in) copyhold, on which barn there was left unpaid £50. This money was also paid off at Michaelmas, 1745, by the care and good management, and bounty of the above worthy vicar John Tanner. This barn was surrendered, a little before the Mortmain Act took place, to Mr. Woolmer, of Carleton: Mr. Robert Hayward, jun., and Mr. John Durrant of Lowestoft; in trust, for the use of such person and persons as, from time to time, shall be entitled to the great tithes. It pays a quit rent of 1/8 to the Manor of Lowestoft.

The value of the living is also further increased from the fisheries. The Vicar receives from the owner of every boat employed in the herring fishery half a guinea, and for every boat employed in the mackarel fishery half a dole. When the North sea and Iceland fisheries flourished at Lowestoft, the Vicar was not allowed half a dole for every vessel sent upon those fisheries, but for every voyage which they made annually to those seas, which were not only one, but sometimes two, three and even four voyages. In the begining of the reign of Queen Elizabeth, about fourteen of these vessels, called doggers, were employed by this town in the North sea and Iceland fisheries, which paid a considerable sum annually to the Vicar. But these latter fisheries are now entirely ceased at Lowestoft, and have been so for many years.

This custom of allowing the vicar half a dole is a very antient one, but how long it has subsisted at Lowestoft is uncertain. At Yarmouth, in the year 1484 the half doles of fishing voyages were granted by the assembly to the use of the haven; but this custom, called the half-doles, had been before that time paid to the town even from time immemorial; for the fishermen had always given a whole dole, namely, half a dole to the use of the church, and the other half to the use of the town; and because one half part of the dole was given to sacred purposes, it was called Christ's dole. Probably the payment of the half dole by the fishermen at Lowestoft to the same sacred use, is as antient as that at Yarmouth.

What is meant by a dole is this: from the amount which each boat raises by the sale of mackarel, during the voyage, a sum is first deducted for provisions and incidental expenses; the residue is divided into shares or doles of which the owner of the boat has a certain number, and the net owner the like for his nets, and the remainder is distributed among the boatmen according to their several stations, including the minister's half dole. Thus, if a boat raises £100, take for provisions, etc., £25, then the residue, £76, will be the sum to divide into doles; and if the number of doles for boats, nets and men, together with the half dole to the Vicar, be 150, then the division will be 10s. per share or dole; and consequently, in that case, the Vicar will be entitled to 5s. for his half dole for that boat.

There not being any antient records now remaining, respecting the origin of this noble and beautiful structure, the church at Lowestoft, they being all burnt in the year 1606, when the dwelling-house belonging to Mr. Glesson, vicar of this town, was destroyed by fire, we are unable to ascertain with certainty the exact time when this building was erected; and consequently all the investigations in pursuit of this discovery must be attended with much difficulty and enveloped in the obscurity of probable conjecture.

It is evident, from what has been already observed at the begining of this section, respecting the grant of Henry I that there was a church belonging to this parish in the eleventh century, but how long it had been erected before that period is now uncertain, probably soon after Christianity was first introduced into the kingdom of the East Angles. In those early ages the generality of our English churchs were undoubtedly very ordinary buildings; they were of Saxon origin, some few were built with stone, but the greater part of wood only, and consequently were much inferior to the stately edifices that were erected after the Norman conquest. To determine therefore, what kind of church it was that they had at Lowestoft at that early period is now impossible; all that can be advanced on the point is, that when we consider the barbarous taste which prevailed in that uncivilised age, the infant as well as the persecuted state of Christianity, and the violent commotions which at that time agitated this part of the kingdom, it may be concluded that it was but a mean building, and bore but a small resemblance to the size and elegence of the present structure.

But it may be asked, that if the original church at Lowestoft was a building of that inferior kind as is above represented, by what means was it that the present large and elegant structure came to be erected; since it is evident, that the ability of the inhabitants at any one period was never equal to the accomplishing such an expensive undertaking?

In answer to the question it may be observed That the church belonging to the impropriation of this parish, which made part of the endownment of the priory of St. Bartholomew, by Henry I, was the old original building, which was then standing, and not the present structure. The former of these buildings, was of very ancient date, probably soon after the establishment of Christianity in the Kingdom of the East Angles; therefore it may reasonable be supposed, that at the time when the grant of it was made, namely, in the reign of Henry I, it must be in a very decayed and ruinous state. This grant of Henry I was confirmed by a charter from Henry III, in the year 1230. When, therefore, the priory of St. Bartholomew was in full possession of the church and impropriation of this parish, by virtue, of this charter, they, in consequence of their zeal, or rather religious frenzy, for erecting churches and founding religious houses, which at that time so universally prevailed, the old ruinous church at Lowestoft was entirely taken down, and the present elegant structure erected in its place, through the munificence of the priory and pious ostentation of the times.

Tanner, in his Notitia, says "That Henry I gave churches in Suffolk to the priory of St. Bartholomew, without specifying the names of those churches; yet it may reasonably inferred that the church at Lowestoft was one of them; because, when the grant was confirmed by the charter of Henry III, this church was particularly mentioned.

It is certain that the present church at Lowestoft was erected prior to the year 1365, because Weever has given an inscription which he found in the church, namely,

"ROBERT INGLOSSE, Esquyer,
which died in Anno 1365."

Therefore, it is evident that the old church at Lowestoft was standing in the year 1230, when the grant of Henry I was confirmed by the charter of Henry III; and as it is equally evident, from the above inscription, that the present church was erected before the year 1365, it makes it clearly manifest that the present building was erected some time in the interval between the years 1230 and 1365; and consequently, that the present church of Lowestoft has been built 500 years.

After the church came into the possession of the priory of St. Bartholomew, it was found to be so old and mean a building, and in such a ruinous state, that it was necessary to take it entirely down and rebuild it, and which was accordingly done in its present noble and elegant style. The nave, the south aisle, and the chancel were the first parts that were taken down; but the north aisle was not re-built till some time after. This is evident, from the difference which may be observed in the form of the windows belonging to these aisles; the former being more acute than the latter, which points out a more ancient construction.

An ingenious writer has said that the very obtusely-pointed arches of the windows of our churches, shew, at first sight, that they are of no very great antiquity; for the very sharply-pointed arch, which succeeded the circular one about the year 1200, expanded itself by degrees, and grew more and more obtuse till, towards the reign of Henry VII. it approached the segment of a great circle. This observation tends to confirm what has been previously advanced, namely, that the present church at Lowestoft was wholly re-built at the same time, but that the north aisle was built some time after the other parts of the building. The walls belonging to the south part of this beautiful structure are at this time much inclined from the perpendicular; owing, probably, to the absurd and injurious practice of open graves, both within and without the building, too near the foundations a practice which too much prevails in other places.

[The south wall was rebuilt in 1871.]

The present church was erected chiefly through the munificence and liberality of the priory of St. Bartholomew of London; and, it is also probable that it was indebted to the same society afterwards for keeping it in repair, for when all supplies from those resources were entirely withdrawn, in consequence of the dissolution of the monasteries, in the reign of Henry VIII., the churches that were dependent on those foundations soon fell into decay, as the parishes to which they belonged were unable to support the expense of repairing them. Sometimes the Lords of the Manors belonging to parishes whose churches have been rebuilt, have been liberal benefactors on these occasions, especially about the time when the re-building of Lowestoft church was undertaken. John de la Pole, Lord of Wingfield Castle, was one of the principal benefactors, when that noble tower belonging to the church at Redenhall, in Norfolk was erected; and as the town of Lowestoft and the island of Lothingland were part of the estate of the De la Poles, in the reigns of Henry IV. and V., it might be supposed that this family contributed also to the rebuilding of Lowestoft Church; but not anything appears to confirm this supposition. No leopard's faces (the badge of the De la Poles) are visible in any part of the building, as they are in many places in the tower at Redenhall. The building of this tower was begun about the year 1460, and finished in 1520; but the church at Lowestoft was not re-built till between the years 1230 and 1395; it is therefore probable that the De la Poles were not the proprietors of the town of Lowestoft and the island of Lothingland till after the rebuilding of Lowestoft church. This was the case at Corton and Kessingland, near Lowestoft, after the dissolution of Leystone abbey, and the abbey of the Minorisses, in London; and the church at Lowestoft would have experienced the same misfortune, after the suppression of the priory of St. Bartholomew, had not the town at that time prevented the lands which had been given many years before, for the sole use of this church, being alienated with the impropriation of this parish, and the other endowments of the priory, in the grant which was made to Sir Richard Rich, in the 36th of Henry VIII.

Probably Corton and Kessingland were not altogether in the same predicament as Lowestoft. For as the abbeys to which they belonged were in possession of their impropriations only, their churches were repaired out of the common revenues of those abbeys; whereas the priory of St. Batholomew had not only the impropriation of Lowestoft, but was also, probably in possession of the lands which had been given for the sole use of the church; which lands were recovered again after the dissolution of the monasteries, for their original purposes. For it appears that the church lands belonging to this parish were never under the absolute power of the priory as the impropriation was, although it might have great influence concerning them; this is evident, by the feoffment of the said lands in the reign of Henry VII A.D. 1503, which shews that the right was not in the priory of St. Batholomew; and consequently, might be the reason of their being recovered again by the parish soon after the dissolution.

But notwithstanding the recovery of the church lands, it appears that the town was much distressed after the dissolution of the monasteries, in keeping the church in decent repair. For in the year 1592 the church was in such a ruinous state that it cost upwards of £200 to repair it; out of which sum £68 18s. 8d. was collected of the inhabitants; £100 were borrowed of Mr. Bartlemewe, of Yarmouth, and the remainder was raised (including a provision for discharging the debt) from premiums by granting leases of the town lands under their full value; the situation of the inhabitants at this time obliging them to have recourse to these methods for repairing the church. It also appears that there had been paid by the churchwardens, towards repairing the church, of hayning-money collected in the roads, the sum of £63 18s. 3d. when the lands were unable to discharge the expenses of the repairs and other necessary expenses of the town, exclusive of money collected of the inhabitants. The church has also cost the parish several considerable sums since that time for repairs; so that, had not the town been assisted in repairing this building by the rents and profits of the church lands, that venerable pile had many years since fallen into decay, and mouldered into irreparable ruin.

The ruinous state of the church at this time arose, probably, from the profits of the lands given for keeping it in repair, being applied to other purposes. From the decree of the Court of Chancery, in 1616, respecting the town lands, it appears, that that decree was grounded on a complaint of the inhabitants that the rents and profits of those lands had been alienated to purposes not intended by the donors. That the lands called French's, given for the use of the poor of this town were worth £20 a year, but that the poor received little more than 13d. a week from them. That the lands given for the use of the church were worth £40 a year, but that £10 a year only had been applied to that purpose; and that the overplus of all these lands had been expended in law-suits and divers other business of the town; contrary to the designs of the donors. It was also further complained, that the churchwardens had let the said lands at rents considerably below their value, in order to obtain fines and incomes, which amounted to £210 and upwards. And as the burthen of repairing the church, in consequence of these alienations, fell, in great measure, upon the inhabitants it occasioned an application to the Court of Chancery for redress. Nevertheless, if the distressed condition of the town at this time is considered, as being obliged to raise £120 in 1591, to defend their rights to Annott's school; to raise £120 in 1597, to defend their rights against Yarmouth, respecting the herring fishery; to raise £200 in 1592 to repair the church; also £114 in 1616 to discharge the expenses of the above suit in chancery; may easily account for some measures having been pursued which were not altogether justifiable, but were adopted through absolute necessity.

That part of the town lands which was given for the use of the church, and is chiefly appropriated towards keeping it in repair, and furnishing it with decent ornaments, is the gift of some charitable and religious persons, whose names, at this distant period, are wholly unknown; but, whoever they were, they are justly entitled to the grateful acknowledgments of the parish, as having been the means of preserving it from a burthen which at all times would have been inconvenient.

Under the general denomination of town lands belonging to this parish, are included, not only those above-mentioned, consisting of sixty-seven acres of land, divers tenants, a wind mill, and dole lands, and which were given for the use of the church, but also those that were given for the benefit of the poor. Concerning the lands given to the church, the donor is not only unknown at the present time, but was also unknown in the year 1552, the sixth of Edward VI, when one, John Jetter, the only surviving feoffee, made a new feoffment of the premises, dated 20th June; and who therein said "That he together with divers persons deceased, had them by the feoffment of Nicholas Hughson and William Fly, bearing date 10th November, 1503, 19 Henry VII.

On the 12th June, 1644, when Francis Jessope, under a commission from the Earl of Manchester, pillaged this church of almost all the brass inscriptions, he took up, in the middle isle, twelve pieces belonging to twelve several generations of the Jetters. Margaret Jetter, 1573, widow, laid in the church-yard. The mother, probably, of Anthony Jetter, of Lowestoft, merchant, who was living in the 8th of Queen Elizabeth.

The feoffees named in the feoffment, dated October 14, 1678, are: John Arrow, vicar; Aldous Arnold, gent.; Samuel Barker, merchant; Samuel Barker, jun., Hewlin Luson, jun., Dan. Ketteridge, merchant; John Peache, merchant;

William Bell Parker, clerk; John Jex, gent.; William Slop, draper; Robert Reeve, gent.; Samuel Collett, draper; Henry Roman, baker; James Harman, merchant; James Brame, baker; William Pashley, merchant; Thomas Brame, gent.; Aldous Arnold, surgeon; Obed Aldred, bricklayer; John Stannard, rope maker; Thomas Smith, beer brewer; Coe Arnold, beer brewer; Philip Walker, gent.; John Howard, grocer.

The other part of the town lands given for the use of the poor, called French's, consisting of twenty-one acres and a half, were purchased with sixty pounds left by William French, by will, dated April 14, 1529, to buy free lands for the use of the poor; the profits of which lands were to be distributed in the following manner: to thirteen poor people of the town of Lowestoft, thirteenpence every Sunday, after divine service; and three shillings and fourpence to the churchwardens, yearly, for their trouble. About the beginning of the last century, in consequence of the great misapplication of the rents and profits arising from these lands, and also those given to the church, the inhabitants applied to the Court of Chancery, requesting that a commission might be appointed for making enquiry into the abuses, and to redress the same. A commission was accordingly granted, and an inquisition was held at Lowestoft, and in the year 1616 a decree was issued from that court (which cost the town £114 10s.) wherein it was ordered.

I. That the town lands belonging to Lowestoft should be let by the year, or by leases not exceeding seven years, by the feoffees (the churchwardens for the time being, being two) and six other inhabitants.

II. No new leases to be made before the old ones are expired.

III. The Rents to be received by the Churchwardens, and to be disposed of as follows:

1st. That twenty pounds be laid out annually in repairing and ornamenting the church

2nd. To thirteen poor people of the town of Lowestoft, thirteen pence every Sunday, and three shillings and four pence, yearly, to the churchwardens, for their trouble.

3rd. Twenty pounds a year to the poor, including the above.

4th. Ten pounds a year to put out poor children apprentice, and a stock, to set poor people to work; and the remainder of the rents to be disposed of as the churchwarden, and twelve other inhabitants shall think proper, for the public good of the town.

5th. That in all the leases there shall be a reservation of the timber and wood; and that no wood or timber growing upon the premises shall be felled or taken, but for the reparations of the church and the houses standing on the said premises. And all underwood, when felled, shall be sold for the benefit of the poor and reparations of the church, by the churchwardens.

The decree in Chancery declares that this is the true intent and meaning of the donors, and therefore ordered that it should be fulfilled in the most ample and liberal manner. The Churchwardens are required on every Monday in Whitsun week to pass a true account to the new churchwardens, feeoffees, and townsmen under pain of five pounds.

In 1738 the town lands belonging to the parish were let for between £90 and £100 per annum.

In 1644 they were let for the term of seven years, at the rent of £64 only. The rents of lands about this time were much reduced in general, probably from the violent commotions of that unhappy period.

In 1651 they were let for £71 1s. per annum.

In 1734 they were let for £90 per annum.

In 1756 they were let for £93 per annum.

In 1776 they were let for the annual rent of £163 4s. 6d., agriculture being so much improved of late years as to render farming very advantageous. The farming business was in such a flourishing state about this time, that the vicar of Lowestoft, in the year 1776, compounded with his parishioners, for his tithes at 3s. 6d in the pound, according to what the farms were let for; but in 1777 the said composition was 4s. in the pound.

In 1683 the lands realised £138 6s. 6d. per annum.

There is no Church rate in the parish of Lowestoft, the profits arising from the lands belonging to the church being amply sufficient for keeping it in repair. Whether the rents of these lands have always been applied to the uses intended by the donors, is now uncertain, but thus far may justly be observed, that through the great care and assiduity of the vicar, the Rev. Arrow, in appropriating to the use of the Church such part of the town lands as it is justly entitled to, and preventing their being alienated to purposes for which they were never intended by their generous benefactors, this stately edifice is not only kept in proper repair, but rendered truly elegant ; so as to become an honour to religion, a credit to the parish, and the admiration of every stranger.

The town lands contain not only the sixty-seven acres given for the repair and ornaments of the church, and the twenty-eight acres and a half, called French's, given for the use of the poor, in the whole ninety-five acres and a half, which lands are particularly and separately described in the decree of Chancery of the year 1616 (as may be seen at large in the folio town-book, in the feoffment before that decree, and in the feoffment of 14th October, 1768); but also the other smaller donations of lands in Lowestoft, making the whole amount one hundred and four acres, exclusive of the estate at Worlingham, in Suffolk, given by Mr. John Wilde, of Lowestoft for establishing an English Grammar school in the parish, and the lands at Whitacre Burgh, the donation of Mr. Thomas Annott, of Lowestoft, for a grammar school at Lowestoft. The above one hundred and four acres of land are put up to auction every seven years, in the presence of the minister and churchwardens, to be let on leases for the said term of seven years. The overplus of Mr. Wilde's estate, at Worlingham, after founding and supporting the school, and fulfilling other directions mentioned in the will, he gave for such charitable purposes as the minister and churchwardens should think proper. This is further explained by a decree in Chancery in 1754, which says, "that the minister and churchwardens shall have the liberty to apply the overplus in such manner as they should think fit, for the relief of such persons as have large families, and such aged, sick, lame and impotent persons that belong to the said town, and who do not receive any relief from the parish; or to and amongst the testator's poor relations, at the discretion of the trustees. It is also further enjoined by the said decree, that as Lowestoft is a fishing town, the preference shall be given to those children whose fathers go fishing voyages, or any other employment about the fishery belonging to that town, as an encouragement to the said fishery. But if there be not forty boys so qualified, then any other boys belonging to the town, so as to make up that number.

The tower belonging to this church is neither large nor lofty, its height is only 120 feet, including a leaden spire of the height of 50 feet, and it is obvious to the most common observer, that both its height and size bear but little proportion to the building to which it is annexed; neither is there much resemblance between them either with respect to composition or workmanship, for in both these points the church is far superior to the steeple. These circumstances plainly denote that the tower belonged orginally to the old church, and strongly indicate that the latter was a building much interior to the present structure. Some remains of the old steeple are still visible, and are indubitable proofs of its original meanness; and also prove that when the old church was re-built by the priory of St. Bartholomew, the greater part of the tower was suffered to remain, after being strengthened and enlarged by buttresses, and ornamented with a spire, in order to give it a more modern appearance, and bring it to a nearer resemblance with the external appearance of the edifice. At this present time and for many years past, the steeple contains only one bell; but it is evident, from the appearances which still remain, that formerly it contained three. The reason generally assigned why the number was reduced, is, that the steeple was not strong enough to bear them. The weight of this bell is 17 cwt. 2 qr. 17 lbs., and has the following inscription thereon :

"I tell all that do me see,
"Newman, of Norwich, new cast me."

The expenses paid to Mr. Newman, for new casting this bell, including the brasses, amounted to £19 12s. 7d.

The church is dedicated to St. Margaret. It may be here stated that St. Margaret was born at Antioch, and was the daughter of a heathen priest.

Olybius, president of the East, under the Romans, intended to have married her; but finding she was a christian, deferred it till he could persuade her to renounce her religion: but not being able to accomplish his designs, he first put her to cruel torments and then beheaded her. She suffered in the year 278.

The patron is the Bishop of Norwich; it is valued in the King's books at £10 1s., and by Queen Anne at £43 16s. 6d., and is thereby discharged from paying first-fruits and tenths. By the King's books is meant the valuation of all the livings in England, taken in the reign of Henry VIII. In the beginning of the reign of Queen Elizabeth, all livings that were under £10 in the King's books were discharged from paying the first fruits. And in Queen Anne's reign, when a second valuation was made, all livings under the value of £50 per annum were discharged from paying first fruits and tenths, and were also entitled to Her Majesty's bounty. Before the dissolution of the monasteries the annual value of the vicarage of Lowestoft appears to have been £44 4s. 5½d.

The principal entrance to the church is by a stately porch on the south side. In a nich on the outside, was formerly placed, as usual, the image of the saint to whom the church is dedicated. There is also a nich on each side of the former one, wherein other saints were also placed. On the ceiling of this porch is a representation of the Trinity, drawn in the same usual, but profane manner as, Blomefield says, it was on the rood-loft in Norwich Cathedral, namely, the Almighty Father represented by a weak old man, the Redeemer on the cross between his knees, and the Eternal Spirit by a dove on his breast. There are also Ancient shields, representing the crucifixion. On one of them is the cross, with the reed and spear saltyr wise: also the scourge, the nails, and on the top the scroll for the superscription. On the other, only the cross. Over this porch there is a chamber, called the Maids' Chamber. There is a tradition that it took its name from two maiden sisters, Elizabeth and Katherine, who, before the reformation, resided in this chamber; and, by withdrawing themselves from the world, retired to the more tranquil pursuits of a recluse life. It is reported of these sisters, that they caused two wells between the church and the town, called Basket Wells, to be digged at their own expense for the benefit of the town.

The church is situated about half a mile to the west of High street; and the reason of its being erected at so great a distance from the inhabited part of the parish, is the danger it would be exposed to from the sea by a nearer situation; it is probable, that at the time the church was built, the sea approached much nearer to the bottom of the cliff than it does at present. The church is about 43 feet in height, 57 feet in breadth, and, including the chancel and steeple, 182 feet in length. It consists of a nave and two side isles, which are separated from each other by two rows of tall, handsome pillars. The building appears to be a perfect model of the churches of the more early ages of Christianity, which were divided into two principal parts, namely, the nave, or body of the church, and the sacrarium, or according to the more modern appellation, the chancel. The former part being common to the people, as the latter was appropriated to the priests and other "sacred" persons. This separation continued in the English churches till the reformation, when Bucer, at the instigation of Calvin, objected to this division, as making too great a difference between the clergy and the people in the celebration of divine service. In consequence of this objection of Bucer's, reading desks were erected in the nave of the church, for the people's instruction. But though the whole of the service was originally performed in the chancel, yet there were always pulpits in the nave of the church, from whence, on Sundays and holidays, the ministers instructed the people by a sermon; and at the bottom of the south-west side of the middle pillar, on the north side of the nave of the church was a stone pedestal, which, before the reformation, supported the bottom part of one of those pulpits. As all the service was performed in the chancel, so the people, during the celebration thereof, remained in the nave, and were not admitted into the former place only at the administration of the sacrament.

The side isles of those antient churches did not terminate where the chancel began, neither did they extend to the end of it, but extended only about halfway of the chancel; and that end of the north isle which reached beyond the nave was named the prothesis, or side table (a repository for the plate, ornaments, etc., belonging to the altar, and called the prothesis).

In all the particulars mentioned, the church at Lowestoft bears a perfect resemblance to the antient churches; the side aisles extending exactly half way of the chancel; the end of the north isle next the chancel is made use of as a vestry; and there is the same space at the east end of the south aisle, which was used formerly for the prothesis. Before the Reformation the chancels were separated from the nave or body of the churches by screens or partitions. These screens are still remaining in some of our English churches; in Lowestoft church part of it was standing about the year 1710. The doors belonging to these screens (or holy gates as they were called in the primitive times) were always kept shut against the laity, except at the celebration of the sacrament.

There was also a rood loft in this church in the times of Popery. A few years since some bricks falling down from one of the buttresses on the south side of the church, near the chancel, discovered the stairs by which they ascended to the loft. The same has also been discovered on the north side of the church. The rood was the representation of our Saviour on the Cross, with the Virgin Mary on one side and St. John on the other; and was placed on the top of the wooden screen which formerly divided the church from the chancel. This screen, from the use above mentioned, was often called the rood-loft, a small bell, which was rung, probably, at some particular parts of divine service (as at the consecration or elevation of the host, from whence it is called the sacring, or consecrating bell), to rouse the attention of the congregation, some of whom, who sat at the south-east and north-east corners of the church, could not well see what was transacting at the high altar. This bell is different from that called the Saints' Bell, which was hung on the outside of the church, and gave notice to those abroad when the more solemn acts of religion were performing. A small piece of stone work on the outside of the east end of the church, with a small perforation or arch in the middle, for the bell to swing in, is still standing on several of our churches.

The chancel belonging to this church is very neat and elegant. The Rev. Tanner, while vicar of the parish, opened the subscription for purchasing the impropriation, and declared that if he succeeded in his undertaking, he would expend a considerable sum in repairing and beautifying the chancel. Mr. Tanner was successful, and he strictly adhered to his promise; for he thoroughly repaired the roof, raised five free-stone steps the whole breadth of the building, leading to the communion table, wainscotted the east end entirely, as well as part of the north and south sides, and also erected the seats at the west end, and made such alterations as rendered the chancel both commodious and handsome, expending in the whole upwards of £300.

The succeeding vicar, Rev. Arrow, continued the plan of his worthy predecessor in repairing and ornamenting the chancel. He erected a new altar-piece, enclosed the communion table with handsome iron work, opened the lower part of the east window (which before was filled up with brick work), and glazed the same, which caused this window to produce a very beautiful effect when viewed from the body of the church; and from these and other alterations, he rendered the chancel truly elegant. The number of communicants at Lowestoft church on Easter day, 1789, was 122.

There was a custom amongst the primitive Christians (during the violent persecutions which raged in those early ages of Christianity) of having churches underground, in order to avoid the dreadful cruelties which a more open profession of their religion would have exposed them to. In imitation of this antient practice the more modern Christians have also had their subterranean places of worship, which were situated under the choirs or chancels belonging to their respective churches, and where they also deposited the bones of deceased persons, which places where called the under-croft, and from the latter use of them charnel-chapels. There seems to have been one of these charnel-chapels formerly under the chancel belonging to this church. The design of them was for a priest to officiate therein, and to pray for the souls of all those persons whose bones were deposited in that place; but after the reformation they ceased being used for any sacred purpose, and were made use of afterwards only as repositories for the bones that were casually dug up in the church or churchyard.

R

The font in the church is very antient. It is ascended by three stone steps, and on the upper step is an old inscription, almost unintelligible through corrosion. The font is surrounded by two rows of saints, each row consisting of twelve figures; but they were so much injured by Francis Jessope, when he visited the church in 1644, under a commission from the earl of Manchester, as to be almost totally defaced.

On the 12th of June, 1644, Francis Jessope, of Beccles, under a commission from the Earl of Manchester, visited this church, and took away all the brass plates from the grave stones having the inscription "Orate pro Anima, etc." and others of the like nature, except the following: "Pray for the soul of Lady Margaret Parker, who died the First day of March, Ao. Dni. 1507. On whose soul may God be propitious." He also disrobed the stones of many brass effigies. All the brass was sold to Mr. John Wilde, of Lowestoft, for five shillings; although the quantity was sufficient to be run into a bell, which was used for a chapel. On the bell is the inscription " John Brand made me, 1644." The stone work of the font is covered with a handsome piece of carved work erected in the year 1734 by John Postle and Edmund Gillingwater, churchwardens.

About the year 1740, the pews in the church being very old, irregular, and much decayed, the Rev. Tanner, the vicar of the parish, in order to recover it from this disgraceful state, and to ornament it with that decent arrangement of seats, so becoming a place dedicated to public worship, and so generally to be met with in other churches, first set the example of new-pewing the church by erecting (in 1746) six neat wainscot seats in the body of the church, in memory of his wife. On these seats was the following inscription: "In memory of Mary, the wife of John Tanner, and daughter of Robert and Mary Knight, 1746. Not unto us, O Lord; not unto us, but unto thy name be the praise. John Tanner, vicar, desires this to be considered as a monument and pledge of love" In 1747 he added eight more, in grateful acknowledgment of some great mercy he had received from the Almighty. On these seats the inscriptions are "What shall I render unto the Lord for all his benefits towards me. J. T., 1747"; the other is "In memory of Grace Symonds, sister of John Tanner, vicar, 1759." It is supposed he thus shewed his thankfulness, for having been enabled to complete and publish the great work of learning and antiquity the "Notitia Monastica," which his brother, the Bishop of St. Asaph, left unfinished. The town being stimulated by so pious and useful an example, undertook within a few years after, to complete what Mr. Tanner had so laudably began; for in the year 1770 the whole design of new-pewing the church was completed; and by the addition of a very elegant desk and pulpit, is become one of the neatest and best pewed churches in the county.

In the year 1778 a resolution was formed by the minister and churchwardens to erect an organ in the church, and in pursuance thereof, a large gallery was built that year, at the west end of the middle isle, for the purpose of an organ loft; and in 1780 a large chamber organ, which formerly belonged to the late Dr. North, of Shanfield, near Saxmundham, was purchased at the price of eighty pounds, and erected in Lowestoft Church, and is the first instrument of the kind ever placed there.

There was a large brass eagle in the church. It formerly stood at the west end of the middle isle, but was removed into an obscure corner. The original use of the eagle, so general, formerly, in most of the churches, was for the purpose of being used as a litany desk; which part of the Church service, after the Reformation, was read or sung, at a different time of the day, from that where morning prayers were read. Also, possibly, the great English Bible, which, in 1538, Thomas Cromwell, Lord Privy Seal, ordered to be placed open in each parish church, for everyone to have recourse to, was laid upon these eagles. The ardour with which men flocked to read this bible is almost incredible. They who could, purchased a Bible, and they who could not, crowded to read it, or to hear it read, in churches; where it was common to see little assemblies of mechanics meeting together for that purpose, after the labours of the day. Many even learned to read in their old age, that they might have the pleasure of instructing themselves from the Scriptures.

In many parts of the Church are stones with matrices, or moulds, wherein plates of brass had formerly been laid; but all are now disrobed, together with the inscriptions, during the ravages under the usurpation of Oliver Cromwell.

The churchyard belonging to the parish, was nearly square, but not so before the year 1769, for at the south-west corner there was a small piece of glebe land, about a quarter of an acre, which projected into it. The parish had formerly made application to the late Vicar, Mr. Tanner, to exchange it for a piece of equal value; but the answer he always returned was, that he had no right to make any alteration in the property of the church. However, in the year 1769, the parish made an amicable agreement for it with the Rev. Arrow, and it was enclosed with a wall and laid into the churchyard, which made it of a regular form, but the piece of ground was never consecrated. On the death of the Rev. Arrow, the Vicar, in June, 1789, the dwelling-house, of which he was the proprietor, was purchased of his executors, for £550, under the powers of an Act of Parliament, passed some years since, for the better securing the residence of the clergy. But as the Act did not authorise an incumbent to raise more than two years value upon his benefice, and that sum amounting only to £430, the deficiency was made up in the following manner: Dr. Bagot, the Bishop of the Diocese, £20, and the parish of Lowestoft £100; and accordingly the house is now settled upon the Vicars of Lowestoft for ever.

In the churchyard formerly stood across, some remaining fragments of the stone work which supported it were visible a few years since. On the north side of the church is a tomb belonging to the family of the Barkers; in which are interred the remains of John Barker, Esq., a native and benefactor to the town; who died at his house in Mansel street, London, the 1st November 1787, aged eighty years. He was one of the elder brethren of the Trinity House, a govenor of the London Assurance, vice-president of the Magdalen house, and one of the directors of Greenwich Hospital. His body arrived at Lowestoft on the 8th of November; and after laying in state at the Queen's Head Inn till the next day, it was conveyed with great funeral pomp to the burial place of the family; where an elegant mausoleum has been erected, he having left by will £500 for that purpose, and also charged £1000 Bank stock, with the payment of £30 per annum for keeping the same in repair for ever; and what was not wanted of the said £30 for that use, is to be given to the poor of Lowestoft, in bread, at the church every Sunday after divine service. He also gave £200 to the poor of Lowestoft, to be given in coals, etc., immediately after his decease, which was done.

John Barker in his Will says: "I direct that my body be buried in the yard of the parish church of Lowestoft, in the County of Suffolk, in the vault wherin my late wife Elizabeth lies interred; and it is my desire that my executors hereafter named do cause a handsome tomb and monument to be erected over the said vault to our memory; but not to lay out a greater sum than £500 in erecting the same. And it is my intent, that the said vault, tomb, and monument be kept, in every respect, in perfect repair, pursuant to the provision hereafter by me made for that purpose.

"I give and bequeath the sum of One thousand pounds, three per cent. consolidated Bank annuities, unto the Accountant General, for the time being, of the High Court of Chancery; but to, for, and upon the uses, trusts, intents, and purposes following, that is to say, Upon Trust to permit and suffer the minister and churchwardens of the aforesaid parish of Lowestoft, for the time being for ever, (subject to the control and direction of the said Court of Chancery, in case if any misapplication of the said trusts, Bank annuities, contrary to the true intent and meaning of this my will), to receive and take the interests, dividends, and proceeds of the said one thousand pounds Bank annuities, to and for the following uses (to wit): In the first place thereout to keep, maintain, and support the said vault, tomb and monument herein before by me directed to be erected in Lowestoft churchyard, as aforesaid, not only neat, clean and decent, but in all respects in perfect repair. And in the next place, as to what overplus shall remain of such interest, dividends and proceeds, after keeping the said vault, tomb, and monument in perfect repair, I do empower the said minister and churchwardens, for the time being, to lay out such overplus in the purchase of bread, and to distribute the same, after divine service be finished on a Sunday, to and among such persons in low and indigent circumstances, of the said parish of Lowestoft, as they shall think fit objects of this charity. But it is my will and meaning, that my nephews, the aforesaid William Bell Barker and Samuel Barker, and after the death of the survivor of them, the persons for the time being for ever, who shall be heirs at law to my said nephews, William Bell Barker and Samuel Barker, shall, from time to time, have and enjoy the privilege of nominating to the minister and churchwardens aforesaid, twelve of such poor persons to receive the benefit of the said charity; and to which twelve poor persons to be nominated as aforesaid, the preference shall be always given, of having the said bread first delivered to them, anything herein before contained to the contrary thereof, in any wise notwithstanding. And it is my will, that all such expenses as at any time may attend the execution of the said trust, shall be first deducted out of the interest, dividends, and proceeds arising from the said one thousand pounds trust Bank annuities. And it is my further will, that if the aforesaid stock, commonly called three per cent. consolidated Bank annuities, shall at any time be paid off; then, and in such case, the produce of the said one thousand pounds stock shall be re-invested in the name of the Accountant General for the time being, on other Government security, to, for, and upon the like uses, trusts, intents, and purposes hereintofore expressed of and concerning the same."

Mr. John Wilde, of Lowestoft, having, by will, dated the 22nd of July, 1735, given several estates to this town, after the decease of Elizabeth Smithson, for the purpose of a school for the education of children belonging to this parish; and the said Elizabeth Smithson (afterwards Perryson) having departed this life the 3rd of December, 1781, the minister and churchwardens, in pursuance of the trust reposed in them by the said will, on the 21st of March, 1788, began to erect a building, for the purpose of a schoolroom, according to the directions of the said will; which building is thirty-six feet in length and twenty-five feet in breadth, and is situated at the bottom of the hill, on the east side of the Stone House which he gave to the parish by the said will; which house stands on the east side of High street, a little to the north of Rant's score. Under the first stone of this building are deposited several silver and copper coins of his Majesty.

Subjoined is an extract of the Last Will and Testament of JOHN WILDE, of Lowestoft, gentleman, (who died in April, 1738,) bearing date the 22nd of July, 1735:

"Also I give and devise unto the town of Lowestoft, for ever, all that my dwelling-house, fish-houses, yards, gardens, and appurtenances whatsoever to the same belonging, in the occupation of the Rev. Shewell. Also I give and devise to the said town of Lowestoft, for ever that all my meadow, in Lowestoft aforesaid, now in the occupation of John Pope. Also I give and devise unto the said town of Lowestoft, for ever, all that my house commonly called Rotterdam, with the yards, gardens, and appurtenances whatever to the same belonging, now in the occupation of James Pottle. Also I give unto the said town of Lowestoft, for ever, all my dole-lands in Lowestoft, together with all my lands, tenements, and hereditaments (if any there be not before by me given and bequeathed in this my will) whatsoever, which I have, at the time of my decease, in the town of Lowestoft aforesaid. Also I give and devise unto the said town of Lowestoft, for ever, the reversion (whenever it shall happen, after the death of the said Elizabeth Smithson) of all my messuages, lands, tenements, hereditaments, and premises, situate, lying, and being in Worlingham aforesaid, now in the tenure or occupation of Nicholas Matcheston, or his assigns, under-tenant, or under-tenants; all which premises, before by me given to the said town of Lowestoft, I give to the uses, intents, and purposes hereafter in this my last will more particularly declared, limited, and appointed. And I do nominate the minister and churchwardens, for the time being, for ever, hereafter to be trustees of all these my bequests to the said town of Lowestoft, strictly charging and commanding them religiously and conscientiously to discharge their trust, hereby by me given to them as they will answer it to Almighty God another day, in seeing the same performed according to the true intent and meaning of this my last will and testament, which now follows. And, first, my mind and will is, that all the same estates before by me given and devised to the said town of Lowestoft, together with the rents and profits thereof, shall be applied for a virtuous and learned schoolmaster, who shall teach forty boys to write and read, and cast accounts; and also shall teach them the Latin tongue. And my mind and will is, that the said schoolmaster shall be chosen by the said minister and churchwardens for the time being, upon every vacancy that shall happen by death, misdemeanour, or misbehaviour of the said schoolmaster. All which I leave to the discretion and management of the said Minister and Churchwardens for the time being, to place, replace, or remove the said schoolmaster as they shall think proper; desiring them they will act impartially in placing or removing the said schoolmaster, and not choose by favour or affection, but having virtue, religion, and merit chiefly in view. And my mind and will further is, that when all the said bequests, before by me given and bequeathed to the said town of Lowestoft, shall become due to the said (then, and not before), the salary of the said schoolmaster shall be forty pounds per annum; which I will be paid half-yearly to the said schoolmaster, upon the feasts of St. Michael, the Archangel, and the annunciation of the blessed Lady Mary the Virgin, by equal portions in every year. And my mind and will is, that until the death of the said Elizabeth Smithson, the profits of the other bequests before by me given and devised to the said town of Lowestoft shall be at their own discretion, so as the same be expended towards the encouraging of learning; and therefore would have it employed, as far as the rents will go, towards educating children in manner aforesaid. And my mind and will further is, and I do hereby give and devise unto the Minister of the said parish of Lowestoft for the time being, for ever, the sum of one pound and one shilling; and unto the clerk of the said parish, for ever, the sum of ten shillings; and unto the sexton of the said parish, for ever, the sum of five shillings. All which said sums of one pound and one shilling, ten shillings, and five shillings, I will shall be paid out of the rents and profits of all the messuages, lands, tenements, hereditaments, and premises, before by me given and devised, in this my will, to the said town of Lowestoft, for the purposes aforesaid. And I bind all the same for the payment thereof. And my mind and will is, that the said several sums shall be paid to the several **persons** always yearly upon the twenty-third day of December, in every year; but upon this condition, nevertheless, that the minister of the said parish of Lowestoft for the time being, shall always yearly upon the twenty-third day of December in every year, sometime in the forenoon, preach a sermon (except the said day should fall on a Sunday, and then my mind and will is, that the said sermon should be preached on the Monday next following); and his text I desire should be these express words—" Train up a child in the way he should go, and when he is old he will not depart from it." And my mind and will further is, that the said sermon should chiefly tend upon the great necessity of the good education of children, and the ill consequence that attends the neglect of it. And in case any overplus should arise out of the said several bequests before by me given and devised to the said town of Lowestoft, after the said salary of forty pounds to be paid to the said schoolmaster, in manner aforesaid; and the said several sums of one pound one shilling, ten shillings, and five shillings, to be paid to the several persons above mentioned, be fully paid and satisfied, such overplus, if any should be, or whatever it be, I give and devise the same, for such charitable purposes and uses as the Minister and Churchwardens of Lowestoft aforesaid, for the time being, shall think proper to distribute, so as such overplus, if any there be, or whatever it be, shall be distributed every year."

Will of Mr. John Hayward, of Lowestoft, to whom some of the poor were indebted for weekly donation of bread:

"In the name of God, Amen. I, John Hayward, of Lowestoft, in the county of Suffolk, mariner, being of sound and perfect mind and memory, do make and ordain this my last will and testament in manner and form following: First. I commit my soul into the hands of Almighty God, etc., and for settling my goods and temporal estate, I do give and dispose of the same as followeth: I give and bequeath all my messuages or tenements unto Mary, my loving wife, during the time of her natural life. I give and bequeath (after my said wife's decease) unto my son, Robert Hayward, all my houses, out-houses, fish-houses, lands and appurtenances whatsoever, to hold to him for and during the term of his natural life, and after his decease to the heirs of his body lawfully to be begotten. And for want of such heirs, give all the same lands and premises to and amongst all my daughters that shall then be living. To hold them jointly, and to their heirs for ever, so as, and upon condition, that my said son Robert, or his heirs, or my daughters, or such person or persons as shall enjoy my said messuages, lands, and tenements, shall pay or cause to be paid unto my grandson, Samuel Mariner, the sum of fifty pounds, of lawful money of Great Britain, at the age of one and twenty years. And also shall pay yearly, and every year, into the hands of the churchwardens of the parish of Lowestoft, and their successors, for ever, the sum of two and fifty shillings. The first payment within twelve months next after the decease of my said wife, and so to be received yearly by the churchwardens, and employed and laid out twelve pence weekly, and every week in the year, for fourteen loaves of bread, to be by them given every Sunday, or Lord's day, throughout the year, for ever, after divine service in the afternoon, at the parish church of Lowestoft aforesaid, to fourteen such poor people as they shall think fit. Which said sums of fifty pounds, payable to my grandson, Samuel Mariner, and two and fifty shillings, given payable yearly for ever, for bread for the poor, my will is, shall be paid out of the estate wherein I now dwell. And I do make all the same estate liable and subject to the payment of the same, as fully and amply as may or can be. And my will is, that the same may so continue for ever. Except such persons as shall enjoy the same, after the payment of the aforesaid fifty pounds to my grandchild, shall give any other security to the churchwardens and trustees of Lowestoft aforesaid, for the continuance of the payment of two and fifty shillings yearly, for ever, as they, the said churchwardens and trustees, shall think fit to accept." (The dwelling-houses charged with the payment of this donation are situated near the north end of the town, on the east-side, now belonging to the Arnold family.)

"This is a true copy of the clause of Mr. John Hayward's will, which was proved at the Bishop of Norwich's principal office (19th of August 1719), holden in the precinct of the cathedral church of Norwich; where the original will may at any time be seen.

JOHN TANNER,

Vicar of Lowestoft, and one of the executors of the said John Hayward."

A decree, judgment, and orders made sett down by Sir Arthur Heveningham, Sir Miles Corbett, knts., Henry Gawdy, Esq., and Mr. Dr. Sucklinge, doctor in divinity; by virtue of her Majesty's commission to them and others, out of her Majesty's High Court of Chancery, under the great seale of England, directed and hereunto annexed, upon a verdict by force of the like commission, to them and others directed by them, the second day of October, in the four and fortieth year of her Majesty's most gracious and happy reign, taken and returned unto the said Court of Chancery upon the statute made in the High Court of Parliament holden the seven and twentieth day of October, in the three and fortieth year of her Majesty's reign, intituled an Act to redresse the misemployments of lands, goods, and stocks of money, before the making thereof, given to charitable uses, as followeth:

"IMPRIMIS. We do order, adjudge, and decree that the free grammar schoole mentioned in the said verdict shall be and remain a free grammar-schoole, and shall have continuance for ever within the said town of Lowestoft; and the same schoole shall consist of a schoolmaster learn'd in the art and knowledge of grammar, and able to instruct and teach the rules and principles thereof and the Latin tongue, and other things incident, necessary, and belonging to the said art, to be master, tutor, and teacher of the schollars in the said schoole, consisting of forty schollars, and not above, to be taught and instructed within the said schoole.

"ITEM. We do order, adjudge, and decree that the house within the said town of Lowestoft, which is now used for the schoole-house for the said master and scholars. (Formerly there was a school-house for Annott's foundation in the Town Close adjoining to the east wall of the Churchyard, which being in a ruinous state, an allowance was made the master until such time as the Town Chamber was fitted up and made a convenient schoolroom in 1674), shall, for ever, hereafter, continue and be the schoolehouse wherein the schoolemaster of the said schoole shall teach and instruct the schollars thereof; and that Stephen Phillips, now schoolemaster of the said schoole, shall remaine schoolemaster thereof; and that he and his successors, and all other schoolmasters of the said schoole, shall, for ever hereafter be called and known by the name of "Mr. Annott, his schoolemaster." And whensoever, and as often as it shall happen, that the place and roome of the schoolmaster hall become void, we do order adjudge and decree, that the Chancellor for the time being, to the Bishop, for the time being, of the see of Norwich, or sede vacante the guardian of the spiritualities, shall have the nomination and appointment of the schoolemaster of the said schoole within the said town.

"We do also order, adjudge, and decree, that the forty schollars of the said schoole shall be of such children as are or shall be borne within the said towne of Lowestoft, if there be or shall be sufficient of such within the said town to supply and fill up the said number of forty. And for want of a number sufficient of them to supply or make up the said number of forty, then that the children of the inhabitants within the said town, albeit the said children be or shall not be born within the said town, to supply and make up the said number of forty. And if these also neither are nor shall not be sufficient to supply and make up the said number of forty, then that the children of the inhabitants within the hundred of Lothingland and Mutford shall be nominated, elected and appointed to supply and make up the said number of forty; the choise and appointment of which schollars shall be to the said Stephen Phillips, now schoolemaster, so long as he shall be schoolemaster there, and to such as from time to time shall supply the roome and place of the said schoolemaster within the said town; so that he do nominate and appoint to the number of forty scholars, and not above; and that he shall not take for the nomination and appointment so by him to be made above the sume of twenty pence for every scholar within the said schoole.

("Examined by me,) RICHARD MOSS, Dep. Reg."

Writings of great length concerning this school could at one time be seen at the Episcopal Office at Norwich. Probably the original deed of Mr. Annott, bearing date 10th of June, 1570, for founding the school, the commission, inquisition and verdict, as well as the above decree, are included amongst them. Mr. Annott dying without issue, his heirs at law disputed the legality of the donation, and endeavoured to recover the lands, for it is recorded that in 1591 it cost the town £120 to defend its right to this school; and it was in consequence of this suit that the heirs augmented the annual payment from twenty marks to sixteen pounds.

On the vacancy of a mastership of this school, a person of good character, and a member of the Church of England, is presented to the Chancellor of the Diocese by the Vicar and Churchwardens of Lowestoft for the time being, who appoints and licenses the same.

About the year 1670 (when the old school-house belonging to Annott's foundation was decayed) a dispute seems to have arisen between this parish and the Allens of Somerly, respecting a design formed by that family of uniting Annott's school with one founded by Sir Thomas Allen. One Mr. Henry Britten formerly master of the school at Lowestoft, who had been applied to by the town for information concerning this affair, answered as follows:

TO THE TOWNSMEN OF LOWESTOFT,

"Whereas I was desired to give an answer to divers things proposed concerning the free grammar-school at Lowestoft, during the time I had to do with it; to which I answer as follows: I was presented to it by Mr. Thomas London, the then patron, in the year 1667, and chosen by the general consent of the town, with the minister's hand and churchwardens, and generally the whole town; and had also a license from the chancellor of Norwich, with his seal, to receive the profits, and did receive, for divers years, the yearly salary of £16 per annum, paid me by the tenants of the school lands at Burrough. But the tenant being a backward man, was always in arrears, and at last died, and left at least £10 unpaid. Thomas Perry, steward for Mr. Thomas Allen, seized what he had, and I was never paid it. But after that they paid me, and I received it from Sir Thomas himself, at the hall, but most what his steward paid me, but they also kept behind in arrears, but told me I should be paid it,

only desired me to forbear awhile, because the tenant had not paid them. Some while after, old Sir Thomas (Admiral Sir Allen, formerly of Lowestoft), erected a school house. When it had been some while built, and stood empty, Mr. Evans petitioned that he might keep a writing school in it, which being granted soon after, Sir Thomas would have me resign, that he might lay the revenues given to the Latin to his school house, designed for English. In refusing to sign, there being about two years in arrears, he told me I should not have one farthing, if I did not resign, and from that time the money was stopped. He desired also to see writings belonging to the school, which he did obtain of some of the townsmen, which he kept, and they could not be found until such time as we came to agreement, which was many years after. Thus it continued many years unpaid. Sometimes I had promise of payment from Sir Thomas Allen, but he was set off again by some or other. I have had many journeys to Norwich, and applied myself to the Bishop and Chancellor, and had promise of them to do me right, but something or other always happened that it was still unpaid. I had counsel about it, and I was told that I might help myself by the Court of Chancery, if the town would join with me, otherwise they would not assist me. I propounded it and found the town cold, and did not care for stirring in it; so that at last I was forced to agree with them, there being £200 due. With much ado I agreed with them to pay me £100, which I did not receive all, till a year or more after I resigned (in 1696.) Mr. Echard, of Somerleyton, was he that agreed with me, as Sir Thomas Allen's agent. They required me to give them bond to quit all claim of the school, and also to give in my license. And, thus, I suppose, I have answered what was desired. "HEN BRITTEN.
"Needham Market, Dec. 26, 1701."

An extract of the last Will and Testament of JOHN WILDE, of Lowestoft, bearing date the 3rd of April, 1699, respecting the donation of James Wilde, his father, of twelve loaves of bread to the poor of this parish to be given every Sunday, after divine service, in Lowestoft church. Also his own donation.

"ITEM. I give, devise, and bequeath unto my said son John and his heirs, for ever, fifteen pounds, of lawful English money; the interest of which said sum of fifteen pounds, with the rent of the messuage, tenement, and pightle, in the occupation of John Middleton, aforesaid, I will shall be for and towards the payment of twelve loaves of bread, given by my father, Mr. James Wilde, deceased, every Sunday, or Lord's Day, in the year, for ever, to the poor of Lowestoft aforesaid. And for and towards the payment of six penny loaves more, as aforesaid, being my own bequest, to be distributed as aforesaid, in Lowestoft Church, after divine service in the forenoon, every Sunday for ever. But my mind and will is that it shall be in my said son John's power to choose whether he will give securities to the feoffees of the town lands and churchwardens of the said tenement and pightle, and the interest of the said fifteen pounds, or assign and set over the said tenement and fifteen pounds unto the said feoffees, to remain for ever to the use aforementioned, the one of which, my mind and will is, shall be performed and done by my said son John and his heirs, for ever."

ANN GIRLING, widow, by will, bearing date 8th of June, 1584, gave certain premises therein mentioned to the poor of Lowestoft, to be given them in firing.

"LOWESTOFT.—At the General Court Baron, with the leet of Corton, holden on Saturday, in Quinquagesima week, in the 27th year of Queen Elizabeth, A.D. 1584-5.

"To this Court came William Wilde and John Lawne, and brought into Court the last will and testament of ANN GIRLING, of Lowestoft, widow, in which is contained (amongst other things) as follows: *Item*. My barn, house, with the tenement adjoining and their appurtenances, being copyhold of this manor of Lowestoft, I give and bequeath unto Thomas Ward, William Wilde, Nathaniel Arnold, John Wilde, John Lawne, John Wells, and their heirs for ever. ONLY to the use of the honest poor of Lowestoft, to be given by the hands of two of them, in wood, so far as the farm of my said barn and tenement, with the appurtenances, will reach yearly. So much yearly detained only as shall keep the same in reparation sufficiently. And they the said feoffees to see conveyance made from them, when there remaineth but two of them, to others whom they shall think good to the use aforesaid. Or as learned counsel shall best advise; and so from feoffees to feoffees, to the use aforesaid, for ever, as by the said will, bearing date the 8th day of June, A.D. 1584, it doth and may more fully and at large appear. And thereupon the said William Wilde and John Lawne, in their own proper persons, and the other feoffees, namely, Nathaniel Arnold, John Wilde, and John Wells, by their attorney, were admitted, etc."

The premises, named, have many years since fallen into decay; and the ground was, in 1773, the garden of a house situated by the old market, and was let for five shillings per annum."

The abuttalments are thus described in the last admission:—"One tenement decayed, with a barn and garden thereunto belonging, in the west lane, near the old market, between the king's highway upon the south; and the lands of Margaret Whitehead upon the north; and abutts upon the widow Sterry, towards the west; and upon late Stingales, towards the east. In whom it is now vested, is unknown; but the churchwardens dispose of the rent."

## SECTION VI.

### OF THE CHAPELS.

THE church belonging to this parish standing at too great a distance from the general residence of the inhabitants to be frequented by the aged and infirm, it became necessary to erect places for public worship in a near, and consequently, more convenient situation. It is evident that there have been **two chapels in the town** of Lowestoft, and both of them erected before the Reformation. One of them **was situated at the** south end of the town, and was called Good-Cross Chapel. **This building was destroyed by the sea**, without leaving any traces remaining, whereby might be determined either its dimensions or the exact place of its situation. This chapel was not only situated at the south end of the town, but also as far to the east, probably, as the sea would admit of; for it stood between the ocean and the principal highway leading from Lowestoft to Kirkley. The latest account that can be met with, respecting the time when it was standing, is in the reign of Edward VI. These circumstances appear from the following entry in the Court rolls of the manor of Lowestoft: —"At a general Court Baron with the leet, held in the fourth year of the reign of King Edward the Sixth, Laurance Robson was admitted to parcel of land of the waste of the Lord with a house thereupon built, called Good-Cross Chapel, containing in length sixty feet, in breadth fifty feet, **the west head whereof** abutts upon the way leading from Lowestoft to Kirkley, on the surrender of Richard ———. At a Court held on Wednesday next after the feast of the nativity of St. John, Thomas Welch was admitted on the surrender of the said Laurance Robson." The offerings made to the holy cross in this chapel, before **the dissolution of the monasteries, amounted to about £9** annually for the benefit of the Vicar of the parish.

The other chapel situated near the middle **of the town, and** after the dissolution, appears not to have been used for many years as a place of worship, but was suffered to fall much into decay. That part of the building which was next the street was converted into a town-house, for the residence of the poor. At the **north-east corner was an entrance**; where, by ascending **a gallery the** chapel **was entered behind the town** house; and also at this entrance was an isle, which led backwards to the farther end of the chapel. The building seems to have been erected upon arches, as there were cells underneath on each side of the isle; and wherein, probably, in the times of Popery, some persons inhabited; for **afterwards**, one of these cells was the residence of the sexton of the parish. (After the re-building of the chapel in 1698, **the** sexton had a certain sum allowed him **annually** by the parish for the house rent, until the **year 1720, when** a house was purchased for him to reside in.) This appears to have been the state of this antient chapel from the time of the dissolution **of the** monasteries until the **year** 1570; when the inhabitants, experiencing many inconveniences in not having a place for public worship near **the** church, made application to Bishop Parkhurst for a license, in order that divine service might be performed in this chapel, which accordingly was granted; but upon this express condition, that the chapel should be decently ornamented and fitted up for that purpose; that no public **prayers** should be used there than those prescribed in the Book of Common **Prayer**; and that neither the sacrament of baptism nor Lord's supper should **ever be** administered there on any account whatsoever.

To the Parishioners of Lowestoft.

"JOHN, by divine permission, Bishop of Norwich. To our beloved in Christ, the parishioners of Lowestoft, in our diocese and jurisdiction, health, grace, and blessing.

"Know ye, that for the furtherance of devotion, and for the increase of divine worship; and attentively considering and understanding from certain good and weighty reasons to us explained, that the parish church at Lowestoft aforesaid not being so conveniently situated for hearing divine service as could be wished (especially in the winter season,) you are not able to attend. And that you may be enabled to cause public prayers to be celebrated in a proper chapel, in a fit place, and decently ornamented, within the parish of Lowestoft aforesaid, whenever the parishioners of Lowestoft, or the vicar thereof, conceive that divine service may be less commodiously performed in the said church than in the said chapel, WE have granted by these presents LICENSE for celebrating divine service therein; and we have caused this our license to be irrevocable. But provided nevertheless, That no vicar or curate baptize, or administer the sacrament of the Lord's supper, or cause it to be administered in the place aforesaid, but in the church of your parish. Nor that they cause, nor that you the parishioners presume, to assist therein, in the celebration of either of the said sacraments, in any manner whatsoever. Inhibiting, moreover That no other public prayers be there used, or suffered to be thus used, than what are prescribed in the Book of Common Prayer, set forth by royal authority, and by the consent of the whole Parliament, approved and lawfully enjoined. But if you or any one act contrary hereto, we will, that the authority hereby given to you be void and of no effect. And moreover, you offending in the premises, shall be liable to punishment, lawfully to be inflicted, or imposed at our pleasure." "11th November, 1570."

After the granting of this license, divine service appears to have been performed in this chapel until about the year 1674 or 1676; at which time, probably, from its decayed state, it became wholly unfit for that purpose; and the public weekly prayers, after that time, were read in the town chamber, a room over the town house; and in this manner was divine service performed until the year 1698, when the old chapel, from its very ruinous state, was entirely taken down and rebuilt, in consequence of a subscription opened for that purpose. The old chapel was a thatched building.

The re-building of this chapel was undertaken under the care and management of Captain Andrew Leake, (afterwards Sir Andrew Leake; eminently distinguished as a gallant sea commander in the reign of Queen Anne), and Dr. Joseph Leake: and was brought (together with corn-cross and town chamber) into nearly the same state in which they appeared in 1698 at the expense of about £350,

The ADDRESS to the INHABITANTS of LOWESTOFT, Respecting the Re-building of Lowestoft Chapel.

"Forasmuch as I have observed the great danger which may ensue from the weakness and decay of the chapel and town house at Lowestoft, in the county of Suffolk, with many other inconveniences attending the same. And considering the state of the inhabitants of the town at this time to be a proper seaon for undertaking and re-building of the said chapel. Being therefore devoted, not only to employ my time in the management and carrying on so good a work, but also to solicit a free and liberal contribution towards effecting the same, which I doubt not but every honest gentleman will promote, by his generous assistance therein; an account of which receipts shall always be shewn to such as desire it, for their satisfaction, by reason of the many complaints of the mismanagement of former collections. And if any person do, or shall suspect my failure in my answering the sum collected, and deposited in my hands, I do hereby promise to engage to give treble security that the monies collected shall be laid out to the use above mentioned.

"As witness my hand, 7th of June, 1698. Andrew Leake."

The amount collected by Captain Andrew Leake was £152 0s. 6d.; by Dr. Joseph Peake £193 14s. 1¼d. The expenditure was £347 13s. 7d., being £1 18s. 11¼d. in excess of the receipts, and this sum was generously discharged by Dr. Peake, in the presence of James Wilde, Henry Ward, John Wilde, John Peake, John Barker, jun., John Jex, John Barker, Matthew Arnold, Joseph Smithson. The chapel, although much superior to the former building, was, nevertheless, but an indifferent structure. The pews were of deal, the pulpit and desk stood on the south side; and a gallery on the east, west and north sides. In the middle of the building was hung a vast brass chandelier, the gift of Mr. Martin Brown, formerly a merchant at Rotterdam, but was a native of Lowestoft.

The font belonging to this chapel stood originally on the north side of it, opposite the desk and pulpit. In 1763 it was removed to the south-east end of the chapel; and in 1773, when the north end of the corn cross was inclosed for the purpose of a vestry, the font was again removed to the north-east end of the building. Although baptism was not permitted to be administered in the old chapel, yet it was always performed in this chapel from the time it was erected. Elizabeth, the daughter of Samuel Darkin, was baptised here on the 29th December, 1699, and was the first baptised in the chapel. The font was the gift of Mr. John Jex, merchant of this town. It is not clear from what place the font was brought. The town book, belonging to this parish, says it came from Easton Bavent; but the late John Jex of this town, used to declare that it was brought from Gisleham, and was digged up by accident on the lands in that parish, belonging to the above John Jex, merchant, his father. Probably the latter is the fact, as Mr. Jex had lands at Gisleham, but none at Easton Bavent. However, be that as it will, Mr. Jex was undoubtedly the benefactor.

Prayers were read at this chapel every Wednesday, Friday, and hoildays throughout the year. On Sundays, divine service was always performed here in the morning, except when the sacrament was administered, when it was always at the church. Sometimes, in very bad weather, the service was at the chapel on Sundays, both parts of the day

It is not improbable, but that before the reformation there was another chapel in the town besides those two already mentioned. This chapel (if there ever really was such a place appropriated to sacred purposes) was situated on the west side of High street, about thirty yards to the north of Swan Lane. It was an old Gothic building, faced with black flint; was about sixteen feet in height, and twelve in breadth; and had the appearance of a very antient building. What tends to strengthen the conjecture of its being a place originally designed for sacred uses is, that the Rev. Tanner, who was vicar of the parish (and who published his brother's "Notitia Monastica," and consequently was a competent judge of those matters) used to say, that if ever there was a religious house in this town, it was situated opposite to this building If so, probably this building was the chapel belonging to that religious society. The buildings supposed to have been originally a religious foundation, carry with them, some resemblance of an institution of that nature. They are divided by a passage (which was entered by a large door-space, in the Gothic style), having spacious rooms on each side, whose venerable appearance demonstrates their having been formed neither after a modern nor a mean original.

## SECTION VII.

## VICARS OF LOWESTOFT.

IN consequence of there not having been any regular registers of the institutions to church benefices before the year 1299, it is impossible to obtain any information respecting those appointments prior to that period; but after the keeping of those registers, much light has been thrown on the ecclesiastical history of this country: and it is from the assistance derived from those registers that the regular succession of vicars of this parish can be given from the year 1308.

Thomas Scrope, surnamed Bradley, from the town where he was born, descended from a noble family, and very much adorned the honour of his birth by his learning and virtues. He was first a monk of the order of St. Benedict; after that, aspiring to a greater perfection of life, he took upon him the profession and rule of a Dominican; and afterwards he submitted himself to the discipline of the Carmelites. He became Bishop of Dromore, in Ireland, but in the year of his age one hundred, he died in this town of Lestoffe, the 15th January, 1491, the 7th of Henry VII, and was buried in the chancel of Lowestoft Church. On the stone over his burial place was a stone upon which was the effigy of a Bishop in his episcopal habit; his crozier in one hand and his pastoral staff in the other, with several escutcheons of the arms of his family etc., and ornamented with a border, all in brass; but scarce any remains of them are now to be seen, and the matrices wherein they were placed are almost empty.

In 1540 John Blomewyle, was on the presentation of Thomas Godsalve, Esq., instituted vicar. He resigned in 1555, in the beginning of the reign of Queen Mary. Probably he could not conform to the alterations in religious matters made by the Queen at that time; or possibly he might be a married man, and therefore under the necessity of resigning, to prevent being ejected, as was the misfortune of a great number of the clergy in that unhappy reign.

The Rev. Jacob Rous appears to have been minister of this parish during the whole usurpation of Oliver Cromwell. He was vicar, on June 12, 1644, when Francis Jessope was sent with a commission from the Earl of Manchester to disrobe the grave stones of the brasses that had the inscription " Orate pro anima, etc."

The Rev. Whiston, on the 19th August, 1702, resigned Lowestoft, to succeed Sir Isaac Newton in the mathematical professorship, at Cambridge. He was a divine of great abilities and uncommon learning. In 1694 he was appointed chaplain to Dr. Moor, Bishop of Norwich, which he held till 1698, when the Bishop presented him with the living of Lowestoft with Kessingland. A parish (Mr. Whiston said) of 2,000 souls, but not worth more than £120 a year clear. The care of souls was rightly esteemed by him as a concern of the highest importance; he, therefore, set himself sincerely and in good earnest to that great work, discharging the several duties of a parish priest with distinguished piety and unwearied diligence. Notwithstanding that his income was so small, he kept a curate, allowing him £30 a year, and the curate made £30 a year more by teaching a small school. Mr. Whiston set up public prayers morning and evening, every day, at the chapel within the town. He constantly preached twice on Sundays; and at the summer season, at least, had a catechetic lecture at the chapel in the evening, designed more for the benefit of the adult than for the children. To these lectures came many dissenters. This may easily be accounted for when it is considered that the noted Mr. Emlyn had officiated as minister to the Dissenters of the town eighteen months, about ten years before. Mr. Emlyn had adopted the Arian principles, and probably had introduced the same sentiments among many of his hearers, who consequently, were pre-disposed to attend lectures that were given by a minister of the establishment who entertained opinions similar to those of Mr. Emlyn, as was the case with Mr. Whiston. There appears to have been the most intimate friendship between these two divines: for when Mr. Whiston, in 1715, held a weekly meeting for promoting primitive christianity, the third chairman of those meetings was Mr. Emlyn. Mr. Whiston resigned the livings in 1702, and being, by the interest of his friend, Sir Isaac Newton, appointed to succeed him in the mathematical chair at Cambridge, he went and resided in that university; but continuing to retain and propogate Arian principles, he was for his heterodox opinions expelled the university on the 30th October, 1710. In 1747 he left the communion of the Church of England, and joined the Baptists. After engaging in various schemes, and experiencing many vicissitudes of fortune, he died on the 22nd August, 1752, in London, after only a week's illness. His body was interred at Lyndon, near Stamford, Lincolnshire. The inscription placed over him says he died in the 85th year of his age. Endued with an excellent genius, and indefatigable in labour and study, he became learned in divinity, antient history, chronology, philosphy and mathemetics.

Jacob Smith, vicar in 1702, was a native of Scotland, and for conscientiously refusing to take the oaths of King William, he was (with a large family) reduced to all the hardships and miseries of an obscure and necessitous life; but on the resignation of Mr. Whiston, Bishop Moor presented him to Lowestoft. He was buried in the churchyard, close by the north side of the chancel, where a tomb was erected to his memory. And tradition reports that he was the first person ever buried on that side of the church. There was formerly a great partiality respecting burying on the south and east sides of the churchyard at Lowestoft. Many years after the interment of Jacob Smith there was not more than two or three graves on the north side of the church, though subsequently it became as general to inter on one side as on the other. This partiality may, perhaps, at first, have partly arisen from the antient custom of praying for the dead; for as the usual approach to this and many other churches is by the south, it was natural for burials to be on that side, that those who were going to divine service, might, in their way, by the sight of the graves of their friends, be put in mind to offer up a prayer for the welfare of their souls; and even now, since the custom of praying for the dead is abolished, the same obvious situation of graves may excite some tender recollection in those who view them, and silently implore the passing tribute of a sigh.

The Rev. John Tanner, who was Vicar of Lowestoft many years, died in 1759; he was precentor of the Cathedral of Asaph, Rector of Kessingland, and also commissary and official to the arch-deaconry of Suffolk, (in 1725), which offices he resigned as soon as the infirmities of age rendered him incapable of performing them with that care and exactness he had always shewn in their discharge. Among his many antient acts of charity may be mentioned (exclusive of the active part which he took in the re-building of Kirkley church) his purchasing the impropriation of Lowestoft, for the benefit of his successors; his expending a large sum of money in repairing and beautifying the chancel; and also setting the first example in new-pewing the church. He was the third son of the Rev. Thomas Tanner, vicar of Market Leavington, Wiltshire; was educated at Queen's College, Oxford; and obtained his preferment through the interest of his brother, Thomas Tanner, who was many years Chancellor of the Diocese of Norwich.

Rev. J. Arrow who was instituted to the vicarage of Lowestoft in 1760, was born in London in 1733; was educated at Westminister school, and admitted of Trinity College, Cambridge; was formerly a chaplain to the Royal Navy, which he exchanged for Lowestoft, with Dr. Greet, chaplain to Dr. Hayter, Bishop of Norwich, who had presented him to the same, but was not instituted. The Rev. Arrow died the 22nd of June 1789, aged 55 years, and was buried in the chancel of Lowestoft church. He was a person of a very regular life and conversation; zealous in promoting the interest and welfare of the church; and so very conscientious in discharging the duties of his function, that although very ill, yet he preached twice in the last twenty-four hours before he expired.

The Rev. Robert Potter, prebendary of Norwich, was well known in the literary world as the learned and ingenious translator of the Aschylus, Sophocles, and Euripides.

## SECTION VIII.

### OF RELIGIOUS SECTS.

THE town of Lowestoft has been much distinguished in religious concerns, for its inviolable attachment to the establishment of the Church of England, as in civil affairs, for its unshaken loyalty to its sovereign. Nevertheless, it is not without its sectaries, which, at different times, have arisen in the town; the principal of which sectaries is that society denominated Independents or Congregational Dissenters. At what time it was that this religious sect first began to make its appearance in Lowestoft is uncertain. Previous to the year 1689, when the learned Mr. Emlyn came to reside in the town, and commenced as minister to the Congregational dissenters, it was but an inconsiderable body, destitute of a regular pastor, and also of a decent structure for the purpose of religious exercises. (When Mr. Emlyn first came to Lowestoft he had not adopted those religious principles which afterwards proved to him a source of the heaviest afflictions). The congregation of Protestant dissenters at Lowestoft might be considered also, at that time, as a kind of dependent assembly on the Dissenting congregation at Yarmouth; as it was customary for the members belonging to the former congregation to repair to that at Yarmouth at the usual seasons of receiving the holy communion, and was much in the same state of dependence on that society as a chapel-of-ease is on the mother church.

At this early period the Dissenters of Lowestoft had no other building for the public exercise of religion than a barn situate in a lane called Blue Anchor lane, opposite Rant's score; and they continued in this obscure situation till the year 1695, when a decent structure was erected for religious uses. Probably the Society was much increased after the year 1689, when so distinguished a character as Mr. Emlyn became their minister, and in consequence thereof might be enabled to erect this building. This meeting house was erected in 1695 upon a small piece of ground given for that purpose by Mr. James Ward of this town. The eminent Mr. Emlyn was born at Stamford, in Lincolnshire, May 22, 1663. In August, 1674, he was put to a boarding school at Walcot, near Folkingham, where he continued four years, and on Sundays was the constant auditor of the noted Mr. Brocklesby, the then incumbent of that parish. Mr. Emlyn's parents were of the established church, and were very intimate with the very learned and worthy Dr Cumberland, then minister at Stamford, and afterwards Bishop of Peterborough, but being inclined to the Puritans, they choose to educate their son among that sect; for this purpose he was sent, for academical education, in 1678, to Sulby, near Welford, in Northamptonshire, where he continued four years. In 1679 he went to Cambridge; and in 1682 was admitted of Emanuel College, but returned again to Sulby; and in the same year he removed to Mr. Doolittle's academy, first at Islington, then at Clapham, and afterwards at Battersea. He made his first essay as a preacher December 19, 1682, at Mr. Doolittle's meeting house, near Cripplegate. In 1683 he was chaplain to the Countess of Donegal, a lady of great quality and estate in the north of Ireland, but resided then in Lincoln's Inn Fields, London, and the year following accompanied the family to Belfast. While in this station he made a journey to Dublin, and during his continuance in that city, preached once before that congregation of which Mr. Daniel Williams and Mr. Joseph

Boyce were at that time pastors, in a manner so acceptable to the audience, as gave occasion for that people afterwards to invite him to be their minister. A favourable opportunity for this purpose offered shortly after; for Mr. Williams having quitted the congregation at Dublin, Mr. Boyce made some overtures to Mr. Emlyn relative to his succeeding him, which he declined accepting. Mr. Emlyn still continued his station as chaplain in this family; but in 1688, when the disturbances in Ireland occasioned his patron's family to leave that Kingdom, he returned to London. On his arrival at that place, and being out of employment, he was invited by Sir Robert Rich, one of the Lords of the Admiralty, to his house at Rose Hall, near Beccles, and was by him prevailed upon to officiate as Minister to the Dissenting congregation at Lowestoft; which place he supplied about a year and a half, but refused the invitation of being their pastor; for as he disapproved of Ministers changing and shifting from one place to another, so he had determined not to accept any pastoral care but where he thought he should settle, and purposed to continue. It was during his residence at Lowestoft, that, reading Dr. Sherlock's piece on the Trinity, he first began to entertain some scruples concerning the received doctrine in that point of faith. Here also he contracted a close and intimate acquaintance with Mr. William Manning, a Nonconformist Minister at Peasanhall, and corresponded with him during Mr. Manning's life. As both were of an inquisitive temper, they frequently conferred together on the highest mysteries of religion; and Dr. Sherlock's book on the Trinity became a stumbling block to both. Manning even became a Socinian, and strove hard to bring his friend into those opinions, but Mr. Emlyn could never be made to doubt either of the pre-existence of our Saviour, as the Logos, or that God created the material world by him.

King James having fled into France, and Ireland being nearly reduced by King William, the affairs of that Kingdom began to be in a more settled state, and the dissenting congregations assembled in larger numbers. This induced Mr. Boyce to renew his application to Mr. Emlyn, to accept, jointly, with himself, the pastoral care of his congregation at Dublin; and to effect his purpose, wrote him a very pressing letter, and sent it to Mr. Nathaniel Taylor, minister at Salter's Hall, London, who transmitted it enclosed in one from himself, to Mr. Emlyn, at Lowestoft.

Mr. Emlyn being so strongly solicited to accept the office of assistant pastor to the congregation at Dublin, complied with the invitation, and accordingly arrived in Dublin in May, 1691, and continued there until 1702, when his troubles began; for Dr. Duncan Cummins, a physician in that city, suspecting him of heterodox notions, about the Trinity, put Mr. Boyce first upon the enquiry, and went afterwards with him to Mr. Emlyn's house, where the Unitarian freely confessed his belief "That God the Father of Jesus Christ, is above the Supreme Being, and superior in excellency and authority to his Son, who derives all from him." Protesting, however, that he had no design to cause strife among them, he offered to leave the congregation peaceably. But, Mr. Boyce, not willing to take such a weighty matter on himself, brought before the meeting of the Dublin ministers; in consequence of which, Mr. Emlyn was immediately prohibited from preaching, and in a few days obliged to withdraw into England. But some zealous Dissenters, having resolved to prosecute him with the utmost rigour, they obtained a special warrant from the Lord Chief Justice to seize him and his books, and went with the keeper of Newgate to execute it upon him. The Chief Justice refused at first to take bail, but at length accepted of a recognizance, from two sufficient persons, of £800 for his appearance. On his trial he was found guilty. He was moved to retract, which he absolutely refused; and was therefore sentenced to suffer a year's imprisonment, to pay a fine of £1,000 to the Queen, to live in prison till it was paid, and to find security for his good behaviour during life; telling him that the pillory was the punishment due, but because he was a man of letters it was not inflicted. After this he was led round the four Courts to be exposed, with a paper on his breast, signifying his crime. The fine was afterwards mitigated to £70, and this, together with £20, claimed by the Primate, as the Queen's Almoner, was paid. Thus, after an imprisonment from the 14th of June, 1703, to the 21st July, 1705, and on giving security for his good behaviour, during life, he obtained his discharge. Soon after Mr. Emlyn returned to London, where a few friends gathered a small congregation, to whom he preached once every Sunday; this liberty gave great offence to several clergymen of the Established Church, and complaint thereof was made to Archbishop Jenison; but His Grace, being fully acquainted with the proceedings against him in Dublin, and his accusers not alleging that Mr. Emlyn made the controverted points the subject of his sermons, on the account of his character, was not inclined to molest him. This congregation was dissolved by the death of the principal persons who supported it, and their preacher retired into silence and obscurity, and died July 30th, 1741. Mr. Emlyn was a man of a lively and cheerful temper, of strong parts, and clear way of thinking, of great learning, and abounding in all religious graces; he was a popular and much admired preacher, for he not only had a portly presence, a strong clear voice, and a graceful delivery, but his discourses were, for the most part, rational and persuasive, always concluding somewhat serious and pathetical. He wrote several tracts, which, with his sermons on practical subjects, were collected and printed, in 1754, in three volumes, octavo, to which are prefixed Memoirs of his Life and Writings.

During Mr. Emlyn's residence in Lowestoft, he cultivated the most friendly intercourse with the Rev. Hudson, at that time vicar of the parish; accompanying him in collecting public charities, and would frequently himself with several of his society attend the service of the church, by which means a perfect harmony subsisted between the members of the Establishment and the Dissenters. Nevertheless, his conduct in this respect was not approved altogether by those of his own community. Mr. Emlyn was also intimately acquainted with the Rev. Whiston, vicar of Lowestoft, and a successor of Mr. Hudson; and he was also particularly intimate with Dr. Samuel Clarke, who entertained nearly the same sentiments in religion as Mr. Emlyn and Mr. Whiston.

It is a little difficult to ascertain precisely who the ministers were that officiated at Lowestoft from the departure of Mr. Emlyn to the year 1698. There is an account of one Mr. Manning, who was an occasional preacher in the latter end of the reign of Charles II, or in the time of his brother James; but who this person was, whether he was an ejected minister (as there were several of that name in this country) or some other minister of the name of Manning, does not appear. It is not improbable that he was the Rev. Manning, of Peasanhall, previously mentioned, who was the intimate friend of Mr. Emlyn. Be this as it may, authentic accounts say that the Rev. Samuel Baxter, the eldest son of an ejected minister of Lancashire, settled here as minister to the Dissenters about the year 1698. He left the congregation about the year 1703, and removed to Ipswich. He was succeeded by the Rev. Henry Ward, who left Lowestoft about midsummer, 1707, and settled at Woodbridge, where he died at the close of the year 1734. Mr. Ward was succeeded at Lowestoft by Mr. Samuel Say, in 1707 or 1708. Mr. Say was born in the year 1675, and was the second son of Mr. Giles Say, minister of St. Michael's parish, in town of Southampton, but rejected thence by the Act of of Uniformity in 1662. But after the grant of liberty of conscience, in the reign of James II, he was chosen pastor of a Dissenting congregation at Guestwick, in Norfolk, where he continued till his death, April 7th, 1692. Mr. Samuel Say, the son, received his first education at Southwark; and having discovered when he was but a young man, a strong inclination to the ministry, his father accordingly took care to have him educated in the best manner he could for that purpose, from his earliest years; and about the year 1692 he entered as a pupil the Rev. Rowe's academy at London, where he had for his fellow students Mr. (afterwards Dr.) Isaac Watts, Mr. John Hughes, and Mr. Josiah Hort, afterwards Archbishop of Tuam. When he had finished his studies, he became chaplain to Thomas Scott, Esq., of Liminge, in Kent, a gentleman eminent for piety and goodness. Mr. Say continued in this family three years, and was well esteemed by all for his Christian behaviour and exemplary conversation. From thence he removed to Andover, in Hampshire; but in a short time came to Yarmouth, in Norfolk, and soon after that became a constant preacher at Lowestoft. Here he continued eighteen years, labouring

T

n word and doctrine; but not being able all the time to bring the people among whom he ministered into a regular church order, he never settled with them as their pastor. During the residence of Mr. Say, at Lowestoft, the Dissenters had not the sacrament administered here; but after that Mr. Say had preached at Lowestoft in the afternoon, on Sundays, he would ride to Yarmouth, attended by such of the congregation as were so disposed, and there he administered it. Mr. Say left Lowestoft in 1725, being invited to a co-pastorship with the Rev. Samuel Baxter, of Ipswich, where he remained nine years; and from thence was called to succeed Dr. Edmund Calamy, then lately deceased, in the pastorship of the Church of Protestant Dissenters in Westminister. He removed thither in 1734, and continued in his pastoral relation till April 12th, 1743; where, after a week's illness of a mortification in his bowels, he died at his house in St. James' street, in the sixty-eighth year of his age. He was a very ingenious and sensible man; had great candour and good breeding, without stiffness and formality; an open countenance, and a temper always communicative; he was a tender husband, an indulgent father, and of a most benevolent disposition, ever ready to do good, and relieve the wants of the distressed to the utmost extent of his abilities. He was well versed in astronomy and natural philosophy. This is evident from an astronomical and meteorological journal kept by Mr. Say from the year 1713 to 1734; wherein, among the various occurrences related by him, as an account of the great consternation excited among the inhabitants of Lowestoft at what is called *the first* appearance of the Aurora Borealis. Mr. Say writes: "The market this day is full of discourse concerning a great and unusual light, from seven to twelve last night, seen in Lowestoft, Beccles, and at sea. Women rose out of their beds through fear, others screamed, ships came to anchor fearing an unusual tempest, so dreadfully the sky opened; the angry clouds also seemed, in the imagination of the superstitious beholder, to flash one against another. This curious phenomenon had never been seen either in England or foreign countries from 1621 to 1707, and then only in a small degree; therefore the splendour with which this appeared attracted universal attention. The vulgar viewed it with consternation, and considered it as marking the introduction of a foreign race of princes into this country; so strangely do people perplex and bewilder themselves when they depart from true philosophy, which never fails both to ennoble and enlighten the human mind." He had also a taste for music and poetry, and was a good critic and master of the classics. Soon after his death a thin quarto volume of his poems with two essays in prose "On the Harmony, Variety, and Power of Numbers," written at the request of Mr. Richardson, the painter, were published for the benefit of his only daughter, who married the Rev. Mr. Toms, a Dissenting Minister at Hadleigh, Suffolk. The poems are not destitute of merit, but the two essays have been much admired by persons of taste and judgment.

In the year 1725 Mr. Say was succeeded by the Rev. Whittock, who removed to Kingston-on-Thames in 1733. It was during the ministry of Mr. Whittick, that the dissenting congregation at Lowestoft became a perfectly distinct body, and dissolved the connection which hitherto had subsisted with Yarmouth, Mr. Whittick declaring that unless they became a separate body, distinct from any other congregation, he would leave them. In 1733 Mr. Whittick was succeeded by the ingenious Mr. Thomas Scott, son of a Dissenting minister at Norwich. Mr. Scott, the grandfather of Mr. Thomas Scott, was an eminent merchant in London. He had two wives. By his first wife he had the above-mentioned Mr. Scott, Dissenting minister at Norwich, who had (besides other children) two sons of considerable note in the learned world, namely Mr. Thomas Scott, who was minister at Lowestoft, and Dr. Joseph Nicoll Scott, who was first a Dissenting minister, and published two volumes of sermons; but afterwards practised physic in London, and was well-known by the hand he had in several ingenious and useful publications. He was an assistant to his father in the congregation at Norwich; but embracing the Arian principles, (received there only by a few at that time) his father was under the painful necessity of expelling him from that society. By his second wife he had Dr. Daniel Scott, author of the Appendix to H. Stephens's Greek Lexicon, in two volumes, folio, dedicated to Archbishop

Secker and Bishop Butler—the New Version of St. Matthew's Gospel, with critical notes, etc., a learned and accurate performance—and an Essay towards a Demonstration of the Scripture Trinity. The design of this last work is to prove that the common notion of the doctrine of the Trinity (or the Athanasian scheme) is erroneous. He had the highest esteem for Dr. Doddridge, notwithstanding he differed so much from him respecting the Trinity; and had such a particular regard for that author's Treatise on the Rise and Progress of Religion, that he made it a constant travelling companion. And Dr. Doddridge seems to have held Dr. Scott with equal estimation; for in his Family Expositor he called him the learned, ingenious, candid, and accurate Dr. D. Scott. Mr. Thomas Scott, minister at Lowestoft, in the early par of his life, kept a small boarding school (for ten scholars only) at Wortwell, near Harleston, and used to preach at the meeting house at Harleston once every month. From Wortwell Mr. Scott removed to Lowestoft, where he continued five years; but the keenness of the air being too severe for the tenderness of his constitution, he was under the necessity of leaving Lowestoft about the year 1738, and removed to Ipswich. (The fine air at Lowestoft was at this time, 1730, strongly recommended by the London physicians, as extremely beneficial in many disorders, particularly nervous complaints.)

After Mr. Scott's removal to Ipswich, he became well known to the learned world by several very ingenious publications, particularly by his poetic translation of the book of Job, with critical notes, and some other poetical pieces. But finding, during his residence at Ipswich, the infirmities of age coming on him very hastily, and rendering him incapable of discharging the duties of his function with that care and exactness which he had always observed with the most scrupulous attention, he quitted that town in 1774, and retired to a small congregation at Hepton, in the neighbourhood of Norwich, where he died about two years after. Mr. Scott was succeeded in the year 1738 by Mr. Alderson, who continued pastor till his death, which happened in 1760. Mr. Alderson having a large family, and the stipend at Lowestoft being small, Mr. Elisha Barlow, a dissenter and eminent merchant of the town, was so far influenced by the considerations as to bequeath by will to the dissenting congregation at Lowestoft a considerable estate in the adjoining parish of Mutford, as an augmentation of the salary of the minister; but on this condition, nevertheless, that if Mr. Alderson was not continued pastor, the said estate should devolve to him and to his heirs for ever. In pursuance of this obligation, it was agreed on by the whole body of Dissenters at Lowestoft (in consequence of their great esteem for Mr. Alderson) to draw up an instrument, in which they formally expelled him as pastor, in order to give him a legal claim to the estate and afterwards re-chose him into his former pastoral office. But notwithstanding all these endeavours on the part of the congregation to render Mr. Alderson so essential a service, they were soon after entirely frustrated by the heirs at law of Mr. Barlow, who disputed the legality of the donation on the Mortmain Act, and commenced a suit in Chancery for recovering the estate. The result of this suit was, that Mr. Alderson was obliged to relinquish all future claims whatsoever to the same. This misfortune was an irreparable loss to Mr. Alderson. The anxiety which he suffered during the contest greatly impaired his health and shortened his days; for soon after, as, on the Lord's day, he was preaching to his congregation, he was suddenly taken ill, was obliged to be led home, and died in a short time. Mr. Alderson was a worthy, well-disposed man, of an exceedingly affable and peaceable disposition, much esteemed by the whole circle of his acquaintance; and as he lived much respected, so he died universally lamented.

The Dissenting congregation at Lowestoft appears to have been but very small before the year 1689, when Mr. Emlyn became their officiating minister; after this period they became a more numerous body, and continued increasing till the year 1735, when their number was become very considerable; after that year they appear to have been in a decreasing state, and declined very fast, especially since the death of Mr. Alderso..; for, according to an account taken in 1776, the number amounted to only 35, that could be properly called Independents and Congregational Dissenters. The number of Dissenting families in 1780 to 1790 (exclusive of the Methodists) was under twenty, but the congregation usually consisted of 150 and 200 persons.

While the law suit was pending, and for a short time after the death of Mr. Alderson, the congregation at Lowestoft was under the care of the Rev. Nasmith. After Mr. Nasmith came Mr. Gardner. From 1760 to 1785 about fifteen ministers had charge of the Dissenting congregation.

A digression may be interesting respecting an extraordinary trial, concerning two poor old widows belonging to Lowestoft who were tried, condemned, and executed on a charge of witch-craft.

In the year 1663 Mr. Samuel Pacey, an eminent Dissenter at Lowestoft, commenced a prosecution against two widows, on a suspicion of witchcraft. Mr. Pacey had conceived an opinion that two of his daughters, Elizabeth and Deborah, respectively eleven and nine years of age, were bewitched; and that these two women, whose names were Rose Cullender and Amy Duny, were the cause of the misfortune. In consequence of this suspicion, he caused Amy Duny to be set in the stocks; but not thinking this a sufficient punishment, he caused both women to be apprehended; and at the ensuing Lent assizes, held at Bury, the 10th March, 1664, before Sir Matthew Hale, Knt., Lord Chief Baron of his Majesty's Court of Exchequer, they were severally indiced for bewitching (amongst others) the said Elizabeth and Deborah Pacey; and being arraigned on the said indictment, pleaded not guilty; but being afterwards, after a long course of evidence, found guilty, they were thereupon, on Thursday, March 13th, sentenced to die for the same, and accordingly, on Monday, the 17th of March following, they were executed.

Dr. Hutchinson, in his historical essay concerning witchcraft, has given many pertinent observations respecting this very extraordinary trial; intending thereby to expose its absurdity, and to detect and ridicule the evidence on which the sentence was founded. To give a detail of every ridiculous circumstance that was urged in the course of the evidence, would be both irksome and disgusting; but two of the most material points may be related, which were adjudged to have the most weight, and principally to affect the cause then before the Court; adding thereto the remarks made thereupon by Mr. Hutchinson.

In the course of the trial it was deposed by Samuel Pacey, that his younger daughter Deborah, was suddenly taken ill with a lameness in her legs, was seized with violent fits, and felt the most excruciating pains in her stomach, like the pricking of pins, which caused her to shriek in an alarming manner; and also, that his daughter Elizabeth was afflicted in the same manner, and that they could not open their mouths wide enough for respiration, sufficient to preserve life, without the help of a tap. But Dr. Hutchinson says, there was no necessity for putting taps in the children's mouths when a sufficient quantity of air to preserve life could have been drawn through their nostrils. John Soam, of Lowestoft, deposed, that, in harvest time, as he was going into the field to load, one of the carts wrenched the window off Rose Cullender's house, whereupon she came out in a great rage, and threatened him for having done wrong. The consequence whereof was, that the cart was overturned twice that day; and the last time of loading it, as they brought it through the gate which led out of the field into the town, the cart stuck so fast in the gate's head that they could not possibly get it through, but were obliged to cut down the post of the gate, to make the cart pass through, although they did not perceive that the cart did of either side touch the gate-posts. Dr. Hutchinson says, very true, Rose Cullender might well be in a passion when they ran the cart against her house and damaged it; and an unruly horse or a careless driver might easily overturn a cart two or three times a day; and if the cart stuck so fast in the gate's head so as they could not get it through (though it did not touch the gate-post as they could perceive), what made them cut the post down? These depositions shew the kind of evidence it was on which these poor unfortunate women were condemned and executed, the ludicrous manner in which Dr. Hutchinson has treated it, as well as the contemptible light in which it was regarded by all the wise and discerning part of mankind. But exclusive of the evidence, they had also recourse, during the trial, to art and stratagem; for they caused one of Mr. Pacey's daughters to be blindfolded and to be touched by one of the supposed witches, in order to discover what effect it would produce; and on using this experiment, the girl fell into a violent rage, and gave the Court what they deemed the most evident demonstration of the criminality of the prisoners. Nevertheless, Mr. Sergeant Keeling seemed so much dissatisfied with this proof, that he thought it not sufficient to convict the prisioners; and therefore Sir Matthew Hale privately desired the Lord Cornwallis, and Mr. Sergeant Keeling to try the experiment in another place, and by a different person; but notwithstanding they perceived the same effect, yet these gentlemen, on their return into Court, declared, that from what they had discovered, it was, in their opinion, that the whole of the charge was groundless, and without any foundation. This was a favourable circumstance in behalf of the prisoners, as it tended to acquit them, and it actually stopped the proceedings of the Court a considerable time. At last, however, it was resolved to take the opinion of Dr. Brown, a physician from Norwich, and who was desired by the Court to give his sentiments concerning the prisoners, whether he really thought they were witches or not. The doctor's evidence amounted to this: "That he was clearly of opinion that the two girls were really bewitched; for that in Denmark there had been lately a great discovery of witches, and from some books that had been published in that kingdom, it appears that the witches there had used the same methods of afflicting persons as had been practised by the prisoners." This evidence of Dr. Brown turned the scale against these unfortunate women, and appears to have been decisive.

The eyes of all the sensible and inquisitive part of the nation were fixed on this very extraordinary trial, and waited with impatience the decision of the Court. They were full of expectations that the point would be so fully discussed as finally to determine it, and leave no room for posterity to engage in any farther controversy concerning these notions. But this was reserved for a more enlightened age; for it appears that nothing but perplexity and confusion ensued thereupon. The judge himself was so far from being satisfied with the evidence, that, on the contrary, he was extremely doubtful concerning it; and was under such distressing fears and apprehensions during the trial, and proceeded with such extreme caution therein, that he forebore summing up the evidence, but left it to the jury, with prayers to God to direct their hearts in so weighty a matter. Accordingly the jury, after withdrawing about half-an-hour, returned with their verdict, which pronounced the prisoners guilty. After this the judge gave the law its course, pronounced sentence of death upon them, and they were executed very soon after.

Thus were these two unfortunate widows, whose only misfortune was either the poverty of their circumstances, the deformity of their persons, or the weakness of their understandings, sacrificed to the superstition of the age, the insufficiency of the evidence, and the ignorance and credulity of the jury.

Possibly it may be admitted, as some extenuation of the absurdity of this prosecution, to remember that it was undertaken in an age in which the notion of witchcraft was generally received; that not only among the illiterate and vulgar, but even amongst those who were in the highest estimation for rank, piety, and learning.

It was in consequence of this ridiculous notion that one Matthew Hopkins, of Manningtree, in Essex, together with some others, were commissioned by Parliament in 1664, and the two following years, to perform a circuit, in order to discover witches. By virtue of this commission they went from town to town through many parts of Essex, Suffolk, Norfolk, and Huntingdonshire, for the purpose of detecting them; and caused sixteen to be hanged at Yarmouth, forty at Bury, and also as many more in different parts of the country as amounted in the whole to nearly one hundred persons. It is to this absurd commission that Butler alludes in Hudebras, when he says:

> "Hath not this present Parliament
> A ledger to the devil sent,
> Fully empow'd to treat about,
> Finding revolted witches out?
> And has he not within a year
> Hang'd three score of them in a shire?

This Hopkins used to call himself Witchfinder General, and had twenty shillings allowed him for every town he visited. He used many arts to extort confession from suspected persons, and when they failed he had recourse to swimming them; which was done by tying their thumbs and toes across one another, and then throwing them into the water. Thus he went on searching and swimming the poor creatures, till some gentleman, out of indignation at the barbarity of it, took him and tied his own thumbs and toes as he used to tie others, and when he was put into the water he himself swam as others had done before him. This method soon cleared the country of him, and it was a great pity the experiment was not thought of sooner.

Returning from the digression it may be noted that another religious sect which appeared in in Lowestoft is the Methodists. The society first made its appearance here in the year 1761; and was introduced by that great leader of the sect, the Rev. John Wesley, and has continued. In the year 1776 their number was increased to about fifty; they purchased a piece of ground on the north side of Frary lane, and soon after erected a meeting house there, which was opened on the 19th November, 1776, by Mr. John Wesley, who came to Lowestoft for that purpose.

## SECTION IX.

## MILITARY AND NAVAL AFFAIRS.

LOWESTOFT being a maritime town, it is consequently more distinguished for memorable transactions relative to naval affairs, than for those respecting military.

The town having always depended upon the herring fishery for its chief support, has rendered this fishery a constant nursery for seamen; and the great advantages which maritime powers have always received from their fisheries, are too many to be enumerated, as well as too evident to require a demonstration; for the constant protection and encouragement which those powers have always found it their interest to afford them, are indubitable proofs both of their usefulness and importance. But exclusive of the valuable benefits which the nation has derived from the herring fishery, in common with other fisheries, in supplying his majesty's service with a considerable number of useful seamen, it has also received many other advantages in consequence of the several very able and gallant sea commanders with which the town has furnished the royal Navy; and who, by the wisdom of their Councils, and gallantry of their actions, have rendered very essential services to their country, and received the most distinguished honours to themselves.

In the memorable sea-fights between England and Holland during the first Dutch war, in the reign of Charles II, among commanders who remarkably distinguished themselves in those important struggles, were Admiral Allen, Admiral Utber, and his son, Captain Utber, all of whom belonged to this town.

It was that gallant sea-officer, Admiral Sir Thomas Allen, who first commenced hostilities against the Dutch, in 1665, by attacking their Smyrna fleet, consisting of forty merchant ships, of which some were very large, were well provided with ordnance and had four third-rate men of war for their convoy. Sir Thomas had only eight ships with him; but what he wanted in force, he supplied by his eminent courage and conduct; for he immediately attacked them, killed Commodore Bracknell, their commander, took four of their merchant ships, richly laden, and drove the remainder into Cadiz. (In 1661, Sir Thomas Allen was member for Dunwich. In 1668, Sir Thomas was a candidate for the same place, but lost the election. In 1710, Sir Richard Allen was member for Dunwich.)

In the great sea fight off Lowestoft, June 3, 1665, all the three above-mentioned commanders had a respective share in that memorable engagement.

The English fleet consisted of 114 sail of men of war and frigates, 28 fire ships, and several bomb ketches, and had on board about 22,000 seamen and soldiers; and the whole was commanded by the Duke of York. Admiral Opdam commanded the Dutch fleet. The fight began about three in the morning, and for some time victory was doubtful; but about noon, the Earl of Sandwich, with the blue squadron, forced himself into the centre of the Dutch fleet, divided it into two parts, and began that confusion which ended in a total defeat. The Duke of York, in the Royal Charles of eighty guns, and Admiral Opdam, in the Eendracht of eighty-four guns, were closely engaged, and continued the fight with great obstinacy for several hours, wherein his highness was in the utmost danger. Several persons of distinction were killed on board his ship, particularly the Earl of Falmouth, the King's favourite; Lord Muskerry, and Mr. Boyle, son of the Earl of Cork, who were killed with one ball, and so near the Duke, that he was covered with their blood and brains, and a splinter from the last named gentleman's skull, grazed his hand. About one o'clock the Dutch Admiral blew up, with a prodigious explosion; by which accident the Admiral and 500 of his men perished. Vice-Admiral Stillingwert was shot through the middle by a cannon ball; and Vice-Admiral Cortenaar received a shot in his thigh, of which he instantly died. These ships bearing out of the line on the death of their commanders, without striking their flags, drew many after them; so that by eight at night Van Tromp, who fought to the last, and kept fighting as he retreated, had not above thirty ships left with him. This was the most signal victory the English ever gained, and the severest blow at sea that the Dutch ever felt. In this action the Dutch had eighteen ships taken and fourteen sank, exclusive of those which were either burnt or blown up; and lost 6000 men, including 2300 taken prisoners. The English lost only the Charity of forty-six guns, had 250 men killed, and 340 wounded; among whom were (besides those already mentioned) the Earls of Portland and Marlborough, Vice-Admiral Sampson, and Sir John Lawson, who died of a wound in his knee, though he survived the battle. Among the wounded was Mr. Howard, youngest son of the Earl of Berkshire; he was landed at Lowestoft, where he died of his wounds on the 6th of June following, and was interred in the chancel of Lowestoft church.

As soon as the battle was over the English retired to Southwold Bay to rest; where they received fresh orders to sail again as soon as possible in search of the Dutch fleet. Accordingly on the 5th July, the fleet steered from the bay to the coast of Holland. The standard was borne by the Earl of Sandwich, and the Blue flag by Sir Thomas Allen, having for his Vice and Rear-Admirals Sir Christopher Minnes and Sir John Harings. (On the fourth day's fight in the first battle in the following year, Sir Christopher Minnes having received a shot in the neck, remained upon deck and gave orders, keeping the blood from flowing with his fingers an hour, till another shot came and put an end to his existence.) The design of the expedition was to intercept de Ruyter on his return with the Turkey and East India fleets, or at least to take or burn the merchant ships, of which they had certain intelligence. But they succeeded in neither of these attempts. De Ruyter returned unexpectedly by the north of Scotland, and arrived safely in Holland. The fleets, consisting of twenty sail, took the same northern route, in hopes of avoiding the English, but receiving intelligence at sea that this would prove very difficult, if not impossible, they took shelter in the port of Berghen, in Norway. This port was easy of access, and covered only by an old castle; the Danish governor, indeed, promised to protect the Dutch as much as possible, and the Dutch, to facilitate their intention, landed forty-one pieces of cannon, which were disposed on a line before the fort; after they had taken this precaution, the Dutch formed another line across the bay, consisting of their largest ships, and in this defensive posture they waited the arrival of the English. It was not long before the English appeared; for the Earl of Sandwich having received advice of the Dutch fleet having put into Berghen for protection, detached Sir Thomas Tyddiman with fourteen sail of men of war, (one of them was the Guernsey, commanded by Captain Utber), and three fireships to attack and destroy them. Sir Thomas appeared at Berghen on the 1st of August, 1665, and though he executed this expedition with great courage, yet, having the wind against him, and the enemy making a prodigious fire from the castle, the line, and the ships, he was forced to bear out of the bay, which he performed without the loss of a ship, though he had five or six ill treated; one of which was the Guernsey, Captain Utber, who was unfortunately slain in the engagement. (Against the south wall of the south isle of St. Margaret's church is a small monument with the inscription "Neere unto this place lyeth ye body of captaine John Utber, commander of His majesties fregat the Guernsey. In which, valiantly Fighting in the defence of his King and countrey, against the Dutch and Dane at Berghen, he was unfortunately slayne, ye 2nd Augusti, 1665. Ætatis suæ 22.")

In the great sea fight in 1666, which lasted four days, it is probable that both the Admirals Allen and Utber had their shares in that remarkable engagement, thought they are not particularly mentioned. For when the fight was over, and both fleets had retired to their respective coasts to refit and prepare for a fresh engagement, on their proceeding to sea again, the English fleet consisting of eighty men of war, great and small, and nineteen fireships, were divided into three squadrons, under the command of Prince Rupert and Duke of Albemarle; and the second squadron of this fleet was commanded by Sir Thomas Allen, who had under him Sir Thomas Tyddiman and Rear Admiral Utber.

The Dutch fleet consisted of eighty-eight men of war and twenty fireships, and was divided into three squadrons, under de Ruyter, Evertz, and Van Tromp. On the 25th July, about noon, the English fleet came up with the enemy off the North Foreland. Sir Thomas Allen, with the white squadron, began the battle by attacking Evertz. About one o'clock Prince Rupert and the Duke of Albemarle made a desperate attack upon de Ruyter, and after fighting about three hours were obliged to go on board another ship. During this interval, the Admirals Allen, Tyddiman, and Utber, in the white squadron, had utterly defeated Evertz; his Vice-Admiral de Vries, and Rear-Admiral Keenders, being both killed. The Vice-Admiral of Zealand was taken, and another ship of fifty guns burnt. The Prince and the Duke, who were both in the same ship, fought de Ruyter, ship to ship; disabled the Guelderland of sixty-six guns, one of his seconds; killed the Captain of another, and mortally wounded two more, after which the Dutch squadron began to fly. De Ruyter's ship was so miserably torn, and his crew so dispirited and fatigued, that he could make but little resistance, and nothing but the want of wind could have hindered the English from boarding him. De Ruyter continued his retreat all that night, and the next day Prince Rupert and the Duke of Albemarle pursued him as fast as the wind would permit. A fireship was then dispatched to bear down on the Dutch Admiral, and missed very little of setting him on fire. At last they approached so near to each other as to cannonade a second time, when De Ruyter finding himself so extremely oppressed, and his fleet in the most imminent danger, that in a fit of despair he cried: 'My God, what a wretch am I among so many thousand bullets! is there not one to put me out of my pain?' By degrees, however, the Dutch drew near their own shallow coast, where the English could not follow them. On this occasion Prince Rupert ungenerously insulted him, by sending a little shallop, called Fanfan, with only two guns on board, which, being rowed near to De Ruyter's ship, fired upon him for two hours; at last a ball from the Dutch Admiral so damaged his contemptible enemy, that the crew were forced to sheer off very briskly, to save their lives.

This was one of the greatest victories obtained at this war. In this battle the Dutch lost twenty ships, had four Admirals and a great many captains killed as to common seamen, the number slain was computed to be 4,000, and 3,000 wounded. The English had only the Resolution burnt, three captains and about 300 seamen killed.

In the same year, when the Dutch and French fleets were endeavouring to form a junction, Sir Thomas Allen, with his squadron, attacked the French fleet, and having boarded the Ruby, a fine ship of 1000 tons and fifty-four guns, he carried her in a short time. This bold attempt so intimidated the French ministry, that they scarce ventured their fleet out of sight of its own shore afterwards.

The first Dutch war being ended, Sir Thomas was sent, in 1669, with a stout squadron, into the Mediterranean, to suppress the insults of the Algerines, where he did his country very eminent services, and was the last employment he ever engaged in. (The Algerines had been committing depredations for many years on the English merchants, so that it now became absolutely necessary to check and chastise them. Among the unhappy captives that were enslaved by falling into the hands of these Infidels, was one William Wilde of Lowestoft, who whilst he was in slavery, wrote a letter to Mr. John Wilde, his father, of which the following is an extract:—"From the prison at Constantinople, 22nd November, 1663. Dear Father, In all duty I do send you salutations, with my loving mother; having yet place left me to mourn for your sorrow for me in your old age and grey hairs, when usual comfort is expected from children; but it is the Lord's hand, let him do with me what pleaseth him. For six months past I have had but little rest. I was chained in the galleys by the leg, and also both hands together, besides a chain to my back, as the other slaves; with all which I was forced to row. My allowance is bread

U

and water; and I am exposed, naked, to the extremity of both heat and cold. I write you the truth, but not all; it would wear out a pen of brass to do it. Now that you may know the occasion of our falling into this calamity, I shall observe to you, that upon Whitsunday last, in the morning, we saw thirty sail of galleys coming into the bay towards us; we weighed and towed about two miles, it being calm where we lay. The galleys coming within us, cast themselves in a half moon, and began with us. I was laid on board by the Bassa himself; the remainder of his squadron, with his nephew, forming the body of his strength, laid round me. Five laid me on board, and three of them thrust their prows [a kind of boltsprit at the head of a row galley, on which is fixed a large gun] into our ports. The general or bassa, once; the admiral another; and one more. The others laid upon their oars, discharging their prows, and boarding us with great clamour. Our ship was on fire all over our heads, which happened on his boarding us, from a wad out of his cursed piece, which shot a bullet of thirty-two pounds. We cleared ourselves of the galleys, supposing to have overcome the fire, otherwise they should have perished with us. At last I caused a barrel of powder to be brought and placed abaft the mast, on the gun-deck; then drawing all my men to the fore part of the ship, I caused it to be fired, and so blew up all, that the enemy might enjoy nothing. The fight continued from eight or nine in the morning till twelve or one in the afternoon, the half of which time they were on board us. Amongst the greatest of my afflictions, this stands first before me:—my care at home. My two boys are forced to turn Turks, to my infinite grief. I do beseech you, show love to my wife and children, by which (if I do live to see) your great love will be shown to me. Committing you to the protection of the Almighty, I rest, your dutiful son and poor captive, WILLIAM WILDE.")

After Sir Thomas had honorably finished the Algerine war, and in pursuance of his instructions, appointed Sir Edward Spragge to command in his place in the Mediterranean, he returned to England, where, for the many services he had rendered his country, he was created a baronet, 14th December, 1669. But having been constantly engaged in the most active, as well as dangerous scenes of action, and being worn down with fatigue, and crowned with success, he was under the necessity of withdrawing himself from the service of the public; and having acquired a handsome fortune, he purchased the estate of Somerley Hall, and removing thither from Lowestoft, it became afterwards the place of his future residence, thereby exchanging the dangerous and tumultuous scenes of war for the calm and undisturbed repose of rural retirement. During the residence of Sir Thomas at Lowestoft, he lived in a black flint-stone house on the east side of High street; where, on that side next the sea, he caused a small round tower to be erected, that he might be enabled to command an extensive prospect of the German Ocean, an object of great consequence during the Dutch wars. He buried a daughter in the north-east corner of the north isle of Lowestoft church, where a handsome monument is erected to her memory.

Another valiant and experienced Admiral belonging to Lowestoft, and who remarkably distinguished himself by his gallantry in the service of his country, was Sir John Ashby.

King William had no sooner ascended the throne of this kingdom than he found himself obliged to engage in war with France, who had sent James II over into Ireland with a considerable force, escorted by a fleet of twenty-two sail of men-of-war.

His Majesty's affairs in England were at this time in so critical a state, that it was some time before he could provide a force sufficient to cruise on the coast of Ireland. At last Admiral Herbert, who commanded the English fleet, in the begining of April, 1689, sailed for Cork, with a squadron which consisted of no more than twelve ships of war (one of which was the Defiance, Captain Ashby) one fireship, two yachts, and two smacks. On the 29th of that month he discovered a fleet of forty-four sail, a convoy that followed King James; on the 30th, he saw them standing into Bantree bay; he lay off that place till morning, and about break of day resolved to attack the enemy. The French detached their merchant ships to land the supply at a place down the bay while they engaged the enemy. The English fleet was reinforced to nineteen ships. The French fleet consisted in the whole of twenty-eight ships. As the English had the wind, they could have avoided fighting if they pleased; but the Admiral exerted his utmost efforts to get into the bay, and come to a close engagement. About ten in the morning, on the 1st of May, the French bore down upon the English, when the battle began. The fight was pretty warm for two hours, but then slackened, because a great part of the English fleet could not come up, but they continued firing on both sides till about five in the afternoon. Admiral Herbert had no opportunity of bringing his whole fleet to engage, as the wind would not suffer him to enter the bay, and consequently was under the necessity of keeping out at sea all the time of the engagement, therefore the dispute was very unequal; but about the hour before-mentioned, the French fleet stood in the bay, which put an end to the fight.

This is the battle of Bantree bay, which, though inconsiderable of itself (since the English, who had certainly the worst of it, lost only one Captain, one Lieutenant, and ninety-four men, and had about three hundred wounded), is yet magnified by some writers as a very important stroke. The French had one ship, called the Diamond, set on fire, and two others so much damaged as to withdraw from the line. The affair, however, was certainly of no very great consequence; and the small advantage that was claimed by the French was more to be ascribed to a favourable wind and superior force, than either a want of courage or conduct on the part of the English. After the action Admiral Herbert bore away for the Scilly Islands, and having cruized there for some time returned to Spithead; on which occasion the King himself went down to Portsmouth, where, to shew his determination to distinguish and reward merit, though not pointed out to him by success, he declared Admiral Herbert Earl of Torrington, and knighted Captain John Ashby and Captain Cloudesley Shovel; giving, at the same time, a bounty of ten shillings to each seaman, and making a provision for the widows of such as had been killed in the action. Sir John Ashby was also presented with a gold watch, set with diamonds.

The French were so elated with the small advantage gained in Bantree bay, as to boast, that the next summer they would insult the joint fleets of England and Holland; therefore, both the honour and safety of the kingdom depended upon taking such measures as might disconcert their designs. In consequence of this necessity, a resolution was formed of assembling early in the Spring a large fleet in the Channel; especially as that part of the nation in the interest of King James where almost everywhere in motion, and waiting, in all appearance, for nothing but the sight of a French fleet, on the coast, to take up arms and declare against Government; but it was so late before the Dutch sent their fleet to sea, and the English fleet was desirous of forming a junction with the Dutch before they put themselves in a condition of sailing that it considerably retarded the operations. But the conduct of the French was very different; for on the 12th of June they put to sea with their grand fleet, consisting of seventy-eight men of war, and twenty-two fire ships, the whole fleet carrying upwards of 4,700 pieces of canon. On the 13th of June they steered for the English coast, and on the 20th appeared off the Lizard.

Our Admiral, Lord Torrington, who was then at St. Helen's received this intelligence with the utmost surprise; and he was so far from expecting the arrival of the French fleet on the English coast that he had not sent out any scouts to the westward for information. However, he put to sea with such ships as he had on the 24th of June, and gave orders that all the English and Dutch ships which could have notice should follow him. The next morning he found himself within sight of the enemy, and the fleets continued looking on each other for several days. It is certain that the Earl of Torrington did not think himself strong enough to venture an engagement, and in all probability the rest of the Admirals were of the same opinion. In this fleet Sir John Ashby was Vice-Admiral of the Blue.

The whole strength of the English and Dutch fleets together, consisted only of fifty-six ships; his Lordship therefore, seeing that he was outnumbered by above twenty sail, was not willing to risk his own honour and the safety of the nation upon such unequal terms, but the Queen, who was then Regent, sent him orders to fight at all events, in order to oblige the French to withdraw from the English coast. In obedience to this order, his Lordship, on the 20th of June, as soon as it was daylight, gave the signal for drawing into a line of battle, and bore down upon the enemy. The signal for battle was thrown out at about eight o'clock, and the engagement began about nine. The Dutch squadron, which formed the van of the united fleets, fell in with the van of the French, and threw them into disorder. About half-an-hour after Admiral Russell, and Admiral Ashby with the Blue squadron, engaged the rear of the French very warmly; but the Red Squadron, which formed the centre of the fleet, and was commanded by the Earl of Torrington, did not come up till about ten; and this occasioned a great opening between the Blue squadron in the rear and the Dutch in the van, which the French taking an advantage of, caused the Dutch to suffer very much.

In the night the Earl retired to the eastward, with the French pursuing him as far as Rye; from thence he retreated towards the river Thames, where, on going ashore, he left the command of the fleet to Sir John Ashby. The French were as much censured for not taking every advantage which this victory afforded them, as the Earl was blamed for the defeat; for the French retired to their own coasts, and after the beginning of August were no more seen in the English Channel.

The Earl of Torrington, as soon as he came to London, was examined before the Council, before whom he vindicated his conduct with great presence of mind. He assigned two reasons for his behaviour in this important transaction: the first was, the ill-grounded contempt the English and Dutch officers had of the abilities of the French fleet at sea; the second was, that he had acted to the best of his knowledge in saving the fleet, and that he had much rather his reputation should suffer for a time, than his country should sustain a loss which it might never be able to recover; but the Council were so far dissatisfied with these reasons, and they committed his Lordship to the Tower; and that they might appease the clamours of the populace, and make some satisfaction to the Dutch, they appointed a committee to repair to Sheerness, in order to make a thorough enquiry into the real causes of this disaster.

The fleet, after this misfortune, was put under the command of Sir Richard Haddock, Vice-Admiral Killegrew, and Sir John Ashby; who had orders to put the fleet into the best condition possible, which being executed with the utmost diligence, they had, by the end of August, a fleet of forty-one ships of the line under their command, exclusive of the Dutch. Yet, notwithstanding all their activity, it was very late in the year before they were in a capacity fit to undertake any essential service, and by that time it became necessary to lay up the larger ships.

The assiduity and administration to rectify all the errors and miscarriages which had lately happened, and, to retrieve the honour of the nation, was very visible in 1691, when the utmost efforts were exerted to send a large fleet to sea early in the spring. In order to effect this purpose, the week after that the Earl of Torrington was dismissed from his command, Edward Russell, Esq., was appointed Admiral and Commander-in-Chief; and in the fleet which was got ready for service in the spring, Admiral Russell, in the Britannia, commanded the Red squadron, having for his Vice and Rear-Admirals Sir John Ashby and George Rooke, Esq. But the French having orders to avoid fighting, nothing material was done this year.

The last employment Sir John Ashby engaged in was the great sea-fight off Cape La Hogue. Lewis XIV finding it impossible to prosecute the war in Ireland any longer with success, came to a resolution of employing the forces in that country, consisting of 20,000 men, some other way; with this view, he concerted with malcontents in England an invasion on the coast of Sussex.

On the 16th of May, Admiral Russell sailed from Spithead in order to meet the French fleet. The English fleet consisted of ninety-nine ships. The Blue squadron was commanded by Sir John Ashby, who had for Vice and Rear-Admirals George Rooke, Esq., and Richard Carter, Esq. The French had only sixty-three ships, having under their protection a fleet of three hundred sail of transports, well provided with every necessary requisite for the invasion.

On the 17th, the scouts to the westward of the fleet made signals for discovering the enemy; in consequence thereof, orders were immediately issued for forming a line of battle.

On the 19th, the fleet was in proper order for battle about eight in the morning; having the Dutch in the van, the red in the centre, and the blue in the rear. About ten o'clock the French fleet bore down upon them with great resolution, and about half after eleven, the Royal Sun, the finest ship in France carrying 106 guns, began the fight with Admiral Russell, within three-quarters musket shot. The French exercised their guns very briskly till about one o'clock, when they began to tow her off in great disorder. The fight continued till four in the afternoon, when the French taking advantage of a fog began to retreat. About eight in the evening it grew foggy again, and part of the blue squadron having fallen in with the enemy, engaged about half an hour, till the French, having lost four ships, bore away for Conquest road. In this short action Sir John Ashby's Rear-Admiral Carter was killed; who when found himself mortally wounded, recommended to Captain Wright, who commanded his ship, to fight her as long as she could swim.

The English continued the chase till the 22nd, when, about eleven in the forenoon, the French Admiral, in the Royal Sun, ran ashore and cut away her mast. He was followed by some others of his fleet, and were all afterwards destroyed. In the evening a great number of the enemy's ships were seen going to La Hogue. On the 23rd the Admiral sent Sir George Rooke, with several men of war, fireships and all the boats in the fleet, to destroy these ships, consisting of thirteen sail of men of war, besides a great number of transports, etc. Sir George having manned his boats, went in person, to encourage the attempt; when he burnt six of them that night, and the other seven, with the transports the next morning.

Sir John Ashby, with the blue squadron and some Dutch ships, pursued the rest of the French fleet till they ran through the race of Alderney, among such rocks and shoals where the English pilots refused to follow them. Sir John has been much censured for his conduct in this part of the transaction, though probably without any reason, since some of the ablest seamen in England were of opinion, that nothing could be more desperate than the flight of the French through that dangerous passage. And though despair might justify them in attempting it, yet the bare possibility of success in following them might be equivalent to the danger of the undertaking.

Besides the Royal Sun of 106 guns, the French lost another ship of 104 guns, one of ninety, two of eighty, four of seventy-six, four of sixty and two of fifty-six guns. If Sir John Ashby had been so fortunate as to have come within the reach of those who took shelter in St. Maloe's, the English would almost have annihilated the power of the French by the sea; as it was undoubtedly a most glorious victory, and too much praise cannot be given by the British nation to those gallant commanders who achieved it. Queen Mary was no sooner informed of this victory than she sent £30,000 to be divided among the seamen and soldiers.

After the battle, Sir John Ashby was left with twelve ships and three fireships, in conjunction with a Dutch squadron of the same force, with orders to proceed to Havre de Grace, and to endeavour the destruction of such part of the French fleet as had taken shelter there; which service they were unable to perform; the situation of the enemy and the violence of the weather rendering it impracticable.

Admiral Russell, with the remainder of the fleet, returned as soon as possible to Spithead, in order to carry into execution a design which had been meditated, of making a descent on the French coast. But the ministry and the sea and land officers not concurring in what manner the descent was to be made, it came to nothing. However, the Admiral sent Sir John Ashby, with a stout squadron, to endeavour, if possible, to intercept the French Fleet which was every day expected to sail from St. Maloe's to Brest; but in his passage he received orders from the Queen to return, and, therefore, in obedience thereof, was obliged to come back in a few days to St. Helen's.

On the 4th of November the King opened the sessions of Parliament: on which occasion he took notice of their great success, and also of their great disappointments at sea. On the 11th, the House of Commons thanked Admiral

Russell, in the strongest terms, for his courage and conduct in the battle of La Hogue; but, nevertheless it did not prevent a warm representation of the opportunities that were said to be lost, after that signal advantage. The Admiral entered into a circumstantial relation of the whole of that transaction, and furnished the House with all letters, papers, and instructions that were necessary for their information.

After Admiral Russell, Sir John Ashby was examined concerning his not executing the orders that were given him to destroy the French ships that had sheltered in St. Maloe's. But Sir John acquitted himself so handsomely, and set the whole affair in so clear a light, that he was informed by the Speaker, by order of the House, "that having observed his ingenious behaviour in his detail of his conduct in that engagement, and received the amplest satisfaction, he was dismissed from any further attendance on that House."

Bishop Burnet speaking of this battle, says, that if Sir John Ashby had pursued the six-and-twenty French ships, which afterwards got into St. Maloe's, by all appearance he might have destroyed every one of them. This very illiberal reflection on the conduct of Sir John is an evident proof of the malevolence which too often actuates the spirit of party; and shews that the most brilliant actions, when executed by commanders whose political principles happen not to coincide with certain writers, are too often tarnished through the malignity of the historian. The conduct of Sir John Ashby in this memorable transaction is so far from being liable to the censure of Bishop Burnet, that it is capable of being vindicated and applauded for its wisdom and prudence. For a naval writer speaking of the battle of La Hogue, says, "that to attempt to destroy the French ships that had sheltered in St. Maloe's, would not only have been extremely dangerous, but wholly impracticable. For soon after this action, when we meditated a descent upon the French Coast, and had received advice that twenty-five sail of French ships were in the port of St. Maloe, Sir George Rooke was dispatched to make soundings on that coast, in order to our attacking them; accordingly he gave a particular account of several surroundings near St. Maloe's, and reported, "that not one of the pilots would undertake to carry in any ship of war, or fireship, at St. Maloe's, though he offered a hundred pounds encouragement to each man."

Sir John Ashby died at Portsmouth, and was there interred; but his body was afterwards taken up and buried in Lowestoft church, where a handsome monument is erected to his memory.

The next eminent sea officer belonging to Lowestoft, who demands notice for distinguished bravery, is Sir Andrew Leake.

On the 4th of May, 1702, her Majesty Queen Anne, soon after her accession to the throne, declared war against France and Spain. In consequence whereof, the grand fleet was immediately got ready for sailing, in order to carry into execution a plan, originally concerted by King William, for an attack upon Cadiz.

On the 19th of June following, the fleet, commanded by Sir George Rooke, having Vice-Admiral Hopson, in the Prince George, carrying a red flag at the fore top-mast head; Rear-Admiral Fairbourne, carrying the white flag at the mizen top-mast head of the St. George; and Rear-Admiral Graydon, carrying the blue flag in the same manner in the Triumph; who were also accompanied by five Dutch Admirals, sailed from St. Helen's. The strength of this fleet consisted of thirty English and twenty Dutch ships of the line, exclusive of small vessels and tenders, making in the whole about 160 sail. The land forces embarked in this expedition consisted of 9,663 English, and 4,138 Dutch, amounting in all to 13,801 men.

As the epectations which the public had conceived from this prodigious armament were very great, so, consequently, they were exceedingly disappointed at being informed that the attempt upon Cadiz had proved unsuccessful.

However, Providence afterwards put it in the power of Sir George Rooke, before he returned to England, to render his country a more signal and important service than it could possibly have received from a successful attack upon Cadiz. Captain Hardy, of the Pembroke, being sent to water in Lagos Bay, before he returned received intelligence there that the Spanish galloons, under the convoy of a French squadron, had put into Vigo on the 16th of September. Captain Hardy hastened with the utmost expedition in his power to convey the news to the fleet, which he did not meet with until the 3rd of October, and even then the wind blew so hard that he found it impossible to speak with the Admiral until the 6th, when he informed him of the intelligence he had received. On this information Sir George called a council of war immediately, in which it was resolved to sail as expeditiously as possible to the port of Vigo, to attack the enemy. In order to effect this purpose, some small vessels were dispatched to reconnoitre them and discover their force, which was effectually performed by a boat belonging to the Kent man-of-war; and from this intelligence the Captain understood that Monsieur Chasteau Renault's squadron of French men-of-war and the Spanish galleons were all in that harbour. Sir George was unable to arrive off Vigo before the 11th of October. The passage into the harbour was not more than three-quarters of a mile over, and was defended by a battery of eight brass and twelve iron guns on the north side and on the south side was a platform of twenty brass guns, and twenty of iron; and also a stone fort, with a breast work, and French ships before it mounting ten guns, and containing in it 500 men. There was also extended from one side of the harbour to the other, a strong boom, formed of ships' yards and top-masts, fastened together with three-inch rope, very thick, and underneath were hawsers and cables. The top chain at each end was moored to a seventy-gun ship. Within the boom were moored five ships of between sixty and seventy guns each, with their broad sides fronting the entrance of the passage, so as to fire with the greatest execution upon any ships that should attempt to come near either the boom, forts, or platform. The Admirals removed their flags from the great ships into third rates, the first and second rates drawing too much water to enter the harbour. Sir George Rooke went from the Royal Sovereign into the Somerset; Admiral Hopson out of the Prince George into the Torbay; Admiral Fairbourne out of the St. George into the Essex; and Admiral Graydon out of the Triumph into the Northumberland. A detachment of fifteen English, and ten Dutch men-of-war, with all the fire ships, frigates, and bomb vessels, were ordered to go upon this service. The Duke of Ormond, to facilitate the attack, landed 2,500 men on the south side of the river, about six miles from Vigo. Then Lord Shannon, at the head of 500 men, attacked the stone fort at the entrance of the harbour; and having made himself master of the platform, mounting forty pieces of cannon, the French governor, Mons. Sozel, ordered the gates of the place to be thrown open, with a resolution to have forced his way through the English troops: but though there was great bravery in this order, yet there was but little judgment; for immediately upon its being obeyed, the grenadiers entered the place sword in hand, and forced the garrison, consisting of French and Spaniards, in number about 350, to surrender prisoners of war. These attacks were of the utmost consequence to the fleet, as our ships, in attempting to enter the harbour must have been excessively galled by the fire from the platform and fort.

As soon as the British flag was seen flying from these places, the ships advanced; and Vice-Admiral Hopson, in the Torbay, crowding all the sail he could, sailed directly against the boom and broke it, and the Kent, with the rest of the squadron, English and Dutch, entered the harbor. The Torbay, who first struck the boom and broke it, was so entangled therein that it was impossible to extricate her from it. The enemy, perceiving her situation, were determined to exert their utmost efforts to destroy her; and in order to execute their design the more effectually, dispatched a fireship, which immediately laid the Torbay on board. In this dreadful situation, having a fireship grappled to her side, the enemy playing upon her with cannon, and at the same time so entangled with the boom that it was impossible to disengage themselves and escape, all subordination was disregarded, and every man was permitted to provide for his own safety in the best manner he was able. Nevertheless, in this very alarming situation, Providence interposed in their behalf, and rescued them from the impending destruction which threatened them; for when the fireship blew up, a large quantity of snuff which she had on board extinguished the flames, and soon after they were able to disengage her from the boom, and repair, as well as circumstances would admit, the damages she had received. It may, possibly, appear a little extraordinary that the fireships should have so large a quantity of snuff on board as to extinguish the flames, but it is to be remembered, that she was originally a merchant ship laden with that commodity, and on this pressing emergency, converted into a fireship. The Torbay, though not absolutely destroyed in this action, yet was so extremely damaged as to be reduced almost to a wreck; her fore top-mast was shot by the board, most of her sails burnt or scorched, the foreyard burnt to a coal, the larboard shrouds, fore and aft, burnt at the dead eyes, several ports blown off the hinges, her larboard side entirely scorched, one hundred and fifteen men killed and drowned, out of which were sixty who jumped **overboard as soon as they were** grappled by **the fireship.** Admiral Hopson, **when he found his ship in this** disabled condition, left her, and hoisted his flag on board the Monmouth. The loss in this action (exclusive of the Torbay) was very inconsiderable considering the resistance of the enemy, and the great advantages which we obtained. In this attack upon Vigo we burnt five French men of war from **seventy-six to** forty-six guns, one of twenty-two guns, and another of eight guns. We also took and brought home four ships from seventy-six to sixty-six guns, and there were also taken by the Dutch six ships from sixty-eight to forty-two guns. There were likewise taken and destroyed seventeen galleons. The French and **Spanish** ships **had** been twenty-five days in Vigo harbour before our fleet **arrived** there; during this interval they unladed the best part of the plate **and rich** goods, and **sent them up the country.** The galleons had on board twenty-eight **millions of pieces of eight, besides** merchandise, which was thought of equal value. Of the **silver, fourteen** millions were saved; and of the goods, about five millions. Four millions of plate were destroyed with ten millions of merchandise. The fourteen millions of silver **and five** millions of goods were brought away by the English and Dutch fleets.

Her Majesty gave a signal testimony of the high sense she entertained of the merit of Admiral Hopson, for his gallant behaviour in breaking the boom at Vigo; for she not only conferred upon him the honour of Knighthood, but settled upon him a pension of £500 a year for life, with the reversion of £300 a year to his lady, in case she survived him. The Queen conferred on Captain Leake also the honour of Knighthood.

**On the 4th** of May, 1703, the grand fleet consisting of thirty-five ships of the line, was sent into the Mediterranean, under the command of Sir Cloudesley Shovel. The Grafton, of seventy guns, one of the ships of this fleet was commanded by Sir Andrew Leake. On the 30th of September, Sir Cloudsley sent five ships, namely, **two thirds,** a fourth and fifth rate, with a fireship, under the command of Sir Andrew, to Lisbon, and from thence to Oporto, etc., to take under his convoy such merchant ships as were bound for England; and having a fair wind and good weather, he arrived safe in the Downs on **the 17th** of November, and there happily escaped the great November storm **that** happened a few days after.

In the year 1705, a large fleet of men of war, under the command **of Sir** George Rooke, was sent into the Mediterranean for the assistance **of Charles** III, King of Spain. In this fleet the Grafton, of seventy guns, was commanded by Sir Andrew Leake; and the Monk, of sixty guns, by **Captain Mighells,** both of Lowestoft. From a variety of unforseen accidents and disappointments, Sir George was unable to perform any essential service to his country in the **former** part of this expedition; and being apprised of the reflections he would be exposed to from his enemies, upon his return to England, for having spent the summer with so formidable a fleet without performing any important action, he called a council of war, on the 17th of July, in the road to Tetuan; where, having delivered his opinion that it was highly requisite they should resolve on some important action that would be of signal service to their country they accordingly, after a long debate, came to a resolution of making a sudden and vigorous attack upon Gibraltar.

The fleet got into the Bay of Gibraltar on the 21st of July; and the marines, English and Dutch, to the number of 1800, were landed, under the command of the Prince of Hesse, on the isthmus, to cut off all communication between the town and the continent. His Highness having taken post there, summoned the governor, who answered, that he would defend the place to the last extremity. On the 22nd, the Admiral, at break of day, gave the signal for cannonading the town. The Grafton, commanded by Sir Andrew Leake, was one of the ships sent on this service. The Monk, Captain Mighells, was in the fleet, but not engaged in the attack. The cannonading was carried on with such vigour, that 15,000 shots were expended in five hours, when the Admiral perceiving that the enemy were driven from their batteries at the South Mole Head, and that if we were once possessed of them, the town **must be taz**en, he ordered Captain Whitaker to arm all the boats, and to **attempt** making himself master of them. This order was no sooner issued, than Captain Hicks and Captain Jumper, who where nearest the Mole, pushed **on shore** with their pinnaces, and actually seized the batteries before the **others** could come up. The Spaniards, perceiving this advantage, immediately sprung a mine, whereby two lieutenants and forty men were killed, and about sixty wounded. However, the English kept possession of the great platform till they were supported by Captain Whitaker and the seamen under his command, who very soon made himself master of a redoubt between the Mole and the town; on which the Admiral sent a letter to the governor to surrender, who on the 24th capitulated, and the Prince of Hesse took possession of the place. This attack upon Gibraltar was planned by the Admiral, and it was executed wholly by the sailors; consequently, all the success and honour of the undertaking must be attributed to the valour and conduct of the British seamen. In the execution of this design, nothing contributed more to its success than the furious cannonade previous to the attack, which obliged the Spaniards to abandon their posts; for the general officers, who inspected the works after they were in possession of the English, declared that they might have been defended by fifty men against as many thousands.

After the taking of Gibraltar the fleet sailed to Tetuan, in order to take in wood and water. On the 9th of August the fleet sailed again for Gibraltar, and had sight of the French fleet, which they resolved to engage; but the latter declined an action, and endeavoured to avoid the English. But Sir George pursued them with all the sail he could make, and on Sunday, being within three leagues of them, the French brought to, and forming a line of battle, lay in a position to receive him. The French fleet consisted of fifty-two ships and twenty-four galleys, commanded by the Count of Toulouse, High-Admiral of France. The English fleet consisted of fifty-three ships. A little after ten in the morning, Sir George bore down in order of battle, and throwing out the signal for engaging, began the fight. The fire of the enemy fell very heavy on the Royal Katherine, the St. George, and the Shrewsbury. About two in the afternoon the van of the French gave way to the English, and the battle ended with the day; the enemy retreating to leeward, and towing off their ships by the assistance of their galleys. Our fleet employed every manœuvre **for** two days, to renew the fight, but to no purpose, for the French assiduously avoided it, and at last bore quite away, which is an evident proof that the victory was the indisputable claim of the English.

In this great battle, called the Malaga fight (from its being fought off that port) that brave and valiant officer, Sir Andrew Leake, was unfortunately slain. After Sir Andrew had received his fatal wound, and was carried down to the surgeons to be dressed, his heroic soul fired with the love of his country, and burning with an insatiable thirst for glory, would not suffer him to remain inactive; but despising death, though surrounded will all its terrors, he wrapped **a** table cloth around his wounded body, and though possessing only the small remains of life, he placed himself in his elbow chair, and gave orders to be carried again upon the quarter-deck, where he bravely sat and partook of the glories of the day, until he nobly breathed his last. Sir Andrew commanded the Grafton, of seventy guns and 440 men. In this fight he had thirty-one men slain and sixty-six wounded.

Another British sea-commander belonging to Lowestoft, who by his conduct and gallantry in the service of his country, acquired the distinguished honour of Vice-Admiral of the Navy, was James Mighells, Esq.

In the year 1697, the sieur Pointis, the French Admiral, in his return from his successful expidition against the Spaniards in the West Indies, in which he had acquired as much plate and other effects as were computed to be worth

v

£1,200,000 sterling, thought himself safe when he arrived off **Newfoundland, as** he had not received the least intimation of our having a stout **squadron in those** seas, under the command of captain Norris, and which would have **been able to** have given a very good account of Pointis and his Spanish plunder, **had they** been so fortunate as to have met with him and engaged him.

Captain Norris, from the first advices that he received of the **arrival of a** French squadron in those parts, conjectured that it was the squadron **sent out** after him from France, with a view of intercepting him in his passage, or attacking him at Newfoundland; however, shortly after he received the most authentic information what squadron it was, also an account of its strength, and that it was conveying to France the rich plunder of Carthagena, in the West Indies. Captain Norton was transported with this ad**vice**; and immediately calling a Council of war, shewed the great uncertainty **of** meeting with the enemy if any delay was permitted, and urged **with** vehemency **the** necessity of immediately sailing in pursuit of them. Other com**manders, however**, did not appear in such haste. Many difficulties were apprehended, **and many** objections started; and therefore the determination of the council was, **to** continue in their present situation, and expect the French in close quarters. But fresh advices successively arriving, confirming the truth of his former intelligence, **it** occasioned the summoning of repeated councils of war; but in all these deliberations, Captain Norris, who was eager for fighting the enemy, experienced the mortifying misfortune of being still over ruled; so that by these repeated delays, arising from **the** irresolute decisions of the councils, the sieur Pointis with his rich booty, was suffered to escape, and arrive safe in France.

The several councils of war which were held on this occasion consisted of **eleven** land officers, and thirteen sea officers; the former were all unanimous against fighting; of the latter, eight were for it, and five against it. It is necessary to be observed, concerning this transaction that Captain Mighells, who commanded one of the ships belonging to this squadron, was among those who voted for fighting.

The whole business was in the ensuing session of Parliament, examined in **the** House of Lords; when, on a full view of the evidence, their Lordships came **to** the following resolutions:

"Die Lunæ, 17th April, 1699.

"1st.—It is resolved, by the Lord's spiritual and temporal in Parliament assembled, That the squadron commanded by Captain Norris, at St. John's, in Newfoundland, not going out to fight Pointis, on the several intelligences given, was a very high miscarriage, to the great disservice of the king and kingdom.

"2nd. It is resolved that the joining the land officers in the council of war on the 24th July, 1697, was one occasion of the miscarriage in not fighting Pointis."

The first action wherein Captain Mighells had an opportunity of signalising his bravery, is represented as follows: Real-Admiral Dilkes having received orders to look for a grand partee, said to lay in Cancalle Bay, on the cost of Normandy, sailed from Spithead on the 24th July, 1703, in **pursuit** of them. Having dispatched the Fly, Captain Chamberlain, for intelligence, he was informed, that a fleet of about forty sail were plying towards Granville. The Admiral resolved to sail immediately after them; and having discovered them, determined to attack them at break of day the next morning. He followed them as far as the pilots would venture, and found them to consist of forty-three sail of merchant ships and three men-of-war. On the approach of the English fleet, the French stood in for the shore; and the Admiral being come within four feet of the water which the ships drew, thought it too dangerous to pursue them any farther with the larger men-of-war; and, therefore, having manned all the boats of the fleet, they attacked the French, and so far succeeded, that by noon they had taken fifteen sail, and burnt six; the remainder stood so far into the Bay, that, according to the judgment of the pilots, even the smaller ships could not attack them. Hereupon, **the** 27th, in the morning it was resolved, in a Council of War, that, under cover of the Hector, Mermaid fireship, the Spy brigantine, a ship of six guns, taken the day before from the enemy, and a ketch fitted as a fireship, all the boats in the squadron should enter the harbour and renew the attack.

This service was performed between ten and eleven in the morning, the Admiral being present, accompanied by Captain Fairfax, Captain Legg, and Captain Mighells, as also by Captains Lampries and Pipon. Out of the three men-of-war which the enemy had, one of the eighteen guns they burnt themselves; one of the fourteen guns was set on fire by Mr. Paul, first Lieutenant of the Kent, who, in this service, was shot through the lower jaw, and had four men killed; and the third of eight guns, was brought off. Seventeen merchant ships more were burnt and destroyed; so that of the whole fleet only four escaped by getting under the command of Granville fort. The Queen, to testify her gracious acceptance of so cheerful and effectual a service; and to perpetuate the memory thereof, as well as recompense the gallantry of those who rendered it, ordered gold medals to be struck on this occasion, and to be delivered to the Admiral and all his officers.

The next remarkable action wherein Captain Mighells was eminently distinguished for his conduct and bravery, was the great Malaga fight on the 13th of August, 1704. In this battle he commanded the Monk of sixty guns, 365 men. In this memorable action Captain Mighells gave a most signal instance of true magnanimity and British valour; for the French Admiral having ordered the Serieux of seventy guns, commanded by M. Champmelin, to board the Monk, which he attempted three times, yet he was as often beaten off again by Captain Mighells, with the firmest resolution and courage; and notwithstanding the French, after every repulse, had their wounded men taken off, and their complement restored by their galleys, yet this gallant Captain as constantly cleared the decks of the enemy, and at last forced them to bear away. In these several attacks the Monk had thirty-six men killed and fifty-two wounded, among the latter was Captain Mighells.

The Monk was probably lost near Lowestoft a few years after. In 1719 the Monk, man-of-war, sixty guns, Captain Clinton, coming out of the sea, ran upon Corton sands. The Captain and men left her (except the master and twelve men) and came ashore at Lowestoft. In the night the ship went off the sands, and the master and men brought her up in Corton roads; but afterwards she went ashore at a place called "Old Almonds" (between Corton and Gorleston) where she was totally lost.

In the year 1711, Captain Mighells was again in the Mediterranean, in the Hampton-Court, man-of-war, under Sir John Jennings. The Admiral, after he had appeared off Barcelona, and had taken on board the King of Spain, whom he had landed at Genoa; and had also proceeded to Leghorn, to procure such a supply of stores as that place would afford, sailed for Port Mahon. On his arrival there, he was informed by the Captains of two ships, that they had heard a great firing all the night before. On this intelligence he sent the Chatham and Winchelsea the next morning to try what they could discover; who soon brought him intelligence that the Dutch Vice-Admiral, with his squadron, was in the offing, together with five ships of ours. The ships belonging to the English were the Hampton Court, Captain Mighells; the Nottingham, the Sterling Castle, the Charles galley, and the Lynn; which came from the coast of Catalonia, and in their passage had fallen in with two French men-of-war; the Toulouse and the Trident, each of fifty guns, and four hundred men. The Hampton Court came up with the first of them and engaged her two hours; and to whose commander she struck, at the time when the Sterling Castle came within musket-shot, which was about ten o'clock at night. But the Trident, by the advantage of light winds and the assistance of her oars made her escape. The masts of the Hampton Court being much injured in the fight, they, by the violence of the weather, came next day all by the board, so that she was towed into port by the Sterling Castle.

Captain Mighells, for the many eminent services rendered by him to his country, being made a Rear-Admiral, was appointed a Rear-Admiral of the White, 1718, in a strong squadron sent to the Baltic, under the command of Sir John Norris; this squadron, consisting of ten ships of the line, left Southwold bay on the 1st May, having eighteen sail of merchant ships under convoy. On the second, at three in the morning, they took their departure Lowestoft light-house distant six leagues, and on the 14th May arrived safe at Copenhagen; where, the same day, Sir John Norris had an audience of his

Danish Majesty, by whom he was received very graciously; and soon after he sailed, in conjunction with the Danish fleet, and blocked up the Swedes in their harbours, and returned to England again about the latter end of October.

On the 17th December, 1718, war was declared against Spain; and in the beginning of the following year, the nation was under the greatest apprehension of an invasion; and on repeated advices being received of the great preparations made in Spain for that purpose, every necessary precaution was taken to defeat their designs, Sir John Norris set out on the 5th of March, 1719, for Chatham and the Nore; and Rear-Admiral Mighells, for Portsmouth, to forward the fitting out such ships as were in those stations, and to take them under their command. On the 8th of March the Earl of Berkeley kissed his Majesty's hand on his being appointed commander of the fleet, which was then fitting out with all expedition. The Earl sailed from St. Helen's to the westward, and after joining Sir John Norris, sailed to the coast of Ireland; from thence he returned on the 4th of April, having dispatched Vice-Admiral Mighells with the Windsor, Monmouth, and Antelope, to the coast of Galicia for intelligence, and then left the command of the fleet to Sir John Norris.

Soon after, advice was received that the fleet of Spanish men-of-war and transports, crowded with men, but wanting all necessaries, had sailed from Cadiz for the Groyne, where they were to be joined by other ships and transports, but had been dispersed in a storm, and driven into different ports, terribly shattered and disabled; some without masts, and others were reduced to the necessity of throwing their horses, stores, and guns overboard, which totally frustrated the designs of the Spaniards to invade England.

The English, being determined to retaliate the insults threatened by the Spaniards in the preceding year, against the British coasts, formed a resolution of sending a fleet and army to the coast of Spain; the former under the command of Vice-Admiral Mighells; the latter under Lord Viscount Cobham. On the 21st of September, 1719, the ships of war and transports, having on board the forces consisting of about six thousand men, sailed from St. Helen's.

The Admiral arrived upon the coast of Galicia in the month of September, and continued cruising three days in the station appointed for Captain Johnson to join him; but receiving no intelligence of him, and the danger of lying on that coast at that season of the year, with transports, rendering it necessary to take some measures of acting without him, and the wind being fair for Vigo, he came to a resolution of sailing to that port.

On the 29th of September, they entered the harbour of Vigo and the grenadiers being immediately landed, about three miles from the town, drew up upon the beach. Lord Cobham went on shore with the grenadiers, and the regiments followed as fast as the boats could carry them. On the 1st of October his Lordship moved with the forces nearer the town; this motion of the army, together with the motion of some parties that were ordered to reconnoitre the town and citadel, gave the enemy some apprehensions that preparations were being made to attack them, whereupon they abandoned the town and retired to the citadel.

On the 3rd a bomb-vessel began to bombard the citadel, but with little success, by reason of its great distance; but in the evening the large mortars and the cohorn mortars between forty and fifty of them, great and small, being landed at the town, and placed on a battery, under cover of fort St. Sebastian (which had been taken from the Spaniards) began in the night to play upon the citadel, and continued it four days with great success. On the fourth day his Lordship ordered the battering cannon to be landed, and, at the same time his Lordship sent to the governor a summons to surrender, signifying, that if he staid till our battery of cannon was ready, he should have no quarter. Colonel Ligonier was sent with this message; but found that the Governor had the day before been carried out of the castle wounded. The Lieutenant-Colonel, who commanded in his absence, desired leave to send for directions, but being answered that hostilities should be continued if they did not send their articles of capitulation without any delay, they soon complied.

On the 25th and 26th of October the forces were all embarked again; on the 27th the fleet put to sea; and on the 11th of November Admiral Mighells, with the men of war and most of the transports arrived at Falmouth, with the loss of only two officers and three or four men killed in the fleet, and about three hundred men killed, died, or deserted in the army. The enemy had above three hundred killed or wounded by our bombs. There were found in the town and citadel a great number of fine brass cannon and mortars, several thousand cannon shot, muskets, barrels of gunpowder, and an immense quantity of other stores and ammunition, which were shipped on board the fleet; besides destroying 153 pieces of iron cannon, sixteen brass cannon and mortars, and a large quantity of other stores; and the treasure brought into the Tower of London was computed to be worth £80,000 sterling It is remarkable, that the arms and the stores thus taken and destroyed were originally designed for the intended invasion of England the preceding year; but from this successful expedition every design of that nature was rendered totally abortive. This was a very humiliating blow to Spain, and convinced them and the rest of the world, that the English spirit was so far from being depressed by the threatening insults of its enemies, that it was not only capable of planning, but of really executing that invasion which our enemies only meditated.

This expedition to the coast of Spain appears to have been the last service that this great officer was engaged in; for being now arrived at his full meridian glory, and worn out with fatigue in the service of his country, he exchanged the tumultuous scenes of war for the more calm and undisturbed enjoyments of a retired situation. He died on the 21st of March, 1733, and was buried in Lowestoft church, where a handsome monument is erected to his memory. The following is a copy of the inscription: "To the memory of James Mighells, Esq., late Vice-Admiral and Comptroller of the Royal Navy, whose publick and private character justly deserves remembrance, if courage and conduct in a commander, fidelity and diligence in a commissioner, sincerity in a friend, usefulness in a relation, love and affection in a husband, care and indulgence in a parent, and the strictest justice and honesty to all men, deserved to be remembered. He died March 21st, 1733, aged 69 years."

The last naval officer belonging to Lowestoft at the same period, who remains to be mentioned, and whose conduct and bravery, as a commander, is justly entitled to notice and esteem is Captain Thomas Arnold.

The Arnolds have been a flourishing family in this town from the reign of Queen Elizabeth. In 1584 Nathaniel Arnold was one of the feoffees for Ann Girling's donation. Thomas, his eldest son lost £375 13s. by the great fire in 1644.

The most memorable action in Captain Thomas Arnold's life, wherein he displayed the greatest valour and magnanimity, was in the great seafight in the Mediterranean, in the year 1718.

About the middle of March, 1718, Sir George Byng was appointed Admiral and Commander-in-Chief of His Majesty's fleet, and to command the squadron designed for the Mediteranean, to act against Spain, in order to protect the neutrality of Italy. On the 3rd of June, the fleet, consisting of twenty-two ships of the line, etc., sailed from St. Helen's; about the latter end of the month it arrived in the Mediteranean, and in the beginning of July was in sight of the Spanish fleet consisting of twenty-seven sail of men-of-war, great and small with fireships, bomb-vessels, etc. On the approach of the English, they went from them along way, but in their order of battle. Early in the morning of the 11th, the English got pretty near up to them. The Marquis de Mari, Rear-Admiral, with six Spanish men-of-war, and all the galleys, fireships, bomb-vessels, and store ships, separated from their main fleet, and stood in for the Sicilian shore; upon which the Admiral detached Captain Walton, of the Canterbury, with five more ships after them. In this engagement Captain Walton took four Spanish men-of-war, a bomb-vessel, and a ship laden with arms, and burnt four men-of-war, being all the Spanish ships that were on the coast. In the meanwhile Admiral Sir George Byng pursued the main body of the Spanish fleet.

The Kent and Superbe (the latter being commanded by Captain Streynsham Master, whose first lieutenant was Mr. Arnold), together with the Grafton and Orford, being the fastest sailing ships, having orders to make what sail they could, and to place themselves near the four head-most ships of the enemy, were the first that came up with them. The Spaniards began the action by firing their stern chasers at them; but the English ships having orders not to fire unless the Spaniards repeated their firing, made no return at first; but the Spaniards firing again, the Orford attacked the Santa Rosa, which some time after she took. The St. Charles struck next, without much opposition, and he Kent took possession of her. The Grafton attacked the Prince of Austrias (formerly called the Cumberland), in which was Rear-Admiral Chacon; but the Breda and Captain coming up, she left that ship for them to take, which they soon accomplished, and stretched ahead after another sixty gun ship, which was on her starboard while she was engaging the Prince of Austrias, and kept firing her stern chase into the Grafton.

About one o'clock the Kent and Superbe engaged the Royal St. Philip the Spanish Admiral; which, though supported by two other ships, and all of them kept a continual fire, yet made a running fight of it till about three in the afternoon, when the Kent bearing down upon her and passing under her stern, gave her a broadside and fell to leeward of her. After that the Superbe bore up to the Royal Philip; but Captain Master (who commanded the Superbe) being diffident concerning the most successful method of attacking her, consulted his first lieutenant), Mr. Arnold, who told him, "That as the eyes of the whole fleet were upon them, expecting the most vigorous efforts in the discharge of his duty in that critical moment; he therefore advised him to board the Royal Philip immediately sword in hand." The council of Mr. Arnold was immediately put in execution; and as his office of first-lieutenant obliged him, he boarded the Royal Philip, sword in hand, and shortly after carried her. Mr. Arnold received such a dangerous wound in this service, in one of his hands and arms, as rendered him almost useless afterwards. At the same time the Barfleur being within shot of the Royal Philip, and astern of her, and also inclining on her weather quarter, one of the Spanish rear-Admirals and another ship of sixty guns, which were to the windward of the Barfleur, bore down upon her and gave her their broadsides, and then clapped upon a wind and stood in for the land. Admiral Byng, in the Barfleur, stood after them till it was almost night; but it being little wind, and they galeing from him out of reach of his cannon, he left pursuing them, and stood away again to the fleet, which he joined in the night. In this action the Essex took the Juno, of thirty-six guns, the Montague and Rupert took the Velante, of forty-four guns. Vice-Admiral Cornwall followed the Grafton, to support her, but it being very little wind, and night coming on, the Spaniard galed away from the Grafton. Rear-Admiral Delaval took the Isabella of sixty guns. The English received but little damage in this battle; the ship that suffered most was the Grafton. Captain Haddock, and being a good sailer, her Captain engaged several ships of the enemy, always pursuing the headmost, and leaving those ships he had disabled or damaged to be taken by those that followed him. Several other men-of-war, fire ships, bomb vessels, etc., were taken and destroyed in this action. As for the prizes that had been taken, they were sent to Port Mahon; where, by an unlucky accident the Royal Philip took fire and blew up with most of the crew on board; but the Spanish Admiral had been before set ashore in Sicily, with some other prisoners of distinction, where he soon afterwards died of his wounds.

As soon as Admiral Byng had obtained a full account of the whole transaction, he dispatched his eldest son to England with the intelligence; who, arriving at Hampton Court in fifteen days from Naples, brought thither the agreeable confirmation of what public fame had before reported, and on which the King had already written a letter to the Admiral as under:

Sir George Byng—Although I have received no news from you directly, I am informed of the victory obtained by the fleet under your command and would not, therefore, defer giving that satisfaction which must result from my approbation of your conduct. I give you my thanks, and desire you will testify the same to all the brave men who have distinguished themselves on this occasion. Mr. Secretary Crags has orders to inform you more fully my intentions, but I was willing to assure you that I am your good friend.

GEORGE R."

"Hampton Court, August 23, 1718."

Mr Byng met with a most gracious reception from his Majesty; who made him a handsome present, and sent him back with plenipotentiary powers to his father to negociate with the several Princes and states of Italy, as there should be occasion; and with his royal grant to the officers and seamen, of all prizes taken by them from the Spaniards.

The Spanish Court was extremely chagrined at this unexpected blow, which had almost totally destroyed the naval force which they had been at so much pains in equipping, and therefore were not slow in expressing their resentments; for they immediately made themselves masters of all the English ships that were in the port of Cadiz, and seized all the effects of the English merchants that were at Malaga. These hostilities occasioned a declaration of war against Spain, in form, on the 17th of December, 1718.

Soon after this battle Mr. Arnold was appointed Captain of the Spy sloop of war, and sent express to the West Indies; but his ship was so very unfit for the voyage that it was expected he would never return. However, he was so fortunate as to arrive safe again in England, and was afterwards appointed to the command of the Fox man-of-war, and ordered upon the Carolina station; but on coming home again, finding his friend Lord Torrington dead; (Sir George Byng was created Lord Torrington); and all his hopes of promotion entirely frustrated, he resigned his command in the navy, and retired to Great Yarmouth, where he ended his days, August 31, 1737, aged 58 years, and was interred in Lowestoft church, where a monument containing a just representation of a brave and gallant officer is erected to his memory.

These are the accounts of the many valiant sea commanders who formerly belonged to the town of Lowestoft, and who by their wisdom, conduct, and gallantry, have not only adorned the annals of their country, but have cast a lustre upon the place of their nativity, and obtained the most distinguished honour to themselves and their posterity.

Lowestoft being a maritime town, it is more distinguished by important events relative to naval affairs, than those respecting military transactions having occurred, which were of considerable importance, such as have given evident demonstrations of the loyalty of its inhabitants, and of their inviolable attachment to the Government.

In the year 1715, a block-house was standing at Lowestoft, well furnished with ordnance, for the defence of such ships as anchored before the town for the purpose of merchandising, which block-house was destroyed by the sea.

In 1549, as soon as the report of Kett having formed a camp upon Mousehold Heath, Norwich, was received in Suffolk, the common people assembled together in great multitudes, made themselves masters of Lothingland, seized six pieces of cannon at Lowestoft, and brought them to an enclosure at the north end of Gorleston, intending to batter from thence the town of Yarmouth. These designs being perceived by the inhabitants, a party of them were dispatched to set fire to a large stack of hay, on the west side of the haven; which being executed, it occasioned a prodigious smoke, and falling upon the face of the rebels, prevented their seeing the Yarmouth men, who, consequently, fell upon the enemy, whereby many of them were slain, thirty were taken prisoners, together with six pieces of cannon. The prisoners, with the cannon, were immediately carried to Yarmouth, where the rebels were committed to prison, and the remainder of the party being disappointed in their design of seizing the town, immediately withdrew themselves, and taking another rout, joined their leader Kett on Mousehold Heath. Afterwards, Queen Elizabeth gave the town of Lowestoft four pieces of cannon and two slings, in the room of those taken away by the Suffolk rabble, when they went to join Kett at Mousehold.

In 1588, when the nation was alarmed with the apprehension of a Spanish invasion it cost the inhabitants of Lowestoft upwards of £200 towards defending the coast against the enemy, which was applied in the following manner: in fitting out a pinnace, £100; in erecting bulwarks, £80; in mounting the cannon £16; and in purchasing gunpowder £16. Also, in the following year, a warrant was issued by the Privy Council to the men of Ipswich, commanding the inhabitants of this town to concur with them in fitting out two ships of war; the charges attending this undertaking amounted to £2,800, and the share alloted to Lowestoft was £23. The town received also a warrant from the Lieutenant of the county, directing that another bulwark should be erected for its defence. In consequence of this order, it was found necessary to apply the money which had been collected in Ipswich, in erecting this bulwark. But about two or three years after, the Ipswich men made a demand of this money; and for non-payment thereof procured an order of Council, whereby several of the principal inhabitants of Lowestoft were arrested, in order to appear before the Council, and answer the charge of disobedience, which cost the town £60.

During the great revolt from loyalty, the usurpation of Oliver Cromwell, the town of Lowestoft exerted its utmost efforts in support of the Royal cause, and consequently was thereby exposed to the greatest dangers and inconveniences; particularly in opposing and counteracting the violent proceedings of Cromwell and the Parliament, respecting the association of the Eastern Counties. Among the many misfortunes and inconveniences which the town was subject to in consequence of this rebellion, may be reckoned, its being obliged, in 1642, to join with Ipswich, Orford, Dunwich, Aldborough, Southwold, Colchester, Maldon, Harwich, Woodbridge, Walberswick, Gorleston, Manningtree, and Barnham, in furnishing a ship of 800 tons burthen, and 260 men, with double tackle, ammunition, wages and stores.

In 1642, when Cromwell was advanced to the rank of Colonel, and also appointed a Commissioner in the order for settling the militia, the eastern counties entered into an association, and agreed to support the Parliament against all its opposers.

The king, in order to defeat the designs of this association, which the Parliament had confirmed, issued out his commission of array.

Cromwell having by his great skill and management, raised a regiment of a thousand horse, obstructed, with the most indefatigable industry, the levies that were raising for the service of the King in Cambridgeshire, Essex, Suffolk and Norfolk, and hearing that several gentlemen of eminent rank were assembled at Lowestoft, among whom were Sir John Pettus, Sir Edward Barker, etc., with a design of forming a counter association in this county, and also in Norfolk, for the service of his Majesty, he marched with the utmost expedition to Lowestoft, and surprised them the day before that many others were to have met and joined them; and had not their designs been frustrated by this unexpected surprise, probably all the eastern counties would have been rescued out of the hands of Oliver Cromwell and his adherents.

The inhabitants of Lowestoft, as soon as they were informed of Oliver's approach were exceedingly alarmed, and exerted their utmost efforts to put the town in a state of defence, and to dispute his entrance; and in order to this purpose, two pieces of cannon were placed at the south end of the town, and two at the head of Rant's score, but one of the principal inhabitants (Thomas Mighells, merchant, who died in 1695) foreseeing the improbability of a design of this nature being attended with success, and also representing the extreme rashness of attempting it with so inferior a force, as well as the great damage which the town would probably sustain from an unsuccessful opposition, so far prevailed with the inhabitants and members of the association that they declined the resolution of opposing Oliver's entrance into the town. The sum of twenty pounds was paid by the City of Norwich to Sergeant-Major Sherwood's volunteers for their service at Lowestoft, where a design was discovered of a counter-association on the King's behalf, made by Sir John Pettus, Sir Edward Barker, and other loyal gentlemen; and was carried so far, that Colonel Cromwell was in danger of his person, and was very near being taken, had not these volunteers rescued him, by sending for one hundred soldiers from Norwich and also one hundred more afterwards.

In consequence of pacific measures being adopted, Cromwell entered the town without any opposition, and fixed his head quarters at the Swan Inn. While he was here he sent for Sir John Pettus, who accordingly waited on him. After that Oliver had interrogated him very closely respecting the designs of the counter-association, requested that he would inform him to which party it was that he intended to engage himself during these disputes, Sir John, without any duplicity or reservation, declared that he should act for the King. Oliver, so far from shewing the least resentment against Sir John for his ingenuous declaration, highly applauded his frankness and sincerity, and dismissed him with assuring him, that he sincerely wished every man in the kingdom would be as open and sincere in declaring his real sentiments and intentions.

Cromwell by the surrender of the town became possessed of a **considerable** quantity of ammunition, saddles, pistols, and several pieces of cannon; **as many as were sufficient for arming** and supplying with necessaries a **considerable** body of forces.

This **unfortunate event** exceedingly discouraged the King's friends of Norfolk and Suffolk; and it appeared afterwards, that, however artfully Cromwell might conceal his resentment on this occasion, yet, he was far from being sincere, or that those resentments were wholly suppressed by the surrender of the town. For he not only declared that had the inhabitants and those concerned in the counter association attempted to fire upon him when he entered the town, he would have put them all to the sword, but also suffered his soldiers, in a great measure, to plunder the town and live at free quarters. The tradesmen in Lowestoft suffered the greatest injuries by Oliver's soldiers plundering them of their stocks-in-trade, as far as they were useful to the army, without making them any recompense. This misfortune, which happened in the year 1643, together with the terrible fire in 1644, which consumed £10,000 worth of property; the Dutch wars, which followed soon after, and the tedious and expensive law-suit with Yarmouth concerning the herring fishery, almost ruined the town.

In the year 1663 a petition was presented by the town of Lowestoft to the Duke of Albemarle, requesting that the four pieces of cannon then in the town might remain there, in order to guard the coast against any attacks of the enemy.

In consequence of this petition, the four pieces of cannon were permitted by Government to remain at Lowestoft, for the defence of the town; accordingly the inhabitants at their own expense, mounted the same on a platform, and also purchased ammunition necessary for their own security. But this platform being afterwards destroyed by the sea, the town was obliged to present a petition to the Earl of Suffolk, Lord Lieutenant of the County, requesting assistance, in order to enable them to erect another platform which petition was granted.

In 1744 a battery of six pieces of cannon, eighteen pounders, was erected at the south end of the town, for protecting ships in the south roads, and guarding the passage of the Stanford. The cannon were given by Government, but the ammunition was furnished by the town.

On the 14th October, 1745, in consequence of the rebellion in Scotland, a subscription was opened in Lowestoft for the defence of his Majesty's person, the support of the Government and the peace and security of the county; when the sum of £200 was subscribed, advice was received of the victory obtained over the rebels, 16th April, 1746, by his Royal Highness the Duke of Cumberland, only £20 of the subscription was paid.

In 1756 a battery of two pieces of canon, eighteen pounders, was erected upon the beach at the north end of the town, near the ness. These pieces were taken from the battery at the south end of the town. They were never of any great service to the town, for vessels belonging to the enemy seldom approach so near to the coast as to come within reach of the guns. On the 7th of April, 1778, Lord Amherst, accompanied by his brother, came to Lowestoft and examined the forts in consequence of the survey they were making by order of the Government, of the state of all the fortifications on the coast.

In 1782, when England was involved in a war with France, Spain, Holland, and America at the same time, was under apprehension that the British Navy was unable to maintain its superiority as mistress of the sea, when threatened by such numerous and powerful enemies, the county of Suffolk held a general meeting at Stowmarket, where it was agreed to open a subscription throughout the county, in order to raise a sum sufficient for building a man-of-war of the line, of seventy-four guns, to be presented to the Government. The town of Lowestoft subscribed £38 6s. 6d. The sum proposed to be raised was £30,000. The utmost efforts were exerted to obtain the money, and weekly accounts were published in the papers of the success that attended it in the several parts of the county; but it appearing, at the close of the year, that the whole subscription amounted to only about £20,000, it was apprehended that the zeal of the county was nearly exhausted, and that the subscription had arrived at almost its utmost limits. In the beginning of the year 1783, the war being terminated in a general peace, a further subscription became unnecessary, and consequently the subscribers were not called on for their subscriptions.

In the beginning of the year 1781, when the war broke out between England and Holland, there were quartered at Lowestoft two companies of the East Suffolk Militia commanded by Col. Goat, which in the May following were succeeded by a party of the 19th Regiment of light horse. Government seemed to have been apprehensive of this war, and also sensible of the necessity of having recourse to such methods as were proper for securing the eastern part of the kingdom against any attacks of the enemy.

On the 31st. of July Lord Amherst, Commander-in-chief of his Majesty's forces in the Kingdom, in his survey of the fortifications on this coast, after being met at Kessingland by a party of light dragoons from Lowestoft, was escorted to Lowestoft, where he surveyed the forts, which were found to be in a very ruinous condition. On the 13th of August the town was alarmed with the appearance of a fleet of large men of war in the offing, steering a direct course for Lowestoft, supposing them to be Dutch ships, but on a nearer approach they were found to be Admiral Parker's fleet returning from a sharp engagement with a Dutch squadron, commanded by Admiral Zoutman on the Dogger Bank, the 5th August. On the 4th September there arrived in Lowestoft a waggon loaded with powder, shot, &c., guarded by a party of the Huntingdonshire and East Essex Militia, from the camp at Hopton, in order to prove, before General Tryon, four pieces of cannon then lying at the old fort, at the south end of the town, in order to discover whether they were serviceable or not ; when, after charging each of them with 16lbs of powder and an 18lb shot, one of them burst, and flying in various directions, part of it struck a boy on the arm, who happily received no material injury. One part of the cannon, weighing between two and three hundred weight, was thrown into a field at a distance of 175 yards. On the 11th October following, Colonel Deibeig proved also the guns lying at the old fort, near the ness, which had laid there since the reign of Queen Anne, when three of them burst. This month the party of the 19th regiment of light horse quartered at this place, left the town, and were succeeded by two companies of the East Suffolk Militia, commanded by Captain Delane, who continued here till the May following.

Government being acquainted with the ruinous condition of the forts at Lowestoft, and the defenceless state of this part of the coast, immediately formed a resolution to erect several new fortifications at this town, and the principal one to be situated at the north end of the town, on the same spot whereon the old fort formerly stood ; and also to have it much larger. But the premises on which the fort was designed to be erected being town land, Government was under the necessity of hiring it by a lease for a term of years, and also to purchase of different proprietors about three-quarters of an acre of land to add to it, the former spot not being large enough. Half an acre of this land was purchased of Mr. Robert Reeve, and the other quarter of an acre of Mr. Henry Lucas.

On January 7, 1782, the new fort, at the south end of the town was begun under the direction of Captain Fisher, one of His Majesty's engineers. About 300 men (including fifty of the East Suffolk militia), were employed in this work. This fort consisted of a ditch about eighteen feet deep, fifteen feet wide, mounted with chevaux de frize. Over this ditch was a drawbridge between four and five feet wide. The inside of the south-west angle measured seventy feet ; the width of the other angles were 95, 140, 100, and 249 feet. The terrace before the embrazures was four feet wide. The embrazures were eighteen feet wide and eight high. Next the sea was the glacis, extending about sixty-five yards. There was also a breastwork to defend the bridge, about eighteen feet thick and eight feet high. At the north-west angle of the fort was the magazine, it was thirty feet long and twelve broad ; it was sunk beneath the surface of the earth, and was bomb proof, and contained 300 barrels of powder. In the centre of the fort stood the guard house ; this was a handsome sashed building, about seventy feet long and twenty-six wide, having a spacious parade in front. At the south-west angle stood the flag staff, fifty-five feet high on which was hoisted an English jack. The battery mounted thirteen pieces of cannon, ten thirty-pounders, and three eighteen-pounders. The whole battery was finished on the 21st December, 1782. The south battery was distant from the north, three quarters of a mile, and from the east battery upon the beach, seven furlongs; and the distance of the north battery, near the distance of the north battery, on the beach three furlongs.

On the 4th April in the same year (1782) the erection of the fort at the north end of the town was commenced about one hundred yards to the north of the light-house. This battery consisted of a breast-work, having four angles, each of them about thirty feet wide. There was a guard house adjoining, about twenty feet long, and sixteen feet broad. Also a magazine, about six feet square, which was paled round. This battery mounted four eighteen-pounders, and was intended to act with another battery, purposed shortly to be erected upon the Beach near the Ness.

A descent on this coast was so much apprehended about this time that a party of soldiers patrolled through Lowestoft every four hours during the night, in order, if necessary, to give an alarm.

And on the 23rd April following they began to erect the eastern battery upon the hill. It was surrounded by a ditch about fifteen feet wide and twelve deep, over which was a draw-bridge about four feet wide. The south-west angle measured eighty-three feet; the other angles ninety-six, eighty-three, fifty-eight, and twenty-nine feet. There was also a block-house erected, about fifteen feet square, the upper part of which was a guard house. The terrace round the inside of the ditch was four feet broad. The embrazures were eighteen feet wide and four feet high. The magazine was six feet square, and the glacis (which was next the sea) was fifty-three feet broad. This battery mounted six pieces of cannon, four thirty-two pounders, and two nine pounders; and was finished, as was also the north battery, on the 21st December, 1782, just time enough to fire (as it happened) for the general peace concluded the 20th January, 1783. On the 12th August, 1782, in honour of the Prince of Wales's birthday, nine guns were fired from the south battery, four from the north, and four from the east battery; which was the first time of the cannon being exercised. The camp on East Heath also fired three volleys on the occasion.

The real cause, most probably, that hastened the finishing of these forts, was the information which Government had received of a descent intended to have been made on this coast.

In consequence of this intelligence, on the 23rd March, 1782, Captain Fisher, of the engineers, came to Lowestoft, and afterwards went to East Heath, near Mutford Bridge, and marked out the ground for an encampment.

On the 27th following, the Captain requested a meeting of the inhabitants of the town to know whether a sufficient number of men could be raised in order to work the guns at the batteries, provided that a party of the Royal Regiment of Artillery, then quartered in the town, should undertake to teach them their exercise. On the Captain offering this proposal, a subscription of upwards of £100 was immediately entered into by the principal inhabitants, with a design of carrying the proposal into execution, but not being sufficiently encouraged it came to nothing.

On the 29th March, Colonel Deibieg arrived at Lowestoft, and informed the inhabitants that Government had received undoubted information of an intended invasion shortly to be made at three different parts of the kingdom at the same time, namely at Torbay, Newcastle, and on the coast near Yarmouth; and therefore requested to be informed whether the town was able to furnish two hundred men to work the guns at the batteries. On this application a meeting was called of the inhabitants to take the same into consideration, when the answer was, that by reason of the great number of sailors belonging to the town being at that time employed in the navy, it was impossible to obtain the number of men required.

On June 23rd, Lord Townshend, Commander-in-chief of the camp at Warley common, and the coasts of Essex, Norfolk and Suffolk, came to

Lowestoft, and surveyed the works carrying on there, and also the ground intended for the encampment on East Heath. On the 24th his Lordship, accompanied by his aide-de-camps, went to Oulton, and surveyed the dyke there, in order to discover whether that part of the river was fordable by the enemy in case of descent.

July 22nd, the 20 regiment of Light Dragoons, commanded by General Philipson, encamped on East Heath, at the bottom of Fidlers' hill, near Kirkley bridge. And on September 10th, they were reviewed on the Heath by Lord Townshend, the Earl of Orford, General Tryon, and General Philipson.

September 11, eight pieces of cannon passed through Lowestoft for Benacre, to be placed there, along the coast to Harwich as signal guns.

September 25, General Conway, Commander-in-chief of his Majesty's forces, arrived at Lowestoft; and being attended by Lord Townshend, General Tryon, General Morrison, and their Aidede-Camps, surveyed the batteries in Lowestoft, and afterwards reviewed the regiment of Dragoons from East Heath; the regiment of foot and Cambridgeshire militia from Hopton; and the West Norfork militia from Castor, on Fritton Heath.

On the 28th September Captain Heigington's company of the 10th Regiment of Foot came from Hopton Common, and encamped near the Battery at the north end of the town, to be in readiness, in case of necessity, to assist the artillery at the fort, commanded by Captain Marlow.

On the 14th October his Grace the Duke of Richmond, master of the ordnance, arrived at Lowestoft, accompanied by his son Lord George Lenox and surveyed the works.

In Feburary, 1782, Lord North, Prime Minister, and all the other officers of State belonging to his administration, were under the necessity of resigning their respective employments on account of the American war. The many miseries which the nation was involved in, in consequence of this unhappy war, and the opposition which ministers met with in the House of Commons, as being the authors of these calamities, occasioned an entire new ministry to be formed. The Marquis of Rockingham was made Prime Minister; who, dying soon after was succeeded by the Earl of Shelburne; Admiral Kepple was appointed First Lord of the Admiralty, in the room of Earl of Sandwich; General Conway was made Commander-in-chief of His Majesty's forces in the room of Lord Amherst; and the Duke of Richmond master of the Ordnance in the room of Lord Townsend. These circumstances are necessary to be remembered, as they account for the different noblemen and officers visiting the town in so short a space of time, in order to survey the works and review the troops.

Among the various methods made use of in order to alarm the coast on the approach of an enemy were the following: July 18, 1782, about ten at night General Tryon caused skyrockets to be let off at the several places of Caister, Gorleston Heights, Lowestoft East Battery, Pakefield, and Covebithe, intending thereby to communicate an alarm from Caister and Covebithe, the two most distant places, in the same manner as was practised by lighting up beacons. This method was found to answer exceedingly well, as intelligence could by these means be communicated from Caistor to Covehithe in two minutes. September 5, another experiment was made use of by the General to convey an alarm in case the enemy should approach in the night near Lowestoft; which was to set fire to a stack of about fifty faggots of furze, upon a hill, in the bounds of Gunton, and to let off four large skyrockets, so as to be seen at Caister, Hopton camp, Somerly Hall, (the head quarters) and East Ness. September 16, another experiment made, was by firing a signal gun from the East Battery at Lowestoft; to set fire to a stack of furze in the Church lane, and let off some skyrockets. The same methods were made use of at Bawdsey Cliff, and at the several different stations between here and Caister (one of which was the foregoing at Lowestoft) when it was found that an alarm was conveyed in this manner from Bawdsey to Caister, fifty miles, in eleven minutes. September 17, an experiment by daylight was made in making a great smoke. This signal was answered from the camp at Hopton. Another signal was given from the East battery to East Ness, by flash of gun. September 25, an experiment was made to convey an alarm to Norwich from the coast, the camp on East Heath, and from the camp at Herringfleet, by firing skyrockets and cannon, which were answered by other rockets, and platoons of musketry upon Moushold Heath, Norwich. After which, beacons of piles of wood, were set fire to on Herringfleet and Moushold Heath. October 9th a similar experiment was made at seven o'clock in the evening. A chain of signals, by skyrockets and fire beacons, were displayed successively from Coxford lodge, near Houghton, Swanton Novers, near Melton Constable; the heights above Attlebridge; and Moushold Heath, Norwich; to Herringfleet (near the head-quarters at Somerly). These several modes of conveying alarms, in case of an actual invasion, were the most practicable and speedy that could then be made use of in this part of the country.

November 11th, 1784, the camp upon Hopton common broke up, and the Cambridgeshire militia having joined the Light Infantry that had been encamped upon the common at Southwould, went into the winter quarters in Cambridgeshire. At the same time the camp also at Caister broke up, and went into winter quarters at Lynn. And on the 12th the camp upon East Heath broke up, when the troops, together with the 10th Regiment of Foot from Hopton, went into winter quarters at Yarmouth, Gorleston, and Lowestoft. The enemy had not once attempted to carry their intended descent into execution. As the war was terminated on the 20th January following, by a general peace, the fortifications which had been so lately erected in Lowestoft, at a great expense, were allowed to fall into decay.

On the 23rd July, 1785, at four o'clock in the afternoon, Major Money, of Crown Point, near Norwich, ascended from the public gardens in that city, in a car suspended from an air balloon. When arrived at a considerable height, he was not only carried above the clouds, but by a change in the current of air, was driven over Lowestoft, and forced many miles over the sea. About six o'clock, the Major with the balloon fell upon the water, where, after experiencing the most astonishing dangers with the greatest fortitude and presence of mind, he was taken up by a cutter between eleven and twelve o'clock that night, about eighteen miles to the east of Southwold; and the next morning landed safe at Lowestoft, to the great surprise and joy of his friends and the country in general.

## SECTION X.

THE rise and progress of the herring fishery have been previously mentioned and further discussion would be superfluous, were it not to represent more clearly the attempts that were made by some new adventurers, who resided at Dunbar, Caithness, and other places in Scotland; at Liverpool, in the western part of England; and at the Isle of Man, in the Irish Channel; in order to deprive the town of the benefits arising from this antient fishery, and to monopolise them wholly to themselves.

The declining state of the herring fishery at Lowestoft was apparent about the year 1776, that the inhabitants began to entertain alarming apprehensions concerning it. This decline may be attributed to the new adventurers and the war with France and Spain.

The merchants at Lowestoft, in the year 1776, had formed a scheme for sending boats to the coast of Scotland, to fish for the large fat herrings which frequent those seas in great quantities, with the design of bringing them to Lowestoft, to be dried and cured, in the manner practised with herrings caught on the Lowestoft coast. By this means an intercourse was opened between the Lowestoft and Scotch people. In consequence whereof, inquiries were made respecting our mode of curing herrings, and the advantages which we received from the fishery; premiums were offered to our fishermen to entice them to repair to Scotland, during the herring season, to instruct those people in the methods of catching and drying the herrings; and persons were also sent from Scotland to Lowestoft to take dimensions of our fish-houses, their manner of construction, etc., and as they had obtained every information necessary for their purpose, fish-houses were immediately erected in Scotland, the fishery was established there and prosecuted with vigour, and Lowestoft was threatened with the annihilation of its antient branch of commerce, which had been its support for many centuries. The adventurers at Liverpool and the Isle of Man having at the same time formed a design of introducing the art of drying and curing of herrings at those places, the same as in Scotland, the like methods were practised by them as were made use of by the Scotch. But all these designs of the Scotch, however alarming they might appear at first, were of short duration; for the heat of the weather during the fishing season, and the fat and oily quality of their herrings, rendered the fish difficult to cure, and unpleasant to the taste; and consequently their schemes were frustrated. But at Liverpool, and particularly at the Isle of Man, the case was very different. In these places the fishery continues a considerable part of the year, the herrings are taken in prodigious quantities at a small expense, and are not of that oily quality as those are which frequent the coast of Dunbar and Caithness, and consequently are capable of being better cured than those which are caught on the eastern coast of Scotland.

Nevertheless it was generally allowed that the western herrings, though preferable to those caught on the coast of Scotland, in that they were more capable of being properly cured, were yet greatly inferior in quality to those either of Lowestoft or Yarmouth. But notwithstanding the superior quality of the Lowestoft herrings, considerable orders were given for the western fish; and in consequence of the low price they could be afforded at, found a more speedy sale than those from Lowestoft, not only at all the markets in England, but at those also of the different Italian ports in the Levant. The diminution of the price of herrings, especially when accompanied with an increase of their size, were recommendations which had so great an influence with the generality of purchasers of that commodity, that they more than balanced the far superior qualities of richness of colour and excellency of flavour, which have always so remarkably distinguished the Lowestoft herrings above those from any other place.

This success of the western adventurers greatly alarmed the merchants at Lowestoft. The great quantity of fish which they caught, the proficiency they discovered in curing them, together with the greatest success they had met withal at market, exhibited but a melancholy prospect to the inhabitants of Lowestoft.

It was computed that in the year 1776, six thousand barrels of herrings were cured only at the Isle of Man; and in 1777 there were sent from the same place four thousand barrels to the London market only, exclusive of those that were sent to the other places. There were also sent to market that year twenty thousand barrels from Liverpool, and a considerable quantity from Scotland. These prodigious quantities of fish, offered also to the public at the reduced price which those merchants could afford them at (namely, Lowestoft herrings at £15 10s. per last, and herrings from Liverpool at £11 per last) so extremely distressed the Lowestoft merchants, that they were obliged to export the greater part of their herrings at Leghorn, and other ports in the Mediterranean on a venture. But even here also they found that ships from Liverpool, with herrings, had arrived there before them; and in consequence thereof were obliged to deposit their herrings in warehouses till the following year, when they were sold at a great loss. The Lowestoft merchants were also in the same predicament respecting the herrings that remained unsold at the London market; and therefore a meeting of merchants was held at Lowestoft, in order to consult about the most eligible methods of disposing of those herrings, and it was agreed to lodge them also in warehouses there till the succeeding year, which resolution was attended with the same misfortune as that respecting the herrings at the Italian ports to the great injury of the Lowestoft merchants.

Notwithstanding the great success which had hitherto attended these competitors with Lowestoft for the herring fishery, yet it was but of short continuance; for the large size of their herrings, and the fat and oily quality they possessed, though perhaps in a lesser degree than those caught on the coast of Scotland, were such great obstacles to their being properly cured, as could not be surmounted, and evidently proved that they were wholly unfit for exportation, and could only be sent to our English markets, and were not saleable even there, unless they were brought for immediate consumption; and consequently the herring fishery established at Liverpool and the Isle of Man experienced the same ill success as attended that at Dunbar and Caithness, that of being totally abolished, at least so far as respected the curing or making red herrings.

The attempts of these new adventurers have evidently demonstrated that the herrings caught on the eastern coast are the only ones that are capable of being properly cured for red herrings; the colour and flavour of these herrings are superior to those from any other place, and they retain their excellent qualities to a longer period and are preferable to any others either for a foreign or home consumption.

The second cause, which, about the year 1777, greatly retarded the success of the herring fishery at Lowestoft, as well as embarrassd the merchants was the war with France and Spain. By this event the intercourse which the English merchants had formerly maintained with the different ports in the Mediterranean was greatly interrupted, and particularly at the time when the siege of Gibraltar by the Spaniards was turned into a blockade. The usual methods formerly made use of by the merchants at Lowestoft in exporting herrings to the Italian and other ports in the Mediterranean, when we were engaged in a war with France or Spain, was, to convey them to those ports in foreign bottoms; particularly in ships from Holland; but the Dutch, at this time being suspected of carrying English property, were more narrowly watched than formerly as they passed the Straights of Gibraltar and consequently were in the most imminent danger of being captured. But in the year 1780 this difficulty was in a great measure, removed by the treaty of "The Armed Neutrality." This treaty was entered into by most of the commercial powers on the Continent, in order to protect any ships belonging to those powers from the interruptions and depredations they had lately been exposed to, under the pretence of carrying warlike stores, etc. By this treaty foreign vessels were permitted to pass the Straights of Gibraltar without being searched, or suffering any other interruption, but unhappily for the Lowestoft merchants, they not being apprized of the treaty being ratified before the usual time of selling their herrings, and consequently were apprehensive of being liable to the same dangers and inconveniences they had before been exposed to, they at the beginning of the season, sold the greater part of the fish which they should catch this year to the fishmongers in London, whereby they sustained a very considerable loss.

The herring fishery at Lowestoft appears at this time to be **established on the most lasting and permanent foundation; such as promises not only to be** advantageous to the inhabitants, and beneficial to the public, **but also, as** a nursery for seamen, very useful to Government. In fact it is a wise policy of all great maritime powers to establish and encourage, as much as possible, fisheries of every denomination; they being not only of the greatest benefit to individuals, but of the utmost utility to every naval power; for not only the English, but also the Dutch, French, and other foreign nations, from the encouragement of their fisheries, have given evident demonstrations of the truth of this assertion. For this reason the British Legislature has always encouraged and protected its fisheries as much as possible; and the herring fishery has been particularly favoured, but in former reigns as well as the present, with signal instances of its indulgence and protection; as is manifest, not only from the many wise laws, interpositions and regulations of preceding kings, but also from the Act passed in the 26th year of his Majesty King George III., for granting a bounty on herrings, under certain restrictions therein mentioned.

## SECTION XI.

THE Rev. Alfred Suckling, L.L.B., in his "History and Antiquities of the Hundreds of Blyth and part of Lothingland," writes:— "There being no parsonage-house at Lowestoft, in consequence of the fire in 1606, the Rev. John Tanner, who died in 1759, left by his will £100 towards purchasing a residence for that purpose; on condition, however, that his successors advanced another £100, and the purchase was made within a limited time. But Mr. Arrow, who succeeded Mr. Tanner, not complying with the terms of the will, the legacy became void; and Mr. Arrow, in 1762, purchased a very handsome and commodious house on his own account, towards the north end of the town, on the east side, in which he resided during the residue of his life. Mr. Arrow died in 1789, and was succeeded by the Rev. Robert Potter, upon whose institution, Dr. Bagot, the then Bishop of Norwich, and patron of this vicarage, revived the idea of purchasing a parsonage-house; and Mr. Potter and the inhabitants approving the measure, and Mr. Arrow's house, then on sale, being thought a proper residence for the vicar, it was accordingly purchased for the purpose, in 1789, for the sum of £550. To accomplish the purchase, the trustees of certain charity lands in Lowestoft, the rents whereof are applicable for matters appertaining to the church, advanced £100; Dr. Bagot was pleased to give £20; and £430, the residue, was borrowed by the vicar, under the authority of the Act of Parliament to enable rectors and vicars to build or purchase parsonage-houses in those parishes where there are none. It was also thought desirable, that a garden, the property of the late Mr. Arrow, and not far distant from the house, should be purchased; the purchase-money for which was £120, but included in the £550 given. The deeds of conveyance executed on this occasion are in the possession of the vicar.

In 1831, the Rev. F. Cunningham purchased part of a garden and right of way, which cost £77 7s. 3d., which he presented to the vicarage, and likewise put the vicarage-house into a thorough state of repair.

The river Waveney in ancient days sought its junction with the Ocean through Lake Lothing, between Lowestoft and Kirkley. Its channel, which is proved to have been shallow, by the discovery of fossil elephants' teeth, as already related, was open in Camden's time, who calls Kirkley a haven town. Reyce, who wrote his account of Suffolk a few years after, describes it as still navigable, for he says, "and then Leystoffe, until you come to that part of Yarmouth which is on the south side of the river Hiere, do finish the number of our havens." The sea, however, aided by the fury of the eastern gales, gradually raised a barrier of sand and shingle about a quarter-of-a-mile wide, by which all navigation was finally interrupted. Still, whenever a violent storm arose from the north-west in conjunction with a spring tide, the sea would flow into Lake Lothing with great rapidity, and threaten the adjacent low grounds with inundation. To guard against these irruptions, and prevent the consequent damages, a break-water was formed on the sandy isthmus, between Lowestoft and Kirkley, as a security for the marshes which lay contiguous to the river. It is not, however, apparent when this embankment was first complete; for, in a Commission of Sewers, held in February, 1652, a levy was made to repair the breaches effected by the ocean in this bank or walls. These operations must have been imperfectly conducted, for even so late as 1712, a shallow channel was still maintained between the sea and Lake Lothing; for it was then customary for a man to stand there with boots on, to carry children through the water, who went from Lowestoft to Pakefield fair. Subsequently, the barrier was so greatly strengthened, that all apprehension of damage from the ocean had vanished, when, on the 14th of December, 1717; the sea forced its way over the beach with such irresistible violence, as to carry away Mutford Bridge at the distance of two miles from the shore. The writer has been led to assert, in his introduction to the Hundred of Lothingland, from false information, that this was the last attempt of the ocean to regain its ancient passage to the lake. Such, however, is not the fact, for on the 2nd of February, 1791, a remarkable high tide once more burst over the isthmus of sand, and again carried away the bridge at Mutford, built in 1760. On this occasion the salt water flowed over every surrounding barrier, and forced the fishes into the adjoining fields, where they were found, weeks afterwards, sticking in the hedges.

In 1814, Mr. Cubitt, a county engineer, was employed to make a survey, "with a view of ascertaining whether or not it was practicable to open a communication with the sea at Lowestoft," so as to enable vessels, drawing eight feet of water, to pass into the lake, and thence by a navigable canal, to Norwich. In 1821, he published his report, strongly recommending the plan, but estimating the cost at £87,000. After much opposition from the inhabitants of Yarmouth, and the gentlemen whose property lay adjacent to the line of the proposed navigation, a Bill was carried through both Houses of Parliament for making Lake Lothing navigable for sea-borne vessels by a new cut, connecting that lake with the ocean, from Lowestoft to Norwich. The Bill received the Royal Assent, May the 28th, 1827, and the works were commenced in the same year. Though not finally completed to Norwich till September 30th, 1833, they were sufficiently advanced for the admission of the sea, and the reception of shipping, in 1831. On Friday, the 3rd of June, in that year the engineer having made the necessary arrangements for the purpose of bringing vessels into the harbour, the *Ruby*, a beautiful yacht of fifty-one tons burden, and drawing nine feet water, belonging to the writer, entered the lake from the sea under full sail, with her colours flying; and having on board the Chairman, Colonel Harvey, and other Directors. She was followed by the *Georgiana* yacht, of forty-eight tons, belonging to John Fowler, Esq., of Gunton Hall, and by several pleasure-boats and vessels of a smaller class. Some of the circumstances attending the junction of the salt and fresh waters, in the first instance, were remarkable. The salt water entered the lake with a strong under-current, the fresh water running out at the same time to the sea upon the surface. The fresh water of the lake was raised to the top by the irruption of the salt water beneath, and an immense quantity of yeast-like scum rose to the surface. The entire body of the water in the lake was elevated above its former level; and on putting a pole down, a strong under-current could be felt, bearing it from the sea, and at a short distance from the lock next the lake there was a preceptible and clearly defined line where the salt water and the fresh met; the former rushing under the latter; and upon this line salt water might have been taken up in one hand, and fresh water in the other. Lake Lothing was thickly studded with the bodies of pike, carp, perch, bream, roach, and dace; multitudes of which were carried into the ocean, and thrown afterwards upon the beach; most of them having been bitten in two by the dog-fish, which abound in the bay. It is a singular fact, that a pike of about twenty pounds weight was taken up dead near the Mutford end of the lake, and on opening the stomach, a herring was found in it entire. The waters of the lake exhibited the phosphorescent light peculiar to sea water, on the second or third night after the opening. This harbour and navigation afterwards fell into the hands of Government, and were purchased of the Exchequer Loan Commissioners in 1842, by Messrs. Cleveland, Everitt, Lincoln, Hickling, and Roe, of Lowestoft; who expended considerable sums in repairs. They continued in their possession until October, 1844, when they were sold to S. M. Peto, Esq. The present

Act, entitled "An Act for making a Railway from Lowestoft to Reedham, and for improving the Harbour of Lowestoft," was obtained in 1845; and the works commenced in the spring of 1846. The plan is to form a basin outside, or seaward, of the old lock, and entrance, by means of piers, consisting of a frame-work of timber piling—the timber being creosoted by Bethel's patent process to keep out the worm. The frame-work will be filled in with large blocks of stone, varying in weight from one to six tons each block, brought from Kent and Yorkshire. The piers will be about 1,300 feet in length, 800 feet apart, and the entrance 160 feet wide. The basin, so formed, will enclose twenty acres, and the depth of water will average at the top of the tides twenty-four feet. The piers will be finished, and the harbour available for every description of vessel navigating the coast, at all times of tide, in June next. In addition to the formation of the outer basin or refuge harbour, the inner harbour has been dredged; and wharfs, three quarters of a mile in length, are in the course of construction: eight coke-ovens have been erected, and upwards of thirty acres of land levelled for the erection of storehouses, &c. Parrellel with the wharfing, a sea-wall, upwards of a quarter of a mile in length, is being built on the south side of the harbour, as a protection to the works; and an esplanade, a large hotel, and lodging-houses, will be erected as soon as the season permits. An Act to enable trustees of certain charity and trust estates at and near Lowestoft, to carry into effect a contract for a sale of parts thereof to the Lowestoft Railway and Harbour Company, and to grant leases for long terms of years, for building purpose, received the Royal Assent on the 13th of August, 1846.

## SECTION XII.

### ST. PETER'S CHAPEL.

ON the 8th of January, 1832, a public notice was given at church of a town meeting to consider the propriety of building a new and more convenient chapel for the use of the inhabitants; to appropriate for its site a portion of the town land, and to provide the necessary funds. In pursuance of which notice the inhabitants of Lowestoft met on Thursday, the 12th of January following, when it was resolved, that the present chapel having been found unsuitable in size and situation for the accommodation of the inhabitants, it was expedient that a new chapel be erected. That in the impossibility of enlarging the present site, if one more suitable cannot be found, application be made to the Church Building Commissioners to purchase a portion of the town land, opposite Back Street, and abutting on the Beccles road. That the new chapel should contain not less than 1,200 sittings, and that in order to provide a fund for the erection and fitting such chapel, subscriptions be collected; in respect of which, pews and sittings be allotted to the subscribers upon the terms after mentioned; that application be made to the Society for Building and Enlarging Churches, for aid; and lastly, voluntary contributions be collected from the public. That 300 sittings be disposed of under a faculty to be obtained from the Ordinary. That subscribers of £25 each be entitled to one sitting for every £5 subscribed. The pews and sittings to be allotted to each subscriber by ballot, &c. That no expense be incurred relative to providing such a site for building new chapel, until the necessary funds, which were estimated at £2500, be subscribed and raised; and that a committee of inhabitants be formed to carry these resolutions into effect.

Subscriptions for pews were immediately entered into, which amounted to £790, besides donations of £130; of which the Rev. F. Cunningham, the Vicar, gave £100. On the 13th of January, at a meeting held in the town chamber, it was further resolved, that personal application should be made throughout the town for subscriptions and donations, and that applications should be made to different architects for plans and estimates. On the 16th of February, the site of the proposed building was determined on, and the draft of an application to the Incorporated Society for promoting the enlargement, building, and repairing of Churches and Chapels, was prepared; which Society shortly after announced a grant of £600 towards the purposes required.

On the 17th of May, an application was made to Mr. Kitson, the Bishop's Secretary and Registrar, inquiring whether the Marriage Act would allow of the publication of banns and celebration of marriages in the new chapel intended to be erected at Lowestoft, and if so, whether the Bishop would be willing to grant a license for the above purposes. Mr. Kitson's reply stated, that the intended new chapel not being one "having a chapelry thereto annexed," nor, "one situated in an extra-parochial place," did not come within the provisions of the Marriage Act of the fourth of Geo. IV. cap. 76; and therefore that publication of banns and solemnization of marriage cannot be authorised to be performed therein. On the 24th of May, in consequence of the exertions of the Vicar and the principal inhabitants of the town, a sum of very nearly £2,500 had been raised, including the grant from the Incorporated Society; and four days after, Mr. Brown, the architect selected by the committee, attended at Lowestoft with his plans, which were examined and approved, with a trifling exception. After divers tenders and propositions, that of Mr. John Bunn, of Norwich, to build the chapel with white brick, including the palisades, fencing, and boundry wall, for £2,626, was agreed on, and signed on the 30th of July; at which time the sum of £75 was ordered to be paid to Messrs. Reeve, Elph, and Cleveland, the trustees appointed by the feoffees of the town land, as the piece of the site for the chapel; and the further sum of £10, being the charge of the Solicitor of the Treasury, relative to the conveyance.

On Monday, August the 6th, 1832, the first stone of the new chapel was laid in the presence of a vast concourse of the inhabitants and visitors. The committee, the contractor, and architect, met at the vicarage-house, whence they proceeded to the ground. Two hundred and forty children—the Sunday and endowed schools belonging to the established church—had also been brought together. After an explanation of the object of the meeting, the Vicar laid the first stone, in which was deposited a piece of money, of the coinage of William IV., and a plate engraven as follows:

LOWESTOFT.

THE FIRST STONE OF THIS
CHAPEL,
TO BE CALLED BY THE NAME OF
SAINT PETER,
AND ERECTED
BY SUBSCRIPTIONS AND VOLUNTARY
CONTRIBUTIONS, WITH THE AID OF THE
INCORPORATED SOCIETY FOR
BUILDING AND ENLARGING CHURCHES,
WAS LAID ON THE 6TH DAY OF AUGUST,
IN THE 3RD YEAR OF THE REIGN OF HIS
MOST GRACIOUS MAJESTY,
WILLIAM THE FOURTH;
1832;
BY THE
REV. FRANCIS CUNNINGHAM, M.A., VICAR.

JOHN BROWN, ARCHITECT.

After this the Vicar offered up a prayer composed for the occasion, and the whole assembly sang the 100th Psalm. On the 15th of August, 1833, Dr. Charles Sumner, Lord Bishop of Winchester, under a commission given to him by the Bishop of this diocese, proceeded to the act of consecration. Prayers were read by the Vicar, and the sermon preached by the Bishop; the text being taken from the 122nd Psalm, and 7th verse.

The subject of the Prelate's sermon was the *Peace* attendant upon a knowledge of the truths of the Gospel,—that Peace beautifully promoted by the various services of our church, and an application as to the possession of this Peace on the part of those present. A collection was made after the sermon of £56 13s. 6d. On Sunday August the 25th, the Sacrament of the Lord's Supper was administered for the first time at the communion table to 140 persons.

On the 15th of October following, a certificate was forwarded to the Secretary of the Incorporated Society, informing him, that the chapel had been completed in the substantial and workmanlike manner, and was capable of of accommodating 1215 persons, including 900 free sittings. In consequence of subsequent arrangements, these sitting have been increased to 1263; of which 939 are free.

It appears that upon the completion of the work, and the putting up of a bell, weighing about 6 cwt., a sum of £196 6s. 5d. was required for the payment of all the bills and expenses, which the vicar generously consented to advance by way of loan. Of this debt £140 18s. 9d. were repaid; so that the final deficit paid by Mr. Cunningham was £55 7s, 8d. It should be recorded, that an offer was made by Mr. Robert Allen, an inhabitant of Lowestoft, to present to the chapel, glass for the east window, painted by himself at the advanced age of eighty-seven, representing the king's arms, &c. But on consulting the architect, it was judged that this glass was not in character with the design of the building, and that, therefore, plain glass would be adopted to prevent the glare to which, otherwise, the congregation would be exposed. A copy of the original faculty for erecting this edifice is deposited in the chest of Lowestoft, and the opinion of Dr. Lushington and Mr. Kitson, respecting the faculty pews are in the hands of the Vicar; from whose careful and well-arranged minutes of the proceedings adopted throughout the whole business, the preceding remarks have been extracted.

Among the notes attached to these records, it stated that "the proposition is to build a chapel in a parish, where there is a parish church, but so distantly situated from the town, as, under any circumstances, to be of no use, and occasionally insufficient." The particulars are as follows:

"The parish church of Lowestoft was placed upwards of 500 years since in its present situation, under the impression as it is supposed, that if nearer to the sea, it might, at no great length of time, be destroyed by its encroachments. But the sea, instead of advancing, has continued to recede, and now a new town has sprung up on the beach, and the church is left, even in fine weather, out of the reach of a considerable part of the population. In the inclement weather to which so frequently the easternmost point of England is exposed, the church is not opened, and it would be highly inexpedient to hold an evening service in it, at any time. In order to meet the actual necessities of the place, part of a town house has been used by a license of Bishop Parkhurst, as a chapel, since the year 1572, on occasions, 'hiberno præsertim tempore,' according to the original document—when the people cannot without great inconvenience get to church. But this expedient is found insufficient. The chapel will hold between three and four hundred persons, but it is usually so filled, that when it is used, numbers do not attempt to go at all; and many who at all events, will attend a public service, are driven to the Dissenting Meeting Houses. Some peculiar circumstances, connected with the town, make a new provision for public worship absolutely necessary. In the bathing season the church is not sufficiently large for the congregation, and then it would be expedient, if circumstances permitted, to open a second place of worship. Moreover, a harbour, for which the Government is about to grant a loan of £50,000, will, at no distant period, be opened; and Lowestoft, in the course of a short time, will become a commencing point to a navigation, which is likely to extend through a large part of Suffolk and Norfolk. For the persons attendant upon this harbour the church is most inconveniently situated."

In a notice of the new chapel, printed in the provincial journals at the time of its foundation, its architecture was said to be in the style of the Temple Church at London. Wherein the similitude consists, the writer is unable to determine; unless, indeed, the presence of long narrow windows, unaccompanied by the charming proportions and graceful decorations of the proud Crusaders' church, be alone able to constitute its resemblance.

## SECTION XIII.

IN a Hand-book to Lowestoft, published by Mr. Thos. Crowe, in 1853, is the following:

"Lowestoft is, happily for the peace and cordiality of its people, neither a parliamentary Borough nor a corporate town: so that political and party feuds in no degree embitter the charities of private life. These are advantages of which its inhabitants are fully sensible; and if they are disposed to forget them, they are abundantly admonished by the example of a town nine miles to their north, which is a prey to the dissensions Lowestoft is so lucky a stranger to. Another reason for the complete absence of those quarrels and bickerings which are usually found in country towns, is the fact, that the inhabitants of this parish are not called upon to pay church-rates, the lands belonging to the church being amply sufficient to keep it in repair. Many of these unseemly disagreements common in other and less fortunate localities are thus avoided. The Vicar, however, makes a claim for a tithe of fish—about half a guinea on the return of each boat; but with his well-known good nature he has only taken this step *pro formâ*, his unbounded charity and benevolence being one of the "great facts" of the locality. Amongst the other immunities and privileges enjoyed by the inhabitants may be mentioned exemption from payment of toll, service upon juries, &c., granted them by charter of Henry VI., in 1442, and confirmed by Elizabeth and Charles I.

"Adjoining the pier is the Royal Hotel, forming the commencement of one of the finest of terraces, which strikes the attention of the traveller from its elegance and architectural beauty, as the reader will have no great difficulty in discerning through the aid of the artist."

"This superb establishment, the Royal, having been recently erected, with an entire disregard to expense, and under the ablest supervision in every department, comprises all the latest improvements in the cellerage, *batterie de cuisine*, and dormitories; while the coffee and dining rooms and suites of private apartments are most admirably adapted for their respective uses, combining in singular perfection all the desirable characteristics of a first-class hotel and family mansion, without the least encroachment of the one upon the province of the other. The house comprises within itself almost every comfort that can be needed by the valetudinarian, or desired by the luxurious pleasure-seeker. Situate on the very edge of the sea, and the tide receding but very few feet during the day, out of door bathing is nearly at all times practicable at will, the neighbourhood being in every way favourable for it; while salt water baths, at every temperature, are within doors, as well as all the ablutionary appliances available under Mahmoud at Brighton, or the most eminent professors of human detergency at Scarborough or elsewhere. A billiard room of noble dimensions, a large conservatory, partly filled with exotics, and partly with native plants, chiefly indigenous to the horticulture of East Anglia (a district peculiarly rich in this respect), and a well supplied news room, offer potent antidotes to *ennui*. If with these accessories, added to the auxiliaries of a most *recerché* refectory, the attendance being at once unobtrusive and assiduous, and everything which the experience of a long skilled and discerning *maitre de hotel* can suggest for the regalement of his guests, a sojourner at the Royal Hotel, Lowestoft, do not discover a true specific against the blue devils, he must belong to the category of Sir Charles Coldstream's hypochondriacs in *Used Up*, who could find neither tranquillity in a domestic Elyseum, nor excitement in the crater of Vesuvius. Perhaps it may be supposed that the *agremens* we speak of are materially qualified by the undue "inflammation of one's weekly bills." But not so. The pecuniary administration at the Royal is conducted as nearly as possible on the model of the most approved Metropolitan Clubs, combining the maximum of service with the minimum of charge compatible with the high character of the house and the completeness of its appointments. The present proprietor, Mr Samuel Howett, possesses peculiar facilities for conducting it with advantages on this score denied to any other person. As owner for several years of the Royal at Norwich—one of the finest establishments of the kind in England, as the Festival visitors can testify, and as is demonstrated by the constant patronage of the officers of the troops stationed in that city—he has had large local experience of the district, enjoying the respect of many of the resident families, and well known for his business habits, urbanity of manner, and liberal-handed management of all public banquets or private entertainments committed to his supervision. With such a commissariat for head-quarters, as the Royal at Norwich, the Royal at Lowestoft becomes, in his hands, adequate to almost any exigency that can arise, especially as, since last Autumn, its former great capacity for accommodation has been very considerably extended. The view in our illustration is on too small a scale, and is taken from too remote a point to give an adequate idea of the extent or peculiarly commanding position of the Royal; but still it will serve to show that it is a sumptuous-looking pile externally, and we can assure the reader that its interior is of fully corresponding excellence in every possible respect. Another story has recently been added to the original building, and an entirely new wing erected, affording a large number of additional bed-rooms, sitting-rooms, and other appliances of comfort and luxury, all of which are furnished and adorned with unusual taste and elegance. The pictorial establishments will especially attract the attention of the artistical. The accommodation for guests now so ample, however large their number, and the servants' department so well ordered and efficient, that there is no over-crowding, confusion, or inattention. In securing order, regularity, quietness, and promptitude on the part of his domestics, Mr. Howett has proved himself an admirable tactician, and has made his hotel a model of comfort in these important respects. When full of guests it has more the air of a private mansion than an hotel, All conveniences for visitors of rank, such as carriages and horses, &c., are provided in great variety and abundance, the extensive and handsome mews being a very noticeable feature of the Royal. Amongst the recent improvements we may add, that the restaurant has been enlarged and redecorated. Public banquets, or private dinner parties, must be large indeed, if stinted for space in this noble apartment. Connoisseurs assure that for extent, variety, excellent taste in selection, and samples of the choicest vintage, Mr. Howett's wine cellars are unequalled in this part of the kingdom."

"The establishment is conducted on the convenient principal of furnishing the guests with the ordinary scale of charges, which Mr. H. forwards on application to any gentlemen wishing to visit his hotel, The applicant must be fastidious in the extreme if he finds any items in this scale to complain of. As evidence at once of the salubrity of the climate, and of the suitability of the Royal Hotel for the utmost requirements of its various frequenters, it may be mentioned, that Earl Cardigan makes it his occasional head-quarters, (bringing his beautiful Yacht, the famous "Enchantress,") and assembling around him a large circle of his military and fashionable friends; and, on the other hand, the Royal is often occupied by several eminent members of the Society of Friends, to whom its quietude and methodical system of management, no less than the seclusion and healthiness of the locale, recommend it in preference to watering-places of more eminent repute among the faculty. The increasing eclát of the Annual Regatta, the number and value of the prizes, and the celebrity of the Yachts that have assembled and competed on occasion of the last Regatta or two, give promise that henceforth the most "crack" Yachts and most prominent members of the Royal Yacht Club will make an annual visit to Lowestoft, and greatly enliven the season. From its proximity to the harbour and sea, and other attractions, the "Royal" is the favourite rendezvous of the Yacht owners and Regatta patrons, and the most eminent sons of Neptune on their visit to Lowestoft; and frequently, on other occasions, contains a large and distinguished assemblage of rank and fashion.

We are thus particular in dwelling upon the Royal Hotel, not only because it is one of the principal features in the beautiful new town of Lowestoft, but because its character must necessarily have a considerable influence upon those who may contemplate visiting the place. Under the same admirable management of Mr. Howett is the excellent secondary hotel at a short distance, called the Harbour Inn, which is inferior to the Royal only in the splendour of its fittings up; but in all its substantials of comfort and convenience it is wholly impossible it could be surpassed; and it may be recommended unhesitatingly to those of less aristocratic pretensions than the usual inmates of the Royal. In the Old Town, also, there are several inns of great respectability and merit, extremely moderate in their charges, and distinguished by a *naïveté* and heartiness of manner in their proprietors and assistants that will astonish a philosopher as being found at the terminus of a railway—belonging, as those attributes do, rather to the primitive hostelries of Addison and Goldsmith, than to the days of electric telegraphs and *Bradshaw's Time Tables*. In concluding this portion of our subject, we may add, and in no town within our experience are the lodgings, speaking generally, so good, so economic, so unexceptionally conducted, as in Lowestoft—the cost of all household necessaries and rural luxuries being fabulously trifling compared with the tariff in other latitudes, whether on the south-west, the north-west, or even on the Welch coast.

"The sanatory condition of Lowestoft is most satisfactory. Unlike some neighbouring towns, there has been no occasion here for the compulsory clauses of the "Health of Towns Bill." A few years ago, an admirable plan of systematic and thorough drainage was adopted and carried out under the superintendence of Messrs. Lucas, at a large expense,—the situation and physical characteristics of the town affording peculiar facilities for an effective scheme of sewerage. In addition to this, a plan has been resolved on for thoroughly draining the North Beach, and thereby preventing the possibility of effluvium arising from "pulk holes" in the vicinity of the fish houses."

"Waterworks and Gasworks (at Kirtley), for supplying the south end of the town, have been completed and in operation some time; and, in the course of last year, a private bill received the Royal assent, incorporating a company for supplying and erecting, at the north part of Lowestoft, Waterworks, enlarged Gasworks, new Market Place, Abattoirs, and other appropriate adjuncts, at an expense of £20,000, to be raised by two thousand £10 shares. These shares were immediately taken, chiefly by the inhabitants and promoters of the undertaking, which promises to be a very successful one, pecuniarily, and a signal advantage to the town."

"The new Waterworks are now in progress near the "Church Lane" where the element, according to repute and chemical analysis, is of excellent quality and unusual purity; and the Market House, &c., is speedily to be erected near the present Market square, and upon the new site now occupied by the excellent Queen's Head Hotel, and adjacent buildings.

"To the new Waterworks Mr. Clemence's recently-erected *Soap* Factory, pretty near thereto, would seem an appropriate appendage. If abundance and cheapness of soap and water will secure cleanliness, the inhabitants of Lowestoft must not be classed amongst the "great unwashed."

"The various comprehensive reports of the Directors of the Harbour of the Shareholders show at a glance the progressively improving nature of this locality, and the extent of the trade carried on. They are all drawn up by the energetic and accomplished Captain W. S. Andrews, for several years known as the Captain of the *Medway* West India Mail Steamer, and whose appointment here first as Harbour-master, and more especially as Managing-director of the North of Europe Steam Packet Company, has been a most important auxiliary in the advancement of everything connected with Lowestoft, especially all matters pertaining to the docks and shipping."

## SECTION XIV.

### RECEPTION OF THE CHARTER OF INCORPORATION.

TUESDAY Afternoon, 22nd September, 1885, was the time appointed for the official reception of the Charter of Incorporation. The Town Hall was not sufficiently capacious to accommodate the large number of townsmen who sought admission.

Chairs were ticketed for the following gentlemen, namely, to the right of Major Seppings, the Mayor—Rev. T. A. Nash, James Peto, Esq., Rev. J. F. Reeve, T. Lucas, Esq., E. K. Harvey, Esq., W. F. Larkins, Esq., H. G. Woods, Esq. To the left of the Mayor—The Town Clerk, Geo. Bush, Esq., Sims Reeve, Esq., G. Keen, Esq., W. Chater, Esq., T. S. Allerton. Esq.

Amongst the Ladies were Mrs. Larkins. Mrs. Clubbe, Mrs. F. Worthington, Mrs. J. Worthington, Mrs. F. Seago, Mrs. Warman. etc. Amongst the gentlemen were Rev. Dr. English, Rev. J. Wright, Rev. H. I. Wonfer, Col. H. Leathes, Messrs. T. R. Woods, W. R. Seago, W. Youngman, B. M. Bradbeer, R. B. Nirholson, A. Lawrence, W. T. Balls, B. Preston, F. Seago, F. Peskett. J. Hobson, W. Warman, J. L. Clemence, A. Adams, H. Jefferies, R. B. Capps, S. Howett, R. W. Saul, T. Hobson, T. W. Etheridge, T. H. Leggett, A. Stebbings, W. W. Garnham, J. Swatman, W. Farrett.

The Mayor said: Ladies and Gentlemen, I regret that the capacity of our Town Hall, is not sufficient for the number of townsmen who seek admission. If we were to adjourn to the Market Place that would be only sufficiently large. However, our proceedings will not be very long. I will at once enter on the business before us. My duty to-day is to receive the Charter of Incorporation, which our Moot Gracious Queen in Council Assembled has been pleased to grant us. (Applause.)

Mr. Keen, (of the firm of Messrs. Keen, Rogers, & Co.,) then rose, and was received with applause. He said: I have been honoured by Her Majesty's Privy Council, who have entrusted me with the duty of conveying to its destination the Charter of Incorporation of the Borough of Lowestoft. In parting with it I may be allowed to hope as our native country has prospered and thriven under our Great Charter, and as the various towns and boroughs have prospered under their respective charters, so may the good town of Lowestoft go on to more and more prosperity under this its own charter. (Applause.) Ladies and Gentlemen, I am sure I am speaking the sentiments of the whole Borough when I say I could not place the charter in more worthy hands. (Renewed applause.)

The Mayor then received the black tin box containing the important document. Having taken the Charter out of the box he handed it, amid applause, to

The Town Clerk (Mr. J. E. Cook), who read the lengthy document.

## BOROUGH OF LOWESTOFT.

### CHARTER OF INCORPORATION.

*VICTORIA, by the Grace of God, of the United Kingdom of Great Britain and Ireland, Queen, Defender of the faith, to all to whom these presents shall come, greeting.*

WHEREAS by the Municipal Corporations Act, 1882, it was enacted that if on the Petition to Us of the Inhabitant Householders of any Town or Towns or District in England, or of any of those Inhabitants, praying for the granta of Charter of Corporation, we, by advice of our Privy Council, should think fit by charter to create such Town, Towns, or District, or any part thereof specified in the charter with or without any adjoining place a Municipal Borough, and to incorporate the inhabitants thereof, it should be lawful for us, by the charter to extend to that Municipal Borough and the Inhabitants thereof so incorporated the provisions of the Municipal Corporations Acts.

And it was further enacted that every Petition for a Charter under the said Acts should be referred to a Committee of the Lords of our Privy Council (in the said Act called the Committee of Council) and that one month at least before the Petition should be taken into consideration by the Committee of Council, notice thereof, and of the time when it should be so taken into consideration, should be published in the *London Gazette*, and otherwise in such manner as the committee should direct for the purpose of making it known to all persons interested.

And it was further enacted that where We by Charter should extend the Municipal Corporations Acts to a Municipal Borough, it should be lawful for us by the Charter to do all or any of the following things:—

(a) To fix the number of Councillors and to fix the **number and boundaries of the Wards** (if any), and to assign the number of Councillors to each Ward; and

(b) To fix the years, days, and times, for **the retirement of the first Aldermen** and Councillors; and

(c) To fix such days, times, and places, and nominate such persons to perform such duties and make such temporary modifications of the Municipal Corporations Acts, as might appear to Us to be necessary or proper for making those Acts applicable in the case of the first constitution of a Municipal Borough.

And that the years, times and places fixed by the Charter, and the persons nominated therein to perform any duties, should as regarded the Borough named in the Charter be respectively substituted in the Municipal Corporations Acts for the years, days, times, places, officers, and persons therein mentioned and the persons so nominated should have the like powers and be subject to the like obligations and penalties as the officers and persons mentioned in those Acts for whom they would be respectively substituted:

And that subject to the provisions of the Charter authorised thereby the Municipal Corporations Acts should on the Charter coming into effect apply to the Municipal Borough to which they should be extended by the Charter: and where the first Mayor, Aldermen, and Councillors, or any of them should be named in the Charter should apply as if they were elected under the Municipal Corporations Acts, and where they should not be so named should apply to their first election:

And whereas certain inhabitant householders of the District of the Lowestoft Improvement Commissioners did in the month of January, 1885, petition Us for the grant of a Charter of Incorporation:

And whereas such petition was refered to a Committee of our Privy Council, and one month at least before the same was taken into consideration by the said committee, notice thereof and of the time when the same was so to be taken into consideration was duly published in the London Gazette and otherwise as directed by the Committee:

And whereas our Privy Council have recommended Us to grant this Charter of Incorporation:

We, therefore, as well by virtue of Our Royal Prerogative as in pursuance of and in accordance with the Municipal Incorporations Act, 1882, or any other Act or Acts and of all other powers and authorities enabling Us in this behalf, by and with the advice of our Privy Council, do hereby grant order and declare as follows:

(1.) The District of the Lowestoft Improvement Commissioners as defined in the First Schedule to these presents is hereby created a Municipal Borough by the name of the "Borough of Lowestoft."

(2.) The inhabitants of the said District, and their successors, shall be, and are hereby declared to be one body politic and corporate, by the name of the Mayor, Aldermen, and Burgesses of the Borough of Lowestoft, with perpetual succession and a Common Seal, and may assume armorial bearings (which shall be duly enrolled in the Herald's College), and may take and hold such lands and hereditaments as well without as within the Borough as may be necessary for the site of the buildings and premises required for the official purposes of the Corporation and other purposes of the Municipal Corporations Acts, not exceeding in value the amount of £2500 by the year.

(3.) The Mayor, Aldermen, and Burgesses of the said Borough shall have the powers, authorities, immunities, and privileges usually vested by law, in the Mayor, Aldermen, and Burgesses of a Municipal Borough, and the provisions of the Municipal Corporations Acts shall extend to the said Borough, and the inhabitants thereoeof incorporated by this charter:

(4.) The number of the Councillors of the Borough shall be 24:

(5.) The Borough shall be divided into four Wards, with the names and bounds specified in the First Schedule to these presents:

(6.) Each of the Wards shall elect six Councillors:

(7.) For the purpose of making the Municipal Corporations Act, 1882, applicable in the case of the first constitution of the Borough, we do hereby, so far only as regards the first Burgess List, first Burgess Roll, and first Election of Councillors, Mayor, Aldermen, Town Clerk, and Treasurer for the Borough, fix and order as follows:

(a) The Town Hall in the Town of Lowestoft shall be the place at which any list, notice, or document required to be affixed, on or near the outer door of the Town Hall is to be affixed; and

(b) Both in relation to the matters aforesaid, and also in relation to any such election as aforesaid, which it may be necessary to hold before a valid election can be held under the Municipal Corporations Election Act, 1882, JOSEPH EDWARD COOK, of Lowestoft; or in case of his death, inability, refusal, or default, THOMAS SIMPSON ALLERTON, of Lowestoft, shall perform the duties of Town Clerk; and SIMMS REEVE, of Norwich; or in case of his death, inability, refusal or default, WILLIAM CHATER, of Lowestoft, shall perform the duties of the Mayor and the assessors for revising the Burgess List, and the separate list of persons qualified to be Councillors; and HENRY SEPPINGS, of Lowestoft, or in case of his death, inability, refusal or default, GEORGE BUSH, of Lowestoft, shall perform the duties of the Mayor and Aldermen respectively, as returning officer, and of the Mayor as summoner of the first meeting of the Council, and of the Mayor or Chairman of the Meeting for the election of the Mayor, Aldermen, Town Clerk and Treasurer.

And the said persons shall be substituted in the Municipal Corporations Act, 1882, for the said Town Clerk, Mayor, Assessors, Aldermen, and Chairman, respectively, so far as relates to the matters aforesaid: and

(c) The first meeting of the Council of the Borough shall be held on the ninth day of November, 1885:

(d) The first Councillors shall be elected on the first day of November, 1885, and the first Mayor and Aldermen on the ninth day of November, 1885.

(8.) The years and days specified in the Second Schedule to these presents shall be the years and days for the retirement of the first Aldermen, and Councillors, who shall retire in the manner and at the times therein designated.

(9.) Subject to these presents and the second schedule thereto the provisions of the Municipal Corporations Act, 1882, shall apply to the determination of the qualifications of the Burgesses, the making out, signing, delivering, inspection, completion, publication, commencement, and continuance of the first Burgess Lists and Burgess Rolls, the claims, objections, and determinations with regard to the first Burgess Lists or Rolls the holding adjournments and decisions of the first Revision Courts, the nominations, elections and continuance in office of the first Mayor, Aldermen, Councillors, Auditors. and Assessors, the appointment and continuance in office of the first Town Clerk and Treasurer, the first Meeting, and Quarterly Meeting of the Town Council, and all matters and things touching and concerning the above, and the dates and times in the said act mentioned shall be the dates and times on, at, during within or for which the matters aforesaid, and the various acts and things in relation thereto shall take place, be done, be estimated or be calculated.

## FIRST SCHEDULE.

### METES AND BOUNDS OF BOROUGH.

The Boundaries of the Borough are identical with those of the District of the Lowestoft Improvement Commissioners, and comprise the whole of the Parishes of Lowestoft with Kirkley, otherwise Kirtley, in the County of Suffolk.

### NAMES AND METES AND BOUNDS OF EACH WARD.

### EAST WARD.

The East Ward comprises so much of the Borough as is bounded on the North by the Borough Boundary, on the East by the German Ocean, on the South by the Outer Harbour, and on the West by a line commencing at a point in the Borough Boundary in the centre of the Yarmouth Road, and proceeding thence in a South-Easterly direction along the centre of the Yarmouth Road to the junction of the same with Park Road, and thence in a Southerly direction along the centre of Park Road and Albert Street to the junction of the last-named street with Mariners' Street, and thence in an Easterly direction along the centre of Mariners' Street to its junction with High Street, and thence in a Southerly direction along the centre of High Street and the London Road to the junction of the London Road with Mills Road, and thence in a Westerly direction along the centre of Mills Road to the junction of the same with Clapham Road, and thence in a generally Southerly direction along the centre of Clapham Road to its junction with Bevan street, and thence in a South-Easterly direction along the centre of Bevan Street to its junction with the London Road near the Suffolk Hotel, thence in a Southerly direction along the London Road to the Harbour.

### NORTH WARD.

The North Ward comprises so much of the Borough as is included within a line commencing at a point in the Borough Boundary in the centre of the Yarmouth Road, and proceeding thence in a South-Easterly direction along the centre of the Yarmouth Road, to the junction of the same with Park Road, and thence in a Southerly direction along the centre of Park Road and Albert Street to the junction of the last-named street with Mariners' Street, and thence in an Easterly direction along the centre of Mariners' Street to its junction with High Street, and thence in a Southerly direction along the centre of High Street, and the London Road, to the junction of the London Road with Mills Road, and thence in a Westerly direction along the centre of Mills Road, Love Road, and Love Lane, to the junction of Love Lane with Rotterdam Road, and thence in a Northerly direction along the centre of Rotterdam Road, to its junction with Beccles Road, and thence for a few feet along the centre of the Beccles Road in a Westerly direction to a point exactly opposite the footpath which leads in a Northerly direction towards St. Margaret's Church, and thence to and along the said footpath and along the road or lane which forms a continuation of the said footpath, and runs by and to the East of certain pits to the junction of the said road or lane with the Oulton Road, just South of St. Margaret's Church, and thence in a Westerly direction along the centre of the Oulton Road to the Borough Boundary, and thence, first in a North-Westerly and Northerly direction and then in a generally Easterly direction along the Borough Boundary to the point of commencement before described.

### WEST WARD.

The West Ward comprises so much of the Borough as is included within a line commencing at a point in the Harbour under the bridge over the same and proceeding thence in a Northerly direction to and along the centre of the London Road to the junction of the same with Bevan Street, and thence in a North-Westerly direction along the centre of Bevan Street to its junction with Clapham Road, and thence in a generally Northerly direction along the centre of Clapham Road to the junction of the same with Mills Road, and thence in a Westerly direction along the centre of Mills Road, Love Road, and Love Lane, to the junction of Love Lane with Rotterdam Road, and thence in a Northerly direction along the centre of Rotterdam Road to its junction with the Beccles Road, and thence for a few feet along the centre of Beccles Road, in a Westerly direction to a point exactly opposite the footpath which leads in a Northerly direction towards St. Margaret's Church, and thence to and along the said footpath and along the road or lane which forms a continuation of the said footpath and runs by and to the East of certain pits to the junction of the said road or lane with the Oulton Road, just south of St. Margaret's Church, and thence in a Westerly direction along the centre of Oulton Road to the Borough Boundary, and thence, first in a South-Westerly and Southerly direction and then in an Easterly direction along the Borough Boundary to the point where the boundaries of the three parishes of Lowestoft, Kirkley, and Carlton Colville meet in Lake Lothing or the Inner Harbour, and thence in an Easterly direction along the Inner Harbour to the point of commencement before described.

### SOUTH WARD.

The South Ward comprises so much of the Borough as is bounded on the North by the Inner and Outer Harbour, on the East by the German Ocean, and otherwise by the Borough Boundary.

### SECOND SCHEDULE.

| Persons to Retire. | Date of Retirement. |
| --- | --- |
| The one-third of the Councillors in each ward who are elected by the smallest number of votes shall go out of office on | 1st. November, 1886. |
| The one-third of the Councillors in each ward who are elected by the next smallest number of votes shall go out of office on | 1st. November, 1887. |
| The remaining one-third of the Councillors in each ward shall go out of office on | 1st. November, 1888. |
| The one-half of the Aldermen who first go out of office shall be those who are elected by the smallest number of votes, and shall go out of office on | 9th. November, 1888. |
| The remaining one-half of the Aldermen shall go out of office on | 9th. November, 1891. |

If any Councillors in any ward or any Aldermen have obtained an equal number of votes, or have been elected without a poll, so that it cannot be determined which of them has the smallest number of votes, the Council of the Borough shall, at the first or second quarterly meeting, and not later, by a majority of votes, or in case of an equality of votes, by the Casting vote of the Chairman, determine who are to go out of office at the times above specified respectively.

In return whereof we have caused these Our letters to be made Patent.

Witness Ourself at Westminister, the 29th day of August, in the 49th year of Our Reign. By Warrant under the Queen's Sign Manual,

MUIR MACKENZIE.

> Here follows the
> Queen's Sign Manual.

The Mayor said he had only one resolution to bring before the meeting, and he would ask Mr. Thos. Lucas, a gentleman well-known to all in former years, and one who was allied with the great promoter of the prosperity of Lowestoft—Sir Morton Peto—to propose it. The town owed very much to Sir Morton Peto and the eminent firm of Messrs Lucas Bros., for its prosperity.

Mr. Thos. Lucas on rising was received with prolonged applause. He said he had been requested by the Mayor to propose "That the inhabitants of the Borough of Lowestoft in public meeting assembled hereby desire to express their great gratification at the grant by Her Most Gracious Majesty the Queen by and with the advice of her Privy Council, of a Charter of Incorporation of Lowestoft with Kirkley; and also their earnest hope that the Charter may tend to the advancement, extension, and prosperity of the town." This was, Mr. Lucas said, a peculiarly interesting ceremony to him. In September, thirty-one years ago, he entered Lowestoft with his friend Sir Morton Peto, and, he ought to be able to say, "Sir" James Peto. (Hear, hear.) The names of the gentlemen who were prominent in the town then were Edwd. Leathes, F. Morse, H. G. Woods, Youngman (father and son), the Gowings, Seago, Balls, Barnard, Howett, and several others. This year happened to be the anniversary of the introduction of the Improvement Act of 1854, and of the formation of the Improvement Commissioners. On looking over the list who formed that body in 1854-5, he noticed that eighteen of them were no more, and not a single one of them was a member of that Commission at the present time. There might be some persons who knew Lowestoft thirty-one years ago, and if so, it was only those who could properly appreciate the stride it had made. He knew Lowestoft years before that date, when the inner harbour was first formed, and there were very few houses on the south side. The progress, north, south, east and west of the town was remarkable. Instead of the very small harbour which was made thirty years ago, Lowestoft now possessed one of the finest harbours in the kingdom. Lowestoft had a magnificent fleet of fishing vessels, worth any person coming from London to look at. The Railway Company had done great things for Lowestoft. It used to be considered a great feat to get from London to Lowestoft in 5½ hours, now the journey was accomplished in three hours. An important interest connected with the town was that of the visitors. He was sanguine that following the inauguration of the Charter of Incorporation more accommodation and conveniences would be provided for visitors. Some of the requirements, though considered as luxuries in former times, were now regarded as necessities. He would, if he might, ask the gentlemen who would form the governing body of the town to turn their attention to the drainage. It was quite true he was interested as an owner of land on the south side, but that was a mere bagatelle and did not weigh one iota with him, because he could dispose of it in twenty-four hours if he wished. But he never lost the touch of interest he felt in Lowestoft. He would compare the growth of Lowestoft with the growth of another place. Just before Sir Morton Peto (one of those far-seeing men) bought the harbour at Lowestoft, he did a similar thing at Folkestone. That place was very much like Lowestoft, with a few houses and few people. They did not receive Sir Morton Peto nor himself with open arms; in fact they were christened "foreigners." The people there could not see that it would be an advantage to make any effort to improve the place, nor to encourage those who were willing to help them. After a time the people saw the advantages the place possessed, and they struck out boldly, houses sprung up in all directions, and mansions were there which had recently been occupied by Princes. There were baths, assembly rooms, club rooms and tramways up the cliffs. It was proposed to have a National Art Gallery there in 1886, and for that purpose a guarantee fund of £50,000 was required. £38,000 of the amount was guaranteed within two months, and he believed the whole amount would be guaranteed very shortly. His object in mentioning Folkestone was because he believed Lowestoft was capable of doing a great deal more than it had done. He did not mean by that that Lowestoft could raise a guarantee fund of £50,000 in a short time, but he would say there ought to be pluck enough in Lowestoft after receiving the Charter, to do certain things which very much required to be done. The drainage question he would leave in the hands of the Corporation. (Laughter, and hear, hear.) A great want in Lowestoft was Assembly Rooms, where high-class entertainments could be given. Something was wanted for the amusement of young people, and for that purpose Assembly Rooms were required. He was prepared to say that if good club rooms were near the harbour, Lowestoft would be favoured with visits by the largest yacht clubs. He had seen as many as thirty yachts, between sixty or seventy tons each in the harbour at one time, and he would ask what reason was there that such a sight should not be seen in the harbour again. (Hear, hear.) Medicated and other baths were wanted, and they should be near the reading rooms. Within the last week he had been in the company of the Chairman of the Great Eastern Railway Company. He discussed with that gentleman his opinion as to what ought to be done in Lowestoft. He felt bound to say that no gentleman could possibly offer to meet the town with more liberality and kindness than Mr. Parkes. (Loud applause.) Of course, Mr. Parkes could not commit the railway company, nor would he commit himself. Mr. Parkes however expressed his desire to co-operate for the benefit of Lowestoft on the condition that the townspeople did their part. If the people intended Lowestoft to be what it ought to become—namely, a first-class watering-place, the inhabitants must drop their little differences and co-operate together. The prosperity of the town was far too important a matter to be impeded by personal differences. He had a temper, and he knew it, but he schooled it, and during his thirty-six years connection with Lowestoft he had had transactions with all classes of men—Tory, Radical, Nonconformist, and Churchman, and he hoped he had never offended one of them nor had one of them offended him. (Hear, hear.) If he did not agree with a man, that man had just as much right to an opinion as he (Mr. Lucas) had. He always respected the opinions of his opponents. (Applause.) He urged that in electing the corporation they should not care to what party a man belonged, but that they should put aside all personal feeling, and elect the very best men they could find. They had no right to think of anything, or of anybody but the prosperity of the town. If that line was followed out, the Charter would be, in his opinion, a great blessing to the town. If at the beginning they took an opposite direction they would make a mistake. When the list of candidates for the first Board of Commissioners appeared it represented every class. He advised a similar course with regard to the New Town Council. Let every class be represented by the very best men. Then they would give tone, dignity and go, to the whole thing. In the Mayor they required a gentleman of long experience, energy, high character, integrity, and means. (Laughter.) The last-mentioned qualification was an important one. If Lowestoft started well under the Charter, it would go on well, but if it started badly, it would take a long time to get right again. He had this week paid a visit to the Lord Lieutenant of the County (Lord Stradbroke), at Henham, and although his Lordship was very old, he enjoyed good health. (Hear, hear.) His Lordship desired him to convey to the town (through the Mayor) his warmest congratulations on it becoming a Borough, and he wished Lowestoft continued prosperity. Viscount Dunwich would have attended the reception of the Charter, but he was away from home. In conclusion Mr. Lucas said—I should like to couple the name of my brother (Mr. C. Lucas), with what I am about to say. If you will help us we will go out of our way to help you. If the new Corporation should not think it worth to go on making improvements I shall make my bow and say farewell. We are quite prepared to assist in promoting

**the** North end as well as the South. If you go round the district, as I have been doing, there is not a single building put up for a first-class residence. What we have done for Kirkley is for the good of the town, and I would beg of you to remember these things. After a passing reference to the Railway Company, and Sir Morton **Peto,** and prophesying a great future for Lowestoft, Mr. Lucas (who became Sir Thomas Lucas) resumed his seat amid loud cheers.

The **Rev. J. F.** Reeve seconded the resolution, which was supported by the **then** Rector, **Rev. T.** A. Nash, and, on being put to the meeting, was carried **with** enthusiasm.

**Colonel** Leathes proposed thanks to the chairman, Mr. E. K. Harvey seconded, **and the** vote was accorded with acclamation. The Mayor replied, and Mr. Lucas **then** eulogised **Mr.** W. Youngman for the very great interest he took in the Borough, and the exertions he had made to promote its prosperity.

Mr. B. M. Bradbeer called for three cheers for the Queen, and these having been given, the proceedings closed with cheers for the Mayor.

## SECTION XV.
## LATER PROGRESS.
### BY A. E. MURTON.

IN compiling a history of any place, a stop must be made somewhere, owing to the exigencies of publication. The details of Lowestoft's past have been recorded, and brought up to, perhaps, the most important point in her career, viz., the granting of the Charter of Incorporation in 1885; and it only now remains to show how it has fared with the Borough since. It may at once be said that its record has been one of steady progress. It has continuously grown in favour as a health resort, and in the year 1897, when this book was published, it had attained a high position among seaside watering places—a position that must be more than maintained if the powers that be will only work well together with a single eye for the benefit of the town. Since the granting of the Charter the population has considerably increased. In 1881 the census showed 19,696 inhabitants; in 1891 this had increased to 23,347, and in 1897 it was put, for the purposes of compiling the health report, at 25,590. So it may be safely said that since the date of the Charter, the Borough has received an accretion of fully 5,000 persons. The growth of houses has been in a corresponding ratio. In 1891 there were 4,242 houses in the parish of Lowestoft, 998 in Kirkley, and one in Gunton, making 5,241 for the Borough. At the end of 1896, this number had risen to 6,430 in round figures—an addition of nearly 1200, which must be considered very satisfactory.

The complaint made by Sir Thomas Lucas, as set forth on the preceding page, namely, that there is not a single building put up for a first-class residence, has to a great extent been remedied, for during the last four years some very fine houses have been built, especially in South Lowestoft. These have immensely raised the rateable value of the Borough, and given it greater prestige in the eyes of wealthier seaside sojourners. This activity in providing large, commodious, and well-arranged residences does not promise to abate for awhile, for the builder is busy on Kirkley Cliff, where splendid houses are already accomplished facts. The Grand Hotel, built by Mr. John Whaley, stands boldly on the brow of the Cliff. It is a palatial place, splendidly furnished and decorated, and well patronised. In other parts the Borough has extended—notably in the West, where hundreds of houses suitable for the working classes, have been erected. In the North there is also progress in this particular, and with the advent of the Great Eastern and Midland & Northern Joint Line Station, this beautiful portion of lazy, lovely Lowestoft, will rapidly go ahead. Indeed, at the present rate of progression, it is not difficult to forsee the day when Lowestoft shall extend to Corton on the North, Oulton and Carlton Colville on the West, and Kessingland on the South.

There have not been any very great upheavals to disturb the even tenour of Lowestoft life—the record is that of a peaceful, but none the less powerful, forward movement. As a fishing port it has greatly advanced, and in this connection mention must be made of the splendid accommodation afforded by the Great Eastern Railway, in the shape of the Spacious Herring and Mackerel Market and Trawl Market, and Waveney Dock, which were opened on the 1st October, 1883, by Lord Waveney. Even the capacious trawl dock proved inadequate, and in 1892 it became necessary to provide additional berthage and quays for the trawlers, the new dock facing the London Road being constructed. The number of fishing boats and smacks sailing out of the port are constantly receiving additions, and it is the proud boast of Lowestoft that she possesses the finest fishing fleet in the world, manned by crews of brave, hardy seamen, who are ever ready to render assistance in saving life. A notable instance of this grand trait of the "toilers of the deep" was the rescue of the 20 survivors of the North German Lloyd Liner *Elbe*, bound from Bremen to New York viâ Southampton, which sunk about 40 miles off

Lowestoft, after collision with the SS *Crathie* in the early morning of the 29th January, 1895. By this awful catastrophe 360 lives were lost. The 20 survivors escaped in an open boat, were sighted and taken aboard the Lowestoft smack *Wildflower*, and landed at Lowestoft in the afternoon of the same day.

The old order is ever changing, giving place to new, and so it came about that the swing bridge which was placed over the harbour waterway in 1830, was found to be inadequate for the vastly increased traffic. This has now given place to the present fine and commodious structure and approaches, which have been provided by the Great Eastern Railway at great expense.

Improvements have been carried out on all hands. The sewerage of the town has been brought up to date, and a new outfall has been necessitated. It has been considered necessary to groyne the North Beach to prevent the incursions of the sea on the Denes, which are prized by the inhabitants and visitors in general as a public walk and recreation ground, and by the fishermen in particular as a place whereon they can dry their nets. The incandescent light has been adopted in the main streets of the Borough, and a fine theatre, provided by public-spirited townsmen, was opened on April 26th, 1897.

Belle Vue Park possesses the Jubilee Memorial. When, in 1887, the question of providing a lasting record of the Queen's Jubilee was talked over, a proposal emanated from Mr. Arthur Stebbings, a member of the Town Council, that a bridge should be built across the ravine which separated the Park from the North Parade. Assisted by several other gentlemen, he raised a goodly sum. But Mr. William Youngman, J.P., an Alderman of the Borough, who was its first elected Mayor, and who has benefited his native town to a great extent, came forward and gave the bridge, which stands as a substantial and useful reminder of the Queen's Jubilee, and of Mr. Youngman's munificence. This gentleman also placed the splendid East Window in St. Margaret's Church, and has offered to build a Children's Wing to the Hospital as a Diamond Jubilee Offering.

Educationally, Lowestoft has progressed. A School Board was formed in 1893, and since that year handsome new schools have been built, where a sound education is given. The need for higher instruction was felt, and to meet it the Corporation are about to provide a fine Technical School on Clapham Road.

Movements having for their object the moral and physical well-being of the community have not been neglected. The commodious rooms of the Young Men's Christian Association on London Road have been erected, containing a comprehensive gymnasium, given by Sir Thomas Lucas, and a Home for the Young Women's Christian Association is being built. A fine residence facing the Park is utilized as a Convalescent Home, and Connaught House in High Street has become a Church of England Home for Waifs and Strays.

An incident worthy of note is the visit which Mr. W. E. Gladstone paid to the locality on May 19th, 1890, when he was the guest of Mr. J. J. Colman at "The Clyffe," Corton. He addressed an audience of 7000 people at Norwich on the previous evening, and received an address on Lowestoft Station, to which he replied in a speech of half an hour's duration. From that time till the following Tuesday, Mr. and Mrs. Gladstone remained at "The Clyffe," and on leaving by special train for Hawarden Castle, the Right Honourable gentleman, who was then in his 81st year, was presented with an album containing 50 photographs of the principal views in the neighbourhood. During his stay he expressed himself as "delighted with the place and the people," to which Mrs. Gladstone added that she agreed with all her husband had said.

The late Duke of Clarence (Prince Albert Victor) was a visitor to Lowestoft in 1885, when he stayed with Lord Claud Hamilton, the present Chairman of the Great Eastern Railway Company.

The narrow part of High Street, which has for long proved a great inconvenience, owing to the obstruction to traffic, thereby stopping the growth of this part of Lowestoft, has been widened, and smart places will undoubtedly take the place of the somewhat tumble down houses and shops, relics of "ye olden time," which formerly existed. While the work of demolition was in progress, an ancient crypt was found to extend some distance beneath one of the buildings. The roof is groyned and arched, and rumour has it that the crypt is a portion of a subterranean way leading from the Cliff to the Church. Be this as it may, the discovery is an interesting one for the antiquarian to ponder over, and it should be carefully preserved.

The fine old Parish Church of St. Margaret's was completely **restored in** and about 1870, when the Rev. W. Hay Chapman was Rector, at a cost **of over** £5,000. Thanks to the engergy of the present Rector, Hon. Canon Charles D'Aquilar Lawrence, the sacred edifice has been entirely re-roofed at great cost. St. Peter's Church at Kirkley has also been restored, beautified, and added to, mainly through the munificence of Mr. E. K. Harvey, J.P. A fine new Seamen's Church and Institute has been erected in Suffolk Road under the auspices of the Missions to Seamen Society. This building is the gift of the Misses Hume, **in** memory of their **late brother, the** Rev. H. S. Hume, M.A., a beloved Vicar of St. John's, who died on November 9th, 1895, after **an** energetic and useful ministry in Lowestoft, of not quite three years.

In the early part of 1897 a Bill was **promoted in Parliament by the** Midland and Great Northern Joint Lines **for the purpose of making a railway from** Yarmouth to Lowestoft, entering the town **across** the Denes. The scheme also provided for a Dock at Gorleston. It **was** felt that this would attract **a good deal of fishing** trade from Lowestoft, besides which, it would ruin the **Denes, and destroy the future prospects of** North Lowestoft. The Council, by a majority of three, **were in favour of the Bill, but a** large public meeting protested against it. A petition **was got up and largely** signed, with the result that the Midland & Great Northern **dropped their Bill,** and made a compromise with the Great Eastern Railway, to have **joint running powers over** a new line, which they, too, proposed making from Yarmouth **to Lowestoft,** by a route which will go **to** the West of the town and join the present **main line near** the Coke Ovens Signal Box. There will be a Station on the Yarmouth **Road, which** will also be used jointly Thus Lowestoft will be in direct com-**munication** with the Midlands.

Lately, Lowestoft Harbour **was a** source **of trouble owing to the periodical** accumulation of sand at its entrance. To obviate **this the Great Eastern Railway** Company will carry out extensive works, by which **the North and South Piers will be** considerably lengthened, and the Harbour space greatly **added to. The necessary** Bill for the purpose has passed through Parliament.

Another event of the last few years is the building **of the** splendid Reading Rooms and Concert Hall on the South Pier, this handsome and well appointed building taking the place of an older structure which **was destroyed** by fire on the night of June 29th, 1885.

It will be seen that Lowestoft has not stood still. **There is no** reason why she should not go **on** in her onward march; and there can be **no** question but that the chronicler of the future will have plenty of material at his command wherewith to continue the History **of** Lowestoft.

---

PUBLISHED BY ARTHUR STEBBINGS, 56, HIGH STREET, LOWESTOFT.

www.ingramcontent.com/pod-product-compliance
Lightning Source LLC
Chambersburg PA
CBHW021733220426
43662CB00008B/834